FLEEING THE HIJAB

FLEEING THE HIJAB

A Jewish Woman's Escape from Iran

~~~~~

Sima Goel

GSPH

GENERAL STORE PUBLISHING HOUSE INC.
499 O'Brien Road, Renfrew, Ontario, Canada K7V 3Z3
Telephone 1.613.599.2064 or 1.800.465.6072

http://www.gsph.com

ISBN 978-1-77123-050-6

Cover art, design: Magdalene Carson

Printed by Image Digital Printing Ltd.
dba The IDP Group, Renfrew, Ontario
Printed and bound in Canada

Library and Archives Canada Cataloguing in Publication
Goel, Sima, 1965-, author
Fleeing the hijab : a Jewish woman's escape from Iran / Sima Goel.
Issued in print and electronic formats.
ISBN 978-1-77123-050-6 (pbk.).--ISBN 978-1-77123-100-8 (epub).--
ISBN 978-1-77123-101-5 (mobi).--ISBN 978-1-77123-102-2 (web)
1. Women--Iran--Social conditions--20th century.
2. Women refugees-- Iran. 3. Jews, Iranian. I. Title.
HQ1735.2.S56 2013   305.40955   C2013-906800-7   C2013-906801-5

FSC

To the loving memory of my parents,
who gave me their best.

To my husband, Eugene,
for his unwavering love and support.

To my sons, Eric and Daniel,
who encouraged me to tell my story.

And to those who still have to fight
to have their voices heard.

Contents

Foreword

by Rabbi Dr. Reuven P. Bulka, C.M.

There are times when, after reading a book, you are driven to meet the author. This is that type of book. The author tells her life story in painstaking—and yes, painful—detail. The story of Sima Goel is in no small measure a microcosm of the Jewish people. As you read this riveting chronicle of survival, a miracle by any measure, you get a sense of the resilience, the courage, the emotional upheaval, that colours Jewish history. And you want to meet and spiritually embrace the author—a true heroine; even more so given her age when she encountered the ugly face of evil and resolved to escape its tentacles.

There is no equivocating, no glossing over, no sugar coating. The feelings of the author are laid bare for all to absorb: the desperation, the frustration, the anger, the disappointment. There are heroes and villains, advantage takers and true helpers, friends who suddenly become enemies, the usual family dynamics exacerbated by continuing crisis. It is all here in this rich and enriching book.

Amazingly, this is not a book written in anger. It is more a lament, a lament of the full Jewish life once enjoyed by the author and her family, a life turned upside-down by unconscionable evil. And to the end, or more precisely, the new beginning, there is not a trace of vindictiveness to be found.

This is not a book about religion, but there are precious nuggets of how Judaism was once lived, so beautifully, in Iran. And it is a book about faith: faith in God, abiding faith in a better tomorrow, and the profound understanding that faith in God demands that we do our best to make that tomorrow happen.

Sima's story is happening, as you read this, to people of all faiths living under oppressive regimes that deny members of faith communities other than theirs the right to freedom of religion. Sima's is the story of a life that easily could have turned ugly, and so many times was on the edge of the abyss, but never sank into the abyss. Thankfully, Sima, who in her early years could not speak a word of English, tells her story with moving eloquence.

How Sima landed up in Canada is the final part of the story. It makes us better appreciate Canada, and most important, challenges us to cherish freedom and to fight for it in whatever forum we are able. The things we take for granted — a room of our own, a bed to sleep in, roach-free food, regular meals, friends, tranquil schooling, religious freedom, freedom of movement, etc. — will all be more fully treasured once you read this book.

And you, like me, will wonder what it is in Sima's DNA that enabled her to endure the enormous physical and emotional torture of her youth. You will wonder, but more important, you will be uplifted.

Rabbi Dr. Reuven P. Bulka, C.M.

Preface

This story will take you from an idyllic childhood in a beautiful and fascinating country through a traumatic escape from hopelessness to freedom.

As I fled my beloved homeland, Iran, I promised myself that one day I would document the whole experience.

Why now?

In 2005, the phone rang at my office. The man at the other end of the line introduced himself as Howard. "I'm producing a documentary movie about refugees, and I'd like to interview you."

I met with Howard, and the interview was apparently such a success that he decided that I would be the exclusive subject for the documentary.

During the filming, forgotten images and scenes and long-buried conversations flashed through my mind. Howard and his film crew were patient when I sometimes had to stop and regain my self-control. But they recorded it all.

Months later, Howard handed me a ten-minute edited version of our interview. He presented the interview in 2007 at a board meeting attended by special guests at JIAS (Jewish Immigrant Aid Services). I sat in. After the presentation, there was not a dry eye in the audience.

In late 2008, I was invited for a preliminary interview to be the guest speaker at a fundraising event. I dusted off the DVD and took it with me. I asked the board members interviewing me if they would like to see another aspect of my life and popped in the video.

As I left the meeting, two women followed me out into the corridor. They asked me if I could speak for "Choices," the largest annual fundraising campaign for the Women's Division of Combined Jewish Appeal in Montreal.

In the beginning of September, I received the confirmation of my speaking engagement: I was now committed to speak about my life to over eight hundred women.

I couldn't sleep that night. The next morning, I went out for breakfast, my head whirling with memories. I had not brought any paper with me, but felt I had to write down what was coming through from the past. I filled every space on the placemat with notes. I cried with every word I wrote, and cried again and again as I reread what I had written. Over the next few days, memories filled every hour of my life. I often woke up crying, and got out of bed to write down the horrific images and details that were flooding to the surface.

Despite the brevity of my speech, there was an overwhelming response from the audience, which told me that now was the right time for me to start on my long-time goal of writing a book about my experiences. I was ready to share with the world what had happened to me and my fellow Iranians.

~~~~~~

In the years since I left, I have watched the situation in Iran go from bad to worse. Despite the image that the media have protrayed, I wanted the Western world to know that Iran is a beautiful country, with an ancient and rich culture, and that, at heart, the people are gentle, warm, caring, and are still willing to fight for freedom.

I felt that someday I would need to share my life story with my children; I wanted to leave them with a written legacy.

My intention here is not to elicit sympathy, but rather to share how we lived as Iranians and what I have learned. We are all human beings; we all have obstacles to overcome. I am hoping that my experiences will be of help or an inspiration to you.

Throughout the book I have made references to God. I am a believer. I do not intend to preach or impose my values on anyone in any way. Judaism has profoundly affected my personal story, especially during the Islamic Revolution. In no way do I wish to criticize or glorify any one religion. I do believe that religion is a private matter. But your religion should not infringe upon my freedom, or mine upon yours. The same can be said of all values and opinions. Compassion, tolerance, and respect are necessary to maintain peace.

I am honoured for the time you will put into reading my story. I hope that in the end you will share the message with the ones you love. If you do, this will justify what I have experienced and why I was spared so many times. Allow me to take you on my journey.

Cast of Characters

Baba	Bijan, my father
Mamán	Parisa, my mother
Farah	My older sister
Soraya	My younger sister
Cyrus	My older brother
Aria	My younger brother
Baba Esghel	Baba's father
Naneh Jaan–Jaan	Baba's mother
Ammo David	Baba's oldest brother
Ester	Ammo David's wife
Ammeh Ashraf	Baba's eldest sister
Ammeh Nilofar	Baba's second-eldest sister
Uncle Naser	Ammeh Nilofar's husband
Baba Bozourg Moishe	Mamán's father
Naneh Zivar	Mamán's mother
Khaleh Mahin	Mamán's sister
Khaleh Ladan	Mamán's sister
Khaleh Shaheen	Mamán's sister
Khaleh Nastaran	Mamán's sister
Daii Faramarz	Mamán's brother
Daii Saaman	Mamán's brother

All names have been changed to protect identities.

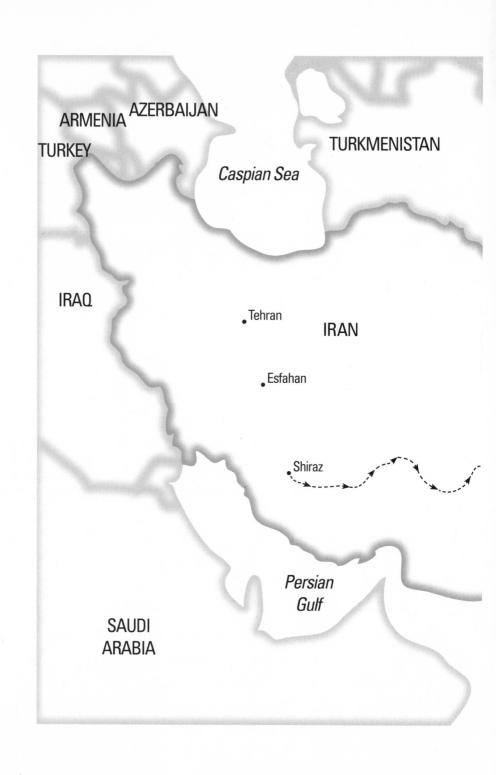

Uzbekistan

TAJIKISTAN

CHINA

Our Escape Route

AFGHANISTAN

Islamabad

Rawalpindi

Lahore

Zahedan

Quetta

INDIA

Karachi

Arabian Sea

PART ONE

Home

There are so many gifts
Still unopened from your birthday,
There are so many handcrafted presents
That have been sent to you by God,
The beloved does not mind repeating,
"Everything I have is also yours."
There are so many gifts, my dear,
Still unopened from your birthday.

Hafez of Shiraz (1325–89)

Shiraz

To me, Shiraz is more than a spicy, blackberry-and-plum-flavoured red wine.

Shiraz was a place touched by the golden light of the sunset streaming over the mountains onto its blue-glazed houses. It was an essential aroma of hookahs smoked by wizened old men crouched in its tea houses.

Shiraz was my home.

Shiraz was also the home of my family, of Baba, my father, and of Mamán, my mother.

Shiraz was the home of my grandparents.

Shiraz was the home of my great-grandparents, of my ancestors for the past 2,500 years, before the Shah of Iran's dynasty, before the advent of Islam, before the conquests of Darius the Great.

Shiraz has been home to Jews since the Babylonian Conquest in 597 BCE.

Shiraz has been home to my Persian Jewish family forever.

In my eyes, Shiraz was the centre of the universe and the most fascinating part of it. Most of the year, from almost anywhere in the city, I could see the snow-capped mountains that surrounded our green, fertile valley. Snow fell on the mountains far away, but never in the city.

Shiraz was renowned as the capital of Iran for many centuries. It was famous for its beautiful women, whose exquisite eyes and eyebrows were captured in the poetry of Iran's prominent poets. A glass of red wine was another subject immortalized by poets. One may wonder why, in a Muslim country, the poets would write about wine. Wine, specifically a glass of red Shiraz, rendered people more transparent, more authentic, more empathetic. So the poets believed.

The poetry of Iran and of Shiraz runs in the veins of every Iranian.

As a young child, I was expected to memorize and recite the words of our most important poets. Poetry was part of our very existence. It filled out our speech, ran through our thoughts, gave us our understanding of life. Iran's two most famous poets, Sa'adi and Hafez, were born and lived in Shiraz, the place that inspired their widely known poetry.

Even in death, these two were immortalized, their tombstones located in popular mausoleums that were considered sites for pilgrimage. Shiraz was known as the city of poets, wine, gardens, and flowers.

Shiraz was also celebrated throughout Iran for its lush gardens brimming with brilliantly coloured, heaven-scented roses and its cascading stone water fountains.

The Shiraz that I was born into was unlike any other part of Iran or any other part of the world. For me it was a paradise.

> The only friends who are free from cares
> are a goblet of wine and a book.
>
> Give me wine . . . that I may for a time forget
> the cares of the world.
>
> *Hafez of Shiraz*

>>>>>

> The grapes of my body can only become wine
> After the winemaker tramples me.
> I surrender my spirit like grapes to his trampling
> So my inmost heart can blaze and dance with joy.
> Although the grapes go on weeping blood and sobbing
> "I cannot bear any more anguish, any more cruelty."
> The trampler stuffs cotton in his ears: "I am not working in ignorance.
> You can deny me if you want, you have every excuse,
> But it is I who am the Master of this work.
> And when through my Passion you reach Perfection,
> You will never be done praising my name."
>
> *Mevlana Jelaluddin Rumi (1207–73)*

᠈᠈᠈᠈᠈᠈

Winemaking has been a ritual in Persian Jewish families for the past thousand years. From the day the last bottle was filled to the day before next year's winemaking began, Mamán and Baba heatedly discussed how many bottles would be needed for the next batch. The day of wine-making was a big ordeal in my house. We dreaded the day Baba would bring home the grapes. I could not contain myself. "Why do we have to make wine? Why can't we buy from the liquor store?"

"Making wine brings prosperity to the home. It is a *mitzvah*.[1] Our people have always done it, and we carry on the tradition," Mamán mumbled. By her tone, I believed she was also trying to convince herself. "Help me wash the tubs; soon you three girls will have to trample the grapes."

Baba visited the market frequently before he bought grapes. He tasted them from different farms in the market to make sure he liked their flavour and their texture. Red, juicy grapes were the only candidates for winemaking.

In the middle of the autumn, Baba warned us that he was going to buy the grapes that day. "Be ready to get started as soon as I return." He came home with a truckload of local red grapes bursting with seeds. These local grapes were from the same vines that made the world-renowned Shiraz wine. The same grapes that when turned into wine became the subject of poets' adoration.

"There are at least ten boxes of grapes; it will take forever to crush them," Soraya, my younger sister, complained.

Mamán had no sympathy. "Don't worry. Sima will start, and as long as she sings her rhyme, the job will go quickly."

I stomped and sang cheerfully while officiating at the grape-crushing ceremony. "*Paie man paie pashe kare Mamán tol nakesheh*." ("My feet are as light as flies' feet, and Mamán's task should be light and speedy.")

My brothers Cyrus and Aria were not interested in the ritual. They continued to bicycle around the garden.

The three musketeers took turns stomping on the grapes. The soft, cool grapes under our feet revealed another side to their nature. Sharp little stems poked viciously at the skin on my feet. As the crushing continued to release the heavenly burgundy juice, my feet turned red. Hours went by, and Mamán inspected our work from time to time,

---

1   A religious obligation or good deed.

studying our labour, and what we were unable to crush with our feet, she squeezed with her hands.

The entire neighbourhood dropped by when we made wine: Naneh Jaan-Jaan (Baba's mother), Ammeh (Aunt) Ashraf (Baba's eldest sister), Ammeh Nilofar (Baba's second-eldest sister). I suspect the visit was an excuse for an inspection, to make sure that the steps were properly followed. The sweet smell of the grapes mixed with the October weather was the promise of cool winter on its way.

Though Mamán and Baba often disagreed with each other, they managed to work well together on this project. They were too busy to argue. After Mamán and the aunts were satisfied that all was in order, Mamán called to Baba, "It's done. I need you to help me take the vat downstairs. Help me transfer the crushed grapes into the container!" Together they transported the crushed grapes down into the dark, dingy cellar and transferred the mash into two big barrels, a difficult task. This was nerve-racking, because if the grapes fell on the floor, all our hard work would be wasted. Whatever fell to the floor instead of into the barrels was useless.

They re-emerged from the basement, arms stained red up to their shoulders from the juice.

From then on, it was a few weeks of wait-and-see. The juice remained on the bottom while the skins formed a mass of pulp on top. Mamán visited her barrels of wine daily, lifting the cotton covers, smelling and tasting to check on their progress. I watched her going through each step patiently and could not figure out how she knew when the wine was ready. Unfortunately for Mamán and Baba, almost half the time, their wine would turn into vinegar. That was a reason for blame.

"Baba screwed up!"

"You are the one who always messes things up!"

Neither of them ever found out what had gone wrong and how to prevent it from happening in the future. But they continued blaming each other. It was a risky labour.

Mamán then poured all the juice into a deep clay barrel, mixed in sugar, and covered it. The pulp was used to make vinegar, which was used for different types of homemade pickles: cucumber, herb, eggplant, garlic, and apple. The pickles were popular with meals. Mamán insisted that a daily dose of pickles with romaine lettuce was her ticket to longevity and health. She went through a lot of pickles.

Mamán kept all the wine bottles in the cellar, lined up according to the year the wine was made. It was homemade wine, authentic, and a symbol of pride. The wine was served every Friday night for Shabbat.

Regardless of the time of year, our family gathered around the table for Shabbat dinner. Mamán toiled in the kitchen all day long. Friday was never long enough for her to do everything she wanted to do. The two hours before sundown on Friday afternoon were chaotic in our home. Mamán shouted to us to help her finish the cooking, cleaning, and bathing so she would be on time for candle-lighting.

She covered her eyes with her hands as she said the blessing over the candles and often she would cry, praying silently. Then she clasped her hands and joyfully proclaimed, "I feel close to God." These words she repeated every Friday.

Baba recited the blessings over the wine and the flatbread; then we dug into the best meal of the week. The Shabbat menu remained the same, week after week: fried fish, boiled chicken, rice, and stew. Mamán cooked enough food to last us all Saturday and well into Sunday. She never cooked on Saturday. It was the biggest sin to create fire.

I tasted the results of our winemaking labour for the first time when I was six years old. My parents thought I was mature enough to drink the four small shots of wine for the Passover Seder. The sweet wine flowed down my throat like velvet. To my surprise, I didn't become drunk.

Or was it grape juice disguised as wine? How could a six-year-old's stomach take the wine without becoming drunk? But no one ever admitted that it was grape juice. Baba was proud that I had fulfilled the requirements of the Seder and drunk "the wine."

~~~~~~

Mamán and Baba's marriage was the product of an arrangement that had come to fruition in spring 1963. If love marriages ever happened, I never knew of them. My grandfathers, Baba Esghel and Baba Bozourg Moishe, were brothers. Both fathers agreed on the marriage and announced it to Baba and Mamán. Baba and Mamán were neighbours and had played together as children. They were attracted to each other physically. Baba was charming and tall, with thick, dark, curly hair and a full black moustache. Mamán was of medium height, slim and beautiful, with a beauty mark on either side of her chin. Mamán was eighteen and Baba was twenty-eight when they got married.

Baba's older brother had been married off a couple months earlier and Baba was the next one to be married. Mamán's older sister was already married; her younger sister was engaged but could not marry until Mamán was married and out of the house. It would have shamed the family to have Mamán stay at home. So Baba Bozourg Moishe approached his brother, Esghel, and both decided that marrying off their children would be a good idea.

Mamán and Baba each had eleven siblings, and so our extended family was very large. Mamán's side was made up of three boys and nine girls; Baba's side consisted of nine boys and three girls: a perfect match.

Mamán felt superior to Baba because she had earned a degree in nursing. Baba did not continue school past Grade 5. He had been working in construction and as a handyman since the age of thirteen. Baba Esghel was a construction worker and he needed help to support his family. Baba was talented and liked working with his hands. He accompanied his father to work as his assistant.

ORT, a Jewish organization, offered opportunities to teach trades to young men. It was perfect for Baba; he decided to become a carpenter. He spent the entire day at school, where he learned carpentry skills and ate lunch. He spoke fondly to us of the lunches at ORT. To feed twelve kids at home on a day worker's salary was difficult for Naneh Jaan-Jaan. Money was scarce, and great thrift was practised.

Baba had accumulated a nice pot of cash by the age of twenty-eight. At the time he and Mamán married, he owned his own house. This was a good selling point for the match. Not that they had a choice in the matter. It was unheard of in the Jewish community of Shiraz to stand against an arranged marriage. Nobody ever had.

Baba's workshop was located in a room inside the entrance to our house; he was always home. Our house was his castle. The best way to furnish his castle was with Persian carpets and a garden full of rose bushes. Baba stated, "A Persian carpet is like a bottle of wine: the older it gets, the better it looks and feels." The carpet's design was proof of the carpet's origins. Tabriz carpet was made of the finest wool or silk and tightly knotted. Shiraz carpet was made of thicker wool, not as tightly knotted. We owned a variety of carpets. Baba was a proud Shirazi. We had to have Shirazi carpets in the house. The big, knotted, rectangular burgundy carpets were threaded through with flower, sheep, goat, and bird designs. We were always in the midst of nature.

Baba was renowned for his cleanliness and tidiness. His belief was, "If a house is tidy, and everything is in place, it will look like a castle." Unfortunately, on the issue of household order, Mamán and Baba had very different viewpoints and standards.

Baba's touch was visible throughout the house and garden. He cleaned the rooms, swept the garden tiles, and watered the plants and trees. Wonderful rose bushes, pansies, and carnations bloomed non-stop amid other colourful, fragrant flowers, and the fruit trees brought forth masses of blossoms and lavish harvests. It was as if the roses and trees wanted to give their best to their loving caretaker.

Mamán was a nurse who worked in several different clinics. She was known among her colleagues and bosses as an exceptional employee, but with one flaw. She was never on time, was the last one to arrive on the job, and usually the first to leave, excusing herself because of her five children. But she never arrived home quickly enough; a Jewish woman's "real" job was to be a homemaker. The ones who did work did not have five children.

When I came home for lunch, I hoped she would come home so I could see her for a few minutes. Sometimes she arrived but sometimes she did not. Sitting on the stoop, I observed the comings and goings of the people who lived or worked nearby. The three musketeers were the street patrol.

I missed Mamán when she was not home. She called us her little chicks because we followed her everywhere: on shopping trips, in the kitchen, to the bathroom. We must have suffocated her with too much love. She was never alone. We even fought about who should be walking on her right and left sides when we went out.

My sister Farah was born in 1964, a year after my parents' wedding, fourteen months before I appeared on the scene. We grew up almost like twins. Farah was Baba's favourite; he called her his *"gole sare sabad,"* his most precious flower. She was a strikingly beautiful child with thick, straight black hair and bangs that framed her dark eyes.

Farah was particularly loved by Ammeh Nilofar, who was single and lived next door with Naneh Jaan-Jaan. Ammeh Nilofar was a regular visitor in our house and doted on Farah, lavishing her with love and compliments. She included me as the tag-along when she played with Farah. She was number one, and I was well aware of my place.

My younger sister, Soraya, was two years younger than me. She had gorgeous black eyes, with long eyelashes; her tightly curled hair was similar to Baba's side of the family, making her a perfect Goel offspring. She was full of energy and did her chores quickly, which also made Baba very proud of her.

Farah, Soraya, and I were known as "the three musketeers" in our neighbourhood. Mamán contributed to the image by sewing us matching colourful flowery outfits. We loved the flowers in the garden, and when we were outside the house, we were dressed in flower print fabrics with small orange flowers. We went everywhere together.

Mamán worked long, hard hours as a nurse, and was exhausted when she arrived home from work. Endless evening hours were spent on needlework or sewing clothes for us. Mamán had no interest in doing housework. She believed that girls had to be able to fend for themselves, without being reliant on others, and was determined to teach us all the skills necessary to run a household, whether for ourselves or for a family.

Growing up, the three musketeers became domestic interns in training. We took over many of the household tasks as soon as we were capable. Farah cleaned rooms, Soraya swept the garden tiles, and I washed pots and dishes, some of which were bigger than me. We also accompanied Mamán when she went grocery shopping. No labour was off limits. As far as Mamán was concerned, we could do anything, as long as we didn't injure or kill ourselves in the process. "Yes," she replied, "of course you are capable. Go ahead and prove it to me and to yourself."

Many times I came across Mamán while she was cooking or sewing, tears rolling down her cheeks. She was miserable: overwhelmed with five children and a full-time job. So I joined her in her crying spells until at last she stopped. I dreaded finding her in this state.

Mamán and Baba fought over every little thing. He criticized her cooking: "You waste food!" "The meat is not cut properly!" And her organization: "The yarn and thread and material should not all be jumbled up in one bag like that!" I hated when he started on her. It frightened me when they raised their voices. Mamán could never admit she was wrong. She always tried to put the blame back on Baba. Mamán never forgot what Baba said or did. But she always forgot what she had said to him and how she had hurt him, too. Mamán had selective memory loss.

The family was polarized. Baba considered me Mamán's daughter, as if he hadn't fathered me. "You are just trying to chummy up to me, but I know you will take her side like always," if I tried to please him.

Everything I did, from my special efforts at cleaning, or working hard and doing well at school, or being particularly polite to my elders, was done to win Baba's affection. But although he loved me, he wasn't able to show it the way he showed it with Farah.

>>>>>

Mamán and Baba were not happy about having three girls. Three girls meant three dowries; three weddings to pay for in full, and more important, our family name would not be carried on by daughters. A family legacy could not continue if there was no boy in the family. Fortunately for them, the next two children were boys. My first brother, Cyrus, was born four years after me. Baba was delighted, as this meant his family name would be carried on; it was extremely important that he prove his manhood by producing a son. He was all smiles and happiness for days. Cyrus was named after Cyrus the Great; in Persian this translated as "King Cyrus." King Cyrus, who reigned in Iran in the sixth century BCE, was respected for his achievements in human rights and his influence on both Eastern and Western civilizations.

Mamán's and Baba's families visited our home when Mamán arrived from the hospital. The *brit milah*[2] celebration in our garden a week after Cyrus's birth was hugely exciting for the three musketeers. In their exuberance, Baba and Mamán sent out invitations to everyone and went full-out for the celebration.

On the morning of Cyrus's *brit milah*, we heard a strange knocking on the door. I answered. A crippled man confronted me. His right leg and half of his left leg were missing; he had no left arm and no right forearm. He could only move around with his crutches. I had never seen him before, neither in my home, nor on the streets, nor anywhere else. He asked to see Baba, who was not at home. He insisted on waiting for him. We invited the beggar into our house, but he adamantly refused.

"I will wait in the garden until he arrives. No matter how long it takes." While he waited for Baba, he let his repulsive body slide onto the tiled floor. We were more frightened by his lack of teeth than by his missing limbs. Sympathy mixed with horror engulfed me as he waited for Baba.

Whenever a Jewish boy was born in Shiraz, the same disabled Jewish beggar came to claim his due, and took exactly fifty *tooman* from the

---

2   Religious ceremony of circumcision on the seventh day of life of a Jewish boy.

newborn's father. You could buy flatbread for one-tenth of a *tooman*, or a kilo of yogurt for one *tooman*. I could buy a small bag of Cheetos for one-fourth of a *tooman*. Fifty *tooman* was a lot of money.

On Baba's arrival home, he came face-to-face with the crippled man. His reaction was more sympathetic than ours. Baba happily handed the man the sum he asked for. "I have seen him in the ghetto. This poor man has had a troubled life and he relies on charity for his livelihood." I was relieved to watch him leave our home and disappear from my sight.

Quickly, Baba proceeded to string coloured lights from tree to tree throughout the garden. The lights glittered like precious jewels. The round metal tables and metal fold-up chairs were placed among the flowerbeds and trees. A five-person band, a caterer who presented plates upon plates of traditional Shirazi Jewish cooking, and the balcony that doubled as the dance floor added to the fairyland atmosphere of the biggest celebration the Goel family had ever thrown. The arrival of Cyrus, our King Cyrus, was greeted with unprecedented joy.

Two hundred guests descended on our house for the festive occasion.

A big argument erupted before the relatives arrived over who was going to hold the baby for the circumcision. This was the highest honour a parent could bestow upon a relative. Mamán wanted to give this respect to her father, to honour her side of the family. Baba wanted to give the honour to Ammo David, my eldest uncle on Baba's side; not even to his own father. Mamán insisted Baba should have saved the honour for himself, if he refused to give the respect to her family. But Baba refused to budge. It had to be Ammo David.

I wondered why nothing was happy for the sake of being happy. In the end, Ammo David was given the honour. However, when his own sons were born, he kept the honour for himself.

Aria was born two years after Cyrus. Baba was ecstatic with the birth of a second son. The three musketeers and Cyrus were excited to have a new brother. We five children always played together and we were all the closest friends.

The crippled man came back when Aria was born. I never understood who that man was, how he found out about the births of my brothers, or why he was entitled to this charity. But the adults accepted him without question and gave him the sums he demanded.

❧❧❧❧❧

Ammeh Nilofar lived next door to us with Naneh Jaan-Jaan and Baba Esghel. She spent a lot of time at our house, since Farah was the first niece in the family. She was our favourite visitor to the house. Farah ran right up to her whenever she heard her footsteps. But change was in the air. Baba was helping to find a husband for Ammeh Nilofar. She would not remain single for too long.

Ammeh Nilofar was six feet tall. Iranian men, especially Iranian Jews, are not tall. A groom tall enough for her could not be found in Shiraz. Baba went to Tehran with Ammeh Nilofar to find a suitably tall husband for her. It was a successful mission. Baba did it out of love for his younger sister; he could not know to what degree the favour would come in handy in the future.

Our garden welcomed Ammeh Nilofar's pre-wedding and wedding celebrations in the late spring of 1970.

The three musketeers were thrilled about her upcoming nuptials, because it was our first wedding. But we were also saddened, because her marriage would take Ammeh Nilofar away from us. She was moving to Tehran, where the groom lived.

An engagement party took place not long after, and the date of the wedding was set for two months later, in early summer. Ammeh Nilofar was eager to get married. As was the custom, Naneh Jaan-Jaan had been accumulating pots and pans, dishes, cutlery, linens, and household articles that made up the dowry for her second daughter since Nilofar was born. Ammeh Nilofar entered into this marriage equipped with everything necessary to create a proper home.

A week before the wedding, many traditional ceremonies and customs crowded the agenda. One morning, I walked into our dining room and found the table covered with dozens of shoeboxes, piled one atop the other. It was the custom for the groom's family to provide shoes for the bride's immediate family for the wedding celebration. We peeked into the boxes and found among the variety of women's shoes several boxes of shiny pink satin ones. Grabbing them from the piles, we plunked ourselves on the floor and tried on the pink shoes, trading them around until we each ended up with the right size. I thought I would be the fanciest five-year-old girl at the wedding with my lovely shoes. We developed a fondness for our new Uncle Naser for giving us such a beautiful surprise.

On the wedding morning, the women gathered together to go to Ammeh Ashraf's beauty salon to have their hair done. Both my aunts were brimming with glee. One was soon to be married and the other took pride in showing off her expertise in making the bride look her best.

Our garden was transformed into a fairyland. Baba, Baba Esghel, and Ammo Teimour, Baba's brother, spent the early part of the wedding day stringing coloured lights across the enclosure. Rented tables were set up in the garden, decorated with baskets of fruits, apples, oranges, small cucumbers, pistachios, almonds, and pumpkin seeds. The three musketeers arrived, dressed identically as usual. Our uniform was cotton, puff-sleeved, knee-length pink dresses, made by Mamán, the best dressmaker we knew.

Uncle Farid's band performed at the wedding. The five-piece band entertained with a singer, a violin, castanets, and maracas, and Uncle Farid played the *doumbek*, a Middle Eastern drum with a rat-a-tat-tat beat. Uncle Farid, the shortest man in the family, danced joyfully, squatting style, kicking his legs out from under his big belly.

Women shimmied together, moving their hands, arms, and shoulders, undulating in fluid configurations. I had never seen women's hips move this way, as if there were no bones in their bodies. They snapped their fingers to the music, their voices trilled. It was all too exciting to watch. Men shook their shoulders and heads to the beat of the *doumbek*, eyes twinkling. Men and women never touched each other while dancing, but the air was charged with an electricity I did not understand.

Ammeh Ashraf was a superb dancer and displayed her talent masterfully at the wedding, bursting with joy. I wanted to be able to dance like her one day. I loved it when she used her hands to make a castanet sound, keeping time to the rhythms of the music. She wrapped her hands together to make a kind of echo chamber while snapping her forefingers together. I begged her to show me how to master this trick. It took a long time, and hours of practice, but I learned, thanks to Ammeh Ashraf. She was not only a great dancer but also a patient teacher.

She had other talents. She could blow bubbles from gum that was not bubblegum. Big bubbles. I could never blow bubbles even half the size she could, even with bubblegum. She always chewed gum and constantly blew those enormous bubbles.

I sat on Ammeh Nilofar's lap and wished her good luck in her marriage. I wondered how old I would be when I would wear a beautiful white wedding dress.

Marriage in an Iranian Jewish family was a permanent state of affairs. You arrived at your husband's house wearing a white dress (the wedding dress) and you left it wearing a white dress (the white cotton burial shroud). You did your best whether or not you loved your spouse. That's how it was in my family; that's how it was for everyone around me. I had never heard of a divorced Jewish woman and had never met one. I wondered what a divorced woman looked like.

At ten years of age, I met a woman with a fully made-up face, wearing a short skirt, her long, loose, brown hair flowing down her back. I had seen her walking in front of our house many times in the late afternoon while waiting for Mamán to come home. My child's curiosity piped up, "What is your name?"

"Farkhondeh."

"I am Sima. What are you doing here?"

"I am walking home from work; I am the receptionist for a company."

I admired her sense of style and her fully made-up face. Mamán did not care about her looks and did not have time to appear as good as Farkhondeh, the receptionist. I wondered why she put the grey and blue colouring around her eyes in the middle of the day.

"How many children do you have?"

I assumed every woman her age must be married and have children. That was the case for every woman in my family; the elder ones were married and mothers by their late teens or early twenties.

"I have no children."

"How could that be?" was my innocent remark.

Her face turned bright red; her gaze dropped to the ground. "I was married but I'm going through a divorce."

"Divorce!" That was a taboo word; Baba used that word when he fought with Mamán. "Why?"

"My husband beat me."

I wondered if the makeup was to cover the black and blue bruises on her face from the beatings. Mamán sometimes had those bruises on her body when Baba hit her.

I admired Farkhondeh's courage. It was difficult to be a divorcee in Shiraz.

She became a regular visitor to our home and confided to Mamán, "Men consider me an easy target and want to sleep with me."

I was confused and could not make up my mind which was more of a torture: to be a divorced woman or a miserably married woman. They both suffered eternally.

>>>>>

Mamán and Baba had all five children in less than eight years. Most of my aunts and uncles had five children. Why five? It was to keep away the evil eye. Five was the magic number for the Jews in Shiraz. Muslims also believed in the power of five. Mamán had no time to breathe from one child to the next. She expected Farah, Soraya, and me to help her with our younger siblings. Kids took care of kids. The three musketeers were in charge of looking after Aria when Mamán was not home. Poor Aria must have been made of steel after all the falls he survived without breaking any bones.

Aria was five years old, riding a bicycle in the garden while Cyrus and the three musketeers played hopscotch. A skrrrrreeeech! erupted from Aria. The bike handle smashed into his stomach and he tumbled off the bike. Farah took charge. "Soraya, call Mamán. Sima, call Naneh Jaan-Jaan. We will take care of you, Aria."

Mamán shouted at us that we were irresponsible not to protect Aria. We had to be more vigilant in looking after him, which was not easy. Mamán took Aria to the hospital; he had twisted his intestines in the accident.

He was hospitalized for a week following the accident. The doctors operated on him. Baba was not home, and we could not contact him. When he returned from the farm and found out, he also screamed at us, calling us negligent. Harsh words were thrown our way, a dagger in our hearts. How could a twelve-year-old, an eleven-year-old, and a nine-year-old be responsible for a seven-year-old and a five-year-old? We had to mature fast in that household, and for the most part, we did. But looking after our younger siblings, when the age difference between the eldest and the youngest was only seven years, wasn't the only difference that separated us Goels from our relatives and neighbours.

Most of my aunts were stay-at-home mothers except for Ammo David's wife, Ester, who also was a general practitioner. They were the only family members who had both a butler and a maid. In the entire family, on both sides, the three musketeers were the only children who had specific daily chores. None of my cousins cooked, cleaned, or did the shopping the way the three musketeers did. And we also excelled at school.

Something felt different about my family . . . about me. As if we were living in two different worlds. My family, Baba, Mamán, grandparents, aunts, uncles, cousins, and their friends . . . that was my comfortable world. In this world, I could just be myself. I was reminded by Baba, "Your family will eat your flesh, but keep the bone. No matter how much you fight among yourselves, if there is a fight with others, your family stands by your side, whether or not they agree with you." I never had to pretend I was someone else to be accepted.

Your name is a symbol of who you are and where you come from. As far as I was concerned, my name was Sima, a very common, non-denominational Persian name. But to the outside world, I had to give my last name, too. This was definitely not something to my advantage, as "Goel" immediately classified me as different. My family name was unusual, and it was certainly not Persian. It is a Hebrew name meaning "redeemer." This had been our family name for generations. But people inquired all the time. For most people, it did not matter that I was different, but some immediately asked, "You're not Muslim, are you? Are you a *Jehood* [dirty Jew]?"

Once, when I was six years old, I met a child in the park my family visited on Saturday nights. Jews went to the park on Saturday nights; Muslims went out on Friday nights. It was not written on the girl's forehead whether she was Muslim, Jew, Baha'i, or Christian. She was the same height as me. I assumed since it was Saturday night in the park, she must be Jewish. We were kids the same age, enough of a reason to play together. "Do you want to play?" I asked.

I did not ask her name, because I didn't want to introduce myself. *Names are unimportant*, I repeated to myself. But before we got far in our game, her mother appeared out of nowhere. She looked at me, paused, and barked, "What is your name?"

"Sima."

"What is your last name?"

I dreaded having to answer this question, because if she asked, it meant that the name mattered to her. This had happened before, and it was inevitable that I would not be able to play. My last name had a stigma.

"Goel," I responded softly, staring at the ground.

Maliciously, the mother yanked the girl's hand as if I was about to contaminate her daughter with deadly bacteria. The girl walked away crying. I was hysterical. Mamán listened to me intently. There was no calming me down. I was mad that the mother's cruelty spoiled a good game of hide-and-seek. From that day on, I worked even harder to keep my secret as long as I could, but some people kept prying and pushing until I had to tell them.

That was one of my first recollections of being Jewish, of being different. I wanted Baba to change our family name to a more common one so that a mere name wouldn't separate me from others at first encounter. I never understood why Baba was so stubborn about keeping our family name. Baba Bozourg Moishe, Mamán's father, had changed his last name to a Persian name; no one could tell whether or not they were Jews. But when I begged Baba, the response was a huge, resounding NO. Baba was proud of our family name and heritage. He even convinced me, "Our family name means 'redeemer' in Hebrew. It is a privilege to carry on this family name. It is a holy name."

Baba had strong convictions about who he was. He did not care how others reacted. This was his strength, which was also his weakness. He did not care about what others thought of him — simultaneously a blessing and a curse. He repeated many times: "If someone does not want to be your friend because you are Jewish, then that is not the kind of person you want as a friend. It is ignorant people who think that way."

Certainly not all Muslims felt the same; many held the 8,000 Jews of Shiraz in high regard. They had no qualms about dining with Jews or being friends with them. Many of Baba's customers were Muslim, and the colleagues at Mamán's clinic were friendly to her and welcoming to us when we visited. But there were others, usually uneducated, who ignored this call for respect. They called Jews *Najest*, a word that means "impure, filthy, dirty." When I heard that word, I wanted the ground to open up and swallow me. That tone of voice shrivelled my insides. To me, it was the worst insult in the world. Those who uttered it knew what effect it had and insisted on saying it to Jews to humiliate them.

Mamán also hated the word *Jehood*. We all did. That is why on rainy days she did not go shopping. She especially avoided the Jewish ghetto, Mahaleh, which is where she usually shopped. The ghetto had a poor sewage system. Water accumulated in the alleys and it was impossible to walk through them without getting soaked to the knees. But getting wet was not the only problem. The more serious obstacle was that the ghetto was close to the Shah Chergh quarter, where the biggest and most venerated mosque in Shiraz was located. Because of the proximity of the two districts, when Muslims wanted to attend services at the Shah Chergh, they inevitably had to pass in front of the ghetto.

Ultra-religious Shiite Muslims believed that if a Jew walked out of the ghetto onto the adjacent streets on a wet day, he brought with him Jew-contaminated water en route to the mosque. A Jew who dared emerge from the ghetto with wet shoes or feet was greeted with hate-filled stares and insults. Though few in number, even one stare was enough to demoralize us for days. "Why don't you dirty Jews stay home! *Najest!*" Water is an easy way to transfer impurity. To face the scorn and hatred of the fanatics was not worth the agony. On rainy days, we stayed home.

Though Iran is a majority Shiite Muslim country, many Sunni Muslims, Zoroastrians, Christians, and Baha'i lived here. The minority religions respected each other at all times. Never did people of another minority religion insult us or call us *Jehood*; to them we were *Hayodi* (a member of the Jewish tribe), a more polite way of referring to us. But the poor Baha'i suffered the same anguish as Jews. They also were called *Najest*.

❧❧❧❧❧

Traditionally, Jewish men in Iran were merchants of jewellery or clothing, tradesmen, or labourers. They also were involved in the alcohol trade, music professions and businesses, and moneylending. Mamán later explained to us that the Muslims, especially the Shiite Muslims, were forbidden to listen to or perform music. Traditional Iranian music was kept alive by minority religions, particularly by Jews. Some of the musicians did not reveal their religions to the public; only close friends were aware of their religion. In addition to forbidding its followers from listening to music, the religion also forbade drinking alcohol, making alcoholic drinks, lending money, and profiting from loans. The irony was that their customers were all Muslim.

Baba's father, Esghel, was a quiet man of dignified appearance, with a white beard and a pale complexion. He made a deliberate effort to melt into the background. He was a construction worker on call. He waited daily with other casual workers in a nearby square for a contractor to choose him for a job. Sometimes it was his own brother who hired him. Known as "the *tzaddik*" (wise man), he attended synagogue twice a day, regardless of the day or the season. He was the first one in the synagogue, and the last one to leave. If anyone needed a *minyan*[3] for a house of mourning, he was there. He collected donations for the poor Jews of the city.

Baba's mother, Jaan-Jaan, "dear-dear," was a short, slim woman with a great abundance of energy. I never saw her tire. She was married in 1933 at the age of eleven. Naneh Jaan-Jaan had many miscarriages before her first son, who became Ammo David, the apple of her eye, was delivered successfully. She was only seventeen years old when Baba, her second child, was born.

Naneh Jaan-Jaan was a role model for our family, because no matter what task she undertook, she would complete it effortlessly and with great speed. The result was that when Mamán wanted us to do a chore quickly, she would say, "Be a Jaan-Jaan!" and we understood what she meant.

Naneh Jaan-Jaan was an esthetician who went to private homes to deliver her services. Her schedule was flexible, which meant she could be home to greet us at the door when we came home from school. She was a second mother to us.

Baba, named Bijan, was the second eldest in a family of twelve children. We thought he looked like a movie star. Of average height, he had a remarkable physical presence that made him stand out in a crowd. His most distinguishing feature was his mustache. It was his pride and joy, and he took great care of it. It made me think of a peacock displaying its plumage.

Baba was a stubborn man who carved his own path. He loved to work with his hands, and took great pride in his skills, whether as a gardener or as a carpenter. He chose to become an independent tradesman. This quality led him, as we were growing up, to decide to become a landowner and farmer, something Jews in general avoided.

His workshop was always as neat as a pin. Unlike the way Mamán organized her part of the household, he had a place for every tool and he could reach out blindly with his hand and find whichever tool he needed. He swept up the wood scraps frequently while he worked, so

---

3   The required number of ten men to be present to pray.

that when he left his shop, he wouldn't track dust and chips into the house. We children all inherited our father's trait for neatness.

My maternal grandfather, Moishe, started off as a labourer, but eventually became boss of his own construction company. He was known in the city as "the tallest one." We could always spot him from far away because he stood head and shoulders above everyone else. It was a comical sight to see him walking with his wife, Zivar, who was extremely short. They were known as the cup and saucer. The cup was Baba Bozourg; the saucer was my round and short Naneh Zivar. Whenever we visited them, his glasses would be perched on the middle of his nose, and he permanently clutched a notepad, calculating the day's orders and accounts for his company. It was a family joke that if someone was doing serious calculations or writing intensely, we'd laughingly call him "Moishe." He loved all of his grandchildren and would sit us on his lap and tell us fables as his fingers flew over the abacus.

Naneh Zivar, despite her diminutive size, was a giant personality and a legend among the shop owners in the neighbourhood. They believed she brought them good luck. Every time she entered a shop, it would immediately fill up with other customers. Consequently, all the merchants hoped that she would drop by their shop first thing in the morning, bringing her good luck with her. That is how she became known as a good luck charm. They greeted her warmly, gave her all their attention, and thanked her for gracing their establishment. And they watched the door following her departure, waiting for the crowds.

~~~~~~

Mamán's name was "Parisa." She was fourth in a family of nine girls and three boys, the second girl. She had very dark, penetrating eyes and soft, curly black hair. She was not a vain woman, but the livid scar that ran across her neck and collarbone because of a fall on shattered glass when she was ten years old caused her to be quite self-conscious about her throat. Consequently she always wore high-necked tops.

Also known as the stubborn, intelligent, and ambitious one in her family, she pursued a career above the family's accepted status. If her brothers could go to school, she felt she was also entitled to get an education. As a graduate nurse, she had reached the highest level of academic achievement of all the women in her family. The four older sisters were housewives, and the four younger sisters were office secretaries.

Mamán's eldest sister, Khaleh Mahin, visited us regularly. Mamán and her sisters were like peas in a pod: black hair, black eyes, and low voices. Khaleh Shadi, who, unlike the other sisters, had an exceptional figure and liked to show it off with tight clothes, felt indebted to Mamán because Mamán helped her find a good government job after high school.

Khaleh Shaheen visited us twice a week on Monday and Thursday afternoons. Mamán had a special relationship with her. Her visit meant continuous murmurs of quiet conversation. We were not supposed to hear their discussions. I looked forward to Khaleh Shaheen's visits because she brought us chickpea cookies from the best pastry shop across the street from their house. Her visits lasted hours, with the sisters and girls drinking tea and munching on the cookies.

Daii Faramarz, whose face was identical to his father's, Baba Bozourg's, was my favourite Daii. Mamán was sandwiched in birth between the two brothers. The rough games they played as children left Mamán with the scar on her neck, and she never forgot nor forgave her brothers for it. Daii Faramarz immigrated to America in 1969; the day he left for America, I was miserable. Since the day he left, whenever I saw an airplane, I waved my hand to the sky, hoping that he would see me waving to him.

Daii Saaman owned a record store that was located at the entrance to Baba Bozourg's house. He was the favourite of Mamán's parents. Baba Bozourg Moishe offered him the space for the business and the apartment above to live in. This privilege was bestowed on him and no one else in the family. He was in contact with the young men and women in Shiraz. His shop carried all kinds of music, from traditional Iranian music to Western pop music.

Though Mamán liked her family, she wanted to move out. The only way to move out was to be married. One of the great selling points in the marriage market in Baba's favour was that he owned his own place, a large, twelve-room house with an enormous garden. It was not unusual for newlywed couples to rent for the first few years of their marriages in order to save for a home of their own. Generally, renting was looked down upon, as if one were poor. They were not free to do what they wanted with their property; they were dependent on the landlord's permission.

Waste was not the Goel way of conducting their lives. But Mamán wasn't impressed with the house. Arguments started early in their marriage over those empty rooms, which she realized even a big family would be unable to use. Baba insisted on renting them out to boarders, which made Mamán very uncomfortable. They never resolved this difference of opinion, even as we were growing up and used more of the space.

Set back from the street by a passageway, the big garden contained five orange trees, two apple trees, a pomegranate tree, a patch of red grape vines and many rose bushes. The centrepiece was a large, blue-tiled fountain. The garden was large enough that we could ride our bicycles in and out of the trees along several circular tiled paths. And there was still enough room to hold a party with hundreds of people.

><><><

"A little and a little, collected together, becomes a great deal;
the heap in the barn consists of single grains,
and drop by drop makes the inundation."

Sa'adi

Spring was the aromatic time of year, when the orange trees flowered. Our garden was a breathtaking sight. The three musketeers, along with Cyrus and Aria, collected the orange blossom petals that fell during the night. We dried them tenderly on cotton fabric and dropped the petals into our tea throughout the year. The fragrance reminded us of flowering springtime.

Spring was ultimate heaven in our home and in the streets of Shiraz. Street vendors sold Chinese daffodils, green almonds, and steamed rutabagas in paper bags. The sweet fragrance, the romantic sounds of Persian singers on the radio, and shoppers frantically running around meant the promise of New Year's arrival. Muslim families travelled to be with others in their family; the children wore new clothes to celebrate the New Year. The special menu for the arrival of the New Year made the fishmongers rich. Every Iranian ate herbed rice with fried fish, no matter what the price. I loved this dish.

There were three seasons in Shiraz: Four months of spring, from mid-February to mid-May, where the fragrance of blossoms delighted the sense of smell with every breath; this was followed by the scorching summer, which stretched from mid-May to September, when it was dry and hot — so hot that we fantasized about frying an egg on the sidewalk;

and then the rainy, cool times of autumn and winter.

We cooled off in the garden's fountain during the hot days of summer. The competition between the girls' and boys' teams was not fair; we were the older ones and splashed Cyrus and Aria, soaking them completely. As Cyrus and Aria grew older, they wanted one of the three musketeers to team up with them. Winning was their only goal. Farah agreed to join them, and they won from that day on. Farah was popular among all of us; Soraya and I could not keep her just to ourselves.

In the evening, Baba covered the pool with a wooden board. From this platform we had a view of the night sky unimpeded by the heavy branches of our fruit trees. We lay on our backs and tried to pick out the different constellations. The first time I found the Big Dipper was a huge revelation for me. I had an appointment with the sky every night for weeks, wondering if the Big Dipper would show up.

Summer nights were spent sleeping in the walled garden covered in nothing but linens, amid the warm scent of roses and jasmine blossoms. We woke up to the sounds and fragrances of the garden being tended; the swish of water from the hose when Baba was home, the delicate perfumes of opening flowers and the smell of wet soil. I made our favourite breakfast: scrambled eggs, dill pickles, and tomato sandwiches. The garden was too hot at midday; the sun-drenched tiles burned our feet. The small pool was our refuge from the heat.

The dates of the birth and death of the Muslim prophet and his descendants were school holidays. We had many days off.

On such a day in early fall, we would spend time crocheting or sitting at the knitting machine producing sweaters for the entire family. The afternoons were cool enough for siestas. At that time of the year, the sun's warmth was pleasant, acting as a perfect heater. A wool blanket covered the garden's tiled floor and another one covered us. After lunch, the best way to rest was to lie down on the blanket and to try to fall asleep for a few minutes. My head was the only part not covered by the blanket.

❦❦❦❦❦

Baba purchased a piece of land in 1971 in the country and changed careers. He decided overnight to become a farmer and a landowner. This was unheard of in the Jewish community. Under the influence of his best friend, a single Baha'i man, Golshan, who lived across the street from us, the two of them decided to buy land in the countryside across the road from one another. I was too young to comprehend the consequences of Baba's decision at the time. We could not have imagined how this decision, taken so suddenly, would alter our lives and our relationship with Baba. Our family life underwent a major disruption. Mamán lost all the help Baba had provided as the on-site parent and housekeeping partner; Baba would no longer be around the house during the week.

It was Baba who had maintained the garden at home, helped with the shopping and the cleaning. Because he had his workshop at home, he had always been there when we needed him. Mamán had a full-time job as a nurse and relied on Baba to be around to help. The length of time Baba spent at the farm created a lot of stress for Mamán.

Baba's property was a forty-five-minute drive from Shiraz, near Kavar, known for its waterfalls. Owning a car was a luxury reserved for wealthy people. Baba did not drive, and we did not have a car in the family; he couldn't commute on public buses on a daily basis. He took up residence in the country, returning home on late Friday afternoons and taking the city bus to return to the country on early Sunday mornings. This was a radical change in our lives.

He spent a lot of money and time on the farm, putting up buildings, digging a well, and planting fruit-bearing trees: apricot, apple, and pomegranate. Baba hired Muslim workers to tend the land. They helped him with the planting and harvesting. He believed that on-site supervision was necessary. Otherwise nothing was done properly. His schedule, tied to the land, did not allow him to be home full time except for a few months in late fall and winter.

Naneh Jaan-Jaan offered to take care of Cyrus and later Aria. Mamán brought Aria to her house every morning and picked him up when she came back from work. The three musketeers went to school, and in the summer Mamán registered us in arts and crafts camp. The rest of the time, we looked after each other. Naneh Jaan-Jaan visited our house often while carrying Aria in her arms to make sure we did not hurt ourselves. Both Mamán and Naneh Jaan-Jaan instructed us to run to Naneh Jaan-Jaan's house if we had any problems.

Much later, I learned that the privilege of owning land was not given to Jews before the Shah's White Revolution. Iran at that time was a feudal country, with few landowners and many peasants and tenant farmers. When the Shah needed labourers in the cities to help build his new Iran, he encouraged the peasants to move to the cities by forcing the landlords to sell their land to the government. This forced the peasants and tenant farmers off the land, and they flocked to the cities. The government then sold land in much smaller chunks back to those owners who still wanted to farm. The rest was made available to anyone who had enough money to purchase it. That is how Baba ended up with about fifty hectares of land. That is how the White Revolution had a direct and profound impact on our life.

Baba and Mamán fought a lot. Farah and I were often implicated in our parents' fights, and even if we tried not to be involved, we still ended up hearing all about it. When people are happy, the little annoyances in life roll off their shoulders. When people are unhappy, every little annoyance is reason for an argument.

The land became an additional reason for their already numerous differences and lengthy arguments: from the way the house was kept, to the boarders in the house, and the money wasted on the bottomless pit of land Baba owned and loved. More often than not, it led to deep resentment from both Mamán and Baba because they hurt each other's feelings recklessly. I couldn't understand what made him buy this land. I have tried to put myself in his position to come up with an answer. I have spent hours, days, weeks trying to understand the reason; but the conclusion was that Baba loved fresh air and solitude. He may have been like our shepherd forefathers.

Baba wasn't there to witness our accomplishments or share our milestones. He wasn't there when we came home from school. Instead we witnessed a weary man, bedraggled and dirty, coming in late Friday afternoon to be home for Shabbat and expecting to be served hand and foot.

Too tired to have a conversation, he complained about work. "The workers can't understand proper Persian."

"The kids did really well at school this week, Bijan."

"You look so tired, Baba."

"I work so hard and you don't appreciate my hard work. Mark my word, every inch of this land will be a fortune soon. We will be so rich. I am sacrificing my youth for you. My blood and sweat is poured into this land, and I am doing it all for your future."

Mamán referred to Baba's land as "his mistress," a mistress who took all his energy, both physically and mentally. "The mistress sent you home like a rag, exhausted, dirty with dust from country life, and poor. You come to fill up your pockets with money and rest so you can go back to her rich and refreshed."

Baba hated when Mamán talked about his land that way. He loved the land so much and no one was allowed to refer to it in unloving ways . . . as if the land would be insulted and heartbroken.

The three musketeers did not spend much time with Baba because we were in school on Saturday, the only day he was in town. But Cyrus and Aria saw Baba because the Jewish boys' school they attended was closed on Saturday. The three of them went to synagogue on Shabbat, walking over to the Kosar Synagogue, which doubled as the Jewish boys' school. Naneh Jaan-Jaan served Shabbat lunch for the family. Aunts, uncles, and cousins came together for this weekly event.

Baba expected Mamán to give him all her salary and the money from the boarders; he then decided how much she needed to spend and on what. Mamán, on the other hand, did not like this plan. In her opinion, Baba had no idea how much daily essentials cost and she was often caught short of cash when Baba was in charge. She insisted that she keep her salary for our daily expenses. Baba counted on Mamán's salary to spend on his land.

"I can't reason with you."

"Show me another Jew who is a landowner in Iran?"

"I am proud to be the first."

The argument heated up. Frustrated, each wanted to prove their point. To win the argument! To be right! There was no way Baba would accept the truth about his "love of land."

Mamán cried and screamed. Baba became hysterical. He smashed the tea cups. Hit Mamán. Mamán ran away into another part of the house, crying. Then Baba hit himself, pulled his hair, and wept while he screamed aloud to Mamán in the other room, "I'm so terrible, nobody appreciates me. I don't gamble, I don't do drugs, I don't chase after women, and I've been working hard all week, all for you. I come back after the whole week and I'm tired."

"You think that's hard? I've been with the kids all week and also working full time, and then you come back and complain!" Mamán shrieked back.

I howled and ran to Naneh Jaan-Jaan's house, begging her to come to our house to intervene.

I despised it when Baba and Mamán raised their voices. Nobody won by anger in the long run. He was still my Baba. There were fathers who were worse than him, fathers who were addicted to drugs, gambling, or chasing other women. No Jewish men we knew were involved in those activities, but there were plenty of those men among the husbands of Mamán's colleagues. Baba didn't do any of that; he just loved his land too much.

After a major fight, everyone tiptoed on eggshells around the house. Neither Mamán nor Baba spoke to each other; the silent treatment went on for weeks, sometimes months. The two of them pretended the other one did not exist. Mamán did not feed Baba. Baba did not ask how she was doing. Baba walked in exhausted. Mamán wrinkled her nose and shook her head in disapproval.

Baba had no access to a shower for the entire time he was in the country. His work was physical. He could not have had interesting conversations with his employees; he had not eaten a decent meal the entire week. If he was lucky, he hitched a ride with a villager back to the city; otherwise he had to walk six kilometres on the gravel road to reach the asphalt road where he caught the bus and rode for forty-five minutes to reach the main square in Shiraz. From there, he had to either hail a taxi or walk another half hour to get home.

Mamán yearned to be acknowledged by Baba for all the work she had done on the days he was absent. As far as she was concerned, that was much more important than what he did all week.

Baba, on the other hand, also wanted to be appreciated.

Neither one received what they yearned for so desperately.

When Baba and Mamán gave each other the silent treatment, we children were the ones who suffered the consequences.

Mamán repeated incessantly the words that were exchanged between herself and Baba in the heat of argument.

She neglected to mention how she had also yelled wounding words at Baba.

She played the victim role, a martyr who stayed in the marriage only because of us. "I am sacrificing my life for you."

The last time Baba raised his hand against her, Mamán fought back, "Enough is enough! Don't you ever raise your hand to me again!" and never did he dare touch her again.

Baba resented that he never had the chance to go to university like his older brother. My grandparents could not send all their kids to university. Ammo David was the only one who was granted this privilege; he was a prominent medical doctor in Shiraz. Baba felt inadequate compared to his brother. Ammo David was Naneh Jaan-Jaan's pride and joy. Living next door to his mother, poor Baba constantly heard about his brother's achievements. None of the other brothers could hope to measure up to this paragon of a man.

᠈᠈᠈᠈᠈᠈

A twenty-five-minute walk brought us to the brick-walled Jewish ghetto, Mahaleh. The ghetto's alleys were so narrow that no cars could drive through. The ground was made up of broken tiles; cobblestones were used in the "better" part of the ghetto. Garbage was strewn along the streets; the shops were old and shabby. The shops and houses were owned by Jews and no one else.

The customers were also only Jews. Mamán frequented the kosher butcher, the fishmonger, and a fresh herb store. Muslims never bought food in the ghetto. Food touched by Jews was considered unclean. The merchants relied entirely on Jewish trade, a very small market indeed.

The merchants knew the most detailed information about one another and all the customers; first name, last name, family history, who was related to whom and who was mad at whom. News had to be exchanged; shopping that should have taken only a few minutes could take hours, and Mamán would stop and talk to everyone.

The people Mamán talked to sneered at her while checking us out up and down and sideways, clutching their boys' hands. "Poor thing, she has three girls; three dowries to give." We couldn't wait to get home.

Mamán defended us. "Yes, I have three girls, but they are as good as boys and can do anything boys can do."

This statement, repeated many times in front of us, would come to haunt her later.

᠈᠈᠈᠈᠈᠈

Food preservation and bottling started in spring. The juicing of sour green grapes, used for stews the rest of the year, took place in early spring. Boxes and boxes of sour green grapes were bought in the main market that supplied the fruit shops. Baba arrived with a pickup truck filled to the brim with the sour grapes spilling out of boxes. This was a big undertaking; family members gathered in our house and offered to help. We had to do the same for them on other occasions. Mamán volunteered me to help out our relatives.

The green grape juicing started in the late afternoon when the weather started to cool. First the mountain of sour green grapes had to be washed. Mamán then passed them through a manual meat grinder to crush them. I could not contain myself. "Why don't we crush these sour grapes with our feet? We do it for the wine grapes." Mamán glared at me for asking such an inappropriate question. The answer was obvious. "Wine ferments for months and that kills the bacteria. Sour grapes are bottled and used in cooking." The answer did not convince me but I did not argue the point.

When the fresh light green mush exited the meat grinder, Mamán passed the mush through a strainer and bottled the result. She used a borrowed machine to seal the bottles tight. Up to this point, there was usually no problem but the final step was nerve-racking for Mamán, because she had to put the bottles in a huge pot of boiling of water, and many times during this process, the bottles exploded. Finally, the surviving bottles were transferred to the cellar, for use during the year.

Each month, from late spring until late fall, was allocated to different types of food preparation. Jews did not have access to kosher packaged products. It was important that everyone in the immediate family and the extended family pitch in with various duties. We children all had our specific chores. We helped to juice and bottle sour grapes and sour cherries, pomegranate juice and sauce, make tomato sauce, and lemon juice. Mamán pickled many different types of foods—cucumbers, herbs, apples—and then made quince jam. Everything we made was stored in our cellar for later use during the year.

Preparing food was our entertainment. Television programs were limited to two midday children's shows. Zorro was my hero. In the evening, television consisted of news, adult comedies, and sometimes old movies from the West, dubbed in Persian. Upper- and middle-class families had access to black-and-white television.

But all this did not mean I had no time to play. The three musketeers played hard. We ran and fell often. The permanent scab on my knee was testament to the rough games of hide-and-seek, hopscotch, and volleyball that we played. I wondered if I would live to see the day that I wouldn't have scabs on top of scabs on my knees. Mamán was a firm believer that

"If it doesn't kill you, it will make you stronger." Consequently she never nursed my scabs more than necessary and always pushed me to continue playing and having fun.

~~~~~

Although Mamán encouraged us to do whatever boys did, there was a prohibition that she could not challenge. One such prohibition was riding a bicycle. A Jewish girl in Shiraz was not allowed to have a bicycle. Girls never rode bicycles, based on some old wives' tale that girls were not supposed to participate in many sports since they could lose their "virginity" in an accident. But since Mamán kept repeating that whatever boys do, girls could do, I wanted to ride a bicycle like the boys. Farah had a tricycle, and that was it. The three musketeers took the training wheel off the tricycle and used it as bicycle until it fell apart. We rode round and round until we were dizzy, and the last one still riding was declared the winner. I dreamed of one day having my own bicycle.

"When will you buy me a bicycle?" I pestered my parents continuously. Mamán and Baba promised me a bicycle many times, but the actual purchase was always in the future.

"When you have better marks." I had good marks consistently. But the bicycle never materialized.

Baba yelled, "Don't complain about not having a bicycle. You're lucky to have a roof over your head. You don't have to live like the people in Halabi Abad." Big metal tin containers, flattened to make shelters, ringed the outskirts of Shiraz. The wealthier tenants lived in tents. The richest among them had rugs in their tents. The kids were barefoot; mosquitoes feasted on their lips and noses.

Baba saw what he wanted to see, as if he had selective visual loss. He never mentioned Ammo David's kids, who travelled often, had bicycles, and took accordion lessons. I never dared bring that up though I thought about it often. The comparison was too painful for him. He was compared to his older brother often.

~~~~~

Mamán's hands were full with five kids and a full-time job. But she liked to spend as much time as possible with her sisters. Mamán called her sisters. "Let's go to the park for a picnic!"

Our favourite ice cream store was close to Sa'adi's memorial park, which was adjacent to the Baha'i neighbourhood. This way we hit two birds with one stone. The *bastani* (ice cream) had hard, crunchy, buttery chunks in it, with pistachios, rosewater, and saffron.

We visited Sa'adi's mausoleum. Mamán started to recite several poems from memory; her sisters followed. Their competition was fierce, and Mamán had to win. All five of us were stunned to witness the competitive side of Mamán, a side that we did not usually see. Then we went for ice cream. Mamán was happy; it was a perfect combination of food and culture.

Mamán became a different person when she was in the company of her youngest three sisters, Shaheen, Ladan and Shadi. They were the only ones among her eight sisters who had finished high school and were office workers. Mamán giggled like a teenager when she was in their presence. Her youngest sister, Ladan, was the clown of the family. She made fun of everyone and was constantly laughing. Her laughter was contagious. Mamán was happiest when she was in the company of Khaleh Ladan.

Lunch was the biggest meal of the day. But we had no luxury of a mother at home. Mamán started work at eight o'clock in the morning and finished at one o'clock in the afternoon, in time to join us for lunch at home. Unless she had cooked the night before or slow-cooked the meal on the stove in the morning, we had no hot meals. Once every few weeks, Mamán prepared the stew on a low flame in the morning, to have it ready by the time we arrived home from school. To be ready and at work for eight in the morning was difficult for Mamán. She was often late for work, and the days that she did the cooking before going to work delayed her even more.

At ten years of age, if I wanted to eat a hot meal for lunch, I had to cook it myself. I begged Mamán to teach me how to make rice. There were two ways to cook rice, a foolproof one or the traditional way. Mamán agreed to show me how to make it the easy way. I wrote it down: One cup of rice, two cups of water, two tablespoons of oil, a dash of salt. I was worried about making a mistake and cooking inedible rice.

We had a two-hour break for lunch; it took fifteen minutes to walk home and half an hour to cook the rice. Mamán also gave me instructions on how to make hamburger. I did not want to mess up my first cooking experience.

I repeated to myself all the way home from school: One cup of rice, two cups of water, two tablespoons of oil, a bit of salt . . . Lunch was ready by the time Mamán came home at 1:30. We ate. "Mamán, try it, did I cook it right?"

As soon as she took the first bite, she nodded her head in approval. I was in heaven. My first hot meal was a success! The training started when I was ten years old. Mamán was a firm believer in "teaching us *to* fish, not *giving* us a fish."

I went back to school and bragged to my teacher and my classmates that I had cooked lunch. Both the teacher and the students looked at me as if I were crazy; and what kind of an irresponsible mother lets a ten-year-old cook lunch on a gas stove?

Mamán did not spend too much time in the kitchen. To her, food was important for nourishment; that was all. She was not obsessed with cooking; she had no time for it. Sewing and crocheting were more important to her, if she had any time left in the day.

We bought our baked goods from the pastry shop across the street from Naneh Zivar's house. I loved the muffins and the puff pastries. Since the shops were closed for the afternoon, business hours were extended until eight or nine o'clock in the evening. Baba visited the shop after Shabbat was over and brought home treats for us. He entered the house with brown paper bags and white boxes of sweets, usually when he wanted to make peace with Mamán after ignoring her for weeks. We had figured it out. And it did work. We were happy to have peace in our family again. Mamán and Baba laughed together. She was happy that Baba came to her with kind words and was affectionate.

><><><

I came down with mumps when I was eleven years old. My tongue was swollen, and one side of my face looked like a big watermelon. My skin burned with high fever. All my sisters and brothers gathered around the sick sister. Soraya watched anxiously on one side, Farah on the other. When someone was sick, you could never take care of them too much.

They woke me up. "You have to drink; here is the soup, drink a little bit."

The doctor prescribed penicillin. Shortly after I took the first pill, hives broke out over my entire body. I could not sit or stand. It was impossible to lie down. I scratched myself until blood stained my hands. So many parts of my body were itchy simultaneously that I did not have enough hands to scratch them.

"What happened to you?" Maman exclaimed. "This is an allergic reaction; you must be allergic to penicillin."

Because she was a nurse, she recognized the reaction. She left me with Farah and Soraya and dashed out of the house. Though she dispensed medications to her patients, she had more faith in natural remedies. A special section in the bazaar was allocated to natural remedies to treat all sorts of common ailments. The shop owners / healers were well respected and trusted by the general population. Many of their concoctions, including teas, seeds, and leaves from different plants, had medicinal properties that helped to relieve symptoms, and Maman believed in their success based on her personal experience with these cures.

Maman bought remedies from the healers to help me get well. The healers were older Muslim men, often quite small in stature. There was just enough room in the stall for a stool where one man could sit, for the stall was filled with all kinds of leaves in bags, and stacks of jars, with lots of little spices hanging outside the stall; very colourful and smelly things. I was so intrigued by the strings of strange, dry objects that I didn't realize until I was much older that they were just peppers and flowers and rosebuds strung fresh with a needle and left to dry into dark, mysterious shapes. They would mix a little bit of this, a little bit of that, to treat diarrhea, or to lower your blood pressure. Only the healer knew what was in each jar. I couldn't figure out how they could mix two or three things and make such potent remedies.

This time, though, Maman couldn't bring me with her; she described the symptoms to the healer. When she returned home, she had a multitude of herbs and strange ingredients that she boiled and I had to drink. That cured the allergic reaction and alleviated the mumps. I never took a second dose of penicillin. The healers' concoctions worked very well.

~~~~~

Maman was busy non-stop. All five of us were in charge of our own entertainment, which often ended with rough games. A little fall, a scratch, or a bit of blood was normal, but at times it was worse.

I was eight years old, playing with Soraya in the garden. I fell and hit my face on the edge of a stone step and ripped open the side of my lips while chasing her. Blood gushed out of my face and my hand was covered with blood. Farah was frantic, screaming for Maman, who was usually not home. But luck was on my side that day. Since it was Friday, Mamán was at home and she rushed me to the hospital. Pretending to be brave in the taxi, I tried to talk like the chatterbox I was, but Mamán insisted that I be quiet.

The hospital was clean and modern, and the doctor who attended to me was professional and made me feel safe.

He asked me, "Who did this to you?"

"No one. It was an accident."

"Tell me the truth. I won't tell anyone."

"No one hurt me. It was an accident."

"I need to sew it. Will you be brave?"

"Yes."

He promised me, "If you do not move, I will be able to sew the stitches so well that no one will ever know you had stitches on your lips." I sat on the plastic chair like a robot, unflinchingly. Mamán told me, "Iranian doctors are well known around the world for their expertise and knowledge."

The doctor stitched the left side of my lip. There were no scars from the stitches.

~~~~~

We walked everywhere in Shiraz. The three musketeers walked to school, walked to the bazaar, walked to the ghetto, walked to the park on Saturday nights. Mamán advised us to walk on the main streets, not in the alleys, whenever we were alone. But if the three musketeers were together, we were allowed to walk in the alleys or hail a taxi. Mamán warned us to keep money on us at all times. It was not to spend, but was for emergencies. None of our relatives were as daring as we were. Mamán raised us to be fearless and street-smart. Look around you — be cautious but not afraid.

If, however, time was short, I hailed one of the bright orange taxis. Customers would pile in through three doors and also leave from all three doors. I hailed a cab, haggled over the price, and then jumped in even if other passengers were already inside. There were many stops. People climbed in and out of cabs at random.

If the haggling didn't work out, I would walk. If I got onto a bus, and an old person entered, I was obliged to get up and offer my seat. Not that I would ever ignore that custom, but if someone did, a serious moral lesson followed.

"Didn't your family teach you anything?" "How come you don't have any manners?" "You should be ashamed of yourself." "This is no way to behave," and further scolding.

It certainly was not worth five minutes of sitting.

~~~~~~

All Shirazis look alike: medium frame, dark hair, dark brown or black eyes. I could not tell just by looking at a man or a woman whether he or she was Jewish, Baha'i, Christian, or Muslim. We all have the same features. That was the reason to ask for both the first and last names and where one lived. Jews who lived in the ghetto spoke a Persian-Jewish dialect among themselves. Consequently, their Persian accent was different from other Shirazi Jews, who spoke slower, softer; the words were not pronounced fully.

A few workers from the Philippines on work permits stood out in the street crowds, but they were the only noticeable minority at the time. Anyone who looked different stood out like a sore thumb in our homogeneous population.

Once in a blue moon, I saw someone who really stood out. The most memorable person I ever saw was a blond person, long hair in a ponytail and wearing a beard. I could not tell if "it" was a man or a woman. If he was a man then why did he have long hair? If she was a woman then why did she have a beard? The blue eyes, the height, and the backpack were the few clues that he was almost certainly a tourist.

These tourists looked like creatures from another planet.

But one other thing made them different: they were friendly. I must have been knee-high to them and had to stretch way up to look at them. By eight years of age, I remembered a few important sentences from the weekly one-hour English classes. I went up to these men, tapped their knees and proudly pronounced, "Hi," in English. "How are you?"

With these two phrases, I considered myself to be functionally bilingual, until they answered me, at which point I terminated the conversation with "No speaking English!" and ran away as fast as I could. I wanted to leave the tourists while they still thought that I actually knew how to speak English. Little did they know that I had already used up my entire English vocabulary in a matter of seconds!

American and European tourists visited our favourite places, the Sa'adi and Hafez mausoleums in the memorial parks, and crowded our bazaars.

But other groups of tourists during the summer months were not as innocent. These were the gypsies who travelled through our town, knocked at our door, and begged for food and money. Their natural unkempt beauty and daring personalities made them stand out in any crowd. Gypsies dressed in traditional village fashion in a style called *toon boon*. The women wore embroidered bandanas and multi-layered, colourful scarves and skirts draped over their slim, fit bodies. Their dark skin was a testament to long hours of living in the sun. Their big brown eyes fluttered provocatively at everyone. They looked men straight in the eye, and if they didn't like you, they swore at you. I didn't want to mess around with the gypsies.

Mamán insisted, "Travellers are guests sent from God. They have to be well taken care of." We offered them leftover food, drinks, clothing, and even money.

Gypsies had a bad reputation. They were recognized as artful thieves. I made sure there was nothing valuable showing on my body and in the house when they were around. They always had many kids with them. But I admired their sense of freedom.

Interesting that with Westerners we never saw any women; with the gypsies, there were never any men.

〉〉〉〉〉

We had a very big house: twelve rooms and three kitchens for the seven of us. Baba thought this was a waste of useful space, and we should rent out some of the rooms. Mamán didn't agree. "We have three girls. You can't expect young men to come and go without noticing them. That is like playing with fire." Mamán was unable to convince Baba.

Consequently, we had boarders. Mamán was more than a little opposed to this. During the summer, we often had Arab families from the Persian Gulf, and during the school year, the boarders were male students from the villages around Shiraz.

Visitors from the Persian Gulf countries, Dubai, Qatar, Kuwait, and Bahrain were even stranger than the blond ones. They appeared in Shiraz in the summer, because our weather was considerably cooler than in their own countries. The tourists from the Persian Gulf rented rooms in our house.

The Persian Gulf men wore long, white robes and plain white

keffiyehs on their heads; usually they had short mustaches (not to cover the lips) or beards. The women wore full-face coverings and long brown and black dresses down to their ankles. Strangely, despite the full-face coverings and their long-sleeved gowns, the necklines were cut very low over their bosoms, showing cleavage even on the street as they were walking. I was shocked by their garb; I had never seen any religious Iranian women dressed this way.

The Persian Gulf women never ate with their husbands. The men ate first and the women ate the leftovers. They never used forks or spoons; they used their hands. When they ate, they did so in private, or if in public, they lifted the side of their *niqabs* — the veil or mask that covered the face — to put food in their mouths. I could not stop watching them; they were fascinating. Sometimes I watched them so long and so intently that they noticed and yelled at me to leave them alone.

❧❧❧❧❧

I had become accustomed to seeing crowds of men fighting in the streets on a regular basis. The reason was always the same. A man had insulted or flirted with a woman. Such a man had "no *namus*" (no shame).

Once I watched a fight from the beginning. I saw a man walk by a woman, then turn around and say in a loud voice, "Hey, cutie!" Bystanders heard him, as I did, and rushed over to the woman. One man grabbed the offender by the arm and screamed at him that he should look away from women and not speak insultingly to them. Other men came over and told the grabber to let go. He hadn't done anything so wrong.

Then the men, ripping off their shirts, started to fight; punches were thrown, and knives came out. The original offender was beaten up really badly. Meanwhile, a large crowd of spectators gathered around, and there was lots of shouting. Eventually an older man intervened and told the fighters to say they were sorry.

"You're brothers. Next time have some respect and don't look at women like that. Let's all go home."

A man in the crowd followed the offender. "Make sure not to flirt with women. You could have been killed over what you did."

To avoid any further fights, one man followed the offending party. "I will accompany you. Where do you live?"

If a person was courteous in this way, he was considered "warm-blooded." Those who weren't, and they were in the minority, were considered "cold-blooded" or cowardly. No one wanted such an unmanly label.

Even in the city, with its anonymity, we were never alone when walking. Warm-blooded men came to protect us whether we wanted it or not. It was a matter of principle.

I felt safe in this environment; the helpful eyes and hands were useful many times. When I carried grocery bags from the market down the streets of Shiraz, men offered to help and carried my groceries all the way home. Not for money, not because they were asked to do so, but because this was how men conducted themselves in society. The men did this because they wanted their daughters and sisters and mothers to be taken care of by others with the same respect.

><><><><

My sisters and I attended a Jewish preschool and kindergarten within walking distance from our house. Mamán thought the boys needed to learn Jewish studies, but for the girls, the Jewish school level of education was not to her liking. There was only one Jewish school, Kosar, and its students were mostly boys. Mamán and Baba were in agreement about the boys attending Jewish school. They had both attended the same school as children.

Because Mamán worked with many non-Jewish people she was aware of the best private elementary schools in Shiraz. Doctor Montazeri was the coed private non-Jewish elementary school I attended with Farah and Soraya. We walked back at lunchtime and after school, a short half-hour walk each way. Our neighbourhood was safe enough to do that on our own.

Girls wore navy blue tunics with long-sleeved blouses underneath, and boys wore pants and long-sleeved polo shirts.

The principal, Mr. Montazeri, was a tall, thin man who didn't have a mustache, unlike most Iranian men. That meant that he was not as manly as other Iranian men, and that he was influenced by the West. He greeted us daily in a stern manner that matched his strict look.

I walked up the stairs and saw the principal, whom I greeted like a friend. "Hi. How are you?" I had no idea that I was not supposed to talk to him. He looked down at me from his great height—he must have been at least six feet tall—and did not respond to my four-foot self. As if to say, "None of your business. You are a Grade 1 student." Later I found out from Mamán that I was not supposed to ask the principal any questions; he was not my friend.

I walked up the stairs and past the principal's office into a huge garden full of trees in the middle of school. All around the perimeter were the classrooms. I sat in the garden to eat my snack every day; it looked like an orchard with oak trees. But the trees did not bear any blossoms or fruit. What a waste of a tree!

The vice-principal, Mariam Khanoom, was an unattractive woman in her fifties who wore no makeup and long, loose, Western-style beige dresses that reached down to her ankles. Each morning all of us students lined up for assembly and sang the national anthem, "Salamati-ye Shah," "Health of the Shah," in the garden.

Oh homeland, my life
My passion and my joy
Show your face in the sky
Like the immortal sun
Listen to the pain of my words
I am your companion, singing
All my body and soul
My homeland, my homeland, my homeland, my homeland
Listen to the pain of my words
I am the nightingale of this garden
All my body and soul
My homeland, my homeland, my homeland, my homeland
All with one name and symbol
With different colours and languages
All with one name and symbol
With different colours and languages
All cheerful, happy and singing
Because of the strength of young Iran
Because of the strength of young Iran
Because of the strength of young Iran

We had to stay in a straight line and sing with all our might or we'd be punished. The punishment was to stand on one leg in front of the principal's office. No matter how hard it was to stand still and shout out loud, it was better than the punishment.

We were off school on Fridays, which was the Muslim Sabbath. This worked very well for us, as it gave us the opportunity to help Mamán in preparing for our Shabbat.

For Friday lunch, Naneh Jaan-Jaan cooked and brought us her special meat patties. It was never enough, no matter how much she brought, and Mamán never cooked meat patties the way Naneh Jaan-Jaan did.

On Saturday, before we went to school, she delivered her hot *cholent*[4] early in the morning. It was her love that was packaged in that plate of delicious hot food. Whatever the secret ingredient was, it made the dish delectable. We ate it hot and again when we returned from school for lunch or devoured it on Sunday if there were leftovers. It tasted even better the next day. No one made a better *cholent* than she did.

The three musketeers went to school, and Mamán went to work on Saturday. But Baba and the boys went to synagogue. We did nothing on Shabbat, other than what was absolutely necessary. We didn't cook, we didn't shop, and we didn't clean. My family respected Shabbat in our own way, as did the other Shirazi Jews. Normally, I went home for lunch, but sometimes on Saturdays I ate at school to avoid unnecessary travelling. I brought cutlets with pickle and tomato sandwiches for Sheyla, my best friend, and she brought Pepsi Cola in glass bottles. We sat in the courtyard at school, and had feasts at lunchtime. We pretended we were dining in a gorgeous orchard.

Unless a Jew attended a non-Jewish school or was employed by the government, he or she did not work on Saturday. All the shops that were owned by Jews were closed on Saturday. These included not only those in the ghetto but the shops in the better part of the city, where the more affluent people shopped.

❧❧❧❧❧

Facing our house was an entrance to a labyrinth of narrow side roads and little alleyways. The alleys were much too narrow for cars, and we used them as shortcuts to get to different parts of town. One famous alley was called "Resentment and Peace." This cobblestone passage was so narrow that only one person could walk through it at a time. If you encountered someone you were on bad terms with coming toward you in the opposite direction, it was impossible to pass each other without touching, so you

---

4   A dish of slowly cooked meat and vegetables.

had no choice but to smile and make peace.

At six years old, I walked with Mamán, Farah, and Soraya past a building with a high, wide staircase leading up to the entrance. On either side of the stairs were giant gold statues of lions that looked as if they were going to attack me, they looked so real.

"What is this building for, Mamán?"

"The Ministry of Justice."

"Can we walk another way so that I won't have to walk in front of the scary lions?" Later, I found out the lions stood for power and justice.

Within a few blocks was another government office, a peculiar-looking building because it stretched along one very long block and was guarded by men with huge guns. There were no shops or businesses nearby. At odd times, I saw a car come in or out of the fenced building but at no time could I see who was in the car. That building and whatever happened inside was a big secret.

"Mamán, what is this building?"

Her voice dropped almost to a whisper. "It is the Shirazi headquarters of SAVAK, the Shah's secret police." Mamán, who always answered my questions fully, didn't explain any further. And I didn't ask. There was some reason I shouldn't. The fear instilled by SAVAK seemed to hover over everyone whenever the name was mentioned. Though life was good during the Shah's reign, there was also an undercurrent of fear.

The Shah was generous to Jews because Jews did not involve themselves with politics. Jews were loyal to the Shah and did not challenge the status quo. Jews were well aware that in a society in which we were a minority, we had to adhere strictly to the rules and regulations of the government. After all, the Shah had been good to us. He allowed us to move up the socioeconomic ladder that had been denied us until his reign. We were allowed to go to university, we were able to rise in the civil service, and we were able to practise Judaism without discrimination. We could live almost as equal citizens.

The Shah had great ambitions for Iran, and what better place to show them off than in the schools? Teach the new generation English so they can fend for themselves on the international market.

~~~~~

English was the official second language of Iran. At school, one hour per week was devoted to English. It is almost impossible for Iranians to pronounce the "the" and "w" sounds, and although I practised them diligently, I was never able to say them correctly. According to my teacher, they came out as "D" and "V," as if I were missing a muscle in my tongue. I walked into my English class once a week, and no matter how hard I tried, I was never able to pronounce English words properly. My English teacher spent hours trying to teach me proper pronunciations. She repeated words to me that I was supposed to say back to her, but I managed to distort them with my thick Iranian accent. When I tried to say "mother," it always came out as "moder." When I tried to say "the" it came out as "deh." I memorized material she gave us, but I could never pronounce the words properly.

Mamán repeated, "Teachers are like candles; they give of themselves to their students in order to illuminate the dark." We respected and looked up to our teachers. Whether it was math, biology, or chemistry, I loved the learning process. It was expected that good students would tutor other students. Through grades 1 to 3, our teacher assigned the five best students to help the rest of the class every day and tutor them. We had a competition for which group did best on exams. I had five students in my group and was happy when my classmates did better on their tests because of the work we did together. It made us proud to help our classmates.

One boy in the group I tutored brought me candies every week for helping him in school, and then one day he stopped bringing any. I had a sweet tooth that needed to be satisfied, so I decided to start eating any candy I could get my hands on.

Relatives would bring boxes of candy when they visited. I could not help but devour them. Mamán forbade me to eat the candies, so I devised a plan I thought would allow me to eat them without her ever knowing. I approached the pile of boxes every day, and I chose to eat from one of the boxes on the bottom. To make sure that no one could tell the box had been opened, I cut a little hole in the bottom of the box and extracted the candies, while the top layer remained intact. Eventually, all the boxes were emptied this way. Mamán kept asking me where I was getting all the candies. "Aj-d'ari, the student I tutor, brought them for me."

My mischief eventually became apparent to Mamán when she wanted to visit a friend's house and decided to bring a box of candies. When Mamán picked up one of the boxes, she realized what I had been doing. The look on her face struck fear in my heart. Not knowing what to say, I mustered up the nerve to say that a mouse must have done it.

"You mean the mouse didn't touch the top layer?" Mamán smacked me in the face for lying and eating all the candies.

Mamán ignored me for a full day. She did not answer any of my questions and forbade the rest of the family to talk to me. I was to be punished for what I had done. It was a torture that worked. I learned my lesson: A fly can escape once, twice, but eventually it will get swatted.

In third grade, Wednesdays were special days. My teacher took the entire class to the Art and Culture House. The students walked in a double line for ten minutes from school. Our teacher walked beside the line. We were allowed to bring snacks with us that day. In the morning I put my snack into my handmade Persian carpetbag. I was the only student who owned a handmade snack bag made of wool; it looked like a carpet, and I felt quite "cultured."

In this culture house, we had hands-on experience with different crafts. I brought home string bags and colourful paper chains and shared them with Mamán, who also wanted to learn how to make these decorative items.

The highlight of the school year was the carpet weaver. A woman from a small village outside Shiraz came to demonstrate the weaving techniques used in making the unique Shirazi-style *killim* (rough rugs) and carpets. She wore a traditional dress with layers and layers of skirts and a long-sleeved dress over all. Her headband and scarf were embroidered to match the dress. She had a huge, colourful carpet comb and wove the wool masterfully to create the rugs.

Part of the training for young girls was to learn to shop and cook. Mamán made certain that we had many opportunities to learn these skills. She gave us a hundred *tooman* (thirteen dollars) and told us to go to the market and buy whatever fruit we liked. These shopping excursions were fun. Thursday and Friday mornings were a special time in the market. Farmers brought their donkeys to carry the extra load of fruit required to satisfy the pre-Shabbat crowds — both Muslim and Jewish — who stocked up in preparation for their holy days. The donkeys, serving as extra display racks for the merchants, were positioned in the middle of the market between the rows of regular shops. The huge bags on either side of their saddles were filled with apples, oranges, and pomegranates. The screaming donkey owner yelled, "Juicy apples, two *tooman* per kilo, hurry and buy before they are finished!"

We budgeted and made sure that with the hundred *tooman* we bought enough fruit and vegetables for the week. Romaine lettuce was Mamán's favourite for salads; at times we had to go into every shop to search for it. If it was out of season, then the one shop that had it took advantage of this and charged much more for it. Apples, prunes, white cherries, and sour cherries were my favourites. The shops shut up tight at noon, when the Muslim religious services began for the Sabbath.

Mamán taught us how to look for good quality and good prices. If our purchases were too heavy, we would find a strong-looking man in the fruit vendor's shop and ask, "Could you help us carry our bags home?" This was a common practice among Shirazi women. Mamán considered it safe and instructed us to ask for help if we needed it.

Upon our arrival, Mamán inspected our purchases and gave us tips on what we could do better next time. "The apples are crisp. Good. The oranges are juicy. Be careful next time because the herbs are wilted."

><><><><

Mamán was my idol and I looked up to her. I knew intuitively when she was stressed or happy. Even though she hired help when the housework became too overwhelming, for the most part, she divided the housework among the three of us. My job was to clean the dishes after meals and put the kitchen back in order. I had to wash all the dishes, which was not a problem; it was the big pots and pans from the Shabbat meal that were hard to wash. They were huge, and the pots had meat or stew stuck to them. I had to make sure to clean them well to make Mamán happy with my work. But my little hands were not strong enough to scrub the food residue as well as I wanted. I had to soak them again and again in more hot water, and by the third time, the pots were sparkling clean.

The three musketeers tried hard to help Mamán as much as we could. We knew how busy and tired she was. Mamán was a public health nurse; she administered vaccinations, held pre- and post-natal clinics, and worked in the rehabilitation of drug addicts.

I had seen comatose men asleep on the streets, syringes in hand. Mamán told me they were drug addicts who were harmless when they had their fix. But these same addicts were dangerous if they had no money and needed drugs; they turned into monsters. Opium was the most popular drug, but heroin, which was also around, was scarier. Opium was popular among wealthy Muslims, but heroin had a stigma attached to it, and those who were addicted to it were doomed. "Never touch drugs or cigarettes." Mamán's words were etched into my brain through repetition. No one in my family smoked, and drinking took place only at parties or at Shabbat and holiday meals.

She tried very hard to help the drug addicts break their addiction by means of methadone treatments and counselling. Once, when I was ten, I accompanied Mamán to work. This was the first time I saw her in action as a nurse at the drug rehabilitation clinic. I was wide-eyed and full of questions for both the patients and the doctors. The first patient of the day was a handsome young man, unlike the drug addicts I saw on the streets begging for money, or the unconscious ones with syringes in hand. This man was well-dressed and well-spoken. He was handsome and clean-shaven, with well-groomed hair. He looked rich. He told me how drugs had ruined his life.

"Why did you start?"

"I hung around with the wrong group of friends."

I was shocked, because the reason I struck up a conversation with him was that he did not look like most of the other addicts.

"Never touch drugs. Drugs will destroy the life of everyone who comes into contact with them, including mine. Do not let that happen to you."

To this day, I remember this clean-shaven man and his advice. Encountering a drug addict and getting advice from him had more of an impact on me than anything Mamán could have said.

Mamán had a secret to tell me on the way home from the clinic that day.

"Daii Faramarz is coming to visit. We will pick up the rest of the family and go to Naneh Zivar's house to see him."

"Why you did not tell me before?" I protested.

"Because you would have driven us crazy. You are so impatient."

I loved Daii Faramarz, who to my great disappointment had moved to America a few years before. He was my favourite uncle, a kind, intelligent young man who made me feel special. Each time I had visited Naneh Zivar's house, where he lived, he would ask me what new things I had learned and would expand my knowledge on whatever subject I had brought up. He was a wonderful teacher with the gift of making me feel brilliant.

Mamán was right; better that I did not know till now. Like any Iranian, I believed that in the West, butlers in suits came around with silver trays stacked with hundred-dollar bills, and asked each person how many they wanted. I could just imagine the boxes of gifts he would bring me. I thought he would have a hard time to carry my gifts, so I insisted that we should visit him with Mamán and all my siblings.

I waited, waited, and waited some more in Naneh Zivar's house when we went to visit him. *Where are my gifts?* I thought silently to myself. He had no gifts for me. I was furious at him. He had forgotten me, because he did not bring me any gifts.

I wondered if the tree with the hundred-dollar leaves was real or just a figment of everyone's imagination.

~~~~~~

Mamán spoke often to us of the importance of carrying on our Jewish traditions. Our family had been Jewish for centuries, and she did not want us to be the ones to break the continuity. Under the Shah, we Jews had lived and thrived without persecution. We were moving up the socioeconomic ladder; the number of Jewish doctors, engineers, and merchants was higher than ever in Iranian history. However, Jews did not get involved in politics out of fear. We ignored what was missing: freedom of speech, freedom to choose democracy. We felt loyal to the man who had granted us this level of liberty.

The Iranian New Year (Noe-Rooz) usually coincided with Passover. "It is for you to continue to remember our people's history in Egypt as slaves. This is how we remember our past. This is how we remember who we are. Always remember that you are a Jew." Though Mamán loved Iranian New Year, she fussed more over Passover.

~~~~~~

Much excitement was going on at Naneh Jaan-Jaan's house because she and Baba Esghel were to visit Israel in 1974 to meet their two sons who had left Iran in the late 1960s. Enthusiasm soared in the family before they left, because this was their first trip out of Iran and their first visit to the holy land. There was even greater enthusiasm when Naneh Jaan-Jaan and Baba Esghel returned from Israel, and Baba sacrificed an animal to celebrate their return from their "pilgrimage."

Baba brought a sheep from his farm. The ritual slaughterer came to the house in the early morning, to avoid the heat of the day. First the animal was enticed with water to move into the shade of a tree, where it was to be slaughtered quickly while the traditional prayers were recited. The blood was to drain onto the ground under the apple tree. Sheep's blood was believed to enrich the earth and make the tree grow stronger. Nothing was wasted: the meat, the heart, the lungs, the legs, the intestines, even the testicles were used. The last item made me laugh all the time. The testicles were grilled for women who wanted to become pregnant and who wanted to have boys. Disgusting. The breasts were given to nursing mothers to improve the flow of milk.

Though we pretended to play, we were very aware of what was going on. It was awful. We hated to watch those animals take their last breath and die. We also disliked the work involved in cleaning, washing, salting, and re-rinsing the animal parts after the slaughter. Mamán never looked forward to all the work she had to do after the animal was sacrificed.

Naneh Jaan-Jaan's souvenirs from Israel for Baba were a holy prayer book in Hebrew and a *tallit* (prayer shawl) and several types of packaged pickled meats and sausages; and for Mamán and the five of us, a jar of Nutella. That glorious brown goo, so delicious and soft, was a real treat, unlike anything we had ever tasted. I had never seen Nutella before or since in Iran. We didn't much care for the vacuum-packed meats; no one quite knew what to do with them.

Ammeh Nilofar and her husband and children visited us from Tehran that Passover to welcome Naneh Jaan-Jaan and Baba Esghel back from Israel. Ammeh Ashraf and her children, and Ammo David and his children also came to Naneh Jaan-Jaan's house to celebrate Passover.

The preparations were endless. The women kept busy grinding the turmeric and pepper spices by hand in Naneh Jaan-Jaan's stone mortar and pestle. My favourite chore always was roasting almond and pistachio nuts on top of the gas stove. But this time, Mamán did not let me come near the nuts. "By the time you finish roasting, there will be no nuts left for the holidays." I loved nuts and could eat them until I was sick.

The morning before the first Seder, Baba Esghel visited our house and probed into all the corners of the house, hunting for small crumbs of *chametz* (leavened flour-based foods such as bread and pastries) that may have been left on the floor, cabinets, or table. Mamán was relieved after he left and announced that we were indeed ready for Passover.

The best part of Passover was when about twenty cousins, aunts, and uncles gathered together and sang *Dayenu*. As we sang, we hit each other with green shallots to pass good luck to each other. The fun and laughter that ensued made all the work worthwhile, though Mamán and the other women were worn out from the preparations.

The day before Yom Kippur, a chicken was bought for each member of my family. Baba swung our personal chicken over the head of each member of the family three times. I was struck by fear. What if the chicken decided to "let loose" while Baba swung it? It was believed that the chickens took away any potential bad luck in the coming year, and this action ensured a happy and healthy New Year for all of us. The chickens were then taken to the ritual slaughterer's shop, killed, and donated to the poor. I was grateful not to have been the target of the chicken's bowel movement, managing to escape every year. This did not reduce the fear, though.

I loved Yom Kippur, a day of fasting for the adults, because Mamán bought the best snacks to keep us children quiet in synagogue. She had a bag full of Cheezies, candies, and cookies. We ran around, shrieking and playing, while Mamán and Baba prayed the entire day.

An hour before the end of the fast, Baba sprinkled rosewater on the women in synagogue to prevent them from fainting. It was a kind gesture on Baba's part. He was charismatic and handsome and when he wanted to be charming, he was great at it. The women looked him up and down, then at Mamán, shaking their heads as if to say, "What is *wrong* with this woman who does not appreciate such a kind, thoughtful, and loving husband?"

Mamán, on the other hand, did not like it when Baba performed this act of kindness in public because it made her jealous. "If you could be so kind to strangers, why don't you practise more kindness at home?"

Baba could be gracious at home, also, but he was almost never home. On odd Fridays when he was home early, Baba brought us lemonade in the *hammam* because Mamán would scrub us one by one from head to toe. That ice-cold, homemade lemonade was a marvellous treat. At Yom Kippur as well, Baba prepared his wonderful lemonade with his secret ingredient. No matter how hard we tried, we could never make it like his.

~~~~~~

Yom Kippur of 1973 was unlike previous Yom Kippurs. Baba did not walk to the synagogue equipped with his usual bottle of rosewater. Mamán did not bring with her the usual bagful of goodies with which she kept us quiet in synagogue. Just before we walked to synagogue, she threw a few apples in a bag. This was serious.

Israel was at war. I had never heard of war before. It shook me. War was bad, very bad. It meant bloodshed. I did not like what was shown on the TV news: the tanks, the guns, the attacks, the hostility. I loathed war.

Israel had been attacked, and for that, a special prayer was included in the service for Israel's soldiers.

Mamán and Baba were distraught over Israel's precarious situation. Mamán spent longer than usual praying as she lit the candles before going to synagogue. She was terribly worried for the soldiers in Israel. The tears rolled down her cheeks and there was no stopping their flow. Mamán asked us to pray, too. "God listens to everyone's prayer. Please pray for peace." I listened to the plea, but no matter how hard I prayed I could not cry the way Mamán did as she prayed.

The hush-hush whispers were unlike normal gossip. Once in the synagogue, no talk was exchanged between adults. Everyone was praying for a quick end to Israel's war with the fewest number of casualties.

One of the girls I was playing with told me to follow her. She had a secret to share with me. I gave her a pinky finger promise that I would not tell anybody. We hid under the staircase. She reached into her pants pocket and pulled out a folded picture of a man, with a black patch covering one eye. She whispered to me, "That is a picture of Moshe Dayan, the Israeli general."

"What happened to his eye?"

"I do not know." Later on, Baba also had the same picture framed on the wall in the dining room.

I had no idea what was going on but sensed that something terrible was happening to the Jews. I was freaked out and started praying for peace. I hated war and confrontation.

That year, Sukkoth was a sad holiday, too.

Usually Sukkoth was my second-favourite holiday. I looked forward to this holiday all year long. Baba and Baba Esghel made a *sukkah* (a temporary hut) in our garden. Baba made a frame with pieces of wood like a freestanding room, from which he hung Persian rugs all around. He put pieces of wood across the top, leaving spaces between them so that we could see the sky. He decorated the roof with big, red, juicy pomegranates, quince pears, persimmons, apples, grapes, dates, figs, and oranges. Walnuts and almonds were strung up and hung across the *sukkah*. The three musketeers were in charge of piercing the fruit with needle and string. Baba praised us; what we were doing was making a big difference in improving the look and magnificence of our *sukkah*. We ate all our meals in the *sukkah* and took turns sleeping in it. Life could not be better than this, to look up at the plentiful fruits and nuts hanging above us from the roof. I loved the Persian carpets spread around. It looked like the best painting—but better, because it was real. Baba and Baba Esghel built the *sukkah* every year until 1971.

~~~~~~

Baba Esghel made every holiday special. He hunted for *chametz* on Passover. He built the *sukkah* on Sukkoth. The pièce de résistance was Chanukah.

Baba Esghel called us to his house, where he lit the *chanukiah*.

He spent the entire day preparing sixty candles on a square table covered with cardboard in a row arranged by yellow, red, blue, and orange. Then he lit a candle for each of his children and grandchildren. As he lit the candle, he held my hand and prayed. He repeated this for every one of us who were present.

By the time every candle was lit, the sight was unforgettable. Each flame shimmered individually, and together they lit up the room. Baba Esghel was afraid of the fire. He escorted us out of the room and gave us special treats. During the year, he had dried apricots, sour cherries, and plums, which he handed us, and they were scrumptious. They tasted so good that I could have eaten an entire bag of them. Baba Esghel rationed them, and maybe that was the reason the taste was exceptional.

This time of year coincided with the winter solstice, which was also a major Zoroastrian holiday. In order to celebrate, it was customary to eat watermelon. In Shiraz, it was impossible to find watermelons, except in season. Baba Esghel had one saved from late summer, which he kept in the cold storage room, and shared with us at the beginning of winter, on the longest night of the year. He had been raised to believe that if you ate watermelon on that night, you would not become sick during the winter. It may have been the power of suggestion, but it worked.

~~~~~~

Baba studied hard to get his driver's licence, but year after year, he failed the test. Mamán wanted to obtain her driver's licence. For her, a licence was a symbol of freedom and independence, even though she had no car. We studied with her many nights and tested her on what the traffic signs stood for. She worked diligently to pass the written and then the practical exams. Baba was not excited that Mamán succeeded so quickly and passed the test, but this was a big achievement, especially for a woman. It was known that the men who did the testing were especially demanding of women. Custom called for celebration. Relatives flocked over for tea and pastries.

In 1972, an Iranian car factory producing a car called the Peykan was built. The new Iranian-built Peykan was a source of great pride among Iranians. Mamán dreamed of owning a Peykan, a medium-sized, four-door car produced mostly in white. But one could not walk into a dealership and buy one, as only a certain number were made every year. The demand was much greater than the supply; as a result, there was a long waiting list of three or more years. Mamán reluctantly added her name to the waiting list. We waited patiently for her turn to come. That day finally arrived in the spring of 1974. I was in Grade 3 when she came home with the good news. Two Peykans had been granted to the clinic where she worked, and a lottery had been set up to choose the recipients fairly. She was optimistic, smiling and happy as if she had won the car already. A week later, she called us from work to tell us that she was the proud owner of a white Peykan. We were out of our minds with excitement.

Before Mamán could drive the car away from the dealership, she had to follow the "traditional" Shirazi ritual for new cars. A car is an object that can cause death for its passengers as well as others. A ritual was needed to ensure that no life would be lost: A "life" had to be sacrificed before the car was driven. Mamán arrived at the dealer's armed with four eggs, to be placed in front of each tire as she drove the car away. This was Mamán's twentieth-century interpretation of a rather barbaric custom. The next day, she picked us up at school half an hour after class was dismissed. Nobody was there to see our triumph.

In our new car, we visited Baba's farm unannounced and picnicked with him. In the evenings, we set off on the road that led to the airport and picnicked there. We were proud to have wheels. Life was the best it could be, the ultimate paradise experience in the best city in the world, Shiraz.

Sitting in the front seat was an honour the five of us fought for. We kept track and took turns. Mamán demanded order or we were not allowed in the car. At night, we covered the car with a white sheet to keep it from getting scratched, or having birds drop little "presents" on it. Not a speck of dust remained on it for long; my siblings and I washed it regularly, to keep it in perfect shape.

Our car was special. It had two horns, a regular honking horn and a horn that sounded like a cow in labour. Nobody respected any kind of traffic rules. Cars, motorcycles, and pedestrians all fought to find their way through the maze of streets in Shiraz. Mamán had to battle to get from one place to the next. She honked the cow horn often, and people scattered in the wake of this angry cow.

Our joy in having a car was short-lived, however. Mamán lent it to a man she barely knew — Heidar, a boarder in our house. He lied to Mamán: "I am on a SAVAK mission, and I will bring the car back in ten minutes." Mamán was naive; since she was honest, she thought everyone was honest. He proceeded to total the car. We were devastated; Mamán was speechless; Baba was furious.

Baba took the man to court, and made sure to put the man behind bars in prison. The rule was to shave the prisoner's hair before he entered prison. Heidar was an ugly man; the only thing he had going for him was his black, silky, smooth hair. Baba was especially happy to see Heidar's hair was shaved off. "He looks like a monster." But it didn't help us get our car back, and Baba forbade Mamán to ever replace the car. She was to be punished for the rest of her life for that careless behaviour. None of us ever forgot the story of the car, and how we had enjoyed it so much for only six months. Mamán never admitted she was wrong. She thought it was Baba's fault that this disaster had happened: if he had been around, if he had not insisted on having boarders in the house, none of this would have happened.

We had many outings during those six months that we would not have had otherwise, and for that I was grateful.

〜〜〜〜〜

On Thursday nights, the soldiers were given a reprieve from duty. They stood out in the crowd because of their shaved heads and their khaki-coloured uniforms with their mandatory high black laced-up boots. And they hadn't seen girls in a long time, which made them salivate over any female, regardless of age, it seemed, whether she was attractive or not.

Mamán asked me to go buy yogurt. I was trying not to spill the yogurt, walking as fast as I could holding the big plastic bowl with both hands in front of me.

A man with a shaved head, obviously a soldier, shouted out to me, "Look at that cutie!"

"CUTIE?" My voice went crazy. *You can think it but you're not allowed to say it out loud to me. You creep!*

I threw the bowl of yogurt in his face. My legs must have grown an extra few inches. I never ran so fast in my life.

"We have no dinner," I announced to Mamán when I reached home.

"What happened?"

"A soldier called me 'cutie' and I threw the yogurt in his face."

She laughed her head off. "Good for you!"

Every Thursday and Friday, more incidents like this happened because those were the days the soldiers were off duty. If Mamán had to go shopping on those days, she was more likely to wear her white flowery cotton *chador* covering.

~~~~~

Many Muslim homes did not have showers, and members of those households used the public Roman baths. There were separate bathhouses for men and women. At eight years of age, I pointed to a place. "Mamán, what is that building for?"

"It is a bathhouse for Muslims only. People of other religions, like us Jews, cannot use it."

Even though there was a perfectly good bath and shower at my house, I was always curious about the bathhouses. Most of the time, the women coming out of there wore black *hijabs*. If a Jew managed to get past the guard without being identified, took a bath, and was afterwards exposed, the owner of the bathhouse had to empty the entire building and purify it. Never have I believed that because of my religion I am not the equal of all other people.

Under the Shah's rule, members of religious minorities were granted government positions. This had not happened in any other period of recent Iranian history. Hoveida, a Baha'i, was the first non-Muslim prime minister, and he was in the Shah's cabinet from 1965–77. This really proved to everyone that minorities had a chance to progress. I liked Hoveida; the pipe in his hand was as much a part of his image as his Western suit. He was a modest and educated man, a true patriarch who wanted Iran to prosper at the international level and who also cared for the individual Iranian. Unlike many other politicians, he was not corrupt; he lived in a small house and drove a Peykan. He was the best prime minister Iran had ever had.

In the beginning, the Shah had discussed the idea of a two-party system. Unfortunately, he had a change of heart in 1975 when he decreed that there should be only one political party — his own. Mamán held discussions with Khaleh Ladan on these changes. "Did you hear? The Shah wants to create a government with only one party. What kind of a political system is that?"

"He is trying to convince Iranians that we're living in a democracy similar to Europe but with only one party. His party. It doesn't add up."

I was not supposed to be listening, but I found it quite intriguing that to the Shah only two types of people existed: those who believed in the monarchy and those who didn't. Then I was banished out of earshot by Mamán and my aunt. I was at this time ten years old.

He then ruled non-democratically through the Rastakhiz (Resurrection) Party. Hoveida, a member of the other party, was eventually forced to step down from his post and was arrested and imprisoned in November 1978 by the order of the Shah as a concession to the revolutionaries, whose popularity was soaring.

Suppression of freedom of thought! You're either with us, or against us. Unreal. The Shah became a virtual dictator. He started to live and act like all the other dictators in history. My aunt and Mamán marvelled over his lunacy.

This was the dark side of his reign. Economic growth came at a high price: the absence of freedom of choice, free speech, and self-expression.

The existence and practices of the secret intelligence agency, SAVAK, created a rising mood of fear and anxiety among the people. SAVAK's ears, eyes, and hands were all over the country, keeping track of everyone's most private thoughts and movements. The prison of Evin, outside of Tehran, was infamous for its psychological and physical torture techniques. I heard rumours that SAVAK burned prisoners' feet with cigarette butts, sodomized prisoners with Pepsi bottles, beat them with sticks, clubs, and belts, and used electric shock. Just the mention of its name made one's flesh crawl.

Iranians were outraged over these brutalities. What crimes did the prisoners commit to deserve this kind of treatment? We didn't know what was wrong, but the whole country felt it and was worried. The Shah's secret intelligence, SAVAK, cleaned the anti-Shah graffiti off public walls every night, but more and more sprouted on every available wall.

Jimmy Carter came to Iran in 1977, urging the Shah publicly to release the 3,000 Iranian students in Evin Prison. He accused the Shah of denying his people basic human rights. He came to Pahlavi University, where the intellectuals and Islamic anti-American students threw rotten eggs at him in protest. It was sadly ironic that Carter had publicly taken up the issue of the student prisoners with the Shah, and this act was ignored by those who should have cheered him, to their own detriment. Demonstrations broke out. The demonstrators believed that the Shah was an American puppet.

This was the first and last time he came to say, "Let them go." The students continued to protest against the political situation and the lack of freedom in Iran. The encounter between Carter and the students at the university was reported at length in *Time* magazine. I could not read English, but I hung around in the news shop and studied the article and the pictures and absorbed their meaning. It was frightening. I wished that one day I would be able to read everything that was written in *Time* magazine.

I was living in a country where there was no freedom, and many thousands of youngsters were in prison because they did not like the politics that were practised in Iran.

～～～～～

Daii Saaman owned a record store adjacent to Naneh Zivar's house. When we visited her, we saw him first. The place was very *au courant*, with Western, Iranian, and especially pop music. The store was jam-packed and music was always blasting at full volume. Many hip young men were in his store; they looked different from the rest of the people on the street. Some of them were very chic; they cared about their image. Others had their shirt buttons open right down to their navels. The girls wore gobs of colourful makeup and pranced around on high heels, wearing short skirts. Their long hair flowed around them in thick, black waves. To me, they seemed to be from a faraway planet.

"Who are your customers? Where are they from?"

"They are intellectuals. These are people who are interested in Western culture. They want to keep up-to-date with what's happening in Europe and the West. They are educated, Sima. They want to learn."

One August day when I visited his store, many customers were milling about, mumbling and crying. They were dressed in black clothes . . . black, the colour of death. Muslims wore black when they lost a dear family member. It did not make sense to me that all the customers who gathered in his shop could have lost family members at the same time.

"Daii Saaman, what is going on? Why are your customers wearing black? Why do they all look so miserable?"

"Elvis Presley died. They are grieving."

"Elvis? Who is Elvis?"

"You must have heard his songs at the wedding. He was very famous. For some of these people, he was their idol."

The sobbing was as if a beloved family member had passed away. The shop was packed, and they were all buying Elvis Presley records.

"Elvis passed away, Sima. We lost a great musician today. They loved him and are here to help deal with their loss. They will be buying his tapes today until I have none left."

Daii Saaman looked worried because by then he already knew something else was going wrong.

❧❧❧❧❧

Toward the end of 1977, Baba, the only Jewish farmer in the area, was anxious about the upheaval, the robberies, the uncertainty. He decided the only way to protect his land and his animals was to stay on his farm as much as possible. We were also scared, living in the city. Baba justified his absence by explaining that in the city we could ask neighbours for help if anything went wrong. He had to be in the country to protect the land and, more important, his animals.

He heard noises . . . hissing . . . whispers. The footsteps of strangers on his property in the middle of the night alarmed him. He rushed out to check on his animals. A group of thieves had drilled a hole in the exterior wall of the barn and were stealing his animals one by one. They intended to empty the barn completely. Baba had three cows and two hundred sheep in his barn. He loved his animals like his children. He would defend his animals with his last breath.

He fought the robbers with his words, hands, and teeth. The cattle rustlers were equipped with batons and they aimed to kill him. They wanted to remove the *Najest*—dirty Jew—who had no right to be there. He was lucky to escape alive. His life was spared for a reason yet to become evident.

Baba hobbled into the garden at home, head bloodstained and bandaged, in the middle of the week. Unusual—he never did such a thing. "What happened to you?"

"Thieves attacked my animals. Stole some. I caught them."

He barely survived this incident. This bloody sight left us worried for Baba's welfare. He was no longer safe on that farm. If they could attack him once, they would do it again. Next time, the thieves would be better prepared.

Mamán nursed Baba tenderly while reminding him that farming was not for Jews. From this encounter, Baba was left with a permanent neck injury.

Simultaneously, his Baha'i friend, Golshan, who owned land across from Baba's property, received an ultimatum from the villagers. He was ordered not to return to his land if he wanted to stay alive. He never looked back. He sold his land for next to nothing.

This was the beginning of the end for Baba's farming ambitions. Baba was devastated. Against his will, he was compelled to sell his animals. He did hold onto the land, however, as if his life depended on it. He justified that by saying the thieves couldn't steal his land. Or so he thought. He hid his head under the sand and pretended there was no problem.

~~~~~

Mamán and Baba continually argued over the boarders. Up to now, Baba had won the argument; but did he win the fight?

The boarders populated the extra rooms in the house. The three musketeers enjoyed chatting with them. Many were smart students from rural areas who were staying in Shiraz to further their education.

A couple of young men stood out. Peyman was a brilliant young man in his early twenties who attended Pahlavi University. His friend Keyvan was in his late teens, finishing his last year of high school. They were often out in the garden skipping rope.

Keyvan skipped constantly. His T-shirt and pants dripped with sweat. Farah and I asked him, "What are you doing?"

"Skipping to keep in shape."

"Do you count how many times you jump rope?"

"My goal is to do at least a thousand a day; but soon I'm going to increase it to two thousand."

"How fast can you do that?"

"As fast as I can. I keep timing myself, trying to beat my previous time."

Soraya joined the conversation. "I want to try it, too. Can we borrow your skipping rope?"

"Not a problem, once I am done."

That was how we became obsessed with skipping.

"How many times did you skip?"

This became our competition: all five of us against him. He won all the time, because he was older than us and had lots of experience.

"Mamán, we're learning how to skip; maybe you should start skipping, too."

"Never mind; this is not for me, it is for young people."

Mamán figured we were safe with him because he didn't smoke, and his buttoned shirt was not open to his navel; she thought there was nothing to worry about when we talked with Keyvan.

When Baba returned from the farm, we announced with passion, "Baba, Baba, we are learning to skip! Keyvan is teaching us."

"What? He's not our friend. Stay away from him. You're not supposed to be friendly with the boarders."

Keyvan was well-built, broad-chested, with thick, brown hair and unusual honey-coloured eyes. He told us what was happening in the universities, which he heard about through Peyman, his roommate. He told us about many students who were leaning toward Islam.

We had many discussions with him.

"Why are they supporting Islamic fundamentalism? Why don't we all just work toward freedom? They can have freedom to worship as they want, but don't say the country should be Islamic, because then others won't be free to practise different religions. If we work toward freedom, we will all be free."

Keyvan brought us books, contraband newspapers, the tape of Vivaldi's *The Four Seasons*, which he had received from the university students.

Keyvan and Peyman ignited the freedom-seeker spark in us. They kept us up to date with the latest news from Pahlavi University.

Our room was plastered with the names and photos of those whom the Shah had executed. We kept the blinds closed at all times to make sure no one peeked in. Keyvan was the one who gave us more details about the torture in Evin Prison. He told us about the electric shocks and burning the soles of prisoners' feet with cigarettes to force them to confess. The prisoners kept their sanity with exercises.

The Shah's government had a wicked side that I had not known existed. All this information was too much for our young minds, but once we knew, we wanted to learn more.

On weekends, Keyvan went away to visit his parents. Baba didn't like that we were so chummy with him.

We read, discussed, and skipped. The three musketeers were becoming intellectuals. The New Life was painful; learning about the dark side of the Shah's government shocked me. The possibility that during my lifetime I would experience real freedom was very encouraging—a far-fetched dream that I kept close to my heart.

Baba screamed, yelled, and blamed Mamán for every little thing, but over the last few weeks Baba had become concerned. Recently, Farah had seemed unusually happy, and Baba was aware of it.

"What is going on with Farah? Why is she smiling all the time?"

"She is in love."

"With whom?"

"Keyvan."

"You were with them in the house. You should not have let this happen!"

Baba forbade Farah to meet with Keyvan, but she was madly in love. Nobody, neither my parents nor the rest of the family, could reason her out of it. Besides, Keyvan was a man with good values. He loved her. He was free-spirited, an intellectual who read books and clandestine newspapers, which he passed along to us. Farah was adamant that she wanted to follow her own path regardless of what people thought.

Farah voiced her feelings. "The heart is not something you can lock and unlock. I love him."

Baba was angrier than ever. He disapproved.

Keyvan was my friend. Many times, I covered for Farah's absence and pretended that she was at a friend's house when she was out with Keyvan.

~~~~~

Throughout 1978, demonstrations and upheavals disrupted the entire country. The *Bazaries* (merchants) and oil industry employees in Abadan, the backbone of the economy in Iran, were on strike. The universities opened and closed, then reopened. SAVAK roamed the bazaars and universities.

Graffiti was spray-painted in red and black on the street walls.

Death to the Shah! Death to the dictator! Death to America! Death to Israel! Long live freedom!

Who was writing these? The next day, all the slogans were spray-painted in white. Groups were fighting to see how fast they could out-graffiti each other.

Mamán listened fervently to Israeli news on her short-wave radio at seven o'clock every evening, followed by the BBC news from London. The two broadcasters updated news about the demonstrations in Iran, the casualties, and the names of groups that were on strike.

At night, the rooftops became the battlegrounds, with shouts of, "Allaaaaaaahu Akbar!" "Allaaaaaaahu Akbar!"

Nobody knew who shouted on the rooftops. The screamers came out at ten o'clock in the darkness of the night, and could not be seen. But the noise echoed throughout the entire city. The fact that it was happening meant change. Meant they had power. Who were these invisible strange warriors? I feared them and did not know what they wanted.

They were the bearers of bad news, of danger, of doom. The growing, unnamed popular power was scarier than the Shah. Something ominous was on the horizon.

Where we once smelled daffodils, we now smelled sulfur from grenades. Bloodstained handprints of injured demonstrators were stamped on the street walls, to point out "murderer, murderer!" Not an inch on the street walls or building walls was free of graffiti.

The Shah declared martial law. No one was allowed in or out of his or her house from sunset to sunrise. Tanks were deployed on street corners. Iran was at war with its citizens. Graffiti continued to blossom on the street walls despite the imposition of martial law. How it could continue under martial law remained a mystery. Burnt tires, debris, burnt American and Israeli flags and newspapers filled every alley. The Shah claimed he ran a democracy. But his prisons were full of tortured prisoners. He executed some, but he could not kill them all. He aspired to save face, nationally and internationally. He was desperate.

Fear displaced all loyalty.

~~~~~~

Staples such as eggs, feta cheese, yogurt, rice, meat, fruits, and vegetables were in short supply. Goods could be transported only during the night because of the martial law curfew, but food trucks couldn't travel at night. Transportation time was restricted. There were shortages of food, but even the food that was available could not be delivered to the customers because of martial law.

Bakeries were open fewer hours; long snake-like noisy lineups of angry and short-tempered people waited for the delivery of essentials. We spent hours and hours in line. Since it was autumn, the days were shorter. The one thing that bothered me the most was the lack of eggs. I could no longer make my favourite dill pickle sandwiches without eggs. Baba brought home animals for slaughter that he had bought from other farmers, and we shared them with our family members.

Meat prices rose on the black market. Because of the shortage, the merchants called the shots. Even at high prices, meat sold in no time.

Bazaars were closed most of the time. Universities were also closed. Many houses were for sale. No one wanted to buy a house under these circumstances. No tourists visited our city at this point. People took their money out of the bank and kept it at home. But homes weren't safe, either. Many robberies took place at night. Power outages became the new norm at night. Something was terribly wrong, but nobody talked about it. Everyone pretended that by not talking about it, life would soon return to normal.

Baba had been pushed to the brink. One Shabbat as he was leaving the house for synagogue, he went to kiss the mezuzah at the door.

He saw a slimy discharge covering the mezuzah. He was devastated. Someone had defaced the mezuzah that was nailed to the entrance of our house. This mezuzah had been there since before I was born. Baba interpreted this act as a bad sign that confirmed anti-Jewish sentiment.

Baba finally decided to put a stop to the boarders in mid-1978. At last he came to the realization that having boarders in the house was not a good idea.

Mamán was relieved. No more boarders in the house.

But Baba brought home new boarders—loud, unruly, feathered ones. Chickens, roosters, and turkeys soon took over our garden.

Mamán was furious. "You are turning this house into a barn."

Normally the chickens were very good and laid an egg each day for us. As the chickens laid their eggs, they shrieked so much I thought they were giving birth to a new planet, but it was just an egg, and only on good days. But since the ongoing tumult of the Revolution, they had been on strike, too. They didn't lay any eggs. They were just as unhappy about their lives as we were.

Mamán's wish to have no boarders had finally come true.

Our world as we knew it was crumbling in front of our eyes. What was replacing it was not promising.

>ᕤᕤᕤᕤ

August 19, 1978. A normal, hot, August night. But the news on the radio was anything but normal. The announcer stated solemnly, "Cinema Rex has been set ablaze and five hundred innocent civilians have been burned to death in the city of Abadan."

The news made my blood run cold. I was paralyzed with horror.

A bomb of darkness exploded over our country.

Five hundred innocent people had been roasted to death.

Iran was petrified.

The unfortunate victims had thought they were going to see a movie in an air-conditioned theatre to cool off from the heat. The vendors had wandered around, yelling "Pepsi, Pepsi, Coca-Cola!" Unknown individuals had silently locked the doors from the outside and set the theatre on fire. The theatre got hotter. Five hundred people were locked inside, screaming, with no way out.

Something terrible had happened; something had gone very wrong. Mamán was glued to both the radio and the television the entire time.

The Shah promised gruesome punishments for those responsible. He designated a committee to investigate.

The Shah was exposed. He, too, knew something was wrong. How on earth had SAVAK failed to get a grip on events? How could they have let this happen in his country?

Who was behind this senseless act of brutality? Though no one said it out loud, most people blamed the action on the supporters of Ayatollah Khomeini. He was the Shiite Muslim extremist leader who had been an opponent of the Shah's liberal reforms since long before he was exiled in 1963.

The Ayatollah declared, while in exile in France, that he would fight for "freedom and liberation from the bonds of imperialism."

No matter who had committed this inhumane act of setting the theatre on fire, the fact remained that we were all scared for our lives. I was frightened and did not want to be in a public place. We were terrified of going outside, being with others, and going to the movies. We did not know who these crazy people were. Who were their next victims? Who were they even targeting?

Why did they do such a terrible thing? I had to find my own answers. I could not sleep. Farah and Soraya were worried, too. We talked among ourselves. Were they going to blow up the bazaars? Were they going to blow up our school? I was thirteen years old and scared for what was coming our way. Mamán was the only one who had answered my questions in the past, and I expected her to have the answers now. I didn't want to show how terrified I was to my younger siblings. Farah and I needed to know.

"Why would they do this?"

"They do not like the Shah."

"Who does not like the Shah?"

"Intellectuals and supporters of Ayatollah Khomeini."

Mamán had no answer for us.

"It could have been me in that theatre; this could have happened to me, and I have to know."

"If SAVAK knows you know their name, they pick you up and torture you. You want to know? I'll tell you so you won't ask these questions anymore."

Mamán spoke to Farah and me in words I had never heard her utter. She was pale. She didn't know whether or not to confide to us the whole story. A quick decision: better to inform us, before we asked a stranger and put ourselves into danger.

She whispered, "For years, the Shah has been keeping very tight control on freedom of speech and freedom of the press. Many intellectuals are in prison and are being tortured. A few have even been executed. You remember the building near Naneh Zivar's house that had armed guards in front of it? That's SAVAK's headquarters. If they think you're a threat, they will take you away." Mamán's voice was shaking. She had never sounded that scared before. "That's why Cinema Rex was set on fire. The militants believe by killing people they can raise international attention. But we Jews don't get involved in politics. Forget about it."

I was traumatized with this news and had no way to understand why killing innocent people was justified. Why was violence necessary?

"Both sides are crazy. It is a competition to see which side can kill more."

Mamán did not like my reaction; she lost control and scolded me. "Enough! Just go to school and get good marks. You can't change the world. We're here living a good life and we don't need anybody asking questions. This is the last time we're talking about this."

Something had changed at the core of my being, and I vowed not to let it rest.

Mamán listened desperately to BBC News and Radio Israel, since there was nothing mentioned about the demonstrations and uprisings in our own media. She didn't want us to hear it, but we eavesdropped anyway.

Baba was at his farm, totally unaware of what was happening. He had his own troubles to deal with.

~~~~~

Farah was attending a high school nearby. The private middle school for girls that I attended with Soraya was made up of predominantly Muslim students. A handful of Jewish students, a few Christians, and a couple of Baha'i girls made up the remaining student population. Yasamin, a Baha'i, had been my classmate for the past two years. She was an appealing girl and very open-minded. Her claim to fame was her thick, curly black hair. It was so thick that it was enough for ten heads. She braided it into two pigtails. How on earth did she wash it?

Yasamin secretly whispered, "I just read an inspiring book called

The Little Black Fish. Have you read it?"

"No. Why are you whispering?"

"It is a contraband book. You can't buy it at the bookstore. I will lend you my copy."

Yasamin brought me the book the following day. She had wrapped it carefully in newspaper so no one could see the title. We planned how best to transfer the book from her knapsack to mine. We needed a secret transfer point. We agreed to switch the book in the washroom stall. "I'll go to the washroom and leave it for you on the floor." I then followed her, picked up the book, and placed it surreptitiously in my backpack. She commanded, "Do not show it to anyone. Swear that if you are caught with the book, you will never reveal who gave it to you."

Excited, I walked as fast as I could, conscious every second of the book lying in my knapsack. But I was also frightened: Was I committing a great crime? Were all eyes fixed on me? I did not tell Mamán about the book. She would be angry with me. And she would have taken it away. My homework was done. I washed the dishes and informed Mamán, "I'll go to bed early; I'm not feeling well."

In bed, I fished the contraband book out of my backpack and, scrunched under the blanket with a flashlight pointing at the book, I started to read.

The story described the life of a little black fish and her family in a little pond. The black fish was very curious; she wanted to see the lake that was connected to her pond. Her whole family blocked her way and tried to discourage her from pursuing her plan. They thought she was foolish to even think about venturing out of the pond. She found her way out of the pond and into the lake, and then, far beyond that, to the big ocean. This experience was very liberating for her. She commented on how her family had been trying to scare her with talk of the dangers. They had no idea what a wonderful experience she had had and how worthwhile the trip had been. She had also met many interesting animals along the way that helped her on her journey to the ocean.

Why was this book on the blacklist? Why did I need to swear to secrecy? A small book with big print and pictures of a fish was contraband! What was such a big deal about this book? Either I was crazy or the Shah knew something I did not know. This book was innocent, as far as I was concerned.

Farah and Soraya read the book, too. Cyrus had a feeling that something hush-hush was happening. Too much whispering was going on. We were able to convince him that it was only homework. He believed us, reluctantly. He was too young to understand the consequences of our parents' finding out what we were up to.

After discussing with Farah and Soraya, I realized that I had to read between the lines. Though this book at first seemed innocent to me, the author was referring to the political situation in Iran. I took to heart the message this book had given me, and it changed the course of my life and that of my family. It did not matter that I was Jewish, or female. What mattered was that I should have the kind of society that would allow me to achieve anything I wanted.

My sisters and I became committed to our fight for freedom: to read whatever we wanted to read and to express our opinions and ideas; to learn and be able to contribute to society. We did not want anyone, the Shah or any other authority figure, to be the master of our lives.

This was how the people in the West lived. Expressing any of these ideas could be reason enough to be sent to prison, to be tortured.

One Peach, a Thousand Peaches, written by the same author, Samadeh Behrang, also became an overnight sensation. The book was about two little boys who wanted to eat a peach — just one — but the big landowner didn't allow them to take a single peach, and they had no money to buy even one. They stole one peach and ate it, and as the juice of the peach covered their faces, they had an epiphany. They could plant the seed far away, and once it grew into a tree of a thousand peaches, all the kids in the neighbourhood could come and eat as many as they wanted for free.

This author had written twelve books, and I read them all. But *One Peach* and *The Little Black Fish* were the best ones.

The Shah did not like any of these books. Especially *The Little Black Fish*, because it celebrated freedom of choice and direct action. The book went from hand to hand discreetly; from child to child and from adult to adult. I learned to my horror that the author had drowned during a visit to the Caspian Sea. Some people believed his death was not an accident. Many similar "accidents" were happening to intellectuals. Consequently, most people believed his "accident" had been arranged by SAVAK.

A week later, I could no longer keep this secret. I had to share this book with Sheyla. She had been my best friend since Grade 2 in elementary school. "Have you read *The Little Black Fish*?"

"Of course. My sisters let me read it months ago."

"What did you think of it?"

"It is a reflection of our political situation in Iran. My sisters have been fighting for freedom for some time."

~~~~~~

I had only heard of the demonstrations — never seen one; never participated in one. I wanted to see a demonstration with my own eyes.

"Farah, let's go see who these revolutionaries are."

"We could sneak out together and go to the university before Mamán comes home from work. Maybe Soraya wants to come, too."

Soraya nodded gleefully.

"Do not mention it to Mamán . . . she will kill us if she finds out."

We three musketeers held hands. Farah was fourteen, I was thirteen, and Soraya eleven years of age. We considered ourselves old enough to have opinions and we had many of them. We marched like little soldiers to Pahlavi University. Thousands of demonstrators were congregating there, men and women, young and old. Some were wearing the black *chador*, but others were dressed in jeans and T-shirts.

Hezbollah supporters filled the air with screams of *"Allahu Akbar!"* Others shouted, "Long live freedom!" That was when the three of us shouted, "Long live freedom!" We were no longer just watching the demonstration. Our fists shook in the air as we screamed with all our might, "Long live freedom!" This sentence electrified my body. The louder I yelled, the harder I waved my fist in the air, the stronger I felt. The contagious fever of freedom had caught us in its grip. I felt free and did not care if I was shot or wounded. At that moment, I became a warrior, along with Farah and Soraya. The hot fury of the protesters with their sweaty bodies became hotter by the minute. The determination in our minds and souls was a stronger weapon than the weapons that the Shah's army relied on. Suddenly, the Shah's soldiers marched in between the demonstrators and began firing.

Bang! Bang! Bang! The gunshots split the crowd of demonstrators into a dozen frightened mini-groups running into the alleyways. "Death to the Shah! Death to the Shah! Death to the Shah!" was shouted by the protestors as they ran, ducking and escaping for their lives.

"Duck!" Farah yelled. I smelled the grenades, dirty and sulphurous. We ran. Farah shouted, "Stay together! Run straight ahead!"

We ran as fast as we could.

I dashed around the corner as quickly as my shaking legs could carry me. Every now and then, I glanced back to make sure that Soraya was following me. Farah shouted at us, "Freedom is fought for! It is never given!" Our lives were now as fragile as three delicate threads about to snap.

The side streets were filled with protestors. "Those bastards! Don't they have families? How could they shoot us? We are Iranians!"

I gasped for air. Farah hugged Soraya for being so brave. She should not have been at the demonstration or exposed to the danger that came with it. But that was Soraya: no one could convince her of anything unless she wanted to do it. She had made up her mind and fought for freedom like an adult.

This outing had been our secret. Neither Mamán nor Baba was supposed to find out. Unfortunately, a friend of Mamán's saw us in the crowd. She called to let Mamán know before we reached home.

Mamán was fuming. "Where the hell have you been?"

"With friends."

Pacing back and forth, screeching at the top of her lungs, "Tell me the truth! I know that you were participating in a demonstration!" The slap came so fast, so unexpectedly, that I could not duck. It hurt so much that I thought her palm was stuck to my face. Her hand left a swollen red mark across the side of my cheek.

She was furious. So were we.

Mamán did not need a new problem. Her life was already full of problems, with Baba, with five kids, with day-to-day living. Now she had to worry about the three musketeers' safety. She broke down and wept. Wept and wept until there were no more tears left in her. We wept along with her. Why didn't we have freedom like the rest of the world? Why did we have to demonstrate for freedom and be faced with bullets?

Word about Parisa's girls and their quest for freedom spread like wildfire in the Jewish community. Naneh Jaan-Jaan came by to scold us. She warned us, "Politics is not for us. If you did not care about your own lives, at least consider how your actions affect the lives of all the other Jewish people in our community. Jews do not rock the boat!"

"Why shouldn't we care about freedom?"

"We do not bite the hand that feeds us. You do not know how good the Shah has been to the Jews. I know. I still remember."

"This argument is not going anywhere," Farah whispered in my ear.

"Don't you know it is rude to whisper?"

"You're right, Naneh. We will be quiet."

We had to agree with Naneh or this argument would have gone on forever. But we still had the fire of freedom burning inside us. As much as we loved Naneh Jaan-Jaan and wanted to make her proud of us, we could not comply with her demand.

We did not want to die in a cage.

There was more honour in dying at a young age for a cause I believed in than to die of old age like a bird that had never left its cage and never flown.

~~~~~~

Every square was filled with angry, frustrated protestors. The demonstrations were no longer only around the university. They were exploding all over the city—merchants, students, teachers, grandmothers, doctors, workers.

The Shah's army deployed more tanks on the streets. More restrictive martial law was declared. "No more than two people are allowed to congregate at the same time. Get your essentials during the daytime. Disobedience will be punished to the fullest extent of the law."

Power outages became a regular phenomenon. Mamán relied on her battery-run radio to listen to the news. We could not watch TV.

"Long live freedom!" "Death to Shah!" echoed in the streets. The two distinct groups of protestors consisted of one group made up of long-bearded men and black-sheet-covered women; the second one of men and women wearing jeans and short-sleeved shirts. The latter were the students. The two groups opposed each other's point of view on most things, but they thought that they could work together in opposing the Shah. "The enemy of my enemy is my friend." They would discuss their differences once their common enemy, the Shah, was vanquished.

They both shouted "Long live freedom!" But the first group also said "Long live Khomeini!" I could not say that, because I did not trust him. He looked ancient. No one could convince me that Ayatollah Khomeini would be granting us freedom.

He had his own agenda. I wanted no part of his agenda.

In the early fall of 1978, my classmate Mojgan whispered, "Did you see him in the moon?"

"Did I see who in the moon?"

"Agha. Ayatollah Khomeini. He is sent from God. The face of Agha is in the moon! See his beard! See his eyes!"

I had never heard of such a bizarre thing. Maybe there was truth to this.

Mamán came home. "At work, people are claiming to see the face of Agha in the moon. Maybe we should look to see if it is true. They say his turban is on the top, he's facing left."

That night, Mamán and the three musketeers looked at the moon and lo and behold, there was the Ayatollah Khomeini staring down at us, beard and all. The power of suggestion.

People thought this was a sign from God that he should be the leader. The thought was frightening.

The air was charged with dangerous excitement. If all went well, this promised freedom, but if it went wrong, it would go very, very, wrong.

Agha was a man of few words. He could not put a complete sentence together.

~~~~~~

In Grade 8, middle school, I had a few friends I hung around with: Mojgan, Yasamin, and Sheyla. Mojgan, Sheyla, and I were good students and studied together. I liked Yasamin because she was also an underdog: she was Baha'i, a minority religion.

I had been to Mojgan's house a few times. Her father was a high-ranking officer in the Shah's military. She lived in the military gated complex with her parents. Lately, Mojgan had kept her distance from Sheyla and me. She ignored us. She befriended two girls in the class who were from religious families.

I whispered to Sheyla, "I was in the demonstration last week. Have you ever been to one?"

"Yes, I have been many times with my sisters. Your mother lets you go?"

"No, she forbids us. But I can't listen to her. I will live with the punishment."

"Are you sure?"

"Yes."

"Then join my sisters and me tomorrow after school. There are two big demonstrations planned for tomorrow. An Islamic demonstration at Shaheh Cheragh—the biggest mosque in the city with a golden dome—we do not want to be in that group. The freedom fighters' demonstration is planned at Flekieh Setad. Dress comfortably. You have to run once the police attack us. Don't tell Mojgan. She is acting weird. I do not know what has gotten into her."

I wore my Adidas sneakers; it hadn't been easy to find a pair. I had begged the shop owner to keep a pair for me as soon as he received his shipment. It took weeks of going back and forth to his store until I bought my precious pair.

Since the upheaval, there was a shortage of Western goods: I could no longer find Dove soap, Nivea, Yardley cream, or Fiji perfume. Smokers could no longer find their favourite Winstons. Levi jeans were the same story. Adidas and Levi jeans were the secret dress code for the secular intellectual freedom fighter.

My heart was racing, frantically trying to beat its way out of my chest, as we marched determinedly toward the demonstration, Farah on one side and Soraya on the other. Thousands of people were marching in the same direction. As I approached my destination, I felt stronger. The group of unknown warriors were my friends. We had common demands. The hope of freedom was like water on soil after a drought. We wanted to drink it in. Our right fists shook in the air. "Long live freedom!" we shouted. The anger in the faces was unforgettable. Though our ages, our genders, our religions, were different, together we demanded freedom. United by one thought. Able to express our humanity as other people expressed themselves around the world.

I was gasping for air. Farah's body pressed against my right side and Soraya was glued on my left side. Everywhere I looked, I met the angry, optimistic people who thought the louder they shouted "Long live freedom!" the faster it would be manifest.

Our enthusiasm was as charged as a high-voltage electric current that could toss off anyone who touched it.

We demonstrators started to move with our fists in the air. "Long live freedom! Long live freedom! Long live freedom!" That voice echoed in my entire being. It sounded so wonderful—as if by shouting it, I had been granted the freedom to express myself.

From the other side of the square, a group of bearded men and black-sheet-covered women shouted, "Long live Khomeini!"

We never barged into their demonstration, but the Islamic demonstrators stormed over and disrupted ours. "You are supposed to be at Shaheh Cheragh. What are you doing here?"

"The whole city belongs to us. We want Islamic democracy!"

The Shah's police released tear gas, followed by the roar of gunshots. Demonstrators were beaten with batons. The only weapons we had were matches to burn anything that was in our path, and small round stones, which we flung at the police. It was impossible to fight bullets with stones.

"Run fast! Go back! These monsters are here to kill us!" The stampede swayed in the other direction.

Farah shouted, "Run! Sima, run! Soraya! Run! Go to Naneh Zivar's house!" We had to move fast. We hid in the alleys. I was enraged!

Naneh Zivar was furious to see us on her doorstep. She figured out what we were up to. She gave us a lecture. "Do not come here again from a demonstration. You are playing with fire. You will be wounded or killed. Think of Mamán. She has suffered enough. She should not be mourning your deaths. Go home. She must be sick over your absence."

In the demonstrations, we were fighting not only the Shah but also the Muslim extremists, who had their own hidden agenda. The whole world conspired against Iranian citizens. No place was safe. The streets, home, school, were all battlefields.

The casualties of the day were not announced on the local radio nor were they mentioned in the local newspaper. The international media, BBC Radio, announced that fifty people had been injured that day.

Military tanks were again deployed on street corners. "Anybody out after dark risks getting shot!" People talked constantly about the casualties—who had been wounded, who had been imprisoned. We were at war: Iranian citizens were at war with the Shah. Fear and uncertainty now affected every aspect of our lives.

〰〰〰

In mid-autumn 1978, our friend Mojgan came to school wearing a head scarf. Overnight she had become one of *them*. She hung around with other girls who wore head scarves, those who came from very religious families.

Mojgan's family wasn't religious. Her mother dressed in the shortest skirts and tightest blouses. Her red lipstick and her blue eye shadow could be spotted from across the street. Mojgan bragged many times, "We had all-night parties in our compound. Only open to military employees, with lots of music and alcohol." She complained, "I do not like it when my father drinks too much. He becomes violent."

The members of Mojgan's family were originally staunch supporters of the Shah. Her father was a high-ranking military officer in the Shah's army. Military officers lived in a gated compound with its own shops. When everything was in short supply, they were taken care of. The Shah knew all about this and supported the army in style, which included plenty of alcohol for their consumption.

It was crystal clear Mojgan's family wasn't taking any chances. They were opportunists and, when the wind changed, they followed the direction of the change. Their purpose in life was not to be loyal to others or to one idea, but to save their own skins.

Mojgan started ignoring me and our old group of friends. I was deeply hurt. Every time I approached Mojgan, she continued her discussion with her new friends and didn't look at me.

~~~~~

Islamic militants hated the Baha'i. In the Baha'i faith, they believe that the last prophet was the Bahá'u'lláh, but Shiite Muslims are still waiting for the arrival of the last prophet. The new, fashionable sport for Islamic fundamentalists in the fall of 1978 was to set Baha'i houses on fire, as well as liquor stores owned by Jews.

Yasamin was very upset. Many of the houses in her neighbourhood, where Baha'i people lived, were set on fire by these militants. She feared the same fate awaited her family. There was no way to comfort her. She had legitimate reasons to be terrified. I urged her, "Forget about the fire for a few minutes. I am scared, too. The Islamic militants threatened to burn my uncle's record store. Let's play volleyball to get our mind off this whole ordeal." Volleyball was her favourite activity. We had a volleyball team at our school. Though Soraya was younger than us by two years, she was a great player. All my friends liked to have her play on our team.

Soraya and I were playing in the schoolyard during lunchtime with Yasamin and Sheyla. For a few minutes, we pretended everything was as it used to be.

Mojgan, like a tribal leader protected on all sides by her henchwomen, scarves around their heads, approached us. With a face like vinegar, Mojgan strode to the corner where we were playing volleyball. She meant trouble. When she had decided to cover her head, she also covered her soul and her reason. She and her friends stopped about five feet away and watched us in silence as we bounced the ball for a few minutes. Then it was Yasamin's turn. Mojgan put out her hand, caught the ball and leered at Yasamin.

"Maybe there's a good reason they are setting Baha'i houses on fire! Ever wonder why?" she sneered viciously.

Yasamin looked terrified. She turned pale and could not speak. She began to stutter. "Wwwwhhhat hhhhave I done wwwrrrong ttto yyyyou?"

Mojgan's words were brutal. "Your religion is what is wrong. You filthy girl! Too bad they didn't burn your house down! Maybe next time . . .!"

She threw the ball away and stalked off. Her gang marched behind her, whispering among themselves. This was the first time I had seen blatant heartlessness from Mojgan. I had considered Mojgan a dear friend. But now, she was worse than an enemy. She had turned out to be mean and evil. I was inconsolable.

I couldn't bear to witness such vindictiveness. This was the second time I was really forced to realize something was going seriously wrong. If these people claimed to be fighting for freedom, why were they burning the houses of innocent Baha'i people? What was the freedom they were fighting for? What was the purpose of their viciousness?

Hot fury washed over me. Peace was what I stood for both at home and at school. How dare she! Instead of sympathizing with the plight of her people, Mojgan had taunted and threatened Yasamin! What did Yasamin ever do to her? What did she know about Yasamin's religion? Throwing the ball on the ground, I ran after Mojgan, screaming at her. "Who do you think you are? You are just a parrot repeating what others have told you. Do you know what the name of your prophet means? What you are doing has nothing to do with peace and tolerance." I had read the night before that when translated into Persian, "Mohammed" means "peace."

Mojgan slowly turned back toward me. I stopped dead in my tracks. All activity in the schoolyard stopped. All eyes were on Mojgan and me.

My voice warned me, *Don't go crazy. You are not the defender of the whole world. Watch your back before someone stabs you.*

In a quiet voice that surprised even me, I explained to her, "Islam is a religion of peace and tolerance. Is this how to practise peace and tolerance?"

I flung my hand toward her friends, and walked away. I was shaking with anger and traumatized by Mojgan's betrayal. To my surprise, Mojgan did not come after me. She and her friends stood, stunned, where I left them. The volleyball players drifted off into another corner of the yard.

Many more words struggled within me to be screamed, but I kept them back. I had already dug myself into a deep hole. What kind of Muslim was she to hurt people like that? No one liked Mojgan except for those sheep she hung around with. But I bit my tongue.

Mojgan marched straight back into the school to talk to "Sister" Fatemeh in charge of religious studies. She reported a convoluted misinterpretation of our argument. I returned to class, distraught. My classmates were surprised that I showed up to the class. Mojgan was not there. My teacher demanded that I should go to the Department of Religion office immediately.

"They are waiting for you."

The department head was seated behind her desk in a small, gloomy room. From head to toe she was covered in a black *chador*. She had a dark complexion, an oversized nose that protruded beneath her *chador*, small, piercing eyes and bushy black eyebrows hanging over them. She really looked like a crow. This religious woman probably thought, ironically, that if she were ever to amount to anything in her life, being active in a fundamentalist revolution would be a real boost. In the school setting, she was able to push herself to the top by sheer fanaticism. Other devout teachers also had made the change from the skirt and blouse to the black *chador*. But they were not as frightening or determined as Sister Fatemeh, the Department of Religion head.

These women, and the hundreds of thousands of others who had made the same change, called themselves "sisters." I called them "black crows." They looked like crows, covered in black from head to toe. The crows in Shiraz were symbolic as bearers of bad news. This new group of crows was also the bearer of terrible news.

The "sister," Fatemeh, had approached the principal, a moderate Muslim, to do something about the behaviour of dirty Jews, and my lack of respect for Islam. She pushed for full suspension.

The principal of the school was sitting in the only chair a few feet away from the "sister's" desk. A gentle-looking man who sported a thick, grey mustache, he found himself in an awkward position. The Department of Religion had gradually taken over management of the school, imposed new, restrictive rules on behaviour, and handled discipline. The unfortunate principal found his authority eroded; he was now not much more than a figurehead. He was ill at ease as I stood trembling before him. I looked across the desk into the hate-filled eyes of the black crow. She stared at me as though I had committed history's worst crime, promising with her stabbing gaze, "This will cost you heavily." Her very presence disgusted me.

"You want to tell me what happened?" the principal inquired.

The words would not come out of my lips. I was frightened. I tried to speak. But the crow cut in.

"She insulted our religion. *Najest*!"

He glanced up at her, and then at me. "You want to tell me what happened?" he repeated.

"I said nothing against Islam," my voice shook. "I told Mojgan to read more."

"See!" the crow screamed at the principal. "She thinks she can run the school! She's a Jew, child of a minority. She stood up for a Baha'i child. She blasphemes the holy Quran. What are these infidels doing in a Muslim school?"

The principal raised his voice, "Do you have anything to say for yourself?"

Whatever I wanted to say would be screamed down and twisted by the crow. And it would worsen my punishment. I shook my head sadly in disbelief. A molehill had turned into a mountain.

The crow cawed viciously, "Sit here until your Mamán comes to pick you up. We called her."

The gossip mill was in top form that afternoon. Soraya didn't leave my side despite my pleading with her to go back to class. Soraya also was scared.

A worm would have been treated better than me by this point. By now the students knew what had happened. Although many approved of my standing up to Mojgan, none of them was going to say so.

"Go back to class before this gets uglier, Soraya," I insisted. "We don't need two girls in the family to be stuck here."

"I'm going to stay right here with you. I don't want to go back to class. I hate Mojgan," she sobbed. She didn't budge. None of the teachers walking by tried to send her back to class.

But I was not looking forward to Mamán's picking me up. I was in for big trouble.

Mamán saw me waiting outside of the principal's office.

She argued with the principal and the crow. "Since when is standing up for justice a crime?"

Fortunately for me, the principal knew I was a good student. I had no history of misdemeanours. So he limited my punishment to three days' suspension.

Mamán complained, "That is too much punishment. She's never been in trouble before."

"I think it will be enough if she's suspended until next week. I assure you, she will never let this happen again. Right?"

He looked at me sternly. I nodded my head vigorously.

The crow held back her malicious words, and shrugged. "If your name ever crosses my desk again, we won't be so lenient. Trust me!"

Mamán was proud that I had stood up for my beliefs, but she scolded me the entire way home.

She reminded me, "Put your emotions aside. You're just one Jewish girl in a Muslim man's country. Men stronger than you get killed. You will be crushed and before you know it I will be mourning your death. You can't change anything."

"But Mamán, Gandhi did it."

"Don't challenge me! You've caused enough problems."

I was not allowed to talk to Farah or Soraya. Mamán didn't want the disease to spread—it seemed I was contagious.

"You know what's going to happen? This news is going to explode like a bomb. You will bring shame to our house. You'll bring shame to our family in the Jewish community. Soon nobody's going to want to talk to us. Why can't you be like everybody else?"

She was conflicted because although she disagreed with the rules herself, she was still unhappy about the consequences this kind of behaviour could bring. Was this tiny dispute among children going to jeopardize my future schooling? Did I have any reason to be alarmed?

Naneh Jaan-Jaan came to visit, and soon after, my Ammeh Ashraf arrived to admonish me. The phone rang off the hook. Cousins, aunts, neighbours, friends of my parents . . . all of them berated me simultaneously.

"Why did you do that? You have to think of all of us, not just yourself when you do something!" complained Naneh Jaan-Jaan.

"You're giving all the Jews in Shiraz a bad name. We all have to suffer for your stupidity!" Ammeh Ashraf yelled. I looked up to see if it was really her. She, who stood up against anyone who she did not approve of, was giving me lessons on proper conduct. This was bizarre.

It was a catastrophic day. I cried nonstop. Mamán came to my defence a couple of times, but that didn't calm them down. Instead they started screaming at her, too, and the entire family erupted into chaotic babble.

Naneh Jaan-Jaan updated Baba on the week's news before he entered the house. Her version, of course. He was screaming his head off as he stormed in.

"It's because of the way you've been raised by Mamán! I knew she was wrong this entire time. She kept encouraging you to help others. Who gave you permission to be the defence attorney for the whole world? It's all this Keyvan's fault; since he's been around, you've all become intellectuals. Who needs to be intellectual? That's garbage."

Mamán chimed in, "You think you can do a better job raising them? You should have been around to do so. Remember those days you were telling everybody about how smart your children are? You don't get to pick and choose."

"Don't you know you are not supposed to speak to your husband like that?"

Mamán started to howl. I felt guilty. Was it right, what I did? Was it worth all this drama? I was beginning to think it wasn't worth causing my family so much pain. The whole thing had gotten out of control.

Keyvan, Farah, and Soraya were proud of me.

Keyvan praised me. "Good work! Keep it up! We've got to stand up for what we believe in."

Talk about making a mountain out of a molehill! This fracas had started as an argument between children in a playground!

That was the last time I saw Yasamin. After that day she stopped coming to school.

~~~~~

Saturday night gatherings in the park had not taken place in months now. Jews were too stressed to socialize, because of the curfew, martial law, and the looting. Daily provisions—bread, eggs, meat, even gasoline—were in short supply. Insane! Iran supplied the world with oil but suffered from a shortage of gasoline for its citizens.

The upheaval caused the economy to fail. Iranian currency became weaker and weaker. The exchange rate for the Iranian *tooman* fell from seven to twenty to the American dollar.

Mamán obsessively tuned in to BBC Radio at seven o'clock at night. She did this by candlelight, because of the power outages. Mamán listened to the radio on battery power. This had been our routine for weeks.

People looked thinner and beaten down.

This was by far the worst that we had seen. Everyone was suffering tremendous stress.

The banks were no longer considered safe. People withdrew their money. Thieves knew that money was hoarded in homes, and citizens were wary of break-ins and theft. We were not safe in the streets or at home. The eyes of the customers in the bakery were sunken with fear. My baker did not joke with me anymore. Paranoia buried itself deeply into our psyche. No one trusted anyone else. Better to stay quiet. I was afraid to be on the streets by myself. We were afraid of our shadows. I kept looking around me to make sure no one followed us. No security was available to us, not from the Shah, not from his new cabinet that changed faster than the weather, and definitely not from the Islamic extremists.

~~~~~

The students handed out pamphlets near the university. I grabbed as many as I could and hid them in my backpack and under my sweater and ran home with them. I never walked straight home in case I was followed. The side streets and the alleys were my friends. Reading this new information in the pamphlet thrilled me.

The voice in my head warned me, "There will be consequences. A good Shirazi Jewish girl should not be getting her hands or her mind muddled with this nonsense." But I didn't want to listen to the warning.

To me, the future of my country was not nonsense.

If in the past someone was caught with any of this literature, he was liable to be tortured, imprisoned, or put to death. During these tumultuous days, however, the Shah had bigger fish to fry and had no time to worry about what schoolgirls were reading.

I had picked up a book about Darwin and was fascinated by his ideas. My family was insulted when I asked them about Darwin at the dinner table. They took it as a challenge, but I was not trying to challenge them. No answer . . . and I was not allowed to ask questions. We Jews never asked questions. We kept the status quo.

"Try not to fall into discussion with her: it's a trap," my aunts and uncles told each other. "She will argue till her last breath."

I wanted to hear every side of every story. The atmosphere was so fear-ridden that even asking a simple question to clarify thoughts in my head was like stabbing my family with the sharpest dagger. I learned that religion was not open for debate—a tough lesson to learn, and family get-togethers were no place for politics and philosophy. I could not discuss this with Mamán or Baba—and definitely not with the teachers. The three musketeers encouraged each other's questions but could not answer them.

My own family and even my extended family provided no reasonable arguments. They stuck me on the blacklist with all the other outcasts.

≻≻≻≻≻

Business in Daii Saaman's record store fell off dramatically during the Revolution. He had been officially warned many times. Islamic militants stormed in for the last time and gave him an ultimatum:

"If you don't want us to bomb your shop, change it into something else." This was serious. To dismiss the threats would be crazy.

He explained this to Mamán when we went to visit Naneh Zivar. "I have to change the merchandise. The Islamic militants detest the type of music I am selling. It is the very thing they want to abolish. Anything that represents Western culture is taboo. They are against it. I have to come up with a new plan before something terrible happens." I had never seen him so concerned. Mamán became agitated on hearing this.

Daii Saaman closed his shop until he could figure out what to do. His safety, and that of his family, was the most important issue.

We were so scared of being looted that we never left the house unoccupied. Mamán left the house only for work and emergency shopping and made sure to hurry back as quickly as possible. She did not want to be harassed or caught in a demonstration. The smell of fire and sulfur wrapped our once beautiful city in a cloud of fear.

The uncertainty regarding our present and future life was difficult to live with. Would the "new government" that was to replace the Shah be any better than we had now? How could we ensure that? Were we getting out of a pothole and falling into the crater? These and a million other questions raced around in my head. I could not keep track of them. The more I thought about the possibilities, the more frightened I became. All indications of what this "new government" would be like were scary. Mamán's words reverberated in my head. "An ounce of something is the same as a ton of it." If the Islamic militants were so intolerant of a different point of view when they were not yet in power, what guaranteed their tolerance if they took over? Would the freedom we had so long fought for become reality? Would this new government seek out and persecute the various religious minorities and political groups? No one dared to speak up or offer an opinion in public; undercover agents could be watching, listening. We had grown used to keeping silent. We didn't know what terrible things were awaiting us—but we knew something bad *was* going to happen.

〜〜〜〜〜

Tourists were history. Nobody wanted to visit our war-torn country.

Whoever had the courage and the means left Iran. My Khaleh Shadi decided she could not take the uncertainty. She left for a week's vacation and never came back. Many people fled to Tehran, and from there to the United States or Israel. Flights out of the country were full. Ticket prices shot up. Airplane seats were unavailable. Time was running out. The hourglass had turned over and the sands were flooding down.

Among the expatriates were tens of thousands of Jews, affluent and intellectual Muslims, Baha'i, and Zoroastrians. People in Tehran sold whatever they could, changed their money, and emigrated to the West. Los Angeles became one of the most popular destinations in the United States (Los Angeles was called "Irangeles" or "Tehrangeles" among the emigrants who settled there). They favoured Los Angeles because its climate was similar to Tehran's.

Because so many houses were for sale, and the economy was unstable, the price of real estate plummeted. Who wanted to buy property from Jews? Not the Muslims; Jews' property was considered impure and cursed. Christians and Baha'i felt jittery about buying new property. There were more sellers than buyers.

Mamán huddled under the candlelight while glued to BBC Radio. Our room was chilly; the winter's bitter cold stabbed us like needles. Shiraz had never been so frosty. Mamán tried to use the heater as little as possible to avoid standing in line for fuel. At our house, we'd always had an abundance of fruit, vegetables, and meat. Lately, Mamán had rationed all the food. It was even hard to buy bread; lineups at the baker's were two hours long. Power outages at nights, food shortages, the fear of looting, and the declining economy . . . living in Shiraz was a nightmare come alive. My beautiful Shiraz had turned into hell.

The Shah had shuffled his cabinet a few times to try to placate the people. But power slipped out of his control. His family had left Iran for a "long vacation." The end of an era was near. The last time the Shah addressed us on national television was on January 16, 1979. Although he normally exuded confidence and poise, during his final speech he was visibly anxious. He was not his usual self. As he spoke, his voice shook and it came across as though he himself did not believe in his speech. No one believed him when he said he was planning to leave the country for a short while and would return soon.

~~~~~

A new fear was brewing inside me. A new government would be headed by Ayatollah Khomeini. His picture was plastered all over the walls of alleys and buildings. Graffiti spread like wildfire.

Long live Khomeini!
Long live Freedom!
Death to America!
Death to Israel!
Death to the Shah!
Death to the Aristocratic Elite!
Salute to the Poor and the Meek!

What did "Long live Khomeini" mean? What did he stand for? Based on his appearance and the way he dressed, he could have been an alien from another planet. How could this bearded old man, covered in a thick, brown cape, ensure the kind of freedom we envisioned? We thought there would be a platform to decide on how freedom would be delivered. Instead, rumours were circulating that we would be forced to wear the *hijab*. Where was the freedom in forcing us to dress the way they wanted? How could they justify this as freedom? This was not freedom, it was just the opposite.

Worried faces and sunken eyes filled the city. We had grown used to this enforced silence. We had endured oppression under the Shah, but now the future did not seem promising at all, despite all the bloodshed. We now had more reason to be concerned. I desperately hoped that a change of government might give us a chance at freedom of speech at last. But the many clues were proof that I was fooling myself.

Ayatollah Khomeini returned home after sixteen years in exile. On the day he arrived in Tehran, February 1, 1979, Muslim extremists throughout the entire country were jubilant, celebrating the return of Agha. Thousands of Muslims poured into the streets. "Long live Khomeini!" echoed loudly. I had never seen such mobs. The black-covered crows shouted, "Long live Khomeini!" The bearded, angry-looking men chanted, "Long live Khomeini!"

Nothing about this small, bearded man with the expressionless face appealed to me.

The majority of Iranians, however, were *not* on the streets. The blood ran cold in their veins, for they knew what the mullahs represented. Islamic militants were so deafening in their exhilaration that no voice of opposition could even be heard in that din.

Traffic halted in the streets of Shiraz. Drivers honked their horns or shrieked with delight. Muslim extremists handed out baked goods and sweets in the streets to celebrate Agha's arrival . . . while the rest of Iran shook with fear at what Khomeini's arrival meant for them. A veil of darkness was settling over Iran.

The entire country sat on the edge of its collective seat, awaiting Ayatollah Khomeini's grand speech about the freedom he was about to bestow on us. We awaited his promises, his platform, and his beliefs. He had said, when he was exiled sixteen years ago, "I will not return until this pawn of America is gone," and he stayed true to his word.

We watched the television and listened to the radio to see what he had to declare after all these years.

As he stepped off the plane, a reporter excitedly asked him, "How do you feel upon returning to Iran?"

He replied in a flat voice, "I have no emotion."

Unbelievable! That alone should have told us everything we needed to know. When I once returned home after a week-long vacation, I checked each corner of the house, thrilled to be back at home. Yet the Ayatollah Khomeini had returned after *sixteen years* of exile—and felt no emotion.

Chaos reigned. I woke up every morning thinking, "Today will be the day. Today will be different. This is the day it will all turn around." There was less and less and less rice, less and less *ghand* (Iranian sugar cubes). The oil workers were on strike. The *bazaaris* were on strike; the university students were on strike. Everybody was on strike.

February 11, 1979. It was dark and overcast at nine o'clock in the morning. This was a strange phenomenon for Shiraz at any time of the year. I soon realized it would an unforgettable day for many reasons. The Shah's army, the Islamic militants, and the intellectuals were out in the streets fighting their last battle.

The Shah had fled a few weeks ago. His most loyal army members were ready to face down the insurrection. They had hoped that they could turn the situation around.

We woke up to the non-stop stutter of guns and the putrid aroma of burnt tires.

"Don't go to school," warned the radio. "Don't go to work." The gunshots echoed across Shiraz all day long. It was hard to breathe the highly polluted air.

Our house was located at the heart of the action. The offices of the Ministry of Justice were on the corner of our street, and Hezbollah forces wanted to take possession of these buildings. We hid behind our garden door as Mamán sternly forbade us to leave the house. Men screamed, yelled, and shouted:

"Long live freedom!"

"Long live Khomeini!"

"Death to Israel!"

"Death to America!"

Of the many slogans I could hear in between the gunshots, the only one I could relate to was "Long live freedom!"

From a crack in the door, we saw movement on the street.

Less than a metre from the garden door, a young man lay on the ground, moaning and calling for help. He held his wounded leg with his hands, drenched in blood which continued to flow in red rivers around him. It soaked the ground beside him.

"*Khoda, Khoda, Khoda!* (O God) Help me, help me, help!"

We cracked the door open. He was bleeding horrifically. I gasped for air. The man was paralyzed, unable to move an inch. In a split second, my sisters and brothers were faced with a life-and-death question: What should we do?

The young man looked up at us. He pleaded to us with his eyes before he slipped into unconsciousness. *For God's sake help me!*

Mamán and Baba, from infancy, had taught us to help those in need.

We knew what we must do.

Farah pushed me out of the way and leapt forward to pull the man into the house.

Cyrus, Soraya, and I joined Farah in grabbing the man by the arms and dragging him into the walkway behind the door. Blood dripped from his leg as we yanked and pulled two hundred pounds of dead weight. We had never seen a wounded human being. Having rescued him, we slammed the door and yelled for Mamán, who was glued to the radio, "Mamán! Help! Blood! Blood!"

Mamán was distraught by the scene she found in the yard. "Bring cotton balls, some material from my sewing supplies."

We watched Mamán as she tended carefully to this stranger. She moved expertly. Mamán ripped open his pants from ankle to thigh. She filled the wounds with cotton balls, wrapping his thigh tightly. As soon as she was done, the wounded man looked up at Mamán, gratitude in his eyes.

Mamán commanded Farah, "Bring me a glass of water, and add sugar to it." Turning to the man, "You bled heavily. Drink this. I have to send you out to get proper help. I did what I could." We never learned the name of our injured victim. He limped out of the door and into the street. He never returned to our house. But we had done our part.

Ambulance sirens screeched throughout the day, picking up the wounded scattered on the streets. We watched as the paramedics took our injured man in the ambulance. There were many casualties on this day; there had been many in the days before. We had seen one wounded man with our own eyes, but thousands were wounded or were dying for freedom. This was the only time any of us witnessed bloodshed first-hand.

Seeing how easily this poor man could have died, we felt the fragility of our own safety.

At noon, the day was as dark as if it were the middle of the night. People ran out into the streets, flitting shadows of murky black. Angry men screamed, carrying batons in their hands, ready to attack the enemy. The sidewalks, the houses, the skies were outlined in ominous shades of black and grey, as if a biblical plague had descended from the heavens.

Mamán kept us away from the door after the incident with the injured man. We were limited to witnessing history being made from the second-floor balcony. The gunshots did not stop, and the shouts did not die down. The smell of burnt tires in no way resembled the delightful aroma of Chinese daffodils that normally heralded the arrival of spring in my city.

Baba remained on his farm throughout the Revolution. I was happy Baba was not in the house because he would have not let us come out of our rooms. But I wondered if any riots had taken place in the country and if he was safe. I prayed for his safety, since we could not contact him by phone in the country; he had no phone line. We could not get onto a city bus to see him, either; all the roads were closed. The city was paralyzed. Only the militants were out on the roads.

At sundown, announcements on the radio confirmed that the forces loyal to the Shah had been defeated. Mamán's expression turned to one of horror. Devastated over the uncertainty, she mumbled to herself, "We got out of the pothole and fell into a well."

The former Ministry of Justice building with those frightening lions in front was ravaged. Smoke-covered men, exhausted by an entire day of fighting and looting, strutted on the streets carrying their trophies — Uzi submachine guns.

Gone were the personal files, the desks, the chairs, the couches.

Only debris and ashes were left.

It was evening before we peeked out the door. Dirty, exhausted men moved past the house with arms full of booty. They carried guns on their shoulders as if they were boxes of pastries. Some carried chairs.

I saw a man who carried doors off their hinges. What was not bolted down was stolen. Finders, keepers.

We had a new government: the Provisional Revolutionary Government, a coalition of Islamic clergy and some democrats. I was scared: What did it mean to have a Provisional Revolutionary Government? The newcomers had not given us any reason to trust them or to believe that they would deliver freedom.

Ayatollah Khomeini appointed his best friends to different positions in the coalition government. I had never heard of Ayatollah Khalkhali but he was a perfect candidate for head of the Revolutionary Court. Ayatollah Khomeini appointed by reputation.

Ayatollah Khalkhali was a key figure who punished anyone with any connection to the Shah's government. Ayatollah Khalkhali shot cats as a hobby. He was a sick man. His brutality earned him a most appropriate position in the new government. Almost immediately, he earned the perfect nickname: Ayatollah Khalkhali, The Bloody Judge. A bad taste formed in my mouth whenever his name came up. My stomach churned when I saw his picture. I could not bear to listen to his voice over the radio.

Ayatollah Khalkhali's goons opened all the files and saw who had worked for SAVAK. The higher the rank, the bigger the prize for those who caught the offenders; execution was their "just punishment." The meek and the poor—*Must az afin*—gained ground. They were ready to take out their anger for the years of being downtrodden. They were going to take it out on *Mustak Behrin*, the middle and upper classes. Anyone whose money they wanted to confiscate was *Mustak Behrin*.

Each day, more people were executed, more cars were incinerated, more battles were fought with the Hezbollah. Squalor and terror ruled the country.

Supporters of the Shah were arrested. These prisoners were generally executed shortly after their arrests; the highest-ranking ones first. Their names were read out on the radio.

For the prize captives, the bloody judge, Khalkhali, was called to render judgment. He also served as the executioner.

Khalkhali's arrival in any city meant death, murder, bloodbaths. He gave the victims the honour of allowing them to die by his hand.

The newcomers seized innocent people's wealth for themselves and executed their victims. Hezbollah members became the nouveau riche overnight. And they came with a vengeance.

In this frightening new atmosphere, men in suits were considered supporters of Western culture. The dress code drastically changed for men; dirty clothing and beards were signs of power. What were the rules? They kept changing, day to day.

There were no laws about what to wear yet; but to be safe, Mamán insisted that we put on a *rosari* when we went out—a square piece of material a metre in size, folded into a triangle, and covering most of the head, then tied under the chin. Our bangs could still show if we wanted them to. It was to respect the mullahs, and to avoid aggravating the extremists. If we were in the extremists' neighbourhood, we pulled the *rosaris* tight around our faces.

We were officially "encouraged" to wear head coverings. This "encouragement" was not yet fully enforced but highly "recommended." I pleaded with Mamán, "Why do we have to wear a *hijab*? We are Jewish; it is not part of our religion." Mamán had no answer for me. She was devastated, too. "I wish I could answer your question. Remember, you participated in the demonstration." Mamán made sure to rub this in my face. "You heard the names of the people they execute every day; soon they will kill those who do not wear the *hijab*. Just follow the rules before they kill you. This is what you and everyone else who participated in the demonstration deserve. You were used like puppets."

I chose to be optimistic, although my inner voice shouted loudly, "You are a fool! This is only the beginning."

Many newspapers popped into existence, like yellow dandelions in the late spring: newspapers of every imaginable political persuasion, from *Farda* (Tomorrow) to *Caricature* (mocking political leaders), to the new Hezbollah daily newspaper, the *Islamic Republic*. We were happy about the freedom of expression. We had never had such freedom.

The *Islamic Republic* published a new list of traitors. Before, under the Shah, the enemy had one face: anyone who did not obey the rule of the monarch. Now people were being killed for a "Conspiracy against God." It was a sticky label. If you were stuck with this label it could cost you your life. Who defined what the "Conspiracy against God" meant? They did. The newcomers. The Hezbollah.

Prisoners had no defence lawyers. Some of the prisoners were accused of working for the Shah. They were simply picked up on the street by the Hezbollah and charged. Most of those caught were wealthy. These prisoners could not defend themselves. They were guilty because Hezbollah said so. Sentences were usually carried out without delay. The prisons were so full that they could not kill people fast enough; new prisoners replaced the ones who had been executed; prisoners with the same fate awaiting them.

Executions were announced daily on the radio at 6:00 a.m. The reporter went through so many names at top speed it was as though the executed were a swarm of flies. But in many cases, this announcement was the first notification of death. It usually was a shock to the victim's family, who had been unaware of the reason their loved ones had disappeared until the morning announcements. Imagine how family members felt to hear of the death of a beloved husband, son, brother, sister, or wife through the emotionless voice of the broadcaster. This list of the executed was confirmed in the *Islamic Republic* daily.

People were rounded up. The new government did not care about keeping face in the world. They hated everyone: they had the key to heaven and they were right. "If you are not one of us, then you are against us," was their watchword. The Islamic government believed the entire world inside and outside Iran was corrupt.

I was outraged by all the brutality that I was witnessing. My only outlet was the hiking trips the three musketeers went on every Friday after the Revolution.

Ever since the incident with Mojgan, I had developed a reputation for being outspoken. Sheyla asked me if I would represent students at an open debate with the principal in establishing a student council.

The principal, Mr. Zamani, agreed to hold an assembly in the school auditorium one Monday morning in late February 1979. He and the teachers sat at a table at the front of the auditorium, and after his introduction, I came forward to give my presentation.

The fever of the Revolution and freedom coursed through my body. I already had a strike against me as an agitator, but I had faith that my friends would come forward if I faced any serious opposition. Our ideas were: The establishment of an exercise program before the start of school in the morning; the right to have a student council, with representatives from each class; and the right to express opinions freely.

Before this, we were not supposed to speak to the principal. No kid had ever talked to the principal openly. We had to stand up straight whenever the principal walked by. His name made us shiver in our seats. I stood face-to-face with him that day and discussed our issues. For the first time in my life, and representing five hundred students, I spoke directly and publicly to the principal. If he was outraged, he decided not to show us.

I trembled with fear that I might not be able to represent the students fairly. It became too hot, my palms were sweating, my heart raced a mile a minute, and my voice turned into a high-pitched squeak. In spite of my internal turmoil, I was ecstatic that of only five Jewish girls in the school, I was the one chosen for the open presentation to the principal.

Once I started to speak, my fear evaporated. The atmosphere was alive, pulsating with the vibrant energy of freedom. The students cheered. At that instant, I felt I represented the entire student body. I did not take this privilege lightly.

When I finished my speech, the students rose to their feet and applauded. Overwhelmed, the principal agreed on the spot to some of our demands. Our first and most cherished demand was granted. "The student council is approved." He called for an election to be held in each class for a representative to sit on the council. Then he asked for nominations from the students for student council president. My name was put forward immediately, along with Mojgan's. We voted by secret ballot the same morning, and Mojgan got one vote. Hers.

I became the president of the newly established student council. Mojgan lost the nomination. Her vinegar face looked pickled.

For a Jew to win an election in a Muslim private elementary school must have been a slap in the face to the fundamentalists. One may wonder what a thirteen-year-old knew about voicing her opinions on freedom. We were children of the Revolution.

Within a day after the debate, the other Jewish girls in school stopped talking to me. They had been advised by their parents to avoid me, as if by association with me they might catch the same disease. I tried to approach them.

"How are you, Mari?"

"I'm studying. Please don't talk to me."

"You're studying now, but why don't you want to talk to me anymore?"

"If I talk to you I'll get in trouble. My parents told me not to be friends with you after that incident with Mojgan."

I made new friends who accepted me for who I was and who also longed for a freer Iran and the right to speak the truth.

A bare few weeks after the Revolution, the school's fundamentalist parents and the religious "sisters" revealed that they were not prepared to accept democratic principles and the election of a Jewish girl in particular. The kind, moderate man who had agreed to our demands and had permitted me to even stand for election was forced to resign. I hoped that his kindness to me in limiting my suspension had not been a factor as well. He was replaced by the "Fatemeh Sister, the crow" in charge of religious studies. In her new role as school principal, she made sure my file, indicating that I was an outspoken freedom-seeker, would follow me everywhere.

A new school election was called, and this time, the fourteen-year-old Hezbollah supporter, Mojgan, won by acclamation, since I was not even allowed to be nominated.

In light of the new freedom, Farideh Khanoom had a brilliant idea. She assigned us a project to do on the life of an Iranian author or poet who had inspired us. I chose Forough Farrokhzad (1935–67). She was my heroine. Inspired by Western and European feminist movements, she became a leader for Iran's feminists. Sadly, she died in a car accident in her early thirties. Her poems about freedom were forthright and bold, and although her work was very popular with the people, neither the Shah nor the Islamic government approved of her. Many people were convinced her death was no accident.

After I completed my presentation, my teacher appeared shocked that I had selected Forough Farrokhzad as my subject. She stared at me in disbelief, wondering how I had mustered the courage to choose Forough Farrokhzad as my idol. Her name was taboo. Luckily for me, my teacher was on the same page as me. She gave me the highest mark, twenty out of twenty. I had done my research carefully and had shown in my presentation that I both understood and thoroughly admired what this audacious woman stood for. The Hezbollah student, Mojgan, took note. Would this achievement come to haunt me later?

⌒⌒⌒⌒⌒

Since February, my sisters and I had met regularly with Sheyla's sisters to discuss the books we read. We planned to go hiking the following Friday with them and their friends. In the secrecy of the mountains, we would have a chance to discuss these forbidden books in greater depth without fear of being overheard. If we wanted to join our friends, we needed permission from our parents. Mamán agreed. Baba was busy at the farm and was not around to be asked.

The three musketeers planned the trip with muted enthusiasm. We dressed in jeans and loose, long-sleeved shirts, running shoes, and the *rosari*, mandatory for all girls. We arrived at the main square in town, Shahrdari, early Friday morning, long before the sun came up. Buses were lined up one after another. Who knew there were so many buses out this early in the morning? Men in Hezbollah clothes climbed onto a bus on the corner. Before the Revolution, I did not like to be near these men. I still did not want to be near them. Since the Revolution, the bearded Hezbollah men had swaggered around arrogantly on the streets. They were the winners, and the rest of us the losers in this revolution.

Hiking had become popular, for many groups of both Hezbollah and young university students. We spotted Sheyla from far away and climbed onto the bus.

Sheyla whispered to me, "This group doesn't care about the religion or gender of its members." To be a woman and a Jew was a curse; the thought was that people who were not prejudiced against these two things must be righteous. The hikers on this bus believed everyone should be treated equally. For the first time since the beginning of the Revolution, I was associating with the right crowd. I could not wait to share with the dozens of young people how lucky I felt to be here in their company.

As we left the city, we saw field after field of red poppies, the symbol of bloodshed and freedom, growing wild in the countryside.

After a forty-five-minute drive, we arrived at the foot of the *Kuh-e Sorud* (Music Mountain). We hiked for three hours. We came across a stream on the mountain at about eleven o'clock and we stopped for lunch. We gathered dry branches for a fire to make tea.

Baha'i, Muslim, Jew . . . boys, girls: we expressed who we were as we sat and talked by the stream. A meadow filled with glorious yellow flowers caught my attention. Chinese daffodils. I was ecstatic. I did not realize these flowers grew wild, and the sight of their sunny faces made me very cheerful. The smell of the daffodils filled the air. I felt so free in that field.

The consensus was that the Islamic government would forbid, penalize, and punish the freedom fighters; but we couldn't let this happen without a fight. Whenever possible, we had to voice our opinions and remind everyone of the bloodshed of the past. It was wonderful to witness how a group of young boys and girls between thirteen and twenty-five years had so many opinions about how the country should be governed. I felt a heavy burden on my shoulders under the pressure of the oppression and deception that had become our reality. But a day of escape from all the real worries invigorated me.

"We must not give up now," Sheyla voiced.

"Many intellectuals also died for this freedom. Why should the Islamic ones be the only ones to have power?" Khatereh shouted.

"Why do I have to wear a *hijab*? I hate it."

"Remember, freedom was fought for throughout history!" Hoomayon exclaimed.

"Has anyone ever wondered who gave the guns to the Islamic militants to fight the Shah?" Mehran, an engineering student, asked. He had been quiet all day. His question intrigued us. Who was behind these mullahs?

At the end of the day, I had more questions than answers to my queries. Goodbyes were reluctantly said as we left our new friends, with plans to see them the following week.

Upon our return, we explained to Mamán that we had gone to stand up for freedom. Mamán was furious, screaming at us to never go hiking again. We had done nothing wrong, but in a society where everyone judges the actions of everyone else, what we had done was bad. It demonstrated disobedience. No parent would want that kind of girl for their son, and no son would want to marry a girl who went hiking with other women and men.

We were well on our way to earning a reputation as freethinkers. Though for some people this could be considered an insult, for us it was a compliment.

We loved the freedom we had felt that day, and fought for it with all our might. Freedom is never given. It is earned, and we would earn it first at home. Mamán was fuming and we were sorry about that, but only about that!

Mamán was torn between two worlds. Mamán and Baba wanted us to forget about politics and freedom. She claimed we were ruining the family's reputation. Baba was furious. Mamán was despondent. Baba threatened to disown us. Mamán at least understood our point of view. Like us, she leaned toward feminism and education, but she knew this new government did not favour an environment in which women could flourish.

We continued to go hiking despite our parents' pleas. The tension in the house escalated. Mamán did not talk to us. Baba did not talk to us. Mamán and Baba did not talk to each other. Baba blamed Mamán and mockingly quoted her: "Men and women are equal; you girls can do whatever a man can do."

Then, to Mamán, "You see what you have raised? They only care about freedom. Who cares about freedom? It is not enough that stronger people than you are killed. They will kill you, too. You are foolish."

A war with Hezbollah and the *hijab* was being fought outside; a war of words and ideas — with a side battle of Farah and Keyvan's love affair — was being fought inside. The highlight of the week was the Friday morning we went hiking despite Mamán and Baba's disapproval.

I pleaded with Mamán, "Why can't I express my opinion?"

"I love you. Your life is more important than your opinions that could get you killed. Keep your opinions to yourself and your head on your shoulders." It was good advice but too difficult for me to follow.

I *detested* the *hijab*. Why didn't men have to wear that meaningless piece of material? Why was I obliged to hide my hair and my face? But if my head had to be female, the rest of me didn't. I defiantly wore my Adidas, long pants, and a long-sleeved shirt. It became increasingly more difficult to find the Adidas because they were American. If you owned a pair of Adidas, it meant you were intellectual, unconventional, and part of the "in" crowd.

Mamán complained, "Look at you! You're never going to get married if you dress like that!"

"As if I wanted to, anyway. That's not feminism; men and women are equal. Why *should* I want to get married? Mamán, *please*." I could not believe how short-sighted she was! As if marriage mattered at a time like this.

Thank heaven I was not interested in wearing high heels. No one could walk in high heels *and* wear the *chador*. It was bad enough to manoeuvre holding the *chador* with one hand while carrying groceries. I could not imagine the agony of wearing the *chador* and high heels.

Students had set up tables and stands around the university to sell books right after the Revolution. The university students thought that with this "new freedom," people would be able to read any book without being suspected of harbouring anti-government sentiment. We took advantage of the opportunity and stocked up. Like a kid in a candy store, all the money I had saved from my allowance was spent to buy as many books as possible. My voice was telling me, *This opportunity will not last for long.* Time proved my voice to be right.

Mamán gave us a fifty-*tooman* weekly allowance (three dollars per week). That money was used for only the most important items, like books or shoes. I wanted to learn and bought ten to twelve books at a time: Freud, Jung, Romain Rolland, Darwin. I also read voraciously the works of Iranian authors: Samad Behrangi and Fourgh Farokhzad, who had both died during the Shah's reign. I woke up reading and went to sleep still reading.

We were conscious of the fact that there might be watchers. There were times when, on my way to university to buy books, I noticed a member of Hezbollah following me. One benefit of wearing the *chador* was that at times like this it served me well. Once in a crowd, I was unidentifiable because of my black *chador*. Those little alleys across from my house were my friends, and I knew them like the back of my hand. In my *chador*, I slipped from one to another, confusing my followers and escaping their surveillance whenever I was leaving or returning home.

We begged Mamán to come hiking with us, but she refused. She wanted to, but she was too torn between her true desires and worrying what other Jews would think and say about her. It must have been a difficult conflict for her.

She complained to us, "You are never home. No one helps me to prepare for Shabbat."

We did our Shabbat chores on Thursday to help her. Nothing could stop us from going on those hikes.

I was heartbroken over the tensions both inside and outside my house. There was no place to turn to vent my frustration at the lack of freedom, except for a few hours on Friday when we hiked. The constant bickering and yelling between Baba and Mamán was agonizing. The never-ending daily list of executions was unbearable. I felt terrible to have put Cyrus and Aria through all the turmoil at home. I was exploding with the tension inside my body. I wished I could run far away where none of these killings, this yelling, these *hijabs*, existed. But my voice reminded me, "You are stuck here. Make the best of it."

So, we three musketeers still managed to hike. The heavy-duty knapsacks were filled with food for all twenty of us. We drank water from the streams and made tea by gathering all kinds of branch bark to make a fire, to boil the water in the smoke-covered metal kettle. Lunch was light: feta cheese, bread, dates, halva or grapes. Keyvan's friend, a girl named Khatereh, and I discussed how the Ayatollah Khomeini had gotten into power. He had supporters, but where had they obtained their guns? And how had they overthrown the monarch? Why had the Shah run away so fast? Why did his international friends who had toasted him publicly not help him?

"Look around. Who do you think has all the money in the world?"

"But why would America help the Hezbollah if they keep on saying 'Death to America'?"

"Sima, don't you know? People pretend they're fighting but underneath it all, they're best buddies? That's all for show, that's for the public, that's for media!"

People who wanted to have control didn't want others to be free in their minds. They couldn't imagine that happiness could come from within, or from gazing at a field of daffodils and smelling the fresh, clean air.

We hiked many times with this group. One of my favourite surprises was when we were hiking down the mountain and came across a full-sized fig tree full of fruit, ripe and ready to harvest. The soft skin of the dark purple fig . . . the ripeness . . . its sweet taste, was a gift to cherish forever. This tree had likely been accidentally planted by a hiker who had dropped a fig here many years ago. A magnificent fig tree now stood at the edge of the mountain, heavy with ripe figs hanging from its branches. It fed us graciously. We ripped figs from the tree and popped them into our mouths with great pleasure and delight.

We had lunch sheltered in the coolness of the caves in the mountains. Ancient lovers' hearts with tender messages carved into stones were proof that people had once lived and loved inside this historic cave. Date seeds scattered over the earthen floor were evidence that shepherds and their flocks had sought shelter in its shade. Who knows how many thousands of years this cave had existed in its remote splendour?

I felt one with nature, blessed to be able to breathe in the fresh air and experience the glorious outdoors.

The beauty of the day permeated our mood. No fights, no arguments, no blame, and no crying. I should have been so lucky to have that kind of atmosphere all the time. But the escape was just for a few hours and only once a week. The other world I lived in was chaotic and run by bullies who believed they were the masters of everyone's life.

Soraya, Farah, and I decided that this was worth the fight we were going to face when we returned home. Neither Mamán nor Baba hiked with us, and we couldn't go on our own; it wasn't fun or safe. Otherwise, we would never have had such experiences. We needed to be part of these groups to stimulate our minds, to plant the seeds of new ideas, to give voice to our frustration.

As young revolutionaries, we talked about feminism. Putting on a *hijab* was a slap in the face of feminism and the equality of men and women; why didn't men have to wear a *hijab*? It was a man's world and a man's word. We were supposed to be their toys. No choice was available to us other than wearing the *hijab*. But I vowed to myself: they can force me to cover my hair, but no one can cover my soul or my spirit. That was my free world. *Hijab* to me was a symbol of oppression that I was forced to wear. But I swore they would never own my mind.

We knew that a law would soon be passed by the Islamic government that women would have to wear head-coverings that covered both their hair and most of their face. The preferred choice of clothing by the government was the *chador*. It is a large semicircle of thick, cotton sheeting, the size of which must be tailored so that the radius of the semicircle is approximately the height of the wearer. The middle of the flat edge is brought from the back over the head to eye level, and the rest of the *chador* is wrapped around the body and held in place by one or both hands, or tucked under one arm held against the body while the other hand holds the material under the chin. The result is that a woman had only one hand to work with or carry things or hold onto a child. Underneath the *chador* I had to wear a head-covering, a long-sleeved dress down to my knees, and long pants.

Why did I have to wear this *chador* (head and body covering) when I didn't even believe in it? Girls had to wear it after puberty because apparently men are very weak, and women's hair and skin aroused them. So because they were weak, we had to be punished by hiding ourselves and protecting them from temptation. No one ever suggested that a little male self-control might be in order.

I wondered: If the scenario were different, how would Muslims feel if a Jewish dress code were forced on them? I did not dare speak out my thoughts. I was already in a lot of trouble.

I wanted them to respect me enough to know that I could choose for myself how to dress. Teach me, if you think your way is better. Don't force your views on me or threaten me if I choose not to go your way.

We talked about *hijabs*, about the daily executions, the crumbling economy, about how only the Islamic fanatics were in power and not the freedom fighters. It was a relief to know that not everybody was under full-on Hezbollah thought control.

~~~~~

Less than two months after the Revolution, on April 1, a national referendum was held. The ballot question was simple: Islamic Republic: yes or no? Unfortunately for us, the Islamic fanatics won by a landslide. Or so they declared. No one other than the Hezbollah counted the ballots. This victory was the beginning of the end of the little freedom we had. Ayatollah Khomeini declared an Islamic republic with a new constitution reflecting his ideals of Islamic government.

The new government needed employees, but they hired only those who had shown repetitive acts of loyalty. People were in heavy competition. They needed new teachers, new principals, new administrators in hospitals; and government workers received many extra benefits. Before this, we were a very close-knit society that looked out for our neighbours. But when someone decided they wanted a job in government, neighbours began watching each other more closely for anything that could be considered *taghou-ti*—pro-Shah, pro-monarchy. Naneh Jaan-Jaan's Hezbollah neighbours produced enormous banners, spray-painted on material saying, "Death to Israel" and "Long Live Khomeini." The three brothers who owned the shop had made the banners for the Shah before the Revolution. After the Revolution, they made sure to be on the side of the Islamic government. They were the spies in our neighbourhood.

The street continually stank of paint. The three brothers were constantly outside, where they worked and spied on us simultaneously, killing two birds with one stone. They became rich overnight off those signs. Their eyes were everywhere and we could not trust them.

Hezbollah kept track of people who participated in the massive demonstrations in support of the government. They kept track of people who attended Friday lunch prayers, where the Ayatollah addressed Muslim citizens who desecrated the American and Israeli flags at the end of the service. How could they keep track of these thousands and thousands? I could not understand it, but they did. They kept a big-brother watch over everyone, and self-righteously killed anyone who disobeyed.

Members of minority religions had no chance to be hired in the new government. We were considered second-class citizens. Under the new Islamic law, if there was a crime and a non-Muslim witnessed the crime, his testimony at court would count as only half the value of a Muslim's. Maybe because they did not consider us as equal humans? Awful.

A week after Hezbollah's victory, it was finally made official. We heard on radio and television and read in the daily newspapers that all women had to wear the black *chador*. Whereas before it had been optional, it was now compulsory. Rumours circulated that acid would be thrown into the faces of disobedient women. The government terrorized the populace to generate obedience. We had no choice but to accept the *chador*, since wearing one was better than being scarred—or even blinded—for life.

I asked Mojgan, "How am I supposed to wear my *chador*?"

"You are joking." She said this with surprise, implying that I was mocking her.

"No, I mean it; I have no idea how to do this, and nobody's around to show me. If I put it on one side, the hair shows, if I put it on the other side, the leg shows, and I don't want any part to show. I don't want acid thrown in my face; how am I supposed to do this?"

Mojgan's eyes shone with happiness that perhaps I had changed my mind and joined her Islamic group. She practised with me, letting me use her *chador* until I could handle it as well as she did.

"First, you fold it in half. Put the middle part on top of your nose, then bring it down, fold a little hem for yourself and draw it across your nose with your left hand. Then the right hand is free to carry parcels and your schoolbag."

I held the *chador* with my left hand. I had to have the *rosari* underneath it because if it was windy or it rained the whole thing fell off of me, and my head would have been naked.

The heat of the *rosari* and the *chador*, the long *manteau* that went all the way to my knees, and the long pants and long-sleeved shirt underneath: every time I left the house it was as though I were preparing for a trip to the moon. It took forever to dress up in these layers upon layers. This was part of the scheme. The Hezbollah militants wanted us to be so consumed by dressing up that we had no time to think about what was going on around us.

They figured anyone who was dressed like a crow would soon think like a crow.

Mamán normally put on lipstick before she went to work, but that changed once the Islamic government came in. She was told at work: no more lipstick. Her dress code changed from a brown knee-length skirt and a short-sleeved, collared beige top with buttons in front to a long-sleeved, loose brown dress to the knee, with long, brown pants.

The dress code changed at school. The colours of choice were black, dark brown, or navy blue—in both winter and summer. Under my *chador* was a steam room dripping with sweat. The worst part was that when it was that hot and sticky, I had additional stress that made me sweat even more. I had to be concerned about my silhouette, too. If the *chador* stuck to me because of the sweat and heat, that was my fault, and acid could be thrown in my face. It was a living hell. What hurt the most was that we had no choice. This was forced down my throat. I was choking.

~~~~~~

Hoveida, the former prime minister under the Shah, resigned from his post in September 1978. He had a chance then to leave Iran but he said he would not leave like a coward. He was convinced, and rightly so, that he had been the best prime minster in Iran's history and he would be granted a fair trial if a new government came to power.

However, he was arrested by the Shah in November 1978. After the Revolution, he remained in prison; he was considered the most important symbolic figure of the Shah's reign. The fair trial that he had believed in did not materialize.

His verdict was decided before his trial ever commenced.

Communication was cut between Qasr, the palace prison, and the rest of the world. Khalkhali did not want to talk to anyone who might want to bargain for Hoveida's life and prevent his death.

Pleas poured in from around the world to free him, to give him a fair trial. Hoveida was shot before he even had a chance to line up for execution. The Islamic government categorized the crime of the victims as "friendship with the enemies of God." Hoveida, our well-loved prime minister, who also had been in trouble with the Shah, was executed on April 7, 1979.

Since when were they the only ones with the key to paradise? How did they know they were the chosen ones and the owners of that key?

The consensus was that Jews never involved themselves in politics and were always supportive of the ruling government. This was the policy that we had practised during the Shah's rule and this was the policy we planned to continue. At its height, Iran had over eighty thousand Jews. Although many wealthy Jews had already left, thousands of Jews continued to live in Iran, mostly in Tehran, Shiraz, Hamadan, and Isfahan. We believed that no one would bother us, because we did not bother anyone.

But that changed. Habib Elghanian was a well-known and respected Tehrani Jewish businessman and philanthropist. His donations to many Jewish charities made him legendary even in cities far from Tehran. The mention of his name was filled with respect. He was known as Mr. Plastic because he manufactured plastic items; he contributed to the economy, employed thousands of people, and was avant-garde in his approach to advanced technological manufacturing in Iran. He had been the elected head of the Tehran Jewish Society since early 1970.

Shortly after the Revolution, he was arrested and charged with spying for Israel. Elghanian was accused of many other crimes, including "friendship with the enemies of God, corruption, contacts with Israel and Zionism, warring with God and his emissaries, and economic imperialism." How could anyone defend himself against these crimes? How could anyone prove his innocence? He was executed on May 9, 1979.

In the eyes of the people who delivered the judgment, his punishment was not severe enough for all his "crimes."

No hearing, no court, no juries. He was convicted. This was the Hezbollah's definition of "justice." The news spread like wildfire. The whole Jewish community trembled with fear. Was history repeating itself?

This was worse than a nuclear bomb. This had fallen on us, we

Jews who had made Iran our home for the past 2,500 years, who had been here longer than Islam. There was no end in sight. It was madness. Anyone could be accused of these crimes. We were labelled as "friends with the enemies of God." The label stuck and cost lives.

How could one defend oneself against these crimes?

Where could one turn for justice? the entire community whispered among themselves in the safety of their homes.

It was a terrifying time. The country was ruled by fanatics, out-of-control maniacs who believed they were the only group in the world who were right.

The execution was a strong incentive for many more Tehrani Jews to leave.

The Jewish community was also angry about the compulsory head coverings. We were fearful of the consequences of disobedience. We were outraged over the execution of Mr. Elghanian and could not express it. We were used to wearing jeans and T-shirts; never anything short or risqué since the beginning of the upheaval. Elderly Jews had always worn some kind of *chador*, but it had always been colourful. The new rules dictated the colour: black. This was not open for discussion. This was it, take it or suffer the dire consequences.

Whether Muslim or not, no woman dared to appear in public without adhering rigidly to the Islamic dress code.

We had to worry about any wind that might be blowing our hair out from under the *hijab*. Forget about makeup; that was ultimate disobedience to the New Rulers. Any little thing set them off. They were insane.

We became paranoid, constantly asking each other, "Do you see any motorcycles? Let's run away to the alleys so they can't follow us."

Questions ran randomly in my mind. If there was a God, why were we being treated this way? Why did God allow these crazy people to rise to power?

Men no longer wore suits. Wearing suits with ties was capitalist, or *taghou-ti*, pro-Shah, which was a crime. Shaved faces were also considered capitalist.

Listening to music was *taghou-ti*, perfume was *taghou-ti*.

Our primary rights as human beings — to eat, to socialize, to think freely — were under *their* complete control and constant scrutiny. *Their* way or no way was the definition of "Islamic freedom," "Islamic tolerance," and "Islamic peace." I guess it was the freedom of the Hezbollah to force the citizens to obey the law! To do what they wanted us to do. To follow their rules.

I felt like a caged eagle with my wings clipped.

~~~~~~

Since we had won the right at Student Council to exercise daily, we habitually gathered in the schoolyard to do morning stretches before the bell rang. We formed small groups based on friendship, but mostly based on political positions on freedom. One group consisted of the children of Hezbollah party members, but there were as many as five other groups, each associated with a political party. I joined different groups each day to do my morning stretches, with the exception of the Hezbollah, just to show my discontent with the new government. I was livid over the killings, arrests, and unnecessary bloodshed. The promise of freedom was buried long before it saw the light of day. I hated being forced to wear the *hijab*. Inside I was churning with an outrage that had no outlet.

The Hezbollah "sisters," with Mojgan as leader, secretly documented who exercised in which group. They followed me everywhere, as if I were some kind of terrorist. For those who sponsored and participated in terrorist activities around the world, having an open mind was considered an act of terrorism. In their eyes, all nonconformists were a threat. Our voices had to be muffled, using every possible tool: verbal attack, suspension, imprisonment, death.

The political atmosphere deteriorated. Living daily with the *hijab* was suffocating me, the lack of freedom was unbearable, the food shortages, the power outages . . . Life was miserable; and just when I thought it couldn't get any worse, it did.

Fifty-three Americans were taken hostage on November 4, 1979, after Hezbollah students led by Ahmadinejad took over the American embassy in Tehran.

"We have conquered the cage of spies. The filthy American spies are being held hostage, now!"

The Hezbollah throughout the entire country were out on the streets, honking their horns, singing and screaming "kilililili!"—a sound that was uttered on the happiest occasions. "It's the little dirty spy house! We've captured them!"

Non-Hezbollah citizens were scared stiff because this couldn't possibly bring any good to anyone. Mamán and Baba whispered to each other, terrified of the consequences for the hostages. Even before the Revolution, we had shortages of gas and food and daily power outages, but this hostage crisis gave reason to expect the worst. The government was provoking a fight with the superpower—the United States—whether we wanted it or not.

This was not promising news to the Jews. We were shaking with fear. Ahmadinejad's face was splashed all over TV and on the front of every newspaper. He became a new face on the Hezbollah scene. Was he the harbinger of doom?

The hostage crisis was the heated discussion of our hiking trip.

"Are they going to be killed?"

"There will be no trial, either."

"Why haven't they hurt them already?"

"Well, what was the reason they took hostages in the first place?"

"They are making all of us look like savages."

"We are not like the Islamic government. We do not like them. Persia was an empire on its own long before the advent of Islam. We are proud, good people, but in the eyes of the world we are Iranian and we will be painted the same ugly colour that should only be used for these fanatics."

I despised fanatics in any shape or form. I detest anyone who forces me to do as he does just because he can. Fanaticism spreads hatred and is ugly. History has proven this time and time again. Why don't we learn the lesson? Fanatics see the world through coloured eyeglasses. There is no room for rainbows in their world. If they could, they would even change the colours of the rainbow.

~~~~~

Most people kept their heads bowed and followed meekly like sheep, without questioning what was shoved down their throat. *They* were going to command us where to go, and we obeyed because this was the easiest way.

But I could not do it. I was bursting out of my skin. The street corners were still wet from the blood of too many people who had died for freedom. The Hezbollah had betrayed those who had died for the ideal of freedom.

The three musketeers hiked every Friday despite Mamán and Baba's condemnation. I fantasized naively that our passionate group discussions could change the world, even though the ones in power were unaware of our disapproval.

Baba arrived home fifteen minutes before us. Mamán and Baba were arguing again—about us, as usual, about why we were not at home.

"I can't control them! They do not listen!"

"It is your fault! You raised them!"

"It is not my fault! I begged you to stop bringing boarders into the house. You think you know how to raise them better? That's it! I'm leaving! *You* take care of them! Take your angels! Let's see how good of a job you'll do!"

Baba yelled back at her, "Good riddance!"

All five of us pleaded with her, "Mamán no, please don't go!"

But it was no use. "Don't you talk to me! You caused all this trouble!"

Mamán packed a small bag and left the house for her parents' place before Shabbat started. She stayed away for an entire month. She did not return our calls and she refused to see us when we went to Naneh Zivar's house to visit her.

Farah, Soraya, and I took over the household responsibilities. We took turns shopping, cooking, and cleaning the house the way Baba liked it. He was happy with the way we did our chores. Soraya asked me one night, "Do you think Mamán loves us? Why did she leave us if she loves us?" Soraya was tormented that Mamán's words were in sharp contrast to her actions. I fully understood Mamán's predicament. She was living in hell, conflicted by her limitations and her ideals, a nightmare with no escape in sight. Naneh Zivar's house was her temporary refuge.

The morning radio news always began with a list of those who had been executed on charges of treason.

I felt helpless listening to the radio announcements. It could be my name announced one day. It could be my parents summoned to pick up my body. Iran's brightest youngsters were among those innocents.

This was one instance where men and women were equal. Though I was disturbed to hear the names on the radio I personally never knew any of these people. I had no close ties with any of the victims. Or so I thought.

Since we did well in our household duties, Baba allowed us to continue our hiking.

Hiking was the only good thing we had going for us. The three musketeers went hiking very early one morning in mid-July 1980. With this group, I was free to express myself. But I had a gut feeling that these hikes would not continue for much longer. The discussions around lunchtime were the proof. Many hikers in Tehran were targeted and arrested, and the consensus was to stop the hiking . . . terrible news, but it was inevitable. I had sensed it coming; I wished I could share that with Mamán. I longed to see her. But she adamantly refused to see us.

The three musketeers were deep in thought after our mountain outing. We silently ran as fast as we could, as if we were being chased by a lion, to arrive home on time before Shabbat to warm up the food we had prepared on Thursday.

But our silence was abruptly interrupted a few hundred metres from our home. Hossein, a young Muslim man, an acquaintance, dropped a bombshell when he solemnly announced: "Your Aunt Ashraf was executed."

We stopped dead in our tracks. For a moment we hoped it was a bad joke.

"Impossible! She didn't do anything wrong!"

The sorrow in his voice confirmed he was telling the truth.

We were paralyzed with shock.

"MURDERER!" we screamed. "MURDERER! MURDERER!"

The night before, Ammeh Ashraf had not come home. She lived in the alley within five minutes of our house. Naneh Jaan-Jaan was worried for her and sat in front of her own house watching the entrance to the alley all night. She knocked on our door a few times to ask if Ammeh had called us. But she had still not come back by eleven o'clock that night.

I had assumed she eventually got home safely. No reason to worry.

Not the case. Our worst nightmare had become a reality.

It was hard to fathom such insanities hitting our family.

Ammeh Ashraf's mission was to make the ladies that came to her salon as beautiful and magnificent as possible. As customers left the salon, they did not wear their *hijabs* tightly. It was not her duty to enforce the *hijab*; the Islamic government had many police designated to enforce this law. But it was reason enough for her to be arrested.

The Brothers of Doom came in early one afternoon and ordered her,

"Close your shop. Give us the key. You're coming for questioning." That was it.

Naneh Jaan-Jaan, Baba Esghel, and her husband searched all over the city to find her. But no one knew where she was. That morning on the radio, at 6:00 a.m., as usual, the list of twelve people executed the previous evening was announced with the arrival of Khalkhali to Shiraz. In honour of his arrival in any city, the number of executions escalated; as if he had a never-ending hunger to see fresh human blood flowing. No wonder he had earned himself the titles of "Bloody Judge" and "Hangman."

To my family's horror, my aunt's name, Ashraf, was listed among the dead.

I loathed hearing that announcement. My poor Ammeh Ashraf, who loved to dance, who could blow bubbles without bubblegum!

My family was grief-stricken. The injustice, the cruelty, and the cold-blooded murder were incomprehensible to us. Why? Why? Why?

That few minutes' walk from the bus stop to Ammeh Ashraf's house felt like a death march. When we opened the door to her house, Mamán, who had been away for several weeks, greeted us at the door. The entire family was on their knees sobbing, tearing at their clothes, screeching, and hitting themselves in disbelief over the senseless killing.

Tears and profanity flowed. Naneh Jaan-Jaan was sprawled on the blood-red Tabriz carpet screaming up at God in protest. Baba Esghel, cross-legged, sat silently reading the psalms, his face devoid of life.

The funeral had already taken place. Baba and Baba Esghel had retrieved Ammeh Ashraf's tortured, black and blue, bullet-riddled body from the city morgue. They washed her body; it was bloody from the bullet wounds. Ammeh Ashraf was wrapped in a white cotton shroud and buried the same Friday before we returned home, before Shabbat.

Baba was devastated; he had looked up to his older sister. He refused to discuss her death and was never the same afterwards. Welcome, Bloody Judge. Islamic or not, this kind of behaviour was more savage and disgusting than that of any of the pagan gods who were worshipped over two thousand years ago.

Ammeh Ashraf had had no idea that she would be one of the sacrificial lambs on Khalkhali's altar.

Ammo David was on vacation in northern Iran, in the Caspian Sea, with his family and Ferideh, my cousin. Ferideh was Ammeh Ashraf's daughter. As they drove back to Shiraz, Ammo David turned on the radio. The names of the people who had been executed that day were announced, one by one, on the radio. Ashraf Goel's name was on that list. Ammo David could not believe his ears. "Did I hear right?" he asked his wife.

He raced all the way from the Caspian Sea to Shiraz, a twenty-hour drive that took him eighteen.

I could just imagine the agony and the shock of my poor cousin in the car to come back to a home from which her mother would be forever absent.

I looked at my other three cousins, who were close in age to us. They were now all orphans — *yatim*. It meant their family was shattered. They had to live with that for the rest of their lives. Whom could they turn to for justice?

Ammeh Ashraf's husband was so traumatized by the news that he refused to talk to anyone, lost in his own world of grief.

My whole family sat shiva at Ammeh Ashraf's house for the week. Christian, Muslim, and Jewish friends visited. Members of the Jewish community gathered in Ammeh Ashraf's house twice a day for prayers. The rooms were so full during prayers that people had to stand outside in the garden.

There had been no trial, no hearing, no jury. She was convicted and the sentence was decided before she was arrested. There was no sense of justice with this Islamic government.

The murderers needed no justification for such deeds.

I have many fond memories of my forty-two-year-old Ammeh Ashraf: her fabulous skill as a hairdresser, her gourmet cooking, and her wit. She knew how to buy the best fruits and the best nuts in the city. No matter what time of year I visited her house, she always had the best, the biggest, the most delicious fruits. She was an excellent homemaker, clean and quick with any task she undertook. She was always there for the whole family. Ammeh Ashraf was a beautiful woman with dimples on either side of her face. She talked frankly about how she felt about ideas, without exaggeration or hyperbole.

The execution heralded the arrival of Ayatollah Khalkhali. It was *normal* for blood to be shed in his honour anytime he visited a city in Iran. That day, my Ammeh Ashraf was one of many victims. She was chosen. Where they usually sacrificed an animal, they sacrificed a dozen innocent men and women.

News of the Shah's cancer, his airplane circling in the sky because no country would allow him to land, and, finally, his death, was plastered all over the newspapers and television.

Iranians didn't believe that he died. We thought this was his latest plot to circumvent justice: to pretend he was dead and be left alone.

But in our home, we had a bigger loss to deal with—Ammeh Ashraf's murder. When I saw what a dreadful place my country had become, I became very angry with the Shah. Had he been a bit more reasonable, a bit more flexible, he would have remained in Iran, alive and safe. He would still be ruling this country, and the mullahs would not be in power. We'd climbed out of a pothole only to fall into a gigantic well.

〜〜〜〜〜

It gradually became apparent that anyone who bought or possessed any Western literature or scientific textbooks had better hide them in a safe place. Because just as the Shah had proscribed books he thought dangerous to his regime, the ayatollahs did not want their citizens influenced by anything other than their own teachings. Although our house wasn't raided, I continued to have nightmares about fleeing down dark alleys and about police breaking into our home and throwing things around, searching in every nook and cranny where we might have hidden books. Good thing they didn't. I had dozens.

The dangers of reading these books were evident, but we could not resist.

Maybe it was as much a form of civil disobedience as it was curiosity. We wanted to know who the best minds were in the outside world and what they were talking about. Among the most coveted authors were Eric Fromm, Sigmund Freud, Carl Jung, and Roman Rolland, translated into Persian. How horribly depressing to be forbidden to read these books that did not in any way incite one to do harm or to think evil thoughts but simply helped one to know more about oneself, one's society, and the world!

The hiking that I loved became increasingly dangerous. The Hezbollah kept track of people leaving their houses early in the morning. They hung around the bus station dressed as civilians as well as in blatant Hezbollah uniform. They interrogated people's destinations as well as with whom they were travelling.

More people in Tehran were arrested. We were not allowed to go hiking with the men, and girls should never hike alone. It was foolish to continue hiking, since the secret service progressively increased their interrogation. I didn't want to get arrested. Against my will, I stopped going to the mountains in mid-1980.

Iran was struck by waves of air strikes. One more worry added to an already heaping plate of troubles.

"Iraq has invaded Iran!" the angry voice announced on the radio on September 22, 1980. "Stay calm. When the siren goes off, run to your shelters. A Muslim mother's duty and obligation is to send her teenage son to walk in the minefields to open the land to the warriors. Anyone who dies at war will go to Heaven."

Shiraz burst at the seams from the human congestion. Afghanis lived on every street corner. Thousands and thousands of families from the southern cities of Abadan and Ahvaz had also fled here since the war began. Countless families were sleeping in the mosques; it was depressing and painful to witness. Affluent people lost all their belongings overnight. Shiraz embraced these homeless people like a loving mother.

Shaheh Cheragh was the main mosque in Shiraz, its dome made of eighteen-karat gold. Many war victims congregated in the mosque and used it for shelter as well as worship. Since the war began, the mosque had been a home to refugees begging for food and water. Families were packed together like sardines. The mosque was so overstuffed that people were sleeping on newspapers under the awning outside. What was once a place of worship had now been reduced to nothing more than a shelter for the hungry and the homeless.

The refugees from Abadan, dark-skinned, shorter, and heavier than Shirazis, were destitute. They were known among Iranians to be entertaining and could use anything as a percussion instrument, but now were too demoralized to sing and cheer themselves up during this grief-stricken time.

There was a further shortage of staples. Coupons for food were issued, and everyone who had a coupon could get a limited number of essentials. Even with these coupons, the lineups were endless. Many times I had to go home empty-handed, because by the time my turn arrived, nothing was left.

The three musketeers were distressed by the suffering of innocent people who had done nothing to deserve this fate. We packed blankets, pants, shirts, sweaters, canned goods, and much more in bags. I swayed like a pendulum balancing the heavy bags on each side. Once I reached the Shaheh Cheragh I distributed the goods among the homeless. But the need was tremendous and it could not be filled; it was a drop in an endless ocean. The face of the city I loved and called home had changed drastically from a famous poet's city of romance to a city of refugees filled with Afghani and Abadani immigrants. The fragrance of the city had changed from orange and rose blossom to the smelly sweat of their dirty bodies. The refugees had no place to clean their clothes, to comb or wash their hair. On rainy days, they were like wet ducks dragged out of a lake, since there was no shelter to protect them from the rain. There was no place for all these people to be.

Afghani men migrated to Iran because they liked the insane new Iranian government. They were devout Shiites running away from communist Afghanistan. The Afghanis stuck together in groups of ten or twelve. Their eyes were tighter, more oriental. Their noses were flatter and their lips were thicker. They spoke some form of Persian but it wasn't clear like ours.

They put down their *sofreh*, a plastic tablecloth on which they ate their bread and cheese, and they slept on the corner of the street; and that was *their* corner. Many times, fights broke out if somebody took their corner. In rainy, cold weather in winter, they took over the houses that were under renovation and became squatters.

I encountered the Afghanis as I walked back and forth to school. When one group of Afghani men stepped away from their corner, another group of Afghanis scuttled onto it, and a raucous fistfight erupted. The government did not intervene; they let the Afghanis practise justice among themselves. The government had other fish to fry. The Afghanis were screaming in an unintelligible version of Persian, their veins popping out of their faces. They looked like wild animals roaring at each other. I didn't stick around to see the end of the fight, but from that day on, whenever I passed that spot at least one of them was sitting glued onto the corner, guarding the spot.

Despite my initial distaste, I felt very bad for them. They ended up doing the jobs that were taboo, such as emptying septic tanks and building houses for small wages. They were far from their families, trying to survive. I could only imagine how terrible their lives had been in Afghanistan if they preferred living here on street corners as despised immigrants to living in their own country.

~~~~~~

Baba Bozourg had not been the same since Ammeh Ashraf's death. He had always been a man of few words, but something had changed deep in his core. He prayed non-stop, day and night. He cried a lot, sat in a corner of the room, and did not move. I wished I could do something to lighten his heavy burden, but it was impossible. No one could. He was heartbroken since Ammeh Ashraf's death.

Naneh Jaan-Jaan was also broken-spirited. She did not visit us as often. She lost weight and had no interest in eating. The entire family dynamic had changed since Ammeh Ashraf's death. She had been the power of our family, a true matriarch. Since her death, we were all grieving silently, each one alone, as if by willing the silence we could lighten the burden that we were under.

Baba Bozourg took ill with a twisted intestine. Despite the attention of his beloved son, Ammo David, his condition worsened. He passed away, grief-stricken, only four months after my Ammeh Ashraf. Baba Bozourg died during Sukkot. Because Baba had been so preoccupied with his land, it had been years since he had built a *sukkah* with Baba Bozourg in our garden.

We held the shiva for Baba Esghel at our house immediately after Sukkot, his favourite time of the year.

~~~~~~

The Iran-Iraq War was in progress, but the schools operated as usual.

Baghdad was a ten-hour drive from Shiraz. Baghdad shot rockets at Shiraz. Most of them missed because we were surrounded by mountains. One day, at the end of November, around noon, I was returning home from school. I heard a loud buzzing, hissing sound. The sound bored straight into my bones and shook me to the core. Within seconds, the siren announced everyone had to run to a safe place. Since Shiraz was warm most of the year, most houses had a cellar that was used in hot weather. This was the only safe place to hide. Not a soul was on the street except for me. I ran home faster than I knew was possible. I had to get home to the cellar, where my aunts and uncles were waiting for the all-clear, wondering what had happened to me.

Despite the government offices located in our neighbourhood, the rockets didn't reach our house.

Poor Naneh Jaan-Jaan had suffered two major losses in four months. Ammo David thought the best idea for Naneh Jaan-Jaan to cope with her grief and her losses was for him to buy her a little dog. Naneh Jaan-Jaan named him Jackson. My old traditional grandmother in her *rosari* walked around outdoors calling, "Jackson! Jackson! Come here!" Since we did not know who Jackson was, we stuck our heads outside to see the handsome, rare tourist we thought Jackson would be. But what we saw was a little white Bichon Frisé, the tiniest, fluffiest, whitest thing any of us had ever seen on four legs. Naneh Jaan-Jaan grew attached to Jackson, and she showered that little dog with as much loving patience as she did with us. How she came up with the name remained a mystery.

That dog was the best remedy for Naneh Jaan-Jaan's losses.

Keyvan's brother's name was announced on the radio among the list. Among the list of executed men, as one of the counter-revolutionaries in northwest Iran, in Tabriz; Hamid's name stood out in my memory. I tried to convince Farah, "Don't worry. Many people have the same name." But instinctively I was certain it was him. Farah tried desperately to reach Keyvan. But she was unsuccessful.

The phone rang. It was Keyvan.

"You won't believe what happened." Long pause. "Hamid was killed."

He cried on the phone.

"He was in a house when the Hezbollah raided the house and they shot him with a bullet to his head." Hamid, at eighteen, had won a math competition for all high school graduates in Iran, and was one of the most brilliant students in the country. Consequently, he was admitted to the university in Tabriz.

His poor parents! His poor mother! I felt terrible for Keyvan. It is normal for children to bury their parents, but for parents to bury their child was the worst curse imaginable. We were fraught with sympathy and grief. Nothing could brighten the gloom felt by Keyvan and his family.

Keyvan did not go to the funeral or visit his parents, because the Hezbollah were waiting to arrest him. The shadows of evil encompassing the entire country grew blacker with each passing day.

Poor Keyvan's father had to drive more than twenty hours to Tabriz to collect Hamid's bullet-ridden body. I cannot imagine the agony and horror he felt during that drive. How can one console a parent whose offspring's life has been destroyed so brutally?

I thought it couldn't get worse. But it did.

﹀﹀﹀﹀﹀

The second language taught in school changed from English to Arabic. Arabic class was mandatory for all students, even for those of minority religions. Arabic is a guttural language, where all nouns are either masculine or feminine. Even their language was sexist. It was a very hard language to learn, and the only use most Iranians had for it was to read the Koran, but for me, as a Jew, it was of no use.

"Excuse me, Zahrah Khanoom." I was not allowed to call her *Khakher* (sister) because I was Jewish. They were only *Khakher* to other Muslims. "Can I learn another language, not Arabic? I'm not planning to visit any of those countries."

This was taken as an insult, another strike against me that would cost me heavily in the future.

The whole class shut up instantly, putting their heads down, pretending they had not heard anything. They could not believe my lunacy. I spoke the words they thought but were too afraid to spit out. The Hezbollah rulers had abolished English as a second language. This kept the young population away from Western influences and information, and kept the citizens under government control.

Every aspect of my being was controlled. From what I wore, to what I ate, to who my friends were. *They* wanted complete thought control. *They* took away our freedom to learn English. *They* treated us like animals, like insects. I believe this was to take control over our minds. Dictators can control the citizens longer when they keep them ignorant.

The merit of a man was no longer measured by his actions, but by the size of the weapon he carried on his shoulder. Many people were arrested on a daily basis. The majority of prisoners were young people who demanded change. The government was not willing to listen.

The three musketeers revolted when Sheyla told us that young women were raped before they were executed. Girl prisoners were raped by prison guards to ensure they were no longer virgins, and therefore could not go to heaven. If the girl were truly guilty, she would go to hell anyway. If she were not guilty, she would still lose her automatic admission to heaven. The men involved, on the other hand, could simply say the prayer that allowed them to take advantage of any female and then be able to rape with impunity.

The government forced mothers to send their sons, even their fourteen-year-old boys, to war, to prove their commitment to the government and to God. It was mandatory for all eighteen-year-old boys to enter the army. I looked at Cyrus and Aria's innocent faces. They, too, would have to participate in the war soon, whether or not they liked it.

The streets were filled with amputees, blind, and disfigured boys who were wounded while they "did their duty to serve God." The images of the war would haunt them for the rest of their lives; they had permanent disabilities that scarred them for life. Hezbollah families were handsomely compensated if a son was injured during the war. Hezbollah mothers were so brainwashed that they forced their teenagers to go to war. They sent their sons to war, to walk on minefields and to get killed. This senseless act guaranteed both parents and their dead sons a spot in heaven. Unheard of! No animal sends her young to be killed. These people had less brains than a four-legged animal.

Otherwise, the families of those who were wounded or killed during combat just had to bear their losses without any government compensation. What if this happened to my family? What would I do and what would be my expectations of others? I would not be able to live with myself anymore. I wanted to run away from myself and all the stresses of everyday life, from the war, from the *hijab*, from the food shortages, from Mamán's and Baba's constant bickering.

We had been betrayed by the promise of freedom. There was no relationship between freedom and the wholesale murders we were hearing about and experiencing first-hand. The freedom we had all fought for was now only granted to the government to kill anyone who stood in their way. The government did not have a higher authority to respond to; they were self-justified in their barbaric way of treating their citizens.

The Iranian people had been lied to. My sisters and I were not obedient little lambs who were willing to accept their lies and remain silent. I began to voice my opinions rather angrily among my friends, and before I knew it, I earned a spot on the official blacklist again, and this time it came at a very high price. Nobody in Iran, especially not a

Jewish girl, should have behaved as I did. Jews kept quiet and tried not to attract any attention.

~~~~~

The universities reopened. The new standards for admission had many near-impossible requirements, such as a close-to-perfect GPA and perfect scores on the entrance exams. The most important prerequisite was to have a clean record. This meant 100 percent obedience and adherence to the Islamic government's rules since its inception. Rarely were applicants of minority religions accepted in university, let alone in medical school or engineering. Pahlavi University, where I had hung around with intellectuals and absorbed the atmosphere, where students had dressed in jeans, and where books had always been available, became unrecognizable. All the male students looked angry with their long, dark beards; female students looked like crows under the long, black sheets that concealed their bodies and made them look identical.

Every Friday at lunchtime, the entire city shut down. The ayatollahs gave speeches over the loudspeaker systems and led the daily prayers in the public square. Good Muslims (their followers) came to listen from all across the city. During the prayers, Hezbollah members, mingling among the worshippers, initiated and provoked the shouting of slogans.

"Death to America! Death to Israel! Long live the Ayatollah!" Their worshippers screamed. They burned the American and Israeli flags every Friday after prayers. I never went near those meetings. I couldn't stand the malicious speeches spouting from the mouths of the devout.

Mamán knew if she wanted to hear the real news, she had to listen to BBC (London) or Radio Israel on her shortwave radio. Owning a radio capable of receiving stations other than those permitted by the regime was also considered a crime.

~~~~~

My physical health began to decline. The Islamic government affected the entire population at a psychological level, but it also affected me personally at a physical level. I could no longer lift my left hand; the only way to lessen the numbing sensation was to hold my left arm close to my body with my right hand. Since I was left-handed, this meant that I was unable to write. This problem affected my performance at school. I was not able to cope with the tremendous stress that I was living under both at home and outside the home. Inevitably, my poor body was screaming at the unjust living conditions I had imposed on her. My left arm was less painful during quiet, peaceful periods, but as the situation around us became more volatile, so did the throbbing and tingling in my limb.

The injustices I witnessed made me indifferent toward school. I no longer had any incentive to try hard for the highest grades, as I had been doing since childhood. Top scores from high school did not guarantee entrance into university, which was now based on completely different parameters that I could never meet.

This meant complete adherence to the law, complete obedience to Hezbollah order, and never asking a question—something I was not good at. I could not be convinced to look at the colour black and swear it was red. I could not hide my head in the sand and pretend there was no sand around. I could not swallow this brutality and the dictatorship of the mullahs under the name of God and Islam. I was choking.

My new attitude was reflected in my report card. There were fewer twenties (equivalent to 100 percent). I was no longer a straight A-plus student.

Mamán was deeply irritated by my attitude and she made sure to let me know. All report cards were posted on classroom windows in the schoolyard. I didn't want her to come and see my marks, but she insisted.

When Mamán saw that I had gotten a "C" in mathematics, she drew back her hand and WHAM! she slapped me hard across the face, in front of all my friends and enemies, including Mojgan. I didn't see it coming, or else I would have run.

Sheyla was there, and Mamán scolded her, "It's your fault—you ruined my daughter! I hate you! Stay away from her! Leave Sima alone!"

At home, she lectured me at great length about the importance of doing my best. It didn't matter what kind of government was in power. She repeated that it was a question of personal growth, and I should always strive for the highest achievement regardless of what political turmoil was fomenting in my country.

By Hezbollah standards, I was far from innocent.

One day, Sheyla and I decided to write our opinion on the walls in the street. Even before the Revolution, graffiti covered almost every surface in the city, and we were ready to add our part to it.

We looked around and made sure we were alone on the street. In the heat of the afternoon, no one stayed outdoors.

As Sheyla kept watch, I furtively took out some chalk and started writing "LONG LIVE FREEDOM" in big Persian letters on the wall on the side of a building. There were many other graffiti on this wall, such as "Long live Khomeini" and "Death to America," but ours was the best one.

We didn't suspect anything. But a mother in a house across the street watched me through the blinds as I scribbled on the wall. She marched into the alley and screamed at us, "How dare you! Don't you know that's against the law? What do you mean, 'Long live freedom'? How can you deface somebody's property like this? Does your mother know where you are? Who taught you to act this way?"

She spotted the new Seiko watch on my wrist. A fourth-grade birthday gift from Mamán. With glittering eyes, she pointed at my watch. "May I see it?" She waited a couple of seconds, then, "Give me your watch this instant or I will call the Hezbollah!" she commanded. "Come back with your mother, and I will give it to her after I tell her what you did."

I never told Mamán how the birthday watch was lost.

I was livid about this government. Sheyla was also furious. Together, we naively thought we would be able to bring the Islamic militants to their knees. We planned another outing. All this behind Mamán's back, on my way from school.

Sheyla and I planned to distribute the pamphlets her sisters had written criticizing the suppression of human rights in Shiraz. Sheyla's sisters were vocal about the injustice. They wrote the pamphlet and made two hundred copies of it on green paper. Our job was to distribute it without being caught.

We snuck into a crowded intersection at rush hour wearing our black *chadors*, fully covered. Throngs of people wove in and around each other. We moved among them without being noticed. Both of us were carrying a hundred leaflets each hidden underneath our *chadors*.

The moment arrived. When I thought no one was looking. I lifted my left arm from beneath my *chador* and tossed the leaflets up in the air as my right hand held tightly to my *chador*.

A secret Hezbollah policeman saw me and came after me with a box cutter. I ran to the street and quickly hailed a cab. But as I entered the taxi, he sliced deeply into the fleshy part of my left hand. I was bleeding in the cab; bright red blood covered my pants under my *chador*. But since black was the darkest colour, it concealed my bloody hand. It did not show the red bloodstain. I wanted to cry. But I had to look composed and calm, because who knew whose side the taxi driver was on?

Invisible spies were everywhere, armed and ready to dispense instant justice. I felt shaky and frightened after this incident. But I stayed determined to follow the cause that had become my obsession.

Mojgan, Sheyla, and I had been going to the same middle school since the fall of 1979. Our friendship had taken a turn for the worse since the incident with Yasamin. Mojgan became the head of the Islamic Student Council. She was in charge of Islamizing the school. Because of our past history together, she had a vendetta against me of which she could not let go. She approached the principal and convinced her that Sheyla and I should transfer to a new school. We could no longer attend the school we had gone to for the past two years.

In the summer of 1981, Sheyla and I were only allowed to register at a school in the southern and poorest area of the city with tougher religious controls. Hezbollah families populated this school. Evidently "the sisters" in the new school expected us impatiently. Mojgan forwarded our files to the new school with a specific note: "Make sure they never make trouble in your school. Watch them like hawks. Assign somebody to follow them at all times."

This move was to punish me and knock some sense in my thick skull that the new government was here to stay. At least for now, I had better give up any ideas of freedom.

Prior to entering the new school, Sheyla and I had decided not to talk to each other while at school. We did not sit next to each other, did not speak to each other during recess, and did not work on any projects together.

Each morning as I entered school, I was thoroughly searched. I had to take my shoes off. The Hezbollah sister patted me down. She was rough with me, searched under my armpits, in the groin and felt me thoroughly. Three crows checked me every morning. They went through my bag, paper by paper. They weren't looking for guns. They were looking for real weapons—pamphlets, anti-revolutionary articles, any sign of freedom-fighting. Knowledge! I was not so stupid as to give them the pleasure of finding the items they were looking for. Each of them hoped the next one would be able to outsmart me and find the "forbidden leaflet." Nothing! Frustrated and angry, they went through the same motions the next day. Little did they know that the pamphlets were safe at home, buried in a jar underground.

The disappointment in their eyes as they searched me grew deeper and deeper as the weeks went by. I was ecstatic to see it.

Sheyla was the other victim in their hands.

In order to make it look normal, every student had the body search, but both Sheyla and I were given special treatment, with the three crows checking us.

This school was much smaller than our previous one, the classrooms rundown and in desperate need of painting. The schoolyard was too cramped. No volleyball court had been erected; in fact, no place existed for any physical activity.

Since Sheyla and I were not speaking, I wanted to make new friends. There was only one girl who piqued my curiosity. She looked particularly unhappy. Not just about the *hijab*, not just about the strict Hezbollah curriculum; she carried around some deep sorrow, visible when she walked. Her shoulders were stooped. She was too quiet, too skinny. Something was particularly wrong with this girl. I asked her, "Are you from Shiraz?"

The words spilled out of her. "I am from Abadan. My name is Marzieh. I migrated with my family because of the war. We lived a good life in Abadan. We had our own home; my father had his own business, a store selling clothing. Then the war started, and we had to pack and leave fast."

"What it was like when the war started?"

Tears welled up in her eyes. She hesitated for a minute, but I assured her that I was not a spy and told her about my Ammeh Ashraf's execution.

She confided in me that when the Iraqi army attacked Abadan, they had first cleared the men out of the area. They took the women hostage, raped them, and then killed them. But Marzieh and her family were lucky to have left before they were attacked.

"We had to run away in the middle of the night. All the shops were closed; we could not drink the water because it was contaminated. We had to crawl away in the middle of the night. We were happy to be alive. Some other people don't have the means to leave."

Marzieh was a constant reminder of the war. I asked her, "How can I help you?" She whispered so quietly I didn't hear her at first. "If you have some extra clothes please bring them for me, but you don't have to if you don't want to. Don't tell my parents I asked you that. They are too proud to ask for any help."

"Where do you live? I will drop them off at your home."

"I live with my parents and my younger sister near the bazaar. Here is the address."

I dropped off my extra clothes at her house on Friday morning. Mamán was too busy to notice the bag in my hand as I left the house. Marzieh waited for me in front of her house. I understood why I was not welcome in her house. The neighbourhood around the bazaar had deteriorated since the Revolution. The stink of urine in the alleys was very strong; garbage was strewn all over the alleys. We kept my parcel drop as our secret.

Much time was devoted to Islamic studies and Arabic. These two subjects were at the bottom of my interest list. I had to learn verses from the Koran, even though I was not Muslim. Fatemeh Khanoom indoctrinated us in the Muslim way of a woman's responsibilities toward her husband, her children, and the household.

No one played during recess. The recess that I had always looked forward to was too boring, since I had no one with whom I could share it. The students ate the little snacks they had and waited impatiently in the crowded playground to go back to class.

When I went to the bathroom, I was followed by Hezbollah enforcers. A sister waited outside to go into my stall even though there were empty ones. She followed me everywhere I went like a malevolent ghost. She checked the stall after I left to see if I'd written anything on the walls of the bathroom stall.

At home, Mamán and Baba argued all the time. They had not figured out whose fault it was that we girls had turned out so concerned about freedom. The school, the curriculum, and the reality that I was under scrutiny all the time made the school environment intolerable. I could not talk to Sheyla and had no friend other than Marzieh. I did not want to talk too much to her either, because this might have gotten her into trouble with the suspicious Hezbollah sisters.

A prison within a prison was the story of my life. I wanted to scream at the top of my lungs, "Can't you see they have gotten under your skin? They want to own our souls so they can control us!" Fury overcame me many times but I silenced it and choked it down. Living under these conditions was living in hell.

I was the only Jewish girl in an all-girls school and I still had to wear a *chador*. The school was for girls only. Why did we have to wear the *hijab* in a school that was run by women only? The Islamic government was paranoid . . . about another woman seeing a piece of my hair? Why? Whom were we hiding from? I was suffocating.

It was depressing because I used to love school and I loved learning, but school had been ruined for me. I hated to go to school, I hated to learn Arabic. I hated the daily body searches. If I had been given the choice to learn Arabic, fine. This, however, was imposed upon me by someone whose beliefs I didn't share. It was a heavy burden. All these restrictions took away any fun from learning and my natural youthful curiosity.

I watched Sheyla from far away. She cried all the time at school. As I walked by her, she sobbed quietly, "My sisters were arrested two weeks ago. They were executed." More sobbing. "I did not want to miss school. I am devastated."

The floor sank under my feet.

But worse was yet to come.

Mojgan had gone further than to simply exile us to a terrible school. She vested in herself the power of a universal judge, and decided to play God.

Mojgan dropped by "old friends'" houses on "friendly" visits. But these were anything but friendly visits. She visited the homes of outspoken students from the list she had created since the Revolution. On a Wednesday evening in mid-autumn 1981, she knocked on the door of Sheyla's house.

"Hi. Is Sheyla home?"

Her mother didn't recognize Mojgan. But she figured she was harmless, that Mojgan had come by to study.

"Yes, Sheyla is here."

Meanwhile, a car with Hezbollah police inside was parked nearby. Mojgan waved her hand. She gave a signal to the messengers of evil in the car to come and raid the house.

Sheyla was pulled out screaming and kicking. Her widowed mother had lost two of her daughters only days before. Her only living child was torn from her and dragged out of the house. Sheyla's mother ran after the army jeep, shouting and crying, but her cries fell on deaf ears and on hearts made of cold, hard steel.

Sheyla didn't show up at school the next day. I knew it was not safe to call her home. Their telephone was tapped.

Keeping a low profile was the only option for me at school. I listened in their Arabic classes, made sure my *hijab* covered every last hair, did the best I could to continue my education.

I was later informed by an acquaintance that Mojgan's visit had been the catalyst for Sheyla's disappearance. Mojgan's behaviour was an example of what was happening all around the country. Fear brought out the worst in many people.

This betrayal wounded me tremendously. Hezbollah believed the whole world had to bow to them and their beliefs. How could Mojgan stoop so low to save her own skin? How could she have her own friend arrested? Mojgan had been our close friend at one time; we had played together in elementary school. How could a child act like that against her classmates and friends? How could she knowingly subject them to torture and endanger their lives?

The only way to explain her behaviour was that she and her parents were terrified by the political atmosphere. To ensure their own safety, they were willing to do anything. Their loyalty to the Islamic government granted them lavish benefits from the state. She must have gotten some kind of sick pleasure out of her betrayal.

These sick, horrendous acts were all committed in the name of God, and the Hezbollah claimed to be God's representative on the planet.

There was no more reading.

There was no more hiking.

I was not allowed to use the phone.

Mamán and Baba didn't care if I liked it or not; they did not want me to be killed. They'd rather I was comatose than dead.

I stopped eating. I would rather have been dead; I might as well have been. Mamán was worried about me, since I was already very skinny and didn't have much fat to spare.

This form of protest continued for a few days, but I didn't gain much ground.

The week after Sheyla disappeared, a shabbily dressed woman I had never met before rang our doorbell. "I want to see your Mamán. Is she home?"

She was nervous, spoke quickly and demanded privacy with Mamán.

They retired into a room for several minutes. When the unannounced visitor left, Mamán's expression was one of complete terror.

"Sima," she whispered in a low voice. "You are in terrible danger. Sheyla was arrested. The teachers know you are her best friend. That woman was your school nurse. She overheard your name this morning. You are the next to be arrested. I do not want you to go to school anymore."

The visitor had been Mamán's classmate in nursing school. At least some decent people still existed. If it weren't for her, I would surely have suffered Sheyla's fate.

We decided that my sisters should not return to school, either. It was likely they had been blacklisted as well; they also had their tendencies to speak out.

That night, I went to Naneh Jaan-Jaan's house and stayed there.

I hid in a room on the second floor that was used only once a year, for Passover. The slightest noise sounded to me like the Hezbollah was coming to grab me. To smash me like a useless bug. Every noise was magnified in the silence. I could hear my own breath. Naneh Jaan-Jaan's little dog barked every time someone passed by the door. Every time I heard a bark I thought someone was coming to arrest me.

I imagined the torture they would put me through when they found me. The Hezbollah men would beat me with a leather belt. They would burn the soles of my feet with cigarette butts to extract a confession out of me. They would insert objects in me. I was going crazy. What would happen to my family? They would come for me, I'd be tortured, my family arrested, our belongings seized, Baba killed, and my brothers sent off to war. I could not sleep. I had only my thoughts to occupy my time. Needlework would have been a useful way to spend the long nights. But if I turned on any lights, the Hezbollah neighbours might wonder who was in the room.

Naneh Jaan-Jaan's house was too close to home to be safe. I thought of fleeing to stay with some friends of my friends.

If Mamán did not know where I was, she would have nothing to confess under torture and questioning.

No options were available to me. My whole world had fallen apart. The highs I felt prior to the Revolution and the promises of freedom had turned into inescapable blackness.

I had lost all pleasure in living and had become a shadow of my former self. I had to disappear. A week of hiding at Naneh Jaan-Jaan's house seemed much longer that it really was. I had no contact with the outside world. Farah and Soraya limited their visits as well, to avoid blowing my cover.

I wanted to pray. But my faith had been challenged. I have always believed in *Khoda* (God) and I was certain that he would not allow this dictatorship to last forever. But time was running out.

None of my own values were reflected in this fundamentalist version of Islam. Hatred and violence was what the Islamic government represented.

I dreamed of liberty; of being able to express myself freely. It was not going to be easy; that was why so many of us had to fight for it. But so much blood was being spilled. What did we get? More deception and more dictators wrapped in brown capes who could not even speak a complete sentence that made any sense. The new government was poor, hungry, and bloodthirsty.

The Shah had been corrupt; his pockets were deep, and he filled them with money. His hands were stained with the blood of his enemies. But his intentions were honourable; he wanted to help his people become a part of the twentieth century.

The newcomers, the mullahs, had bottomless pockets that no amount of money and no amount of killing could ever fill. These religious fanatics were more corrupt than the Shah. They believed they owned the key to paradise. The mullahs believed they represented God in Iran and God in the world. They had ruined my country and would continue to do so until Iran was bereft of all life. The terrible part was that they did it in the name of God.

I never heard of Sheyla again.

PART TWO

Homeless

This being human is a guest house.
Every morning a new arrival.
A joy, a depression, a meanness,
some momentary awareness comes
as an unexpected visitor.
Welcome and entertain all!
Even if they're a crowd of sorrows,
who violently sweep your house
empty of its furniture,
still, treat each guest honorably.
He may be clearing you out
for some new delight.
The dark thought, the shame, the malice,
meet them at the door laughing,
and invite them in.
Be grateful for whomever comes,
because each has been sent
as a guide from beyond.

Rumi

Into the Unknown

November 2, 1981

I slip out of Naneh Jaan-Jaan's house wearing my black *chador*, a few scattered *tooman* in my pocket. The night is darker than ever. Who knows what is lurking in the shadows? I am positive that the Hezbollah are just around the corner ready to jump me. The wind whistles in the background. The headlights of a car zooming along the road loom behind me. I flatten myself against the cold stone wall. At the speed I've been going, I run the risk of tripping on a piece of garbage, falling with a loud thud, sprawling on the ground. *I mustn't make any noise . . . slow down, Sima!* my inner voice screams. *Look normal!* Mamán would say the pigeon's heart beats faster than any other creature's. At this moment my heartbeat is much faster than any pigeon's. All my senses are sharpened like daggers, poised for fight or flight. Either way, until I am in a safe house, any false move can bring me to prison, to hell behind bars . . . to Sheyla's hell.

>>>>>

In early November, I take a taxi and then a bus to arrive at Zari's house. I plan to move in with Parvin's aunt, Zari, her husband, Farhad, and their daughter, Setareh. They live on the other side of Shiraz, in a middle-class suburb. The bus passes through the suburb of Halabi Abad, a slum area, where the houses are made of flattened metal containers. The prison where Sheyla was taken to is a few miles away.

Zari is expecting me. Her house is small, with two bedrooms and a tiny garden. The outhouse is in the garden, as is standard in most houses. There are no trees in this garden. How could this be? A Shirazi house without a tree is strange. Never have I seen a house without a tree in the garden before. I am stunned.

Her house is scantily furnished. There are carpets in each room, not Tabriz carpets, but Shirazi-made imitations. Inexpensive stuff.

Zari is petite, in her early twenties, with long, silky light brown hair. She and her husband, Farhad, do not like what our country has turned into. This is why she has opened her home to me. She says this is the least she can do to help those who loathe the government. Zari is Muslim, of course. Her house is far from my home, and it is unlikely that anyone I know will be in the area. We will pretend that I am a mother's helper.

Only Farah and Soraya know where I am. Mamán and Baba have no idea.

For the first time in my life, I am all alone.

Zari's life revolves around her husband and her four-year-old daughter, Setareh. When Zari wakes up, we clean the house together. She starts cooking right afterwards. She slices the meager portion of *halal* lamb meat as thinly as possible without its disappearing into the stew. I feel bad eating, because there is so little of it—I am taking food out of her daughter's mouth. And it is also not kosher meat. Until today, I have eaten only kosher meat. Zari has her family's mouths to feed, and everything is rationed because of the war. She and her husband are generous and expect nothing in return.

As I take the first bite of the stew, I am overcome by guilt and shame. Mamán would never approve. Surprisingly, it tastes wonderful. There is something about a hungry stomach and slow-cooking meat for hours that makes it so mouth-wateringly juicy.

Zari's husband, Farhad, stays in the bathroom for hours and hours. Zari says, "He's constipated." Every time he has used the bathroom, I see a cigarette butt in there, but there is no smell after he leaves.

Amir, Zari's nephew, and an old friend from my hiking days, visits often. He confides in me that Farhad is addicted to heroin. Zari is suffering quietly. How could she be happy in her marriage, considering the hours her husband spends in the toilet, and lying to her? Zari and Farhad hardly speak to each other. Farhad never thanks her for the appetizing food she makes. Zari is taken for granted. She doesn't think she has a choice—and she is right: she doesn't.

Their daughter, Setareh, asks me, "Why are you here?"

"Because Mommy wants help," I reply.

"Come play with me!" she commands.

From time to time, I call home from a pay phone; one call costs two *rials* (one-tenth of a *tooman*). It's not always easy to find a pay phone, since people stay in the booth for hours, telling their lengthy stories with those two *rials*.

I call once, hang up after one ring, call a second time, let it ring twice, and on the third ring, Farah picks up. This is our signal that I am calling.

Farah and Soraya meet with me sporadically to bring me money. When Mamán is at work, I call them, and they scurry through the alleys to lose any followers. Then they hop into a taxi to come to our meeting place. Every time we see each other, we arrange where we'll meet the next time. Nothing is discussed over the phone for fear of phone-tapping.

In Sa'adi's memorial park, the thousands of flowers are gone, replaced by a few scraggly rose bushes. Farah shows up with Keyvan. The love they have for each other is glowing in their eyes. They cannot touch and they cannot hold hands, otherwise the Hezbollah would be all over them like flies on a dead body. It is already two months since I've been at Zari's. Keyvan advises me not to overstay my welcome at their house. He has arranged for me to live with Khatereh, in Esfahan, for a week.

Khatereh, like Keyvan, is political. She has been our family friend since the Revolution. We hiked many mountains together, post-Revolution. She had to leave Shiraz last year after her brother was arrested as a counter-revolutionary. Khatereh was afraid the Islamic government would also come for her. Now I am in a similar situation. She certainly can empathize.

Esfahan is my next destination, and travelling by bus is my only option. Here I am to live with Khatereh. She rents a bare room in a big, one-storey house, which she will share with me. She has a blanket on the floor, where she spreads her futon. No need to fuss over the sleeping arrangements. I can sleep anywhere on the floor. I end up sleeping in the corner of the room on a blanket.

There are other boarders in this house. The owner, Fatemeh Khanoom, and her family stay in the north side of the house, where the kitchen and bathroom are located. Fatemeh Khanoom's business is renting out the two spare rooms to women only. We are not allowed to use the kitchen to cook or the bathroom to take a shower.

The street layout is different in this city. The streets are much wider and the trees are much larger. I adore *Leili Va MajNoon* trees—weeping willows—named after two legendary Persian lovers. This is the only place where I have seen weeping willows.

Esfahanis are more religiously observant than Shirazis. They are more devout, much more fervent. The black *chador* shows up as a black shadow everywhere I look. Khatereh informs me that the square where Friday lunch prayers take place is so packed that traffic is blocked for miles around. Fatemeh Khanoom doesn't know we are political and, more important, that I am a Jew.

Khatereh pretends to pray a few times a day when she is at home. She suggests, "You should also pray." I know how, because I was forced to learn it at school. I have to pretend to pray so as not to raise Fatemeh Khanoom's suspicions. *Hypocrite!* The voice shouts at me in my head. I do not want to be deceitful, but my life depends on it. The voice reminds me: *Go through the motions; your Jewish roots are too deep to be affected by these motions. Your family tree traces back to thousands of years in Shiraz, and this would not arise where you have come from.* When this voice is reasonable, it is lovely.

Khatereh makes sure to leave the door to her room open so Fatemeh Khanoom can see us. I carefully watch every move Khatereh makes and do exactly as she does. First we wash our hands and feet in the prescribed sequence. Then she spreads the prayer carpet, a small, rectangular, dark red Persian carpet. We pray facing the direction of Mecca, the Muslim holy city. I have to bow and bend many times. Never in a million years would I have thought how awkward and unpleasant it is to be going through the motions of another religion.

I want to leave here. There is only so much I can take; I dress like a Muslim. Isn't this enough? But having to pretend to pray in their way, too? If the situation were reversed, would these Muslims ever agree to pray in my way?

Esfahanis have a reputation for being very snoopy. Khatereh tells Fatemeh Khanoom I am her cousin from Tehran, and I'm too shy to speak to anyone. This might prevent her from asking too many personal questions and noticing my thick Shirazi accent. I try to avoid her as I move in the garden. Fortunately, we have a separate entrance into our room from the garden.

We have no access to Fatemeh Khanoom's fridge or stove, so I adjust to cooking on one little burner in Khatereh's room. At this point in my life, food is just fuel. Since the war began, there is a greater shortage of staples. Even rice and bread are rationed. Most of the dishes we make are vegetarian because of the scarcity of meat. The vegetarian dishes made of tomatoes, onions, eggplants, zucchini, and green beans, with turmeric, make a delicious stew. I like it a lot, and don't mind eating the same thing over and over, every day, morning, noon, and night. I can't afford to be picky.

Farah and Soraya are aware that I am in Esfahan. Calling long-distance on a pay phone is beyond my budget. The telegraph office is too far from where I live. I don't call home from Esfahan.

Away from my family, I long for my sisters and am overwhelmed by terrible guilt that Mamán does not know where I am. My family is the love of my life. These people who welcome me into their homes with open arms are kind. They are Muslim; they don't have any obligation to do this. It is very risky for them. If I am found in their house, they could be arrested, too. They are simply good-hearted people.

As I stroll through the streets, the beauty of the city of Esfahan takes my breath away. It is an ancient city. The buildings are ornate and majestic. It is obvious this was once the capital of Iran. Imam Square is grandiose and spectacular, and the facade of the mosque, which towers above it, displays delicate, hand-carved stonework in fantastic designs. The small blue and white tiles are inset in patterns around the entrance. I am humbled by the exquisiteness that shimmers in front of me.

No synagogue is visible. These days, unless you know exactly where the synagogue is, there is no way to find it accidentally. Its location is not advertised. There must be at least one, but I have no idea how to find it and I do not come in contact with any Jews while I am in Esfahan. I can spot a Shirazi Jew in Shiraz. They speak with a specific accent and usually dress modestly. It is as if we have a radar detector for each other: we know who is Jewish. But in Esfahan, I am lost. I have no idea what to look for.

At school, whenever the teachers spoke about Esfahan, they would add, "*Nesfe Jahan*." Esfahan is so magnificent that for anyone who visits and sees its wonders, it is as if that person has seen half of the world. I am enveloped by its splendour and its regal majesty.

One morning, when Khatereh is at work, I visit *Siu Seh Pol*, the Bridge of 33 Arches, built in 1650. This bridge should be on the list of the top ten wonders of the world. Above me, I have the blue sky, and crossing the river that flows through the city is a bridge composed of thirty-three perfect arches, the water moving gracefully beneath them. I have no family here. I know only one person. I am all alone.

As bad as my situation is, I am still free to promenade on this bridge at this exact moment. Bliss fills every cell of my body. My black *chador* blows in the wind, floating around me, barely touching my nose. Despite the blackness of the personal prison that I am carrying around with me at all times, for the moment, I am awestruck at the huge blue sky and the rising sun behind these arches, throwing reflections in the water in millions of colours . . . chromatic fractals in every direction.

For a fleeting second I feel free. The world exists to give me this experience.

Through all the wars, through all the revolutions, the bridge was never destroyed.

I am inspired. Despite all the obstacles, I suddenly see light at the end of the tunnel. Every dark night will end with a bright sun. Freedom! I hope to live long enough to see that day. I want to feel it in every breath I take, even if it is for only a few fleeting moments. To live as a free woman, with no shackles on my body or my spirit! This is what keeps me going during these dark days.

A week has sped by too fast. When I come back to Khatereh at the end of the day, it is for the last time to sleep on the floor of this stifling room. Even though Khatereh has been very welcoming, I am happy to leave because it is too exhausting to pretend to pray. Anxiety grips me again. Where to stay next? I am homeless again. I travel back to Shiraz with my poor, tiny heart in my hands. I am scared. I feel sorry for myself and my little body. I am only sixteen years old. What crimes have I committed that I have to run for my life so much? Finding another place to stay is my new challenge.

After two months of not seeing my family, I have run out of places to stay and have to beg Mamán for help.

January 1982

Even before I left for Esfahan, Farah told me that Mamán was going crazy from my absence. As soon as I return to Shiraz, I visit Khaleh Tahereh and I beg, "Please call Mamán. I need to see her."

Mamán is furious. She gives me a good slap in the face and shouts, "Where have you been all these months? Did you forget you have a mother?" The smacks are so hard, that her hand must have left red marks on my face. As much as I try to be brave, not to cry or show that I am hurt, I can't; tears, unchecked, roll down my cheeks.

Mamán is oblivious to my pain. We are all suffering in silence, and there is no way to lighten the weight or relieve the agony. I'm running out of places to live in and I don't know what to do. "Do not leave," she commands. "I will do whatever I can to help you."

She disappears for three long days.

Ammeh Nilofar's house in Tehran may be the next home for me. She is my favourite aunt. Baba had matched her up with Naser. Years later, she is still happily married. Ammeh Nilofar feels indebted to Baba for helping her find happiness.

Khaleh Nastaran also moved to Tehran after her wedding five years ago. Long before the Revolution, I was invited to my Armenian friend's house for Christmas and Khaleh Nastaran made sure I was presentable. She shared her red lipstick with me.

"I'm going to take you to your Ammeh Nilofar in Tehran," she declares. We travel to Tehran together, a fifteen-hour bus ride. Ammeh Nilofar agrees to let me stay with her, although reluctantly and on two conditions. I will not be allowed to read any books nor speak to anyone other than my uncle and my cousins.

Before Mamán returns to Shiraz, she hands Ammeh Nilofar 4,000 *tooman* for my English course. It is Mamán's desire that I learn English. "You never know. If you can speak English, the international language, it will come in handy in the future." This is puzzling. It is exciting that Mamán wants me to learn English, although why she insists on this, I don't know; it is not as if I can speak English to anyone here in Iran. Ammeh Nilofar, however, is uncomfortable with this idea because she thinks it will open a can of worms; and talking to other students might cause danger for the family.

I live with her for a week and I plead with her, "Ammeh, when are we going to register for the English course?"

"I don't know where it is. It's far from here. The class is full, and we missed registration."

That's right. Smash the dream right to smithereens. Shut up and do as you're told or you're kicked out of here.

Both my aunts live in apartments, both on the second floor, in different parts of the city. I have never lived in an apartment in my life and I find it very small and cramped. There are no apple trees, no orange trees, and no garden. Tehran is the most expensive part of Iran in which to own real estate. That is why people live in such small apartments. They can't afford to own a real house. My cousins Azin and Seppideh share their small room with me. Sleeping on the floor on a folded blanket is the routine for me by now. I can't ask for more.

Mamán suggests to me that I alternate between Ammeh Nilofar's house and the home of her sister Khaleh Nastaran. The only clothing I have with me is my *rosari* and one spare top. I have been handwashing my *manteau*[5] at night in the sink, letting it dry during the day, then washing the other *manteau*, over and over. They have been washed so often that they look worn out but I have no other options. They get so dirty during the day. I have to rinse them many times until most of the filth from the pollution in Tehran's air is gone. There is a shortage of water in Tehran, and I have to be careful not to use too much water. It has not rained for the longest time. With the pollution, the shortage of water, the shortage of food, and the lack of freedom, I am living in a prison with changing prison guards.

Tehran is very busy and crowded; rivers of human beings flow along the sidewalks and roads, the currents weaving in and out. There are too many people, too many roads, too many mean-looking Hezbollah men. I have to push through the crowds; it feels worse than the car traffic. It is human traffic. No matter where I look there are more and more people. They must be growing out of the ground like weeds. To the people here, it seems normal. To me, it is anything but normal. I know Shiraz like the back of my hand. There is no way I could ever know Tehran like that.

People here are not as religious as those in Esfahan or Shiraz. Women are not as strict about their *hijabs*. Half of their blonde hair sneaks out as their *rosaris* slip halfway back on their heads. Iranian women do not have blonde hair. It is certainly dyed. Women wearing red lipstick, mascara, black eyeliner and blue eyeshadow parade around as if they forgot it is no longer the Shah's reign. These kinds of women I have not seen in public since the Revolution. Am I in another country? Aren't they afraid acid will be thrown in their faces and leave them permanently disfigured?

---

5   A loose, long-sleeved and at least knee-length coat.

They are playing with fire. I dare not let any of my hair show. All it takes is one crazy person to leave me disfigured forever.

Ammeh Nilofar is a hard worker. She puts the food on a *sofreh*,[6] is the last one to start eating, the first one to finish her food, and before her family has finished eating, she is already washing the dishes. She is neurotic in her own way. I love her; my Uncle Naser is funny and tries to make me laugh. He mocks the Shirazi accent. "You drag the words out so long. Why do you do that?" I have no idea what he is talking about. Among other things, he loves eating watermelon; he eats it with so much passion and enthusiasm that he gets sick from over-stuffing himself. Azin and Seppideh want to play all the time. Their favourite game is hide-and-seek, but there is nowhere to hide. This place is too small.

Khaleh Nastaran, Uncle Omid, and my two cousins Shahzad and Teimour live in an apartment in a commercial area above a shoe shop. An older single Jewish man lives upstairs. He impresses Khaleh Nastaran because he is an engineer who studied in France. Any man who has graduated abroad is in high demand and supposedly good marriage material. Khaleh Nastaran wants me to meet him. She just wants me to get out of their way and not to stir up any more commotion. If I get married, I'm my husband's problem. I don't even want to think about marriage. She has an expression, "The fly that flies around too much will land on shit." Meaning, if you wait too long to get married, you will become an old maid and get the worst husband—if you are lucky. How cruel of her to talk this way. I pretend I do not understand what she means. This aggravates her and she repeats herself over and over. I continue to ignore her. I live in my own little world.

Khaleh Nastaran and Uncle Omid are less religious than we are. Sometimes they take me with them when they go out on Saturday nights to restaurants. There are no kosher restaurants in Tehran. Going to a restaurant on my own is not something I have ever done, not only because it is not allowed by both Ammeh Nilofar and Khaleh Nastaran but also because it is expensive and I have no idea where to go. For the first time, we go to an outdoor Persian *kababi* grilled-meat restaurant. No Shirazi Jew would ever do that. "You eat non-kosher? We never do that at home!"

They stare at me as if I'm completely unworldly and shrug their shoulders.

6   A tablecloth placed on the floor and on which the food is served.

Outside, under the stars, the night is gorgeous. There are many tables, and they are all full. What to order is my dilemma. Uncle Omid orders a *joojeh kebab* (little chicken) for me. I am delighted that he decides for me. The smell of saffron with lemon surrounds us. The meat is grilled on a long metal skewer over charcoal. When I put it in my mouth, the chicken wrapped in its juice is scrumptiously delicious. If one could taste Heaven, it would taste like this. The royal treatment I receive for a brief few moments makes me forget that I am an exile in my own country.

After a few days of sightseeing, the novelty wears off. I'm at Ammeh Nilofar's house and she witnesses my boredom. She utters under her breath, "I will keep you busy, don't worry."

She is a nurse and makes house calls when injections are due. One couple who uses her services has a dressmaking workshop in their house.

She comes home ecstatic. "I have something for you to do. You're going to learn sewing and dressmaking in the house factory. The owner is doing me a favour to teach you the skills; that is why you won't be paid."

This way, I am off her back, and she won't have to entertain me. Here there are enough eyes watching me that I can't cause any fuss. I'm desperate. My brain is dying. I need stimulation. I want to learn and will accept any conditions to use my mind.

Ammeh Nilofar and I walk for ten minutes to reach the factory. On the second floor of the big house, a short, fat, bald man greets us. He introduces himself as Agha Hassan. Then he barks out the working conditions: "Start at eight a.m. Finish at four p.m., or later. No lunch break. You eat while you work." I'm not getting paid; why do I have to clock in and clock out?

There is a huge table where the material is cut with big scissors. He lights another cigarette. "If you want to work here, you have to be serious. You're learning the basic skills of dressmaking and sewing. This is going to take some time to teach. You won't learn it overnight."

I'm excited about learning: how to pick a fabric for a design, details about how different sizes fit different people, how to make a pattern and sew a dress from beginning to end. It is not what I want to do for the rest of my life, but for now, it will do. Mamán has stamped into my soul that a person can never know too much. It is good to learn. How generous and charitable of Agha Hassan to teach me all these wonderful skills! But

I am suspicious: if he is such a kind person, why is he speaking in such a nasty tone? Something is wrong. It does not add up.

The house has three floors. I walk through the garden to enter the basement. The workers are not allowed to walk through the house. It's off-limits. The whole operation is run out of the basement of the house. There are about twenty machines, and no air conditioner in the basement. Only men work here. They range in age from twenty to fifty years. The dressmakers work as fast as they can and they don't talk to anybody. They are paid by the piece.

At the factory, the star dressmaker is a scary looking Afghani man. I wear my *hijab* all the time especially because of him, since I figure he must be like the other Afghanis coming to Iran. Afghanis love the Islamic government and its laws.

On our way to the factory, I see a group of Afghanis having breakfast at one of the corners at an intersection, seated cross-legged on their blankets on the pavement. Many such intersections have been colonized by these homeless groups. This particular corner belongs to one particular Afghani group. This is where they sleep and eat. I don't want to think about what they use for bathroom facilities.

I hope my star dressmaker does not sleep on this corner. What if I bump into him as he is eating his breakfast there? How should I greet him? Should I pretend not to see him to avoid embarrassment for both of us?

Reza, an intellectual-looking dressmaker who wears round glasses, has a tendency to ask provocative political questions. "Did you hear what's in the news? The government is killing many people, both in the war and in the prisons." Reza is a counter-revolutionary. I try to avoid his political remarks but it is not easy to keep quiet. If I ask him, he will bring me books, but I don't want to provoke Khaleh Nastaran, who searches through everything, or Ammeh Nilofar, who helps me out so much.

I change the subject to a safer theme. "What are Tehran's highlights?" He is excited to inform me about the zoo. "How can one go there by bus?" I can't stop him from talking. He has now found himself a fresh ear to talk to for hours. The other factory workers try to avoid him. As soon as he opens his mouth, the machine operators start working faster, and increase the volume on the radio, blaring out mournful Islamic music. To me, the music is more irritating than his comments, but no one asks my opinion or cares to hear it.

Reza gives me very valuable lessons; I have no idea what brings this on. He says, "The people you love in your life represent a beautiful bowl of antique china; you need to take care of them. Imagine if you have a crack in the china bowl. No matter which master you take it to, the crack will show. The moral of the story: take care of your loved ones and do not take them for granted." I thank him for the lesson and stop talking to him. Ignoring the belligerent stares from the other workers takes too much effort.

These are tough days; even my thinking is controlled. Ammeh Nilofar follows me to work and back every day. She wants to make sure I make no contact with strangers. She and Uncle Naser are terrified that I will start to express my views again and bring harm upon myself and them. She cannot forget what happened to Ammeh Ashraf and doesn't want anything bad to happen to me. The new government has succeeded in establishing such a pervasive atmosphere of terror that no one trusts anyone else. Not friends. Not relatives. Not family. Nobody is trustworthy.

Agha Hassan and his wife, Maryam Khanoom, travel often to Europe, particularly to Paris, to view the latest fashions, which they use as inspiration for outfits acceptable to Islamic requirements. Their dresses are custom-made from silk or expensive polyester for their affluent women clients to wear at private parties.

I become the assistant to a very talented Afghani immigrant, a recent immigrant to Tehran. His name, Shah Gholam, means "king-butler." He is curious about me. But I am too frightened to tell him why I am here.

Excitement vibrates in every cell in my body to be working with the best dressmaker in the whole factory. Undoubtedly, there will be a lot to learn. For a few minutes, I daydream of a day that Maman will be impressed with my valuable skills when I sew a dress for her all by myself.

But soon enough, the truth becomes evident. The dressmaker needs a slave. Agha Hassan and Shah Gholam think I have been given to them as free labour and they are determined to make maximum use of my time and youthful energy. Keeping up with Shah Golem's gruelling pace leaves me out of breath, and despite his promises, I am not learning dressmaking skills.

I am underground with twenty men, sweating in my *hijab*, ironing non-stop or using the overlock machine, working hard for free and having to do it with a smile plastered on my face as if I am enjoying myself.

The house is magnificent. Sometimes, I peek upstairs at the silk curtains, the beautiful sofas and colourful, top-quality Persian carpets covering the floor. It looks luxurious. Shah Gholam sends me there to pick up the cut material, and Agha Hassan is stunned every time he sees me. Probably he sees my wandering eyes. He is such a snob — and rude, too. "What do you want?" he shouts. He acts as if I am intruding, when I am just doing my payless job that benefits him enormously.

Agha Hassan was an engineer, but after the Revolution he lost his job and opened this factory. I hear about his wife, Maryam Khanoom, from other workers, though I've never seen her. How could she live with Agha Hassan? He is malicious. I wonder if he was always mean or if he turned mean after he lost his job. He most likely does not like having the factory in his house; that is why he barks at me any time I come up to get the material for sewing.

Agha Hassan and Maryam Khanoom have a maid in the house who also cooks for them. At lunchtime, the scent of saffron fills the entire basement. Of course none of us is allowed to eat the appetizing food that the cook makes for them. This is not for us second-class citizens.

Ironing in the extreme heat of the basement with twenty sewing machines going at full blast all day is no pleasure. Because of ironing so much, the pain in my left arm worsens. I can't move it; it feels as though my arm is on fire. My only alternative is to iron with my right hand. I am expected to keep up with Shah Gholam's pace, which is very fast. He is aware that I am not being paid and also sees how hard I work. He promises me if I am patient he will teach me how to make a beautiful *manteau* for myself. I wonder if he will keep his word and if it will happen before I become an old lady.

One day when the factory closes early, he says, "Come with me. If you buy some fabric, I'll cut it for you, and teach you how to make a striking *manteau*." I can't believe it; he has kept his word. A noble act, indeed. These days it is hard to find people who keep their promises.

I do not walk with him, lest the Hezbollah brothers stop me. I do not want to get into a taxi with him, either. What if he wants to trick me and he is really not the good-hearted person he appears to be? He is a single man in Tehran. Who knows what he has in mind? I do not want to give him any opportunity for mischief. I am not at all interested in anything other than buying my fabric and sewing my *manteau*. It is better to be safe than sorry. "I will follow you as long as you walk through the main streets to the fabric shop." He agrees.

I stride a few metres behind him for about an hour, making sure to keep my distance the entire time. He steps into a fabric store and I follow. The rolls of fabric are piled all over the table and are almost bursting out of the walls. There is hardly any place to move in this store.

Never have I seen fabrics like this, so colourful, so varied in texture. The silk is soft, smooth and shiny. The woollens feel rough as I run my hand over them. As much as I love the texture of silk, there is no way I can wear it anywhere. A silk *manteau* would outline my skinny body and would contrast with the enforced *hijab*.

The salesman is about thirty, has short, neatly combed hair, and is clean-shaven. He smiles at me. There are not that many clean, groomed men around since the Revolution. They are so rare that when I see one, I notice him right away. "Can you please show me material for a *manteau* and a *rosari*?" He guesses that neither silk nor wool would be appropriate for the *manteau*. That is why he pulls out bulky heavy cotton rolls of fabric. I choose a thick navy cotton fabric. He tells me how much to buy. Shah Gholam approves. The fabric is cut, and I pay and give the fabric to Shah Gholam to take home.

He will bring it to the factory tomorrow, when we will start to work on my *manteau*. I do not want to bring my purchase home to avoid being interrogated by Khaleh Nastaran. Khaleh Nastaran's house is nearby, and that is the reason for me to spend the night there. If she asks what brings me to her place, I will tell her that I finished early and decided to walk to her place. That will be convincing enough for her. She is not pleased to see me again. But that is not new; I am used to not being welcome.

My life is so mundane that I am ecstatic over sewing my *manteau*, a loose winter coat that comes down to my knee, with many fine details on the collar and the sleeves; it will actually have buttons on the front. This is going to be the highlight of my stay so far in Tehran. Finally I have a chance to learn how to make a dress from start to finish.

Agha Hassan is not happy that I'm making my own *manteau*. But I am entitled to it, since I have been working weeks for him and have not been paid a penny. I stay longer to sew it myself. Nobody else in my family has such an intricately worked *manteau*. It is obvious it is special. I wear it with a matching headscarf, a *rosari*, and it looks incredible. I love this coat. It's all I have to show for my exile in Tehran.

~~~~~~

Uncle Naser's nieces Afsaneh and Sahar, who are in their late teens, invite me to go on an outing with them. The two of them do not cover their hair fully. They look at me with disapproval: why is my hair fully covered? No need to tell them my entire story.

I am planning to have fun today without thinking what brought me to this place. I ask, "Sahar, show me your favourite place in Tehran."

"My favourite activity is shopping."

What an odd answer. I cannot tell her that shopping is the least of my interests and that I don't have any money to spend anyway.

We start out on foot. The street is jam-packed, and I spot something red in a paper bag, marked for sale. Many people surround a short man who is booming louder than any loudspeaker, yelling "*tootfarangy!*" (strawberry). How could such a tiny man have such a powerful voice? Has he swallowed a microphone? What is he selling so enthusiastically? It looks as if he is selling gold at bronze prices. People are gathered around him, anxiously awaiting their turn to buy this "gold at bronze prices." Never have I seen anything like this. My voice nudges me to splurge and buy a bag. For the first time, I taste strawberries, apparently available only in Tehran. These are small, wild strawberries, and very expensive. How can such a tiny red thing be so juicy and delectable? As I put the strawberry in my mouth and take the first bite, the sweet taste, the red juice, and the softness of this new fruit transports me. Sometimes Heaven exists in the midst of hell, and today is one of those days.

Today is a special day. It has been weeks since I have been planning to take myself for an outing. Poor Sima is suffocating in that basement workshop with all the noise and the heat. Ammeh Nilofar thinks I am going to work. She has already checked on me enough times that she trusts me. I pretend to go to work at the usual time, 7:45 a.m., so as not to raise any of Ammeh Nilofar's suspicions. But other plans dance around in my head. Excitement, a foreign feeling beyond my wildest dreams, overwhelms me. If I am caught, I will be padlocked in the house, a real prisoner.

I have to see the zoo. It is a shame to come to Tehran and not see this major attraction. There is no way they will take me there. They are too busy. I live with the consequences. Is escaping to the zoo a silly thing to do?

I walk out of the apartment, in the direction of the factory for about ten minutes, and then at the intersection I jump onto a bus. I am pushed and shoved. I feel the heat of bodies pressing in on every side. The stinky breath of the passengers is all over my face and body. Doesn't anyone ever take a shower? There has been a drought and a shortage of water in Tehran; this smell is definitely from the shortage of water. It reeks on the bus.

After an hour, I arrive at the zoo. It is not far from downtown Tehran, a place with acres and acres of land. Ancient trees guard the entrance, and the zoo is well-kept and clean. At this time of morning, hundreds of visitors are already milling around the zoo. The women are covered from head to toe with the black *chador*, just like me. Men walk around in long pants and shirts with either short or long sleeves. Men are lucky; they do not have to cover up like us. It is hot; I am drenched in sweat. Dozens of kids run around with their parents, the kids pointing out the animals.

Never in my sixteen years have I visited a zoo. There is so much to see and do that I don't know where to look first. My eyes are opened so wide that I am scared they will fall out of my face.

For the first time I see zebras, elephants, tigers, and different sizes of monkeys. I am most stunned by the lions. They look just like the bronze lions I used to see in front of the courthouse as a child in Shiraz. Lions symbolize power and freedom. We should treat them with respect. But here they are in cages. I am suddenly saddened by the plight of these magnificent creatures, lords of the jungle, trapped behind iron bars. They can no longer roam freely over the plains of their homeland. They have been brought here to be spectacles for the entertainment of children and adults alike. So much for the fate of kings!

I wish Mamán, Baba, Farah, Soraya, and the boys were here with me. They would have liked to see the animals, but they, as I, would have been upset to see the animals in cages. The symbolism would have also hit too close to home for them. Who gives the right to the zoo owner to imprison these animals? It is not right. All God's creatures should be free to do what we are supposed to do.

As much as I want to stay here all day, I have to rush back home to return at my usual time. Hopefully, Khaleh Nastaran will not find out. There would be a high price for this disobedience. Visiting the zoo on my own is my new crime.

I long to hike the mountains in Tehran, to see them with my own eyes, to be blown away by their majesty and physical exhaustion, but it will not happen. I live a parasitic life with no control over it. Life is wasted on me now.

March 1982

It has been three months since I arrived in Tehran. Those lions in the zoo and I have one thing in common: we are both not in control of our lives. I hate my present existence, and the despair about the future. Having no one to confide in is taking its toll on me. I keep in touch with my sisters by sending letters through the regular post, but Khaleh Nastaran, who is extremely nosy and doesn't seem to like me, reads all the letters my sisters send me. She says, "So Farah is still seeing Keyvan." Nobody is supposed to know that. Khaleh Nastaran is snoopy and bitter toward me. She is smart but has nothing worthwhile to occupy her mind. My life has become an exciting project for her. She dissects every word I say and every step I take.

I am only sixteen and have no idea how to deal with her personality. She is too complicated. One minute she is funny and we laugh together. The next minute she looks at me with rage as if I have offended her. Too hard to know how I offend her, but I do. It is difficult to believe Khaleh Nastaran is Mamán's sister. They could be totally unrelated, they are so different. She is not the aunt I once knew.

Khaleh Nastaran and Ammeh Nilofar find out from my letters to my sisters that I went to the zoo, and that Shah Gholam took me out to buy material; they call Mamán and say: "We can't take care of your wild daughter." Obviously, this is an excuse; they can't keep me forever. Mamán and I need to come up with a new plan.

Even family ties break down in the face of fear.

Mamán finds out that I have been working for free in the factory. "What, you are a slave?" She is disappointed but knows she can't do anything about it. Mamán rushes to Ammeh Nilofar's door to take me back to Shiraz.

Ammeh Nilofar's and Khaleh Nastaran's families are greatly relieved.

Mamán gives me conditions, too. These are the worst ones yet. I'm not allowed to leave the house. This is a non-negotiable dictum.

"We can't go home directly when we get back. Our neighbours know you're not in town, and they keep asking where you are. We're not going to let them see you arrive home. You're going to your Khaleh Mahin's house. I'll come get you tonight.

"The situation at home is not getting any better. Baba is just as unhappy as ever. I'm miserable, too. We don't know where Keyvan is, and Farah is despondent. Just stay quiet until we figure out what to do."

We sit in silence for a few minutes . . . "And by the way," Mamán adds, "the chickens and roosters in the house are not happy, either."

"What?"

"They're so upset they don't even lay eggs anymore."

We arrive at night and of course I have on my *chador*, so the neighbours won't see. Everyone lives in fear these days; neighbours are spying on neighbours. We know there are Hezbollah supporters in every second house. Mamán wants to be sure that nobody knows I am home.

April 1982

I used to love this time of the year but now there is nothing special about it. The Iranian New Year has come and soon will be gone. Every day is like the day before, and there is no hope that tomorrow will be any different.

Passover was my favourite time of the year but since Ammeh Ashraf's execution and Baba Esghel's death, we no longer celebrate with the whole family. Though "Jackson therapy" worked for a little while, Naneh Jaan-Jaan has lost her legendary energy and her joie de vivre. Now she cries so much that her eyesight is affected. She no longer can see well enough to thread a needle. She used to make variants of halvah for every holiday, special recipes for happy holidays, and different ones for holidays of mourning. Now she makes her halvahs only for mourning days. She commemorates the deaths of family members. She wails the entire time while she is mixing the halvah.

The nuts are too expensive, fruit is too expensive, and meat is scarce. We are all demoralized. Mamán goes through the motions to get ready for Passover with no excitement.

The first Seder brings tears to my eyes over the family members who were killed unjustly, over Baba Esghel's sudden premature death, over my own circumstances. It is a quiet Seder. We don't hit each other with green onions with the same exuberance as Baba sings "Dayenu."

❯❯❯❯❯

We now struggle with yet another slap in the face delivered full-force by the Islamic government. The announcements on radio and television declare that all Iranian citizens must update their birth certificates to ones now issued by the new Islamic government. You cannot use the old certificates to obtain your coupons for rationed food. There is a huge difference in price between buying these items with coupons or at the highly inflated black market price. People with large families or those with no jobs will sometimes buy a rationed item with their coupons and then sell the item for many times the price they paid for it, in order to have money for rent or other necessities. These people make do on even less food. They sell their children's food in a country whose oil revenues alone could feed every citizen efficiently.

For the first time, there is a specific reference to religion on birth certificates. Members of minority religions are referred to as *Agha* (Mr.) or *Khanoom* (Mrs.) on the birth certificate. Shiites' birth certificates are marked *baradar* (brother) or *khahar* (sister). Now I am *persona non grata* not because of lack of personal merit but because of my religion. It is a curse to be a Jew and a female in this Islamic country. What happened to Iran's being the leader of civilization in the world? Now, Iran is the leader of discrimination in the world. Well done; all the other nations progress, we regress.

❯❯❯❯❯

Mamán sees my *manteau* that I toiled over in Tehran, and asks me to make her one like it. She has to find ways to keep me busy. I pretend to know what I am doing and make Mamán a *manteau* similar to mine in dark brown cotton. After all, I have managed to absorb some skills and knowledge of dressmaking by watching Shah Gholam. It actually looks professionally made. A surprise for all of us. Mamán is impressed.

The next few months are as dreary as can be. There are no new books available. Baba has burned almost all of them. The few novels that are left I had already read many times. This is the only thing remaining of our "freedom days" that so many died for. No telephone calls, no friends, no hiking, no music. Classical music is considered counter-revolutionary.

No more boarders are in the house.

No more human contact.

Mamán buys needlework patterns at the bazaars; I do an intricate needle-point of three horses; that's the only way I can get in touch with nature. It is Mamán who taught me how to crochet. While I am confined to the house, needlepoint and crochet become my neurotic obsessions. I hide, scared of my own shadow, afraid of anyone who rings the doorbell or calls on the phone. I am frightened that Mojgan will come to visit; that maybe Sheyla has turned traitor.

I become engrossed in my work as the only way to escape my reality. Hundreds of hours of my life go into making intricately detailed, elaborate patterns with needlepoint and crochet. I spend hours on it.

Are the mountains still as much fun to climb? I will never know. My Chinese daffodils never flower, so I can't even smell them. I miss the fresh air. I miss the people on the street calling out *"chahala badam!"* (green almonds) and the smell of charcoal-broiled corn in salt water. But there has not been anything like that since Hezbollah came to power. We can't even go to the park. Mamán is always with me when she isn't working at the clinic. My siblings try to cheer me up but they're miserable too. Baba thinks I'm going out of my mind, because I'm always crocheting late into the night. He doesn't ask me what's going on because he knows he can't provide any solutions. He's right, of course. He cannot. He wants me to turn the light off so he can sleep better. He wakes up early before sunrise. I can't sleep; my useless life becomes more vivid in the dark when I am lying still, and there is no way to escape.

Families in Iran, Jewish and Muslim alike, marry off a daughter to a man who is able to support a family. Marriage is treated as a business transaction. It is irrelevant whether the girl even likes the man. A wife's job is to satisfy the husband's needs; to cook, to clean, and to bear his children. My cousin Homeira is gorgeous and only fifteen years old. She is a year younger than me. She is married to a man who is fifteen years older than her. Baba Bozourg expects me to do the same. I can't. There is a right time for everything in life. At this point, marriage is not the right thing for me.

Marriage is now out of the question anyway, even if I were to agree to it. No family wants a woman who is hiding from the government. I am a freethinker and a nonconformist. I want to continue my studies, but that is obviously impossible. No normal lifestyle is achievable; the only future open to me is that of a fugitive. I already know I have to get out of Iran, and so does Mamán, but we do not talk about it.

To continue my education is my new obsession. *Do not give up the dream*, my voice insists. At least I can dream. Dreaming hasn't been taken away from me, not now and not ever. This is my free world, between my ears and in my heart. They can take everything from me but my dreams, which are mine and will stay with me to my last breath.

I barely exist. Day by day I am less alive. There is no quality to my life. I feel invisible. To die for a cause would be preferable to a life of this terrifying existence. When someone has a nightmare, she wakes up and realizes it is just a bad dream. But this is a nightmare from which I can never awaken. I am desperate, and there is no hope of change. Mamán knows this is not what she wants for her daughters. She knows I am not stupid, not handicapped, and very thirsty for knowledge. Soraya pours her heart out to us, and we lament how pitiful our lives have become.

Soraya queries, "Do you think we will ever be able to continue our studies?"

I wish I could say yes. I do not want to disappoint her and take her hope away but I can't lie to her. "The three of us are on the wicked blacklist. No school will accept us. No matter where we go in Iran, every school will need a copy of our report cards and with it comes the report from the Hezbollah sisters, the crows. I hope there will be a way to go back to school. For the moment, we have to pray to find the way." I am disconsolate as I express the truth. The weight of the entire world lies heavily on my shoulders. A sixteen-year-old's duty is to study, and that fundamental right has been taken away from us. This world is ruled by bullies. They have power, guns, and prisons.

Mamán and Baba continue to ignore each other. It has been years that their little conversations have turned into howling and screaming on both sides. They have had one too many arguments over whose fault it is that their girls turned out this way. Their values are hard work, honesty, faithfulness, and family unity. But their reactions to the new Iran under Islamic rule are so far apart . . . as if they were from different planets. Baba tends to hide his head under the snow and pretend there is no snow. How can he not see that there is nothing left for us in Shiraz? He thinks if one is busy doing, cleaning, working, cooking, the problems will go away. I know this does not work. I have been very busy crocheting and needlepointing, but my problem, lack of freedom, is becoming more palpable and impossible to live with.

I have no reason to live. Am I some kind of pest that would be easier to crush and walk over? But no, it has to be done slowly and I have to go through the torture. The worst thing for anybody is to take away his or her hope. I can't fight, I can't run, I have to stay still with all these emotions packed inside. I am going to explode like a bomb; the timer is on and it is ticking. And that's why I become sick again. My arm pain is back. It is so painful that I can't let it hang down. I can't straighten it. I have to hold my left hand, which I write with, close to my body with my right hand. And now even the pleasure of sewing is gone because I am incapacitated. All I do is sleep and breathe, sometimes eat, and drift around the house like a ghost.

In Baba's eyes, Mamán has raised us girls to be too liberal; we should not be concerned about freedom — we are supposed to do our work. Mamán regrets that she could not continue her education. She does not want us to have the same regret. These two opposing views about life and child-rearing are at the core of the differences between Mamán and Baba. There is no way they could meet in the middle. Mamán lets us know in Baba's presence that her colleague Morteza's son escaped through Pakistan. Baba snaps, "There is no way I will expose my daughters to that kind of danger. How irresponsible of his parents to do such a thing!"

To me, Morteza performed the greatest act of kindness and devotion for his son. This is not the first time we hear Baba talk like this. He believes it sincerely. "No matter how bad the situation, children have to stay close to their parents."

My thoughts turn elsewhere. I begin to entertain the idea of escaping from Iran. It is nothing but a dream. How did Morteza smuggle his son out? Who helped him? How do we find these people? What do I have to lose? What are my options?

I have nothing. I am hanging by the tips of my fingernails. Day turns to night, night turns to day, and all I do is sit and crochet frantically, as long as I can ignore my arm pain. Waiting for the government to come and get me. Baba yells at me, "Well, now you've lost it. You're going nuts."

He's right. I sit here, constantly working these tiny fiddly things, day in and day out. I can't even go for a walk. I can't read, I can't listen to music, I can't watch any movies, I can't express myself in any form. I can't even wear what I want or talk to my friends, and on top of it all, there's a shortage of food. If I could describe hell, this is how it would be. Life is hell, in its hundreds of ugly manifestations. No matter where I turn, I can't seem to escape the dark cloud surrounding me. I love my country, I love my family, but this Islamic government has turned my beautiful country into a living hell.

~~~~~

Farah is dejected the entire time, and one day we sit down and talk. My voice warns me that something significant is in the works. Farah has been too quiet for too long. What is going on in her head? She opens up to me with her most cherished news.

She whispers to me furtively, "I have a secret . . ."

She glances around to make sure nobody else can hear. I've been her confidante for the longest time. I trust her and she trusts me completely.

"I'm still seeing Keyvan. Remember, his brother Hamid was murdered, and now Keyvan is in a lot of trouble; the government is looking for him, too. He has to leave. He's thinking of escaping through Zahedan. If he is successful, maybe we can follow him."

"Why don't you go with him?"

"I can't. It's too risky. Besides, he wants to make it out safely before he puts my life in danger. He said if he makes it, he'll send word; maybe he'll help you, too. Now you understand why you can't open your big mouth and ruin this? Because if he cannot leave, that means we're stuck here forever."

September 19, 1982

In the early evening, Farah suggests to Mamán, "The kids haven't been out in the longest time. Why don't you take them out to visit Khaleh Mahin? I'll stay with Sima. She needs the company."

Mamán is suspicious as to why Farah is concerned about my brothers but she intuitively understands the reason. She decides to let it slide.

In a few minutes, they are out the door. Miraculously, Farah's plan has worked. I admire her efficiency in planning. It's a weeknight. Baba is not home. Farah stays by the door as they leave and makes sure that it's not locked.

Keyvan watches from the alley as Mamán, Soraya, Cyrus, and Aria leave the house. They don't see him because he is hidden in the shadows, and besides, they wouldn't have recognized him because he looks so different.

As soon as Mamán leaves with my siblings, Keyvan sneaks into the house. Farah ushers him upstairs, into a room on the second floor that nobody ever uses. He is sitting in a room in our house with a mixture of hope and terror on his face. Keyvan looks like a member of Hezbollah: army-design cargo pants, dark, long-sleeved, buttoned shirt. He has grown a bushy, brown beard and so unlike his usual, well-groomed self, he looks messy and unkempt. "When in Rome . . ." Seeing him dressed as the enemy is surreal. It makes me anxious.

There is nothing in this room other than the colourful carpet that Keyvan is sitting on. But the room is alive with emotion. The smell of raw fear surrounds us. But there is also hope. Between Farah, standing in the corner of the room, and Keyvan, with his back against the wall, a bond based on love, anxiety, danger, and excitement is blossoming. The air quivers with their feelings. After months of wretchedness, the strong electric energy engulfs me. I can neither laugh nor cry, though I want to do both. I feel that I am on the brink of an explosion. Farah watches Keyvan, and Keyvan watches me.

I say, "I hear that you're leaving Iran. Farah hasn't stopped crying for a week now."

"Yes. There's no more future here for Farah and me. Evidently you want to come along with us? We're not going on a picnic. It's going to be tough. Are you ready?"

"I am ready. I'll do whatever it takes."

"I'll do everything to help you. Leave us alone. Farah and I might never see each other again and we need to have some private time together." Tears of joy run down my cheeks as I step into the hallway.

He commands me: "If anybody enters the house, cough so Farah can rush down. I should not be seen here by either of your parents."

I think back to a few years ago when he first arrived to rent a room. Who would have known then that this man might turn out to be my knight in shining armour? Poor Farah has suffered so much grief over him, and now he's going to be the catalyst for our escape.

This was the last time I would see Keyvan in Iran.

Farah can't disclose why she's crying. She's inconsolable and whispers quietly, "Keyvan is gone. I'm so worried. He could be killed."

"He was going to be killed anyway; at least now there is hope, and he will survive. You can't do anything now. We have to be optimistic. He is trying, and that is what matters the most."

"If he makes it out safely, he'll take me and you. It'll be a big sacrifice for us. You'll be our chaperone. We will keep the secret until we're sure he's out of danger."

Keyvan has promised her he will call as soon as he is safe. It has been at least a week that Farah has been glued to the phone, willing it to ring.

Mamán doesn't want to let her anywhere near the phone because although she has no proof, she knows what Farah is waiting for. Once Keyvan is safe, if he can't contact her by phone, he and Farah have a backup plan. He'll call a friend and send her here to tell Farah he has survived.

October 3, 1982

Khatereh drops by for a surprise visit in the evening. She is a family friend. I have told Mamán that I stayed with Khatereh when I fled to Esfahan. Mamán thanks her for giving me shelter. She's sitting with us for tea, and we're sharing the polite small talk that passes for conversation since all this began in 1979. We do not talk about politics, although we want to so badly. Does Khatereh have any news of Sheyla? I'd better not ask. My heart feels tied up in ropes. Mamán leaves the room for a brief moment to bring the tea and I see Khatereh lean in with a barely perceptible movement and breathe into Farah's ear, "Keyvan is safe."

Farah shudders with relief. Her transformation is dramatic and immediate. I've never seen such silent happiness. Colour returns to her cheeks, and joy returns to her face. She takes a deep breath and for the first time in many months, I see her smile.

From that day onward she sheds no more tears.

Farah and I contemplate leaving the country. We don't have passports; how can we leave? Our name is Goel, our aunt has been executed, we are on the blacklist, and we are Jewish. They'll find us anywhere we go. There are eyes in all the bushes; the walls have ears. Friends betraying friends . . . everyone is watching.

I'm losing my sanity. I can't do it. Show me the way, but how are we going to escape this hell?

That's enough. We deserve better than this.
Dying is better than living this way . . .
Let's get out of this hell.

October 6, 1982

The house is unusually quiet. In the garden, the chickens are squawking, the cats are meowing. I can hear my own breath. Cyrus and Aria are off at Naneh Jaan-Jaan's house playing with our cousins. Farah, Soraya, and I are the only ones left for tea after dinner. Mamán is deep in thought. She is giving birth to some extraordinary plan. She can't complete a sentence. It is as if she has a bullet stuck in her throat that she can neither swallow nor spit out. We sip our tea. The leaves in the garden rustle quietly. The stars twinkle down at us.

Mamán clears her throat. She looks around nervously, sighing deeply. "Listen carefully to me," she mutters into her teacup, "and don't answer until I'm finished." Farah and I glance at each other, then at Mamán. I am disturbed to notice the change in her face. The creases around her mouth and eyes are deeper than they were yesterday. Her eyes are watery and slightly red. A patch of white has sprouted overnight in her thick black hair. She is only thirty-eight years old but she looks like an old lady. Where did that white come from?

We don't have any idea what the future holds for us. I can't read the expression on her face. There is no sparkle, no anger, no indignation, and none of the familiar impatience.

"Farah and Sima, I love you and I would do anything for you." She pauses. "We all know that the situation in Iran is not going to change in the foreseeable future. There is no way you will be able to go to university. A life totally dependent on parents or a husband is not for you, any more than it is for me. There is no decent future for you here."

Mamán looks up at the sky, gasping for air. Then she takes several slow sips of tea.

Silence.

Farah and I are quiet. We steal looks at each other. Something important is happening. We do not want to push her. We have never seen her so choked up over words, Mamán who never lacks words, no matter the occasion. We tense up.

She studies her teacup as if she is reading tea leaves. "This is very difficult for me to say, but I'd rather you leave Iran than stay. I can't stand to see what is happening to you. Your situation is breaking my heart."

We have to lean forward to hear her. The words astonish us. They must be the most painful words she has uttered in her entire life. Her voice is full of anguish. We can't at this moment understand the strength she has shown in coming to a decision like this . . . that she would prefer us to have a full life even if it means she must let us go. The message is electric.

The silence lengthens. My heart leaps into my hand. Her words strike my ears like the plucked strings of an ancient sitar. Mamán has spoken the thoughts that Farah and I have been secretly nursing for months. She has given us beautiful freedom, the freedom to take our lives into our own hands and find a way to flee our prison. I have to hold back my tears.

"Mamán, Keyvan will be able to help us escape. We can ask his family. They know people."

Mamán has never approved of Farah's choice of a husband. Baba is furious. Keyvan had earned Mamán's complete trust.

"Yes. It will be all right, as long as the two of you go together."

We are beyond joy. We jump up and hug her, and we all cry. The tears roll down my cheeks like raindrops after a long drought on bone-dry soil. The suddenness of hope overwhelms us. We squeeze each other harder. We are oblivious at this moment to any danger. Mamán motions us to sit.

"Baba and I have not been in agreement about many things for a long time. He will try and stop you if he finds out. That is why he won't know until you are out of the country. I have some jewellery I can sell, some savings Baba doesn't know about, some debts owed to me that can be repaid. Don't worry about money. I know you are capable, but do you?"

Blood is pumping back into my body, the feeling of life that has been denied me these past months. I want to climb a mountain, scream from the summit that I'm going to be free. But I can't tell anyone. Not now. Not yet.

Farah is full of her own delight; she will be reunited with Keyvan soon. Soraya squeezes my hand. I kneel and kiss the ground, thanking God for this moment. The three of us hug each other and Mamán. We laugh and cry simultaneously. Lately Mamán has been taking fits any time she doesn't see us for five minutes. Now she's suggesting we leave the country forever. Maybe it is true that mothers *are* connected to their daughters. Maybe she reads our minds. We have never dared say anything to her about our thoughts of leaving.

Soraya sobs uncontrollably. Although happy for us, she knows the three musketeers' days are numbered in Shiraz, in this house. This is a bittersweet moment for all of us.

October 7, 1982

How are we going to collect the information from Keyvan's family and connect with the smugglers? Keyvan's parents must know. But this situation isn't one to discuss over the phone. Baba and Mamán have met Keyvan's parents and have visited them them in person; it is a matter of life and death. For our sake she will do anything.

After his son's death, Keyvan's father was willing to send Keyvan away. Keyvan told Farah before he left to contact his family for information on escaping our homeland. Keyvan's father will help us. Mamán goes alone.

Mamán reports on her visit to Keyvan's family. She sat cross-legged on a Persian carpet in Keyvan's family home having tea, where the information was exchanged that would change our lives forever. "There is a man in Zahedan who can help you. We will send a message to his family. He will call you in a couple of weeks. Be patient. In the meantime, buy American money, very carefully. Say you want to send a gift to some relative outside of Iran."

This isn't an inconceivable lie; Mamán's brother, Daii Faramarz, lives in the United States.

Mamán is in trouble with Baba. They have not talked or acknowledged each other's presence for the longest time. Baba is suspicious of us. We don't mope around the house as we used to. We are more cheerful. Mamán is silent. Baba screams, "Do not think of causing any trouble or disobeying the government or I will be the first one to report you to Hezbollah." The veins on the side of his neck bulge out in his fury. I am afraid he will have a heart attack. We can't imagine he would ever do such a thing. He would not be able to live with himself, but we do not want to take a chance. I hate it when he yells like this. I wish I were deaf so I couldn't hear his shouting. I love and hate him at the same time. By now I am an expert in living with intense emotions.

Mamán hears him and recognizes that she was right in not telling him of our collective decision. Baba must not learn of our plans. She is slowly and carefully exchanging *toomans* for American dollars, selling some of her jewellery, calling upon those who owe her money, and taking out some loans. She must keep to places she trusts, where the merchants know her. She can't do this in the evening; if Baba is home and she's not, he'll wonder where she is. Though they do not talk, he keeps track of Mamán's presence. She can't miss too much work, either, because she will be taking some days off to take us to Zahedan when the smugglers call. She buys us special new shoes for the escape.

Farah has a magnificent antique 18-karat gold braided bracelet, a gift for her fourteenth birthday from Mamán and Baba. She loves it. Mamán sells it, because it is a rare piece and she gets many times the price she paid for it. Every dollar counts. Farah is upset, but who needs a gold bracelet when you can't be free?

Mamán is highly stressed. The furtive money-changing expeditions, the selling of the jewellery, and her personal dread about the loss of her daughters take away all her energy. Will Baba find out about our secret plan?

Naneh Zivar, her mother, who has been chronically sick, takes a turn for the worse. Since Mamán is the only nurse in the family, our grandfather Baba Bozourg always calls on her when Naneh takes a bad turn. He calls in the middle of the night, on Shabbat, any time, any hour. Mamán is on duty twenty-four hours a day. Evidently, the end is near. Mamán is fighting many battles at the same time. Naneh Zivar is dying; her two daughters are leaving. Farah and I now have to face the thought that if we leave, we will never see Naneh Zivar again. We beg Mamán to give our love to our grandmother, to tell her we look forward to seeing her soon, to promise her we will try to visit if we can. Naneh Zivar knows what my life is like.

Lies from her daughters to her mother! Just one more burden she has to bear. She mutters, "I hope when the end comes, I will be in Shiraz." I don't know how she copes, but she does.

October 26, 1982

Shahram, the contact for the smuggler, calls in the evening. At last! He tells Mamán he has received our message and he will call back with information within the next few weeks.

November 7, 1982

The phone rings early in the morning. Bad news travels fast; now I am experiencing it. Naneh Zivar has passed away.

Mamán jumps out of the bed, weeping out loud. She was aware that the end was near but never thought it would be this soon. She orders Soraya and Farah to go with her to Baba Bozourg's house, to greet the visitors when they come back from the cemetery. No unmarried woman is allowed to go to the cemetery unless it is for the burial of one of her parents. It is a bad omen. Close relatives and friends help prepare the food at the shiva house, since the mourners are forbidden to work. Our role is to receive condolences from the family, friends, and guests. Soraya does an exceptional job; she is kind, quick, and gracious.

Mamán leaves early in the morning and comes home very late at night. I am lonely. It's punishing to be at home all by myself. My relatives are at the shiva. Do they miss me? They know I am at home, but pretend they don't know. If the Hezbollah informant in our neighbourhood sees me, he will report me to the Islamic guards. Fear of being spotted has paralyzed my family and me so much that I cannot go and pay my last respects to my Naneh Zivar, whom I loved. The government of Iran has made my home into my prison.

Naneh Zivar left us too early. She was only fifty-five years old. I was never that close to her. She was round as a ball. I had the reputation of managing to kick and bump into her accidentally no matter where she was sitting. She was my unintentional victim all the time.

November 30, 1982

Mamán receives a phone call this afternoon. We have been waiting impatiently for almost four weeks for this particular call. It is Shahram on the phone. No details are discussed over the phone, but we know from Keyvan's father it will cost approximately forty thousand *tooman* (US $1,000) for each of us.

Shahram says, "I will see you and your daughters in Zahedan on December fifth."

Six days' notice. Time is too short. But Mamán has been preparing for a few weeks. She is more at peace with herself now that Naneh Zivar has passed away. The timing of her death was such that I am confident that she is watching over us and will help us from the other side. Is that why Mamán's mind is more at peace?

Baba has made it clear he doesn't want to hear of anyone leaving. He cannot stand the thought of the dangers that might await anyone who tries to escape. He is not going to be told. I will not risk losing this miraculous opportunity by being talkative and letting something slip out. My lips are sealed tighter than Evin Prison's doors.

It is getting harder and harder to hide our happiness at escaping. Mamán shops and cooks. She finishes all the preparations for our departure. In the brief six days we have been given, we have to prepare ourselves emotionally for the separation: from our parents, our family, our city, from the country that has embraced my family forever.

December 2, 1982

We need to see our aunts and uncles for the last time. A dangerous undertaking, but we are compelled to take a chance. We casually drop by the homes of many of our relatives at night, when we know neighbourhood "watchers," who live next door to Naneh Jaan-Jaan, are at home in bed. In their eyes, anyone who does not like this government is a traitor. They will report that I have been seen on the street if they know, so we pull our *chadors* completely over our faces as we walk by. Who would have thought that *chadors* would be useful in our escape?

If we could tell my aunts and uncles why we are here, they would wish us "*Safar Be Kheir*" (have a great and safe trip) and bestow gifts on us. Here we are, going on the most terrifying adventure of our lives, and we can't tell anybody what we are doing or where we are going. We can't even say goodbye. Nobody can wish us *Safar Be Kheir*.

My Ammo Bashi has seen one of the needlepoints I have been working on during the many months I've been trapped at home. During my conversation with him at his house, he asks me, "Have you finished that magnificent needlepoint picture of the three horses in the field that I liked so much? I'd love to buy it from you. Would you take 10,000 *tooman*?"

I am deeply flattered and also tempted. Ten thousand *tooman* is over US $250. That kind of money could certainly come in handy. I do not want him to know I need money. Does he have some idea that we are planning to run away? Is this his way of saying he'd like to help? I am very appreciative, but know that I mustn't give him any inkling of the truth. "I'd like to keep it for myself. But you can come and look at it any time you want."

We visit Khaleh Mahin and Saltanat at Zinat's house, so we see the entire family at the same time. They are surprised to see me. Though they do not say anything, I can see they seem scared by my presence in their house and must wonder at the reason for the visit. They are not stupid. I wish I could tell them that what happened to me in the past few years is going to be over soon. This is my farewell visit. I will most likely never see them again, at least not in Iran, if I survive the escape. I wish I could ask them for forgiveness if I ever offended them. But I can't do any of that.

I ask Khaleh Mahin to give me the recipe of the rice dish she served months ago to Mamán. She beams with excitement at being asked to share her recipe. She's proud of her skills as a cook. Much explanation goes on while we all pretend to listen carefully. None of us registers any of the information, but she seems happy to be on a pedestal for a few minutes.

I think they would like to ask questions, but don't dare. They know my story, but pretend they don't know, and we pretend we don't know they know. They know about Farah and Keyvan, but they don't mention it.

They offer us tea. We drink in the garden. We make polite conversation. I can't concentrate or follow the gossip about who is doing what. I am not interested. I don't care if the price of rice in the black market is a few *tooman* up or down. To them, it is important. Right now, I have life and death issues to think about.

I will soon be leaving my lovely, poetic city. I wish I could put a little earth from my garden into a jar and take it with me, a symbol of my connection to my deep roots, as a proud Shirazi. But I cannot take anything with me. My memories are etched in the deepest part of my heart. Despite what has happened to my country, I will always remember that Iranians and Shirazis have a truly rich and beautiful culture, where poetry is not just for the poet but is part of everyone's blood.

My mind is wandering again.

Enough!

Enough is enough!

Only we know that these visits are our final farewells.

December 3, 1982, morning

It's Friday . . . our last Friday in Shiraz, in our home, in our own garden.

How life has changed over the past few years! Our garden was awash in rose bushes in red, pink, yellow, and white, with their sweet heavenly perfume, and the many petalled sour orange and apple trees. The rose bushes are now gone. Of the six sour orange trees, only two have survived the Revolution and the water shortages.

Mamán wants us to remember this day forever. She starts the day frying onions, making our favourite omelette. The smell of frying onions fills the whole house. No matter how often she prepares this dish and no matter how much she cooks, we are never satisfied. She cries the entire time she chops the onions. Are all the tears truly because of the onions? Mamán sends Cyrus off to buy fresh, hot flat bread from the bakery. He looks puzzled. Why is she insisting he go this early in the morning? Usually he goes to the bakery at lunchtime.

The tea is brewed; Mamán picks a few sour oranges from the tree and calls everyone to the last breakfast in the garden.

A blanket covers the tiled floor. On top of it she places the *sofreh* (tablecloth) where we all sit crossed-legged. Mamán divides the omelette into almost equal portions; she gives the biggest portions to Farah and me. Aria starts to whine. "Why are they getting such big portions? We're the growing ones, not them. They are already grown up." Mamán promises to give them the biggest portion the next time she makes this dish. I savour every bit. The onion omelette with sour orange juice is mouthwatering: sour, salty, and wonderfully succulent.

Every corner of this house holds a tale of my childhood. I look at Cyrus's bicycle in the corner of the garden with sadness. I would have loved to have my own bicycle. How hard I worked during my elementary school in hopes of getting a bicycle as a reward for a perfect report card!

I do not want a bicycle anymore. I just want to be free, and it will take more than a bicycle to make me free now.

Mamán calls me. She has called me a few times, and I haven't heard her. I am deep into my childhood recollections.

The apple tree is staring at me. I loved to climb this tree and to read my books. It was under this tree that my white goat was killed. When Baba had the barn in his farm filled with animals, I saw the whitest goat, with the longest hair, and fell in love with him. Baba said, "That is your goat." But one day, Baba brought him home to be killed and used as meat for stew. He told me that he had no choice. How I wept that day for my little friend! To this day, I do not like to eat goat meat . . .

Straight to the left, the pomegranate tree stands; it also has its own story. Every year in the spring, I would look at it daily, count its red blossoms, stroke their softness. I thought I was encouraging its growth but I now think I was bothering it. Last year, I saw one small pomegranate on the top of the tree where I could not reach it. It was too high for me even with a ladder. I salivated over the taste of it, but one day I saw the pomegranate become a meal for an ugly black crow. The loud, dreadful black crow that we all hated had a feast. I wished that special pomegranate had been eaten by pigeons instead. I like pigeons. The crows are nasty. They are said to be bearers of bad news.

Mamán shakes me out of my reverie. She reminds me the day will fly by, and there are too many things to be done. We each have our chores. Farah sweeps and dusts the rooms. I have to help Mamán in the kitchen; Soraya sweeps the garden. We all help hang the washing. Even though we have a dryer, Mamán likes to air-dry the laundry.

It is a good thing Baba has been at his farm these past few days. The atmosphere at home is too uncomfortable for him; no one talks much to him.

The biggest challenge today is cooking. Usually, Fridays involve an overwhelming amount of cooking, but today Mamán has to cook twice the usual amount. She also expounds feverishly as she works. She insists that Farah and I listen carefully and take note.

She soaks the basmati rice in salt water. The meat for the stews is defrosting on the table. There is a shortage of meat and chicken, and for some time we've rationed our consumption, but today Mamán is going all out. *Ghormeh sabzi* and *fesenjoon* stew, slow-cooking chicken, and some rice dishes for tomorrow are in various stages of preparation. She also prepares our favourite fish, river trout, which crackles and sizzles with oil and turmeric. There has to be enough for Baba, Soraya, and my brothers for Saturday and well into the week; and for us to take with us on the bus.

While we listen to the fish fry, she talks non-stop about traditional Iranian foods and methods of cooking; about good nutrition and proper diet.

For lunch, Naneh Jaan-Jaan brings us the hot meat patties she knows we love. She is unaware, however, that we are eating them for the last time. A week from now, even if I survive, there won't be meat patties for Friday lunch. I won't be hearing the familiar footsteps of Naneh Jaan-Jaan walking in the garden or hear her voice calling, "Come eat while they are still hot." There is no one in the world who can offer the kindness and unconditional love of my Naneh Jaan-Jaan. I wish I could tell her how much I love her. I can't. I want to scream it out loud. I want to hug and kiss her and tell her I'm sorry I have to leave, that I will miss her, that I am so grateful for her being my Naneh, my grandmother. But I can't. I choke down the feeling. Life and living just hurt too much. The meat patties stick in my throat. I can't enjoy the meat patties anymore. Tears, unbidden, roll down my cheeks.

About five months ago, during my "house arrest," Mamán brought home one stem of a purple-heart plant, some snips of wandering Jew (mother-in-law's-tongue), and a clipping of coleus with red, yellow, and green patterned leaves. The bits were placed in a jar of water. The stem of the purple-heart quickly developed roots; it became my first potted plant. Within a short time, I had twenty pots of beautiful plants.

An empty room on the second floor of our house was turned into a greenhouse of sorts. This room has plenty of natural light. The wooden bench was positioned so the sun shines directly on the flowerpots. It was important that all my plants have enough sun. I watered all the plants regularly, and turned them toward the light. These plants have been my only contact with nature over the past months.

This room is filled with love. I hope these plants will not feel that I abandoned them like a mother whom circumstances has forced to abandon her children. Soraya comes upstairs with me when we take a break from cooking. I want to show her how to take care of them. They do not need a lot of water. What they need is a daily visit. It was the loving tender care I lavished on them that helped them grow so fast. I envy them; I wish I had the same opportunity to thrive. How could one little stem of mother-in-law's-tongue turn into this beautiful garden? I touch them and apologize to them for leaving their lives.

In the way I loved my plants, Mamán has loved me unconditionally my entire life, but she can no longer give me what I need to flourish. Sometimes we must let go of the people or things we love because we love them so much that we cannot bear to see them die. To me, this is the full expression of unconditional love; I am blessed to feel it with every fibre of my being.

The day flies by. We take long, hot showers, especially Farah and me. We do not know when we will have our next ones. The smell of the food fills not only our home but wafts out into the street. There is a fantastic feast in our home tonight. Mamán always used to say that the secret ingredient in cooking is love, and the success of her cooking depends on what mood she is in. If this is true, I have never seen Mamán so emotional before today. She cried the entire day. I wonder if the food will taste as good as it smells.

December 3, 1982, 3:00 p.m.

One last thing remains to be done. Mamán waits until Cyrus and Aria take their showers. She whispers to Farah and me, "I have to show you the American dollars and the gold coins that you will be taking for the escape." Up to this moment, I knew we would be leaving very soon, but now it hits home. This is real, and we are really leaving.

It is no longer a dream.

I have never seen American currency. All I know is that it is green. Mamán pulls out a bag from the freezer and draws out a handful of paper currency. She shows it to us and counts it. I am astounded. Unlike Iranian paper currency, all the denominations are the same colour; the one-dollar bill and the one-hundred dollar bill look alike.

Mamán warns us to be careful about that. She explains that she tried to obtain mostly hundred-dollar bills, to save space. "I am going to stuff these bills into menstrual pads. You each will have to wear one until you reach Pakistan. No one must know you have money with you. I will be carrying the third maxi-pad, and will divide that money between the two of you in Zahedan. Now contain yourselves. I know you are afraid, but try your best to hide it. Act as normal as you can in front of Baba until we leave.

"I will stuff the pads and give them to you tomorrow before we leave the house. We will rest as much as we can tomorrow. It's Shabbat, and no one will think anything is different. We need to leave right after sundown."

She is out of breath. She weeps as she instructs us as to what to do.

Farah and I observe each other. The same tears welling out of my eyes are also welling out of Farah's. The floodgates have finally burst. Mamán scolds us and offers us water. She is afraid that the boys will find out. We splash water on our faces and laugh. During these past few days we move instantly from tears to laughter. I feel unstable.

December 3, 1982, 4:00 p.m.

Mamán and Baba are still not speaking to each other.

We know why she is crying, but Baba and our brothers don't.

Baba arrives home from the farm before sunset. This gives him enough time to get ready for Shabbat.

Mamán, as usual, ignores him, and he doesn't greet her. But he does call out to us, and we dash into the garden to welcome him.

"Hi, Baba."

"What are you smiling about?"

"Nothing, Baba."

"Why don't you take off your dirty clothes and I'll see that they are washed," Farah cuts in quickly. Baba looks surprised.

"I'll make you some tea. It'll be waiting when you come out of the shower." He is puzzled by our gracious welcome and frowns as he shuffles into the house.

He comes back half an hour later. Mamán watches as Farah and I give him a cup of tea. Baba looks at us, then at Mamán, then back at us.

"What's wrong with your mother these days? Her eyes are always red and she looks pale. Who is in trouble now?"

He sits cross-legged on the carpet and sips at the tea. Does he really expect us to answer? I reassure him. "No one is in trouble, Baba. Enjoy your tea."

I am furious. I cannot comprehend how he can be so oblivious to what is going on under his nose. Baba is in his own little world, and so are we. There is such tension in the air right now that I can see it. I can smell it. Its bitter taste leaves me choking. Harsh words rush to escape my lips, and I swallow them with difficulty. Inside, I am annoyed with him, but I can't show it.

It breaks my heart to know it is not Baba himself who is our enemy, but rather his fear of the Islamic government. He believes that the only way to protect us is to keep us under his wing no matter how smelly, distressing, and suffocating life is here. He prefers to ignore this atrocious odour that we know won't dissipate as he hopes. It is awful that we can't tell him our plan.

Baba muses aloud. "If you would go and get yourselves husbands, then you'd have something valuable to do in life."

His words pierce my heart like a knife. How dare he condemn us to such a life? How dare he have daughters and then absolve himself of any responsibility for their well-being? I cannot bear to listen. White-hot fury builds up behind my eyes. My internal screaming deafens me.

I am frightened. Maybe he really suspects something and is not letting on? Maybe he is weakening in his resolve to keep us under his wing? I want to tell Baba about our plan; I want to take him into my confidence. He is my father. But I can't.

Inside, I cry copious tears, endless tears. Babá can't shake the values he was taught. In his world, women are parasitic. They must rely on men for their sustenance. They cannot stand on their own two feet. The irony of his wife's self-sufficiency is lost on him. He only resents it. I want to hug him, to tell him it is not his fault that we have turned out differently than what he expected. I want to tell him that I won't be dependent on him, that I will become somebody he can respect as a human being and not "just" a woman, if I survive the coming challenge. But, no, I keep my emotions bottled up tightly inside. I want to meet him in the future as an equal, not as a subservient woman.

Mamán alone knows what a good job she has done in training us to be self-sufficient women with both traditional skills and values and a modern outlook. We simply have minds of our own.

For this night, I want everything to be pleasant. I want to cherish this last Shabbat forever.

The *ghormeh sabzi* is still simmering. Before she lights the Shabbat candles, Mamán draws Farah and me close to stand beside her. After saying the blessing in Hebrew, she makes a personal prayer, asking God to hear her and to take care of her precious daughters. More tears spill from her eyes, down her cheeks, and over her two beauty marks as she prays. With each tear she looks more like a goddess in my eyes. She must be connected to a bottomless well. How many tears can be stored inside a human being? It takes all my strength not to cry with her.

December 3, 1982, 7:00 p.m.

We gather around for dinner. Mamán's beautiful flower-patterned *sofreh* (tablecloth) is spread on the floor. We girls help to bring the food to the *sofreh* is spread. As usual, Baba recites the prayer over homemade wine and flatbread. Then he intones the prayer over the fried fish. Finally, it is time to eat the food Mamán has been preparing all day.

Mamán watches Farah and me closely, and keeps insisting we eat, eat, eat. She knows this is the best meal that we will eat for a long time. But I can't eat. I am too nervous. However, my eyes are still hungry. My eyes are bigger than my stomach tonight. I pile up a huge plate of rice and stew. Baba looks at my plate and raises his eyebrows. He knows there is no way I can eat all this. He hates when we leave food on our plates. I try to force myself to eat what is on my plate and I can't. Baba takes my plate and finishes the leftovers. "If you take a little bit of food on your plate and finish it, you can always take more. The food will not run away. What's gotten into you tonight?" I look at Mamán's plate, which is still full. Poor Mamán, she can't eat, either.

I wash all the dishes and tidy the kitchen. I clean the kitchen extra well. Soraya will have a lot of work until Mamán returns. I do not want to leave her my work. Will I have to wash as many big pots in my new home, wherever it might be?

In the bedroom that Farah, Soraya, and I share, we stay up very late, talking about our dreams and the special moments we shared. We reminisce tearfully. This is the last night I will sleep in a bed in my child-hood home, in the bed I have always slept in with my sisters. We each have our own room, but we always end up sharing this one. This bed is so soft. I'm going to remember this softness as long as I live.

December 4, 1982, 1:00 a.m.

It dawns on us now what this separation really means. We sob in each other's arms as we three musketeers spend our last hours together.

December 4, 1982, 8:00 a.m.

Mamán goes to work. She has to, to avoid raising any suspicion. Poor thing, how she can concentrate on work today?

Farah, Soraya, and I are in the garden, talking about the eruptions in our lives over the past five years. Baba, Aria, and Cyrus are getting dressed in their Shabbat suits in preparation for synagogue.

Soraya is tormented by mixed emotions. "How will I survive with-out you? I wish I could come with you. Promise me you will write?"

Farah shushes her. "Stop, don't talk about this. You know Cyrus with his antenna. He's going to detect something. If we're not careful, he'll tell Baba, and we won't be able to leave at all."

An idea occurs to me. Has Mamán spoken to Soraya about how to handle the first reactions to our absence?

"Soraya," I say, speaking of Baba, "when he notices that we are missing, do not tell him where we are until Mamán comes back. Pretend you are just as worried and you do not know where we are. Try to prevent him from going to the police to look for us. Tell him that the whole family will get into trouble if he does. You'll have to stall him as long as possible, at least a couple of days."

December 4, 1982, 10:00 a.m.

Naneh Jaan-Jaan comes over. She says, "I brought you *cholent*. Eat it soon before it goes cold."

I agonize inside. I love her so, but can't say goodbye.

"You visited your uncles. What was the occasion?"

"We hadn't seen them in the longest time. Sima hasn't been able to leave the house for months. It was getting to be too much for her. She needed to get out and socialize."

"Are you going to sit in the house your whole lives? Farah, have you given up on Keyvan? I haven't seen him around lately. You girls are so pretty. It is time you found good Jewish husbands and started to live your own lives. Wouldn't that solve the problem?"

"Naneh, whatever you say."

She isn't expecting this. "What do you mean, whatever I say?"

"We love you and we're sorry for causing you so much anguish." She shrugs her shoulders and walks away slowly. She does not know what to make of our avoiding an argument today.

This is the last time I will ever see Naneh Jaan-Jaan. I gaze at her and try to fix her image in my mind. She has always dressed modestly. She wears her long dress with many skirts, and underneath she has loose white pants, tight around the ankles. Even before the Revolution she would cover her hair with a white *rosari*. A few of her white hairs, like snow, stick out today. Whenever she washes her hair and she feels good, we are lucky to see two white braids slipping out from the *rosari* on either side of her face. She is petite, but she's a dynamo. I admire her heavily wrinkled face. To me, each line is a sign of wisdom. Even after losing her beloved daughter Ashraf, Naneh Jaan-Jaan still knows how to be the warmest, kindest person. She always says, "I had to pay a very high price to earn each of these wrinkles you see, and I'm proud of every one. One day you'll be proud of your wrinkles, too." At this moment, she is the most beautiful and honourable person I know.

As she shuffles toward the door, I see her shadow disappearing, one footstep at a time.

December 4, 1982, 1:00 p.m.

The hour of departure comes closer and closer. Time is dragging. Mamán comes home in the early afternoon. She looks as if she has been through the wringer. She can barely walk. She eats some cold rice with cold stew. Although she pretends today is no different, she insists we take a nap. She knows that is the best thing to do. Time will go faster and we all need the rest. She disappears into her room.

As much as I want to nap, I cannot. Every cell in my body is super-charged.

I am restless, itchy; hot and cold at the same time.

My mind flies back over the past thirteen months. Mamán has really been wonderful. She tried her best to fight my despair and boredom. I must have been a terrible strain on her, but she didn't let on. Where would I be today without her unconditional love and concern?

A sense of gratitude envelops my entire being, and I am thrilled to be able to experience whatever is going to happen, regardless of the outcome.

I am taking a major step to becoming the master of my fate.

Farah hasn't slept, either. We slip out of bed and decide to do something we have not done for a long time. We'll try to fill our last hours with cherished memories. We're going to play with our brothers.

Though I love both Cyrus and Aria equally, Cyrus will be more upset when he finds out that we have left. I have been tutoring him in math. He likes it when we work together. He will miss us so much.

We descend into the garden. "Can we play with you guys?"

"Are you sick or am I dreaming? You want to play with us? You're too big for our games and besides, you anti-revolutionaries don't like these things," sneers Cyrus.

"You finished analyzing? Can we play?"

We play hide-and-seek with them. Surprisingly, I can still fit into the places I used to hide in many years ago. I hide in the cellar. Cyrus and

Aria are still scared to come down here alone. They will never be able to find me. Finally, they give up, and I slowly climb back up the steep stairs. They are not happy to lose the game, not to their older sister; it is not cool at all.

"You're really a great person, Cyrus. You're really smart." I grin at him.

"You guys are weird today. What's up? Are you going to see Keyvan, Farah?"

"Keep it down!" Farah pleads. "We are in trouble even when we are kind to you."

"I'll tell Baba, I'll tell Baba!" Cyrus sings.

"Be quiet! You don't think we're in enough trouble already?"

"See?" I complain. "Even when we compliment you, you are suspicious."

Ten-year-old Aria doesn't know what to think.

December 4, 1982, 4.00 p.m.

The tension in the house is so thick that Baba would rather not be around us. He visits Naneh Jaan-Jaan often. He feels better when he doesn't have to look at us. When he is at home, he is impossible. If he sees us sitting doing our needlework, he asks why we have nothing better to do. When we say nothing or do nothing, it also irritates him. I feel I am under constant scrutiny. I have to watch my words. I can't seem to do anything right. Even my greenhouse annoys him. He shouts, "So many flowerpots in that room will cause too much humidity and ruin the room." He is right, but there is no way I am going to give up my greenhouse. This is my only connection to nature.

We count on his visit to Naneh Jaan-Jaan tonight, as usual. Everything depends on Baba following this weekly routine. If he doesn't go, my life is ashes! Finally, he peels himself out of his chair, announces that he is going to his mother's for dinner, and walks out the door. I can't contain my heart. It is soaring into the sky. Mamán serves dinner, and afterwards, when we are ready to leave, she tells Cyrus and Aria, "We are off to visit your Khaleh Mahin. You can manage by yourselves until bedtime. Girls, get dressed."

Trying to appear natural, we scatter to our rooms. I climb upstairs to visit my plants one last time. A voice in my head says, "All the events of the past year were just a preparation for this exact moment." Now I want to leave, leave everything behind, my home, my family, my city, my life . . . to start fresh somewhere in this world if I manage to stay alive.

I will be free.

I am leaving the cage created by my parents, by my city, by my country's fundamentalist laws. I will be free to listen to any kind of music, to walk in the streets alone, to talk to anyone I want to talk to, to read what I want to read, to study what I want to study, and to become whatever I want to become. I will be free, and tonight is the first step toward that goal.

Only God knows how I long to be free.

December 4, 1982, 5:00 p.m.

Mamán tousles Cyrus's and Aria's hair, kisses them lightly, and says to us, "Once in a while you girls can be affectionate with your brothers. Kiss them goodbye."

Our attempts to kiss them elicit squeals and squirming.

"Let me go," complains Cyrus, as I grab his shoulders from behind. "What is this? Family hug time?" He gropes at my *chador* and pulls it down over my face. "Leave me alone! You girls are disgusting!"

I hear Aria struggling with Farah, who is also trying to "show" her love. We giggle as we wrestle with them. Soraya tries to tickle them while we kiss them. At that moment of childish scuffle, the dark fears for tonight and the future seem to vanish.

"What brought all that on?" asks Cyrus, as we straighten our *chadors*. "Are you planning to leave Iran?" Farah and I stare at him, unmoving, as silence abruptly pervades the room. Cyrus is a perceptive person for one so young. He knows something significant is in the works.

Mamán motions to us to come. Cyrus looks at her, then at us. "What's going on? Did something happen that I should know about?"

"Nothing's wrong," she responds firmly.

Mamán tells Cyrus and Aria she'll be home soon. She's just going to take us to visit Khaleh Mahin. Baba is still at Naneh Jaan-Jaan's house next door. We are wearing long pants, long-sleeved shirts, long *manteaus*, *rosaris*, and black *chadors*. I am shaking as I hide American money and gold coins under my clothes in the maxi-pad. I had hidden things — books or pamphlets — in my clothes in the past but never money or coins. My world is turning upside-down.

I am bursting out of my skin. The entire world's eyes are on me. The Hezbollah will inevitably interrogate me to show them what I am hiding. How can I look normal when I am so electrically charged? If there is a way to get a voltage reading of my body now, I am sure it would be at a record high.

We travel lightly so as not to raise any suspicion from: the Ayatollah, my brothers, Baba, my relatives, neighbours, strangers. We say a normal goodbye to Cyrus and Aria. Cyrus is still untrusting.

"Why can't we come, too?"

"I can't walk into someone's house with five kids. Next week will be your turn."

The only way to get him off our backs is to suggest a race between him and Aria to see who the fastest runner is. This race has been run many times, but Cyrus never loses his chance to take the challenge again.

They amble off to the garden, leaving us alone.

December 4, 1982, 7:00 p.m.

I look back at the garden for the last time as I approach the door. I am leaving seventeen years of my life here, and walking into the unknown, hoping it will be better than this.

We don't take a taxi because we don't want anybody to notice we are nervous. Soraya accompanies us to the bus station. To the slaughterhouse? As we walk, I imagine that when my weight is on the left foot I am full of inspiration and hope. When my weight shifts to the right, fear, blood, and death flood my mind. The consequences of our attempt to escape, if we are caught, are chilling.

The autumn evening is dark and cool. We slowly make our way toward the station. We don't walk in a straight line. Taking the Alley of Peace and Resentment, we know it is the last time we will follow this narrow, winding pathway. These alleys always come in handy when one does not want to be followed. But tonight, this alley feels too tight. The houses are so close they almost touch each other overhead. I am going to suffocate as the walls on either side press against my body.

There are windows that open onto the alley, and we must avoid being noticed by the people who live here. I feel like a cat walking on hot bricks. I'm afraid the sound of my beating heart will wake up the neighbours. Each contraction vibrates intensely. Can't my heart beat more quietly?

Every once in a while, I squeeze one of Soraya's arms. I feel terrible for her. The three of us have been best friends our whole lives, walking side by side together all the time, and now she is walking to the bus station with us, and will return home without us.

Soraya looks at me with eyes that say, "You're going to get me out of this hellhole, too?"

Our eyes answer hers, "Don't worry, we swear—if either of us survives."

The main bus station is a gigantic rectangular space, out in the open air. The bus station is a lot more crowded since the last time I was here. It is packed with people, and there are at least ten buses parked against one side of the enormous space. In front of the buses are small, pistachio-green metal booths. The destination of each bus is indicated in the front window of the booth, and the drivers periodically shout out their destination and departure time into microphones. The air is filled with their booming voices.

The noise is deafening. People cry hysterically because their loved ones are leaving for the war; the goodbyes are long and sad. When buses arrive, disembarking passengers shout out greetings to those waiting for them, some ecstatic, some proclaiming grief, some joyful and excited. You have to howl to be heard above the din.

People make animal sacrifices right in the station to welcome back the arriving travellers, so the blood and feathers of sacrificial animals are spread thickly on the ground beside the buses. The fresh blood of a chicken drips onto the pavement. A family celebrates the safe arrival of their son from the war. This is a common tradition; people make animal sacrifices to welcome and honour their loved ones who have been gone for a long time.

Beggars congregate at Shiraz's bus stations, playing to people's superstition that if you give money to a beggar, you'll have a safe trip. One particular beggar rivets me. I hold back a scream at the sight of a man sitting on the ground, leaning against one of the booths, accompanied by a crippled child asking for money. Usually the beggars are disfigured, blind, or missing an arm or leg. But this man has a squashed face. His face is unrecognizable as a human face. He has no nose. He has no legs and only a stump of a left arm. He is blind. He is just a torso with a faceless head. Obviously he is a war victim. We have been seeing more and more of this type of terrible human tragedy. The contrast between my life this night and his life forever overwhelms me. This man is trapped in a prison from which he will never be freed. I look at Mamán. She drops coins into his dish.

The only colourful things here are the green booths and a vendor with a donkey selling Darab oranges. He shouts, *"Poorteghal Darab!"* These are grown in a village near Shiraz. Oranges are good things to take on the bus, and Darab oranges are the juiciest, sweetest, and biggest oranges in this part of the country. There are several passengers buying from him. Earlier in the day, there would have been many more vendors, but at this late hour, he is the only one.

Mamán buys two kilos of the oranges. She comments that this year, Darab's oranges are plentiful because the weather co-operated. Some years, we hardly get any crops. I do not feel like eating them, but I am happy he is selling them as we are leaving Shiraz. The oranges will be a pleasant memory, and who knows, they may come in handy.

The driver of the Zahedan bus reaches for his microphone and screams into it, "Zahedan in fifteen minutes!"

Why would anyone go to Zahedan? We avoid conversation with other travellers. We suspect that some of them may be like us, heading there on the first leg of an escape from this country. There are others, half-exhausted, who may be going to meet family or return to family in a city that isn't notable in any way, that has lousy weather, where there are no tourist attractions or important historical landmarks. Unlike Shiraz, Isfahan, and Tehran, in the history of Iran, Zahedan has never been a capital. One doesn't see Zahedan in any travel guides. No newspaper has a list of the top ten places to visit in Zahedan. The tired, worn-out look on the voyagers' faces is testament of many long years of stress and difficult living.

The travellers express raw emotions on the bus station's platform . . . howling, weeping, sobbing quietly. I am tormented by the sadness in Soraya's eyes. I wish I could take it all away. I can't. There is no other way—the only way is to leave it all behind and embrace the unknown. Soraya holds us, crying softly. We hug her for the last time and try to hold back our tears.

We try to make ourselves invisible as we approach the bus cautiously. The travellers who are moving in our direction do not have the happy, shining eyes of those who are heading to Tehran or Esfahan. The anxious-looking men and women surround our bus. They avoid any eye contact whatsoever. Or is it just our imagination?

December 4, 1982, 8:00 p.m.

Mamán pays cash for tickets for the three of us at the green metal booth, and the driver lets us on. The bus driver's dull, black eyes rake us from head to toe as we reach the top step. He is a heavy man, maybe in his fifties. He is not wearing a uniform, and because of his short sleeves, I can see a tattoo on his arm in Arabic. *Allahu Akbar.* God is great. Tattooed men are frequently ultra-fanatic fundamentalists, so we have to watch ourselves carefully. He will certainly be keeping an eye on us.

We don't have any luggage to check. Mamán has everything in her handbag, some crocheting and some snacks. The bus is spotless and modern. It is so clean that I conclude it must be very new. The upholstery is red-striped corduroy. Mamán chooses seats for us in the middle row and we sink down into their softness. There is an individual air conditioning vent above every seat, but I notice no one has dared to turn it on, despite the thick, hot, motionless atmosphere in the bus; probably for fear of breaking it.

We blend in with the rest of the passengers, all of whom speak Persian, with the exception of a few small-eyed Orientals, who are sitting in the back of the bus. The Orientals come to Iran for work, of course, but why these men are going to Zahedan is a mystery. Is there work for these people?

Snoopy people on the bus try to engage us in conversation, "Where are you going? Why? What will you do there? Who are your friends? Who are you going to see?" Everything is everyone's business. If a discussion is opened with an Iranian, especially a Shirazi, they are going to find out who your grandparents are in no time. Before you know it, they are discussing your ancestors. Everybody's a judge and everybody's on trial. To discourage this, Mamán pretends to be unfriendly. But beware of sounding too unfriendly, or they will be suspicious. It is a delicate balance. We need to avoid the other passengers. Who knows if they are to be trusted? It is difficult, but the cost of making a mistake and talking too freely can have dreadful repercussions.

December 4, 1982, 8:15 p.m.

The bus driver yells out *"ALLAHU AKBAR!"* and starts the engine.

Soraya is standing outside all by herself. Her shoulders are slumped, making her look like a shrunken doll. All I can see of her face, behind the *chador* pulled over it, are her eyes, wet with tears that glitter in the lights of the station. I don't want to think about the expression around her mouth. It would break my heart, I know. Someone has just pulled a rug out from under me, and I fall into darkness. I have left my heart with Soraya.

But I mustn't show any feeling, despite the anguish that bleeds inside me. I must look normal. I mustn't cry. This is the hardest thing I have done yet. I look at Farah and think that she also must be bleeding inside.

The Hezbollah road police make random spot checks along this route. We will be questioned about our destination and the purpose of our trip. When exactly this will happen, we do not know.

Are we going to be stopped once, twice, ten times?

How can one really prepare for this?

~~~~~~

We have our answers ready in case the Hezbollah stop us. We will say we are going to visit relatives in Zahedan for a few days. We have money rolled up in the maxi-pads we wear, as well as taped to our bellies and thighs.

If they stop our bus, the first thing they do will be to check us for gold and money. If one is only travelling within Iran, obviously there is no need for American dollars.

If they decide to do a body search, we will be found out. We will be arrested. We will be condemned. A Jewish woman with two daughters has no business travelling outside Iran. How would we explain this money? Having gold coinage on you is a crime at all times, even within the country. It is a blessing that it is harder to search women than men. Only men do the searches in the middle of the night in the wilderness. They cannot put their hands on a woman's body.

There are times when our weakness becomes our strength.

To be a woman in this country is not an advantage, but tonight it is.

To leave Shiraz, we must pass through Koran's Gate, built to bless travellers and assure them of a safe trip. It is the only entrance and exit to the city. I have passed through this gate hundreds of times; I have always thought that I would return. It has always seemed to me that the Hafez and Sa'adi mausoleums are the centre of the universe and that my children and my grandchildren would play in those parks as my grandmother, my mother, and, subsequently, I did.

I have always thought that the last time was going to be in the distant future. This time, as the bus passes through Koran's Gate, there is no turning back. I am really leaving Shiraz. My beloved homeland is nothing but a memory now. The thought of never being able to return to Shiraz terrifies me. Not until these monsters are gone. I want nothing to do with it. But I will always remain a proud Iranian and a humble Shirazi.

I vow to myself not to let the past few years blot out my vision of the real Iran. I will remember only the ancient and fascinating history of this land of my birth and childhood. I will recall only the beautiful old buildings, the rivers, the bridges, the gentle climate, and the colours of the bazaars.

The neighbourhood I grew up in, the kindness of my friends, the hospitality of the strangers, and the fact that I could ask for help even from people I never met before will remain with me forever. Little treasures that I will keep close to my heart. Every person who lived in my street was my friend, other than the heartless Hezbollah brothers. I will remember the warmth and hospitality of the people as they were before this ugly, thick, black cloud descended upon my homeland.

Outside, it is completely dark. Vague silhouettes of black mountains are carved against an even blacker sky. There is no light. Despite my fear, I wish I could scream out to the stars how happy I am and how close I am to my destiny. But I can't even say it aloud to Mamán and Farah, let alone scream it. All my emotions are trapped within my own mind. The clear weather is a lucky omen. At this point we need reassurances, even from nature, that we will be safe.

The bus driver stops after four hours at a service station to let people eat and use the bathroom. The bathrooms at these stations are never clean. Even women have to squat over a hole in the ground to do their business. There is no water at this time of the night to wash hands. I avoid using the bathroom unless it is absolutely necessary.

Typically the rest stops are where the police come around to check. Luck is on our side so far tonight. But the night is young and stretches ahead of us.

Mamán spends her time either crocheting or pretending to sleep. What is going through her mind? I can only imagine that worst-case scenarios are running through her head. Her face appears serene, however, as she sits and works on her mind-numbing, repetitive craft. Her hands, however, move more quickly than usual. She is competing with all her might to win the gold medal in Olympic crocheting. Does she think the bus will arrive faster in Zahedan if she crochets faster?

Time crawls by.

Farah and I pretend to be sleeping. Our faces are always covered.

What's waiting for me on the other side?

Will there be another side?

Will I live?

Will I be raped?

Will I be tortured?

Will I ever see my family again?

I call upon a prayer that Mamán taught me, invoking the help of Jewish holy men. *Ya Elhade Rabi Meir Ba'la'ness, Ya Elhade Rabi Meir Ba'la'ness.* It has always worked in the past and I have complete faith it will work this time, too.

We pull into the second service station. Hezbollah police stand around in their cargo pants with machine guns slung over their shoulders. We climb out of the bus under their watchful eyes. A young, shabbily dressed man with a heavy dark brown beard catches their attention.

"Where the hell do you think you're going?" They pull him over, roughly, to the side of the bus and start questioning him rudely.

"What are you doing, you stupid donkey?"

"Give me your bag, you coward."

We move quickly into the building. This kind of behaviour by Hezbollah is completely normal to us by now. Everyone pretends nothing is happening. We ignore both the police and the unfortunate victim of their attention. The Islamic government has trained us to save our own skin and only our own skin. I am terribly sad and infuriated to witness this cruelty. I wish I could scream in the Hezbollah's ears and ask him how heaven couild be guarded by a filthy, nasty egomaniac like you? But if I treat him as he treats others, I would be just like him. And that I won't do.

When we return to the bus and the driver calls out his *"Allahu Akbar,"* the young man's seat is empty.

We pretend to sleep. I guess I really did sleep a little. Later, I am jolted awake as the bus stops without warning. Two motorcycles pull up beside it. One inspector, a man in Hezbollah uniform with dirty hair, bushy, black beard, Uzi slung across his shoulders, marches onto the bus. He stomps down the aisle. The sound of his boots hitting the floor reverberates in my ear. He stops at every seat. We pretend to sleep. I hope he won't try to wake us up. He rudely questions every child, man, and woman. The passengers' voices shake as they answer. He finally stomps over to where Farah and I are scrunched down in our seats, trembling like leaves.

"Where are you going?" he barks at Mamán. "Who are these sleeping women? Does your husband know you are gone?"

He shouts in our faces to wake us up. He orders us to follow him off the bus for a body inspection. He is convinced he has caught criminals in action. I pretend I am deep in sleep; he reaches his dirty, bloodstained hand toward me to shake me awake.

The bus passes over a bump. It jolts me out of this so-realistic nightmare; I am drenched in cold sweat. Luckily, I don't scream. Mamán feels me jump and stares at me wide-eyed. It isn't at all unusual for me to wake up in a cold sweat from nightmares. We have heard horror stories about the dreadful things that happen to travellers. We are lucky nothing worse happens to us.

As the sun rises, I begin to see the desert around me. The barren sand stretches on as far as the eye can see under the cloudless sky. There are no rivers, no lakes. There are no shrubs, no trees . . . no plants. Nothing is moving out there. Even the occasional houses look different; they are just shacks made of metal or mud, with no ornamentation. The entire scene is dirty beige and grey.

There is no life.

How can someone live out here?

December 5, 1982, 6:00 a.m.

The bus stops again, this time for morning prayers. All passengers leave the bus. The men and women move into separate groups a short distance from the bus. They stand to say their morning prayers in the sand at the side of the road. Normally before prayers one has to wash hands and feet in a prescribed sequence, but travellers are exempted. They go through the motions of washing, but without water. They spread their oval prayer rugs on the sand, all bending and bowing. For our safety on this voyage, we ought to pretend to follow the rituals and try not to draw attention to the fact that we are Jewish, but we don't. Is this stupid of us? Are we going to have to pay for this?

The Muslim prayer ceremony and Muslim prayers were obligatory at school. I hated so much that I was forced to learn them. I only pretended to pray when I was in Esfahan. I will pray the way I want, not the way I am told.

Are these people really pretending or are they sincere? Are they compelled by fear of human retribution to do this? How can they justify in their minds obeisance to God, and then go off to murder people?

Mamán, Farah, and I quietly recite our morning prayer in Hebrew, while we pretend to be sleeping in the bus. We do not need to put on a show. Prayer is a personal matter and not a matter of public display.

When the prayers are over, the passengers climb back in and start off again. The bus driver shouts out *"Allahu Akbar!"* again. I wonder if he really means it, or if it is part of his job description. Then I remember his tattoo and shudder.

December 5, 1982, 11:30 a.m.

Finally, "We are arriving in Zahedan. Everybody awake! Collect all your belongings; make sure nothing is left behind!"

As we pull into the station, *"Allahu Akbar!"*

At last we arrive at our stop in Zahedan. The bus station here is much smaller. There are only two buses parked on the pavement by the station. With turtle-like speed, our fellow passengers disembark.

We clamber out.

Next to us, the passengers shuffle into the station as though they are sleepwalking.

The men here look shorter and broader, with rounder faces. A few women are moving about in black *chadors* that completely cover their faces. There are many, many beggars. Mamán slips one unfortunate soul some money for good luck, but that doesn't stop the others from gathering around us. In the corner, a mother sits with her baby. The baby has flies all over her face; the mother's face is wrapped in a *hijab*. She begs. They are so poor. My heart breaks to see the baby's face as a feast for flies.

December 5, 1982, 12:30 p.m.

The one other bus that was at the station when we arrived eventually pulls out. Now it is quiet.

Time plods onward; my heart is racing faster than usual. My breathing is too fast. I am hyperventilating. My mouth is dry.

No one comes for us.

Is this a hoax?

We know that we can't go back.

Are we doomed?

December 5, 1982, 1:30 p.m.

Time is moving on at a brutally slow pace. Seconds feel like hours. I glance surreptitiously at my watch.

The minutes creep on.

The sun beats down on us relentlessly.

It is a sauna under my *chador*.

I am being steam-roasted to death under the blackness of the *hijab*.

It takes all my strength just to stay upright.

At last we see a tall, thin man walking toward us.

He is supposed to meet two young girls and their mother at the time of our arrival by bus, but he is two hours late.

I am mad. I have plenty of complaints for him. "Why are you so late? Don't you know we are in danger?" This is not a good start.

He has thick, curly black hair and small, dark eyes. He comes directly toward us, as if he knows us, and says, without an apology for his lateness, "You are Parisa?"

Mamán nods.

"I am Shahram, the one you spoke to on the phone. Follow me." He leads us out of the station, flagging down an old broken-down cab.

I am scared I will faint from the tension in this taxi. Shahram gives the driver an address. We pile in.

From the cab window, I see people in the streets. They are different from the people on the streets of Shiraz. The women wear long, colourless dresses of heavy cotton with head coverings that show only their eyes. The men wear long-sleeved tunics, in shades of tan and brown, over baggy pants tied at the ankles, and patterned headscarves on top of their heads, which can be opened and wrapped around the ears and neck as needed.

Their faces are darker and rounder than Shirazi faces, and their eyes are not almond-shaped, like ours, but round. It is not hard to pick out the Hezbollah with their cargo pants and the rifles slung over their shoulders. There are many of them in plain view. Zahedan is a centre for human smuggling and fugitive counter-revolutionaries, and they know it.

The weather is strange. It is very hot, but terribly dry. In a few hours, I imagine that the skin on my face is going to split and peel off like the skin of a snake.

After a fifteen-minute taxi ride, expecting the taxi to fall apart momentarily and leave us in the pathway of the other decrepit old cars rattling behind us, we finally arrive at our destination. Gratefully, we tumble out and wait on the side until Shahram pays the driver.

We follow Shahram through a door into the courtyard of a sand-coloured clay house. It was probably a private house at one time. The broken doorknob recounts a story of long use. A common toilet is at the bottom of the garden. Shahram explains that most of the rooms are rented to permanent residents, but there are some rooms that the smugglers use as "safe houses," to lodge their clients until they start their journey.

It is a family business, and only people who know the family can rent there. Apparently no one has asked questions about the changing occupants of the smugglers' rooms. In Zahedan, it seems, as in Shiraz, people have learned not to ask any questions. Even we three Shirazis manage to keep our millions of questions to ourselves.

Shahram leads us to a room, unlocks the door for us. He pours his heart out. "I am Keyvan's friend. I lived in Pakistan for the last year, but I ran out of money. That is why I came back two weeks ago. I am from Zahedan. Our house is in a village about two hours from here. My mother sold all her jewellery to pay for my return to Pakistan. I do not want to stay in Pakistan. This time, with this money, I will leave Pakistan."

Farah utters the words, "Thank you for taking us back with you. How is Keyvan?"

"I met him in Rawalpindi. He came back with me to Quetta three weeks ago. I walked back to Iran with the smugglers. He is the one who convinced me to come back. He is right; there is nothing to do here. This country is hell. Keyvan is waiting for you in Quetta.

"I can't say more than this. It is better the smugglers do not find out I know Keyvan or you. I will tell you the reason later. Stay here and await further instructions."

Other than the people on the way from the bus station to the house, we don't see anyone else. We will never know how people here really live. It's probably best that faces not be seen and that comings and goings not be noticed. Shahram instructs us not to attract attention to ourselves in any way. We shouldn't go outside. We shouldn't make noise.

When Mamán demands how long it will be or whether we can go out to buy food, Shahram answers, "Do not leave this room. Your meals will be taken care of. Someone will bring you food. I will come back to see you as soon as I have more information." He walks out and slams the door. We stare at each other, startled. What happened to proper manners men show to women? It seems that manners are a rare commodity these days.

Even the room is inhospitable, with nothing in it except a futon mattress and a folded blanket on the floor. The windows are covered with blinds so nobody can see in or out. There are none of the colourful carpets I have seen in almost every home all my life. There are no pictures on the walls, except the picture of Ayatollah Khomeini staring sternly down at us. I am haunted by him. This room is intended for survival only.

Nothing more.

I feel raw. I don't feel real. I am trapped at the edge of the world, where the refinements of humanity don't seem to exist. There is only bleakness, indifference, hardship, hunger. Is this where my life is going to end?

Shahram left without giving us any indication of when he would be back. Do we have to wait here another few weeks like we did in Shiraz? Will he be back in an hour, a day, a week, a month? What is his role in all this? Who *is* this mysterious man?

December 5, 1982, 3:30 p.m.

There's a knock at the door, and a woman in her mid-forties, short, pretty, of medium stature, enters. She introduces herself as Maryam Khanoom. She offers us a tray of black Iranian tea. She apologizes for the lack of sugar cubes. It is war and there are shortages of all kinds of food. This we know too well.

"I know why you're here. I won't let you starve. I'll try to sneak you some food from our family's rations."

Maryam Khanoom is the only one aware of our presence. She returns some time later with a vegetarian meal for supper. We thank her profusely. Mamán slips some money into her hand, which she doesn't reject. She looks back at Mamán and thanks her as she exits.

My first sortie to the bathroom has me rushing back, chilled to the bone. The temperature in a desert climate drops radically at night. I have never experienced such a severe change of temperature in such a short time. We put our *manteaus* on, then our *chadors*, and then we pull the single blanket over us. So hot by day and so cold at night! How can this still be Iran?

December 6, 1982, 6:30 p.m.

We are waiting.

And waiting.

And waiting some more.

I rush to finish crocheting the dark blue scarf I will use for the journey. Mamán is crocheting obsessively as well. As soon as she sees me finish my scarf, she hands me the yarn to start on the sleeve of the sweater she is working on. We will soon finish crocheting the sweaters for all the family. We will run out of yarn. We are racing against time. For some strange reason, we all seem to believe the faster we crochet, the faster the time will pass and the faster the smugglers will come for us.

We are at their mercy.

Shahram barges into the room without knocking, followed by another man. This new, unknown man doesn't introduce himself. He has a swarthy complexion and speaks no Persian whatsoever. He looks like a clown, compared to the elegant Shahram, who acts as translator. Mamán asks immediately, "When are you going to take them?"

Beady Eyes mutters something in Urdu, and Shahram responds, "We're waiting for an answer about the road, so as soon as we can, we'll come get them."

"How much is this going to cost?"

"One thousand American dollars per girl."

"How are you going to take them there?"

"They'll have to walk about twenty minutes and there will be a car waiting to bring them to Pakistan."

"When do you need the money?"

"Right away."

"I'll give you half right before you leave Zahedan with them. The other half I will send to Keyvan. You will be paid in full when they are safe in Quetta."

"Just wait. We'll let you know."

They disappear, slamming the door behind them again.

By now, we are used to their rudeness. Nothing surprises us.

Mamán is sending her two daughters off into the wilderness. Under such circumstances, what could a mother say to her daughters? She won't even be able to get our bodies back if we die. If anything goes wrong with us, Baba . . . oh, dear. She would be better off killing herself.

We spend two very difficult nights here, shut off in this featureless room. These are our last hours together, our last days in our country where my ancestors have lived for at least 2,500 years. This is where my roots have been forever.

Soon I will be leaving it all behind me like a faraway shadow.

I am going to a place where, if I am lucky and survive, I will be looked upon as a stranger.

A newcomer.

Just like those Afghanis who migrated to Iran. Will I be treated the same way the Afghanis are treated in Iran?

How dreadful.

Now I will be the recipient of all the awful stares.

I fear what lies ahead.

Mamán is putting a guilt trip on us all the while. She is torn between contradictory emotions. "You see what you've done? Sima, you should have kept your mouth shut. Farah, you had to go and get involved with Keyvan. Everything you two have done has made my life harder. I pray for you. As soon as you leave I'm going to fast until I hear that you're safe."

We are all worried about Soraya and how she is managing with Baba. Can she stall Baba long enough? We cannot call home; there is no way to find out.

We just pray and hope; hope and pray.

We also have to be extremely tolerant with the smugglers. They don't seem to feel any urgency. They don't know Mamán has to go back to Shiraz soon. Would they care if they knew? Would it make any difference? Rushing them would be futile. We want to leave under the safest circumstances.

The three of us are a blubbering heap on the futon. Exhausted from the fighting, crying, and mental stress, we all collapse into fitful dreams.

I am living in a beautiful city wearing a skirt and short-sleeved top instead of the suffocating *hijab* and *chador*. I can listen to classical music. I can read the books I want. I am continuing my studies. I love this place. Farah is happy with Keyvan and she also is going to school.

We wake up too early in the morning.

I remember last night's dream.

How will we pass the time today?

Farah and I try to recall our most recent trips, our happy family gatherings. We laugh and cry. Mamán listens carefully.

We remember the Ali Sadr cave. We remember the walnut tree with Cyrus and Aria. That day, we were their heroes. They proudly showed their treasure of 150 walnuts to all their friends and family members. They boasted about their sisters who brought down the nuts by throwing stones at them. We talk about our visit to Sarah bet Asher's grave, and dancing and singing the night away.

Our lives have changed so radically.

I will never find out what happened to Sheyla.

We eagerly wait to leave our beloved homeland. What's wrong with us?

What can we say to Mamán? We don't even want to think about all the things that might go wrong, but if they go right, the reward of freedom is delicious. Fear and excitement, a confusing, exhausting mix of emotions, have us in their grip.

I am glad I am not in Mamán's head right now.

If anything happens to us, she won't be able to live with herself.

Into the Desert

You were born with potential.
You were born with goodness and trust.
You were born with ideals and dreams.
You were born with greatness.
You were born with wings.
You are not meant for crawling, so don't.
You have wings. Learn to use them and fly!

Rumi

December 7, 1982, 4:00 p.m.

Three long days have passed since we left Shiraz.

Shahram knocks at the door. "May I come in?"

Mamán responds. "Yes."

Shahram shuffles in slowly, keeping his eyes glued to the floor. He fidgets and can't stand still. This is not the same man that we met at the bus station. Why such a difference in behaviour? Is he afraid of something?

"I need to ask a favour from your daughters. I have two thousand dollars from my mother. She sold all her jewellery and cashed all her life savings to put together this much money. She wants me to use this for leaving Pakistan. Could you please keep my money until we are in Quetta? Do not mention anything about it to the smugglers. It is our secret."

He furtively hands us the two thousand dollars. "Please hide it well."

He leaves immediately afterwards, as though he has relieved himself of a heavy burden and needs to celebrate his victory.

A few hours later, Shahram barges into our room with two men. This time, his demeanour is like his usual self. He translates furiously from Persian to Urdu in the presence of Beady Eyes from last night, and an unappealing tall man. He is slim; nothing in his face or body is in proportion. His nose is too big for his small face and his lips are too small, and he speaks so softly I can barely hear him. It is ironic that neither of them introduces this new man. We don't ask. We have quickly learned to limit our questions to the absolute minimum.

"Are you taking my daughters tonight?"

Beady Eyes looks at Shahram for translation and mumbles in Urdu, "Only after we are paid. We will let you know when we will leave."

Mamán anticipated this and she has counted the money many times. She reaches in her bag and hands the one thousand American dollars to Beady Eyes, her hands shaking and the sweat dripping down her forehead. She is under the impression that he is in charge of the escape. He grabs the money out of Mamán's hand so fast that he almost drops the stack of hundred-dollar bills on the floor.

Squashed Nose's eyes light up as Beady Eyes greedily counts the money. They both must feel extremely wealthy with this much money for a few hours of work. We are excited, too. We are able to buy our way to freedom. There is a price for everything and freedom for us is now priceless.

I had never seen someone counting money so eagerly. Beady Eyes hands the money to Squashed Nose to count it again, to make sure it is the right amount. They whisper among themselves. Shahram translates, "We have to leave now. Now!"

Mamán escorts us out of the room into the garden. I have been waiting for this moment for the past many weeks and now it is finally here. Mamán embraces us for the last time, praying silently over us. The men stand impatiently in the doorway. We rush out and over to the door. Mamán cries quietly. She looks so sad. I can't bear to look at her.

Before we part, Mamán wraps the blue scarf I crocheted in Zahedan around my head and says, "Don't touch drugs! Stay away from alcohol! Study! That is your passport to the world. Become a somebody! Stay alive! We will meet soon. May God keep you safe."

If I stay another minute I won't be able to leave. My heart is clenched in my hand as I look at Mamán one last time. I may never see her again. The terrified look in her eyes affirms that she is as torn as we are. It is too late to change our minds. The only way to leave now is to go forward. There is no going back.

She kisses Farah goodbye, prays over her, and whispers a few things I am not supposed to hear. We leave the house, accompanying Beady Eyes and Squashed Nose, who are taking us across the Pakistani border to the nearest city, Quetta. No one notices us as we slip out of the courtyard into the street. We wear our *hijabs* over long-sleeved shirts and pants. We carry nothing. We have no identification or objects in pockets or clothing apart from the concealed money. No one can trace us if we are caught. If anyone asks, we are girls with no parents, like bushes growing along the side of the road. If we are caught, we won't reveal where we came from because the government will punish any accomplices, including our parents.

As we leave the house, Shahram follows us. He mumbles to us that he is going along with us as a translator to Quetta, since the two men cannot speak Persian. How thoughtful of the smugglers to have a translator for us.

Shahram warned us before we left the house to keep absolutely quiet for fear that people in the houses around us would hear our voices. We are not to say a single word. The smugglers tell us to keep our eyes on the ground at all times. They will answer for us, as if they are our older brothers who are responsible for our well-being. It is very dark. It is the two of us and the three men, Shahram, Beady Eyes and Squashed Nose.

They do not want anyone to know we are here. It should be as if we never walked over this terrain. We are silent lest we are seen or heard by people inside or around the next turn. At every corner, we expect the waiting car.

Nobody lurks in the alleys, which are connected to each other by stairs. We walk up crackling wooden stairs, down broken stairs; up old, slippery stone stairs, down old stone stairs. One alley leads into the next via more stairs and passageways lined with one-storey houses. This must be the poor part of the city, since there is not much design to the houses. The stink of urine is impossible to ignore, as the dark, isolated alleys are used as substitute urinals. I am too afraid to make any noise as I walk. To bump into boxes of garbage or to crunch over the garbage will have disastrous consequences. A tape runs over and over in my head, "You will never see Mamán again."

It is too quiet outside my head. Inside, my voice yells at me, *How stupid of you to think these men will bring you to Quetta without harming you!* My heart challenges my brain. They are both deafening, wanting all my attention. My heart pounds faster than a jackhammer, and my head whirls with worst-case scenarios. I do not want to listen to my voice anymore. *Enough!* I resort to chanting my prayer in my head. Now I can hear the barking of wild dogs in the distance and bleak, dismal night sounds. The alleys have given way to stony paths that lead toward a new kind of darkness. There are no lights ahead. We keep walking.

Will I ever be able to forget tonight if I survive? The walk and the darkness are imprinting themselves on my psyche, step by torturous step, the inky blackness seeping into my soul. For a chatterbox like me, keeping silent is its own hell. In the desert, sounds travel much farther than in the city. The two men whisper. We don't understand the foreign sounds. I can smell danger. Beady Eyes glances toward us, and the look on his face is very revealing. "I've got you. Now you are at my mercy: you have no way out and there is nothing you can do."

We reach the point where we are willing to break the silence to ask the smugglers about our transport. A twenty-minute walk has already turned into a three-hour hike through an unknown darkness. The town is far behind us now, and we can see no sign of roads or headlights. There is no car. I grow more and more anxious. We are in the middle of the wilderness. The city's flickering lights look so far away. No one is here other than the five of us in the middle of nowhere. No reason to keep my mouth shut. I can't be quiet anymore, but I am. The words stick in my throat, frightened to come out. "How much more do we have to walk?"

"Patience," the two men chide, through the voice of the translator. "There's been a slight change of plans."

"What is the plan now?" demands Farah.

"Where is this car?" I ask.

"There will no car tonight. The car broke down."

A few minutes later, Shahram drops back to talk to us. He tells us its owner was stopped by the Hezbollah on his way to our pickup point. Fearful of the consequences if he was discovered, he decided he wasn't going to drive tonight.

"We're getting in trouble for you. Just walk. The faster you walk, the faster we get there."

Shahram whispers furiously that it is even more important now that we not talk.

This is not encouraging news for us. Not only are we trying to escape illegally, we now have the added risk of a possible informer. Terrible scenarios run through my head at the speed of light, from bad to worse to completely unbearable. What other revelation is in store for us tonight? I am prepared for any surprise.

I almost forget to keep walking. I glance at Farah. She tries to reassure me. "Don't worry, Sima. They will be bad enemies to make at this point. We need them, remember. Let's walk faster."

Beady Eyes insists that the faster we move, the less chance there is of discovery. We have no choice but to continue.

The desert's cold breeze pierces through my skin and bones. We are not dressed for this weather. The wind blows tirelessly at our faces. As hours pass we grow impatient and tired.

Well into the night, we ask how much longer we will be forced to walk. Squashed Nose responds, "Do you see the next mountain? That's where it is."

I have never been so eager to reach the next mountain, and the next and the next and the next.

We will never make it. There is no end in sight.

～～～～

We've been walking in the darkness of Zahedan to the Kavir-e Loot Desert—Desert of the Pirates—for many hours. Every muscle in my body is aching. My sister walks beside me, silent. I glance cautiously at Farah, but she is lost in concentration. I watch as she fights to keep moving. With every step, each foot sinks ankle-deep into the cold, smooth sand. Did someone grind up this sand to make it so smooth? As she pulls her foot out, sand pours off the toe and out of the top, while the other foot disappears into the sand.

Every step we take deeper into the desert is a struggle.

The cold desert wind blows sand in our faces. Hundreds of tiny particles pierce my face like sharp needles. I can't close my eyes, but I can't keep them open, either. Walking is a nightmare under these conditions.

I beg the two men to give us a short break so we can rest. They agree to five minutes. That is all. I lie down on the sand. For the first time in my life I have realized that sleeping on sand is comfortable. I sleep deeply. A kick on the foot is my warning to stand up and keep moving. An animal would be better treated than this.

We are reminded by both men, "Time is of the essence. We have to reach a particular spot by sunrise."

Beady Eyes looks at us scornfully, then at our fancy new shoes, and comments, "No! We must go faster!"

He points at my feet. "Take them off. It's easier to walk."

Over my dead body, I think.

"I don't want to remove my shoes. I am worried that my feet will get cut."

He laughs, shrugs his shoulders, and whispers to his friend, "City girls!"

Shahram, who is walking ahead with them, also laughs. He is barefoot.

The sand rubs against the money hidden in the bottom of my socks. I'm afraid that all that will be left for my future life will be shredded, sweaty, sand-rubbed bits of the paper American money Mamán hid in the brand-new soccer cleats. She thought she was smart because they had no treads, so the sand couldn't stick there. But because of the cleats they plunge even deeper into the sand, which pours over the top and into the shoe. I don't care. There is no way I'm going to confess to the smugglers why I can't remove my shoes.

Suddenly, Squashed Nose sternly commands us to lie down flat on the bottom of a sand dune and be silent. Thank God the desert has valleys marching up and down its breadth. There are small trees scattered about, but the trees are too sparse and even when we find them, they are too small to be used as hiding places. I have to lie as flat as possible with my face to the sand and hope I will be not noticed.

Muscles tensed and hearts pounding, we obey. Lying there terrified, my body pressed tightly into the side of a sand dune, I hear the faint sound of voices ahead.

"*Allahu Akbar, Allahu Akbar.*" Muslims. We can hear murmurs from far off. I remain motionless as a group of about twenty young men move in our direction. They are quite visible under the full moon. They move slowly past, within twenty feet of us, shouting slogans and chanting. They have long beards and mud-coloured clothing. The shabby, bearded image fits perfectly with what is becoming more and more common in Iran. They are so absorbed in their singing that they don't see us.

My most fundamental need, my breath, is almost taken away from me. How can I breathe less when I am so anxious? I am frozen with both fear and fatigue. I can't move any longer. I never thought I would die in the middle of the desert. Poor Mamán! How is she going to collect my corpse? Whom could she go to? Where is Farah? Will she be taken away while I have my head in the sand? We lie still for an interminable half-hour, silent, barely breathing, as the men disappear into the desert.

A jolt in the foot. Ouch! Can't he be a bit more civilized? The smugglers are back. No finesse here.

"Get up."

As I struggle to rise, Farah scrambles to her feet. We run to each other.

We start marching again. Squashed Nose explains, "The men who passed us are Afghanis leaving their homeland. They are on their way to Zahedan to start a new life."

How ironic that our paths should cross tonight. The route we take passes the borders of three countries: Iran, Afghanistan, and Pakistan. Right now, the desert is a crossroads for people trying to escape to a better world. These young men approach Iran looking forward to the very lifestyle we are fleeing from. They sing to warn other travellers that they are good Shiites. If they had seen us, they would have captured us and brought us back with them as trophies for the Hezbollah. I do not want to even think about what would have been the next scenario.

Now as we walk, we strain to hear sounds that will warn us of another encounter with Afghanis. The undisturbed, comforting roar of the wind is a blessing. The pain of our bodies fades into the background, but pain is not a problem. Discovery is now our biggest concern. "We have escaped once, but this could happen again," Shahram warns us.

We are on edge for the rest of the night, straining to hear sounds that will warn us of the Afghanis. We are forced to hide several times. Thank God for the sand hills. I never thought the sand hills could become my protector from the friends of my enemy, the Afghanis on their way to Iran. The mountains are no closer now than they were when we set out at nightfall from Zahedan.

I nudge Shahram: "How long before we meet the transport?"

"That mountain," and he points vaguely into the distance east of us. I am not convinced.

"Which mountain?"

"Third one."

"How far to walk?"

"A few hours. Enough talk!"

Where is Mamán now? How is Soraya dealing with Baba's reaction to our absence? Regardless of the outcome, I am walking toward my destiny. Whatever will be will be. All I can do at this point is to make sure one foot moves in front of the next foot just like a robot. Stop thinking; just walk.

What might have been a challenging, personal pilgrimage toward happiness and freedom becomes a gut-wrenching ordeal.

A few hours?

A lifetime?

I have no idea where we are or if we are ever going to arrive somewhere else. I suspect the smugglers think we might have changed our minds if we had known the truth. That is fine. They don't know how desperate we are to leave.

The affirmations repeat in my head. I will walk as long as it takes. I will get there or I will die. As long as I move in that direction I will eventually get there. What does a day, two days, or even a week mean to me now? I wasted the entire year just running from one house to the next. Now I am actually running from the whole country in the hope that one day, somewhere in the world, I will find a place that I can call my home with pride. There is nothing else to be distracted by.

Glory will come to those who work toward realizing their dream.

Every fibre of my being is working to make this dream come true.

The desert is suffocating, so intrusive on my consciousness, so demanding on my physical strength, that merely surviving each step seems to be the main reason to keep going. We follow these two strangers without question. My optimism convinces me. Hope is the only weapon we have at our disposal.

I must believe that this will turn out all right.

Giving up is not an option.

Going home is not an option.

I will die before going back to that miserable life that was forced upon me.

Each hour feels like a year, each minute as long as a week. The night drags on and on. Is it ever going to end?

The sun refuses to rise.

Will I ever see it rise again? I repeat to myself the mantra, "*Payane shabe siah sefid ast.*" (The end of the long, dark night promises the brightness of the sunrise.)

In every direction rise the sharp, forbidding peaks of black mountains, watching us like hideous monsters as we walk in the night. Even the full moon cannot cast any light on these featureless black slopes. The shadows they cast are just as black, shadows reaching out toward us, ready to swallow us into their depths.

I thought I loved mountains. In Shiraz, mountains were green and friendly, with vibrant flowers growing wild in the meadows, an occasional sparkle from a small stream cascading down a rock face or through the grass. We would sit under the trees and talk about life, a good life, a life of freedom. Mountains then were my friends. But these mountains are frightening. There is no sign of life. They are always on the horizon. They watch us and follow us, and there is no way to escape from them.

The wind hisses around my ears . . . it is in my ears. There is also an echo of wind from the mountains, and the sound of wind crossing the sand, and all these winds roar in my ears, a noisy constant and irritating roar. I try pressing my hands over my ears to block out the sound. Then I am forced to listen to the thoughts in my head, forcing me to feel desperation, forcing me to think we have made a serious mistake, drowning my hopes and draining my spirit. I remove my hands. The wind seems more of a welcome distraction, now; better than living inside my head.

The sand pierces my face like sharp needles. I am afraid I will have cuts on my face from sand shrapnel. I wrap my blue scarf tightly around my face, but the sand still blows into my eyes. I can't cover my eyes. I need them open to see where I am going. Every fibre of my being is being abused and tested to its limit tonight.

Now my attention is grabbed by a new sound, very faint. What . . .? The smugglers and Shahram have noticed it, too. They whisper together. We keep moving and searching for places to hide. The noise seems to grow louder as we walk, breaking through and replacing the sound of the wind, but I still can't make out what it is. We walk some more. The echo gradually becomes louder, but it takes forever before I recognize human voices. I'm in terror that the sound has reached us from so far away.

The smugglers, alarmed, turn back toward Farah and me.

"Stop! Lie on the sand. There's a hollow over there; see there, the shadow under the dune. You!" He points at me, "Go over there. Don't make any noise! Wait till I come get you!" I rush over to the place Squashed Nose points out and bury myself into the shadowy sand. I hear more instructions, but don't dare lift my head.

I wait.

It is quiet except for the voices, which grow ever louder. I close my eyes. I now hear shouting. *"Allahu Akbar!"* Not again. I am shaking. With my eyes closed, I feel I'm back in Shiraz, at one of the Friday lunch prayers. It sounds like the crowds of fundamentalists who gather in the public squares to hear a speech by one of the imams. There may be dozens, or hundreds, or thousands. I can't tell.

What on earth is going on? Is someone shooting a movie out here? Is it an invading army?

A group of a dozen bearded men move across my line of vision, maybe a few metres from where I am lying motionless. They certainly sound much louder than a dozen men. Do they have microphones with them? The desert makes twenty men sound like thousands. The desert is their microphone. The irony is that we are both running away. We have to be as quiet as possible and they as loud as possible. The desert hosts both of us with indifference.

They are so close I can smell the sweat of their bodies. I close my eyes again. I don't want to watch. I don't know where Farah and the others are hidden. If one of us is discovered, then we are all doomed. What if they find only Farah and take her away? I might never see her again. How can I continue without her? I burrow deeper in the sand and wait.

Sweat is pouring off me, drenching my clothing.

I am hot.

I am freezing.

I open my eyes.

I am afraid to move.

I am drooling into the sand.

Is there still enough water left in my body that I can spare so much?

It feels as though I have been waiting here all my life. The Afghanis and their chanting disappear. Beady Eyes stands over me, shaking my legs hard. As we rise from the sand again, we feel the tension and the stress more deeply.

"Get up," he commands. "We're moving."

I push myself up; Farah struggles to get up as well. She has tears in her eyes. "More wasted water, we can't afford it."

Fear is my constant companion. Waves of sheer horror wash over me. At these times I resort to prayer. Mamán had taught us, "When you can do nothing more to help yourself, then that is when you must pray. Pray. Pray."

I pray. I pray with all my might. I ask God to perform a miracle, like the many He performed for our Israelite ancestors as they were escaping slavery and were in the wilderness, on their way to freedom and a new life.

I have a sudden revelation of the profound meaning of that story.

I ask God passionately to bring Farah and me safely to a good land I have never seen.

I promise I will do everything I can to be a decent person, if only He will take pity on us.

I am crying silently.

For the first time in my life, hiding in that moon-drenched desert, I have the feeling that someone is listening.

I glance up at the sky. I am grateful for the full moon, a sign of good luck. I will hang on, no matter what. There is no other option. Walking is the only option.

As the night wears on, my feet hurt more and more. Despite the throbbing, taking off my shoes would be foolish. As we walk, the texture of sand changes from soft, smooth sand to a dry, coarse, rock-filled terrain. There is no chance of stopping so I can rub my feet. I do not want the smugglers to see American money hidden in my shoes.

My toes are numb from the pain. Are my toes going to be able to hold on until I am able to take these hard-toed soccer shoes off? The sand no longer irritates my skin. Is this something to be concerned about? Does it mean gangrene is setting in? I will lose my toes. The doctors will find the American money in the socks, all shredded up, when they remove my soccer cleats. They will laugh. But I will not let that stop me now.

"Keep walking. Keep dreaming big dreams," the voice repeats in my head.

There is a future somewhere, in some distant place. Where living openly in freedom is a way of life. My sisters and brothers will be all around me, with my parents at my side. Mamán and Baba will be proud of us. Surely this one night is a small price to pay.

"We're moving," Shahram barks.

December 8, 1982

The sun rises. We have walked all night. It must have been at least fifteen hours. What if we see the Afghanis now? At night, the darkness was our friend, although I despised it. Now, in the bright sunlight, where are we going to hide? How much farther do we have to walk? Are we going to another planet? There is no one here who will answer my questions. Better I keep them to myself as I have done since I left Shiraz five days ago.

Twenty hours into the journey, in the middle of the following afternoon, with the hot sun blazing overhead, the smugglers tell us, "Sit down and rest." We sit on a big, dark grey rock nearby. It is barren here. There is nothing around us other than mountains and more mountains. Sand and more sand. Scattered rocks. There is no sign of civilization here, let alone a telephone. The desolation, the fatigue, the dehydration, the fear, have drained me of all my energy. I am wiped out. We have walked over a hundred kilometres since we left Zahedan. Squashed Nose's sudden concern for our physical condition is a complete change. Something is wrong. He announces, "The most dangerous part of the journey is over."

Squashed Nose continues, "We crossed the Iran-Pakistan border a couple hours ago."

It is mean of them not to have told us.

As I think this, Squashed Nose seems to read my mind, "You would not have walked had you known we were in Pakistan. Besides, we have to meet the driver here for our lift to Quetta."

We are jubilant. How are we going to inform Mamán? She is dying to hear from us. She has to wait. We have no choice.

Beady Eyes demands, "Now that we have brought you to Pakistan, we are supposed to get paid in full before we go any further."

"What the hell? That's not what we agreed upon! Mamán gave you the first half before we left."

We know the second we give them the money they will feel free to abandon us or worse, kill us. Either way, we lose.

Mamán had warned us this might happen, and no matter what, we are not to give any money to the smugglers or to change the original agreement until we arrive safely in Quetta.

Of course we have the money taped to our bodies, but they must not find it. They must suspect that we are carrying some cash or they wouldn't be asking for it. Farah and I read each other's thoughts and immediately deny having any money with us.

Farah shouts at them, "Keyvan will give you the money when we get there. How are we supposed to get money now? You want us to dig it up from the ground?"

"You should not get any money until Mamán has been notified that we're safe. You are supposed to take us all the way to Quetta. First you say it takes twenty minutes to get to the car and it took twenty hours? You will be paid when we are delivered, as promised."

Beady Eyes and Squashed Nose spend some time in serious discussion. Shahram sits in the front with them, listening. He translates as Farah and I whisper anxiously to each other.

Beady Eyes shouts, "We will drive off with the car when it arrives and leave you here, if you do not pay us immediately."

"We have nothing on us," we insist stubbornly.

I whisper to Farah, "Do you think they're really going to drive off? Are they going to kill us?"

"We have to appeal to them. Even though they are Pakistani they are still men, they will have some kind of honour, just wait."

Farah and I break down, sobbing hysterically. These have been the nastiest twenty hours of our entire lives. The encounters with the Afghanis have left us breathless each time, adding to the stress of possible discovery by the Hezbollah. We are exhausted, hungry, and thirsty. We cry and cry and cry. All we need now is a little compassion, but instead we are faced with more aggravation. Our rescuers are becoming our prison wardens; they have total power over us. There is no way we can hand them the money. If they see the money we are not sure that we will ever arrive in Quetta.

Farah begs them, "How would you feel if your sisters were treated like this? We come all the way here to be left here? Why didn't you ask Mamán for all the money in Zahedan?"

As their argument heats up, the men raise their voices. Shouting continues in Urdu. They gesture, they snarl, and they pace back and forth frantically.

Shahram translates, "They want to be paid or they won't get going. They're afraid they won't get paid. It might have happened to them before."

All form of communication stops. We ignore them and they ignore us. The air is cooler as the sun disappears behind a mountain. I wonder if I will ever leave this spot. We have run out of ideas. We're sitting alone, in the desert, on a rock, disheartened by this betrayal. How can these two men take advantage of our circumstances? Will they kill us to get the money? Will they rape us before they kill us? We can't go back and we can't go forward. We have to settle here. There is nothing here. We will die of starvation. Stop! We have been through so much already. This too shall pass. Hope is the only friend that can sustain us.

Mountains and more mountains surround us. There is no sign of habitation. There is no road. If we are waiting for the car, how is this car going to drive here? It won't fly down from the sky.

Beady Eyes is sitting with Squashed Nose about five metres away from us. Shahram walks back and forth between us, uncertain what to do.

Silence.

My breathing is faint. My skin is dry. The temperature is dropping. It is late afternoon. There is a vague noise from the south. It becomes louder and louder. We are baffled. From far away, something moves toward us. Sounds like a car engine. A car? How is the driver able to drive where there is no road? Beady Eyes mumbles to Squashed Nose. They move toward the sound. We see a beat-up old pickup truck approaching across the desert.

We are expecting a car. What pulls up instead is a rattletrap obviously not safe to drive. It is a miracle that it has somehow made it to this spot. However, since the altercation we are walking on eggshells; we don't dare say anything. What will the smugglers do with us? Are they going to leave us here as they have threatened? We have no idea what is waiting for us.

Beady Eyes mumbles goodbye; he is going back to Iran.

Squashed Nose bids us climb into the back seat of the pickup truck as if no discussion has taken place. Late Wednesday afternoon, we drive off toward Quetta. Squashed Nose and Shahram sit in the front next to the driver.

It doesn't look as though we are anywhere close to civilization. All that surrounds us are mountains. The whole world is just made of mountains, ugly ones. The ones that chase you wherever you go and from which you cannot hide. Are these mountains going to swallow us up? I abhor these mountains.

The men ignore us completely. They do not offer us any food or drink. Squashed Nose tells us, "Cover up. It is for your protection and safety. No one here sees a woman's face. You do not want to look any different than the locals." The Pakistani outfits he throws our way are thick, earth-coloured saris of coarse cotton fabric. There are veils of nearly opaque black mesh to cover our faces, through which we can see but will not be seen. We sit silently in the back seat of the truck as they drive and cover up as we are told.

I ask Shahram, "How long is it going to take before we arrive in Quetta?"

"A few more hours."

Right! Just like last night it was a few minutes of walking. Who knows? I should keep quiet and simply pray.

I try to understand what just happened but can't figure out the argument over the money. How come as soon as the truck arrived, they rushed us to get in? Were they just killing time because they didn't know when it would arrive? Was it all just a diversion for them?

This journey takes us through a part of Pakistan that has to be one of the most primitive parts of the world. The road is not paved. At times there is no road at all. There is no sign of life. There is no agriculture. There are no signs of habitation at all. When we finally come upon a few settlements, we see clusters of scattered huts made out of flattened metal oil cans, or tents.

There is nothing along the road — no garages, no gas stations, no tea shops or food stores. That black mountain range we saw at night is even blacker by day. It is all around us, encompassing us, swallowing us into its blackness.

This driver intuitively knows where to go. There are no roads, no lights, no compasses, no road signs, and no maps. We have no idea where we are. We are at the mercy of the driver.

We have heard that many women are forced into prostitution this way. Many are supposedly whisked away to other countries. Virgins can be sold for thousands of dollars. What is there to stop them from doing this to us now? It is not as if Mamán can go to the Iranian government and say, "I sent my girls to Pakistan, I haven't heard from them, where are they? Could you help me find them?" She would be stoned to death in the town square.

Farah shivers. Her teeth chatter. We have not showered or brushed our teeth in four days. My breath is bad and my mouth is dry. Our skin crawls with our sweat. Sand is stuck to my body from the desert. I smell. My scalp is itchy. I fear lice infestation.

The driver shouts, "Keep it quiet. Can't you see I need to concentrate on the road?" What road? Never have I experienced such wretchedness in my entire life. A sack of rice would be transported with more respect than we are.

The driver stops at a settlement to let us get some food and to pick up gas. The people in these tents and mud dwellings make a few coins by sharing whatever food they have with strangers and fugitives. It is sparse fare. We watch as our host, an old, wrinkly man, builds and lights a fire. The cigarette does not leave his lips. It is made of tobacco he rolled himself; it has no filter. The smell is so strong and unbearable that I start to cough. Squashed Nose, the driver and Shahram join in the smoking. Dark, thick smoke surrounds us. They are having a party while we are choking in this tiny tent.

We wait an hour for the fire to get hot enough to cook rice. It takes forever.

I am thirsty. I am dehydrated. The desire for cool water in my mouth becomes urgent. I ask the host for a glass of water. He hands me a metal bowl of water, and I start drinking enthusiastically. It tastes awful and smells like gasoline. This water is undrinkable. Being thirsty is better than being sick with gasoline in my body. If there is no water here, I can just imagine the state of the hospital and patient care. No thanks. Wait for the meal. Only drink water after it has been boiled.

It has taken the entire afternoon to start the fire and to cook the rice. Finally it is ready. It smells good. I salivate over the thought of eating warm rice. Whenever we visited Baba on the farm the villagers who lived in the tent always made succulent vegetarian dishes. I hope this will taste as good as those dishes . . . Oh . . . no . . . there . . . are . . . moving . . . black . . . spots . . . on . . . the . . . rice. Is it really what I think it is? Roaches! Crawling in the food! Revolting! I love rice; I have eaten rice of many varieties, but with roaches, never!

~~~~~

Our gang of smugglers had a wonderful time smoking their heads off, one cigarette after another, in anticipation of food. The pleasure in the eyes of Squashed Nose and the driver indicates, "This is novel hospital-ity." Is it the rice or the combination of rice and creepy-crawly insects that excites them? It is most generous on the part of our host, the old wrinkly man, to make us rice. He eats only bread dipped in oil. Squashed Nose and the driver seem to find the food delicious. Our reaction is a little less enthusiastic. Hungry as we are, we cannot eat rice with roaches. Luckily, the old man offers us oranges or else we really would starve. The kindness of the host in offering to share his food is much cherished, but to us the cooked food is inedible. Maybe this is a Pakistani delicacy?

We set out again to drive on this unending road. Occasionally, sheep, goats, and dogs cross in front of the truck with their shepherds. The widely scattered dwellings that we see now are just huts or tents propped up haphazardly. I can't comprehend how people can live here. The nights are very cold and the days overwhelmingly hot when the sun is at its highest. It is all so inhospitable. I have not encountered a single woman since I left Zahedan. Are these men living completely alone or are the women kept hidden from the presence of strangers?

Our relationship with the smugglers is still tenuous. As we drive through the desert together, communication between us is practically non-existent. We don't even speak to Shahram.

We continue to drive through the night for many hours. Suddenly, a loud, frightening bang! The truck begins to swerve all over the road and stops. It seems we have a flat tire. There is no one around to help. The driver and Squashed Nose have to change the tire themselves. It takes a few hours of hard work on their part before the job is done. The main driver switches seats with Squashed Nose, who is now driving. Thankfully, it was only a flat tire. It could have been worse, with the state this truck is in.

We start driving again through the night, praying that this is the last time we will have a problem with the truck. But my worst nightmare comes true when the truck suddenly grinds to a halt again. Now we are really doomed. It is not a flat tire. They open the hood and can't figure out what is wrong, let alone how to fix it. We have to wait for another truck to arrive and transport us to Quetta. No one knows how long we have to wait. This fiasco takes place in the early hours of the morning around four a.m.

Squashed Nose shouts, "Get out of the car! Wait over there by the road until help arrives!"

What is the difference if we are in or out of the truck? It has broken down and can't move.

It is too cold for us outside. The men are angry and frantic; we cannot reason with them. How are they going to fix this truck? It is not as if a garage is around the corner and they will send a tow truck to pick us up. We are helpless.

Darkness and cold wind surround us. There is howling in the background. No one talks; the complete silence makes the background noise louder. The smugglers are probably more stressed than we are. The faster we arrive in Quetta, the faster they will be paid.

December 9, 1982, sunrise

The sun rises and warms us up. In the midst of all this chaos in my life, I can still depend on the sun to rise in the morning. It is a magnificent sight. That hideous dark mountain does not look so bad in the breaking dawn. The sky is hazy, not quite white, black, or blue yet, but the sun is rising over the cloudless horizon. For a brief moment, there is hope. We're going to get through this. The sun feels like a good omen: The worst is behind us and soon we will reach Quetta. But is it? The truck is broken down; how will it be over? One minute I am hopeful, the next moment I am terrified that I will grow old here and will never see, never taste freedom. I will never go back to school. I am on an emotional roller coaster.

We are waiting, waiting, waiting. Farah comes close to me and squeezes my hand. She looks deep into my eyes. "Stay strong. We can't afford to lose hope. That is our only weapon now." She knows how to cheer me up. I love my sister.

If I had a book or my crocheting, I would have some distraction, and time would pass faster. There is nothing I can do. There is nothing to look at. If there were an ant house on the ground, I could look at the ants for hours and count them. There is no ant house. Ant counting was my favourite childhood activity. How the ants behave royally with one another and their family. How a little ant can carry many times its actual weight and participate in preparation for the changing seasons. We have one thing in common with ants and that is a sense of family and taking pride in doing one's part. Now my family is Farah and Farah alone. My family has shrunk from hundreds to just one. I am not allowed to even speak to the one sitting next to me.

A relief truck shows up, and around noon we continue on our way. How did the driver of the relief truck know about us, and where to come? The smugglers never speak with anyone.

I need a toilet. This is very embarrassing. There is nothing on the road to welcome travellers. I demand, "Stop the car." Thankfully, we don't eat or drink much; therefore the stops are pretty infrequent. There is no public washroom, no water with which to wipe ourselves. Rocks and bushes are my friends. They will conceal me. Even evacuation becomes a big ordeal for us. The dilemma is: should Farah and I go together? What if they drive off with one of us and leave the other here? If they leave us both here . . . at least then we'll be together. Squashed Nose yells, "Only one person at a time can leave the car for safety's sake." I can't understand his reasoning. Nothing makes sense. It is demeaning and humiliating for both of us.

Farah goes first, and I wait with Shahram, and then I go, and Farah waits with the truck. We decide, "If the truck starts moving, I'll scream at the top of my lungs. And then at least you'll know which direction to run and you'll scream and try not to let them drive off. The screaming might distract them and make them stop."

Luckily for us, they don't try anything, but it's not as if they have given us reason to trust them. We pretend to sleep while in the truck. First Farah dozes off for a little while, and then I wake her up and go to sleep for a short while.

I see Mamán. She is almost blind because all she does is cry. Soraya is miserable, sitting in the garden. She does not know what to do, lost in her own world. Then Beady Eyes calls to tell Mamán we are in Pakistan.

Baba is hysterical when he finds out we have left Iran. He is mad at Mamán for helping us to escape.

The whole family, Naneh Jaan-Jaan and all my aunts and uncles, know by now we are gone. Cyrus whines to Soraya, "Why didn't you tell me they were leaving? I would have been kinder to them." Keyvan sits in the garden talking to Farah. I cannot figure out how he is in Shiraz. I scream. I am just dreaming.

December 9, 1982, late at night

The truck stops unexpectedly in the middle of the night. We wake up with a start. A uniformed man standing alone outside a building in the wilderness with a gun across his shoulder stops the car. He begins to question our companions in Urdu.

He leans into the back of the truck, one hand at the driver's window, while he shines a flashlight into our faces with the other hand. He demands an explanation.

Shahram's voice shakes as he translates. "Lift your veils." I am trembling like a chicken about to be slaughtered. Who is this man? Is he going to deport us to the Iranian authorities? Maybe he wants to see if what the smugglers are telling him is true. We have no idea what to expect.

The official orders Farah and me, "Get out of the car. Follow me." Miraculously, he speaks Persian. "I will interrogate you separately."

"No, please let us stay together." We cry. He agrees.

He instructs Shahram and the smugglers to stay in the car and wait until we return. We are led into a room with bare mud walls and a dirt floor.

Oh, my God, this man looks just like Baba. How is it that Baba's look-alike is put in our path at such a crucial moment? Not only does he look like Baba, he speaks Persian. He is the same age as Baba, with the same thick, black mustache. The uniform, and the belt around his waist, which accentuates his belly, are the only physical differences between them. Baba never wore a uniform. This man wears a light brown uniform. The shirt is tightly tucked over his belly into his pants. He sits behind an old wooden desk, and we are sitting on a bale of hay that serves as a chair. The walls are unpainted clay. He starts to question us. Farah looks so pale, as if she might faint at any minute. Please, God, help us. This is not the time to faint. I am hyperventilating but I need to look calm.

"Are you travelling with these men of your own free will?" For the first time in this journey, we are being treated like human beings. We exist. He is gentle.

"Are you thirsty? Do you want water?" An image flashes into my mind from my childhood. At home, when the *hammam* became hot and steamy, Baba would bring a pitcher of lemonade and leave it just inside the door. Now his look-alike is offering us water. He pours water from his clay pitcher into two metal cups. He is an angel sent from heaven.

He is concerned about us. We both breathe easier for a moment. For the first time since our journey began, here is someone who shows some genuine concern for our welfare.

Instinctively, without actually discussing it, Farah and I decide to trust him and so we tell him our story. The buildup of tension over the last few days is released in a torrent of words. We have to repeat ourselves many times because our frenzied crying, along with his relatively awkward Persian, makes communication difficult.

"Squashed Nose wants us . . . to pay . . . him now . . . We are . . . s . . . c . . . ared of him. We . . . have not . . . eaten for . . . da . . . ys. Plea . . . se . . . help . . . us."

The officer seems moved by our story. He clears his throat.

In a heartfelt tone, he urges, "I want to help you. What can I do for you?"

Farah and I request, "Can we talk alone for a few minutes, please?" We haven't had a chance to talk privately since the journey began. He nods and goes out of the room.

"Do you trust him?"

"I do; do you?"

"Yes. What should we do?"

"Maybe he can help us get to Quetta safely."

"We need some kind of safety net; maybe we should ask him if he will take the money we owe the smugglers for safekeeping until we are safe in Quetta."

We devise a fail-safe system using two identical notes. We will give one note to the officer and tell him that after the smugglers deliver us safely to Quetta, we will write them a second, identical note to bring back to him. We have to put our trust in this honest police officer and give him all the money we owe to the smugglers. We have nothing to lose, and we can feel safer this way. He is our best friend now. The smugglers will have to be on their best behaviour from now on.

Farah slowly turns the doorknob, peeks out with one eye, and motions the policeman to enter quickly. She whispers furtively, "We do need your help. Please!"

"What do you need help with?"

"We want to give you money. If we give them a note to deliver back here to you, with the message that we are safe, you will give the money to the smugglers. If they kill us and try to present a note that isn't worded exactly like the one we will give you now, then you can keep the money."

We ask him for a piece of paper and a pen. He fumbles in a drawer of the desk, and offers us a piece of blank paper and an old black pen. Farah writes: "This is Farah and Sima. We are safe in Quetta. Please pay the smugglers their money. Thank you for your help."

We both sign the note. The policeman looks at it, looks at us, and then nods his head. We memorize the words we have just written. We can't write the second note in advance for fear the smugglers will find it, kill us, and return for their money.

We ask the policeman for a knife; we think there is no way he can have a pair of scissors here. But thankfully, he hands us both knife and scissors. He leaves the room so that we can in privacy release the money taped and stuffed in the various hiding places on our bodies and in our clothing.

"Farah, let me help you." I cut the tape around her waist. It is tightly wrapped — professionally done by Mamán. She cringes as we pull the tape and money off her. Where the money was hidden, her skin is irritated, raw, and red from the sweat of the long walk in the desert, from sitting hunched in the car, and from the skin being air-starved. But Farah is relieved.

It is my turn, now. How am I going to take my shoes off? My feet are bothering me more than the tape, so for the first time since Zahedan, I take off my shoes. My toes are numb. My socks are completely stuck on. There's no way those shoes are going back on my feet now. We rescue all the money, pile it in denominations, and then ask the officer to return. I am terrified that I will have to continue on this journey without shoes. I am sobbing as I explain what my problem is. I don't really think he can help me: I'm sure he doesn't have an extra pair of shoes lying about, but he takes the scissors and gently cuts off my socks.

My feet are unrecognizable.

The nails on my big toes have turned grey. Oh, my God. Will my toes fall off? Will I have to go to the hospital before infection sets in through my entire body? I am terrified of the consequences. I have to stay strong. There is nothing else to do.

The officer then cuts away the front rubber part of my shoes. I can't put them on right away, but at least when I do, I should be able to walk without any more pressure on my toes. I keep them with me. As much as I do not like them, they are my only pair of shoes.

We burst out of the policeman's office feeling much lighter and stronger than when we walked in. Squashed Nose looks at my feet, startled. The policeman commands them to follow him into his office.

We are alone with Shahram. "What took you so long? I was worried about you." Farah outlines our plan to him. He raises his eyebrows. "Wow! That's what you planned to do! Are you sure he can be trusted? What did you do with my money?"

"We kept your money on us. We gave the police officer only the money we owe the smugglers."

"If I had known about your arrangement, I would have said to put my name on that secret note, too. I am not planning to pay them in Quetta." Farah and I are surprised; we had no idea what his plans were.

The police officer comes out fifteen minutes later and strides to the truck. He speaks clearly to us and the smugglers, switching between Persian and Urdu.

The policeman commands the driver and Squashed Nose, "Deliver them to Quetta safely. I have your address in Quetta. If you return to me within five days with the note, you will be paid in full. If not, I will assume some harm has come to these girls and I will seek you out in Quetta." He shouts at them, "Is this clear?" They nod at him like obedient puppies. Their facial expression confirms how scared they are. Both Farah and I are secretly relieved to glimpse the smugglers so frightened. We smile for the first time since we set foot in the desert.

Squashed Nose starts to drive. He inquires, "What was all that about? Why did you change our agreement?"

Farah responds, "Since you already tried to trick us once, we're going to have Mamán wire the officer the money instead of Keyvan. Only when you bring the police officer the note of our safety will you get paid."

We are greatly comforted. But are we really naïve? My chatterbox does not want to be quiet. The more I want to ignore it, the louder it shouts. *You are doomed. Now you have no money and the smugglers will leave you on the side of the road. You stupid girl! How could you do such a thing? Didn't Mamán specifically tell you not to give money to anyone until you reach Quetta?*

Shut up! I do not want to listen to you. I have nothing to lose. I trust him.

The driver offers us a dirty, moth-eaten blanket. As soon as the policeman showed up the blanket popped out. Interesting. I am glad, because my feet are frozen. At least we are warm, now. Why didn't they give us those blankets before? They offer us water. It tastes like gasoline, but at least there is effort on their part. We are no longer treated like sacks of insignificant potatoes. Squashed Nose offers us oranges. Where did those come from? I thought we were out of oranges. At that time of night, and with all the excitement, we do not want to eat. We are just very happy to be warm under this old navy blanket full of holes. We go to sleep. We feel safe, now.

December 10, 1982

The long night crawls to an end. The sun starts to peek out over the horizon. On this road there are no other cars, as if the road has been built just for us. I have a funny feeling in my stomach. This place looks more backward than Shiraz has been since the arrival of Hezbollah. Will I regret burning my bridges behind me?

Every few hours, we inquire, "When are we going to arrive?" "How far is it from here?" They always answer either, "Before the end of the day," or, "In the morning." It is not as if we have a dinner to attend at seven o'clock that we can't afford to miss. We have no appointments, we have no dates, and other than Keyvan, nobody is waiting for us.

We have stayed curled up in this car for the past three days. I have not moved or stretched all this time. One grey mountain succeeds another on the horizon. There is nothing to watch. Nothing changes. I am convinced we are in exactly the same place where we started, but this can't be, since we've faced so many crises: the rice with the roaches, the car breaking down, the encounter with the police officer. Still, everything looks exactly the same.

At noon, we stop at a light brown tent along the road. It is similar to the ones in Baba's village. Light brown is the universal colour for a tent, my inner voice reminds me. A few big pieces of stone lie in a circle around a hole in the ground holding the remnants of a fire. A short, skinny, bearded man in his sixties, with a turban on his head, invites the five of us to enter the tent and, taking a bowl from a table in the rear of the tent, he places it on the ground. It contains an egg swimming in oil. We have never eaten eggs with so much oil. That one egg is probably meant to serve an entire family. It's the oil that they like, here. There is gasoline in the water, and they eat lots of oil with a little egg. We thank them but have to refuse. The smugglers divide up the egg. There is also black tea. That is the only option; better than nothing. The tea is very dark. I take a sip; it is unbelievably bitter. I can't drink it. I know I am being too fussy, but what we are offered is undrinkable.

The interior of the tent is different from the ones I knew in Shiraz. I loved it when Baba would bring us to his farm, and we would stop by the tents of the villagers. They were so bright and lavishly decorated with handicrafts and their own colourful, hand-woven carpets placed on the floor. I always felt warm and cozy in those tents. Here, it is barren. There the ladies would greet us, with their multicoloured skirts and matching bandanas and head coverings. Here, I have not seen even one woman. The men look too old, too wrinkly. In the few local tents we've stopped in, every one of our hosts smoked strong, pungent cigarettes, the ones whose stink penetrates to the bone. I hate this smell.

Friday night has come and gone. There is no lighting of candles. No Shabbat dinner. No blessing over the wine. Tonight is no different than last night or tomorrow night. I am sure the Friday night ritual in my home back in Shiraz will continue regardless of our absence. I miss it already. I hope one day, sooner rather than later, I will be able to light candles and pray as a Jew. For now, this is only a distant dream!

December 11, late morning

Squashed Nose announces, "We will be in Quetta within a couple of hours." He insists that he is telling the truth. I look around. There are more huts by the roadside. Maybe it is the truth. We have been driving for almost four days.

The smugglers take turns driving. Time is of the essence. They want to drop us off in Quetta as quickly as possible and return to the police station in order to be paid. They probably have other clients waiting back in Zahedan.

Throughout the entire four days and nights of our escape, we have had very little sleep. I am lucky to manage one hour of sleep without being woken up by a bump in the road. Sitting scrunched up together like pretzels in the back seat of the car, I now recognize that it is a privilege to sleep in a bed lying down. I have taken it for granted for the seventeen years of my life. I have been lucky to have water to drink, food to eat, a bathroom for necessities, a shower to clean myself, a comb for my hair, and a toothbrush for my teeth. The daily routine that I took for granted all my life is swiftly put into a new perspective.

I realize how little one really needs to be happy and grateful.

December 11, early afternoon

We are wide awake now, wanting to get a good impression of the city as we arrive in Quetta. The driver turns into an alley, pulls up in front of a house, and stops; another minor pit stop on the way to the big city, Quetta?

Squashed Nose says, "We're here. Out!"

Oh. We have arrived in Quetta! Excited, we scramble out of the car. Squashed Nose leads, pushing open the door. We had hoped to be greeted by Keyvan, but he is not here. Farah is distressed. Why is he not here?

What they call a house is a room without furniture. There is a door leading to a garden opposite the entrance. There is a heater on the floor with a hot kettle on it and a few pots piled in a corner. No sink.

The first Pakistani woman we have met enters from the garden. She must be Squashed Nose's wife. For a brief time, I believed there were no women in Pakistan at all because I hadn't seen one since we left Zahedan. Squashed Nose's wife is a burka-wrapped, bossy woman. "The man came many times today, but I asked him to leave. I will send someone to tell him you are here as soon as you settle your account." She speaks gently. When she talks, we turn to look at her but cannot see who is talking. We see a thick black sheet thrown over a lump that moves and gestures. How does one talk to a thing? She moves to the heater. A hand emerges and starts to stir something in a pot. The food is for us. She offers us an egg, another one floating in oil on a crooked metal plate. We are to eat on the floor with the food on our laps.

Squashed Nose demands the note from us. He shouts to Shahram, "Give me the money now!"

Shahram responds, "I have no money."

Farah and I are watching as the argument between Squashed Nose and Shahram heats up. How terrible to come this far and not be free. We fully sympathize with Shahram. What is waiting for him sounds dreadful.

The yelling continues. The men are not shy to display their fist power and foul language as they push him into the garden and separate him from us to a room at the end of the garden. We are not to follow him. Both Farah and I start screaming and begging them to stop fighting. What a welcome!

The woman in black stretches her arms across the doorway to stop us from us entering the garden. If we had not feared for our own safety, Farah and I would have pushed her away. But as newcomers in a strange house in a foreign country, the last thing we want to be are hostages like Shahram.

A children's pool filled with dirty brown water in the garden distracts me. There is hope that a civilization exists here if they have a pool in the garden.

Shahram starts to shriek and kick hard. It is the two of them and one of him. They overpower him. They are shouting so loudly that we easily overhear their conversation in the kitchen. The entire neighbourhood can hear this argument. We are trapped. We have nowhere to go. It is not as if we can distract the black-clad woman and escape. We are in prison again. We have no way of leaving. We know no one. We are damned.

The cracks, bumps, and roars of the men in the room are terrifying. Bang! Bang! Whobop! It sounds like wild lions fighting each other. They are willing to kill anything or anyone that comes in their way. Animals! The screaming, yelling, hitting, moaning, and groaning are intolerable. Farah is crying, and so am I. We both start to shout, "Let him out, you are killing him!" Shahram must be bleeding; he must have broken bones. It is unbearable to witness this cruelty. There is no value to human life here. Farah is eighteen. I am only seventeen. How did I come to be so far away from my family, unprotected? This looks like a scene in a movie of a sort that I would never choose to watch. But no, this is real and it is happening in front of me. I can't change the channel or walk away.

This brutality brings back memories of Shiraz in 1979 and the years following, of people being beaten for no reason. There must be a way to resolve this peacefully. We are both weeping and begging them to stop. Keyvan does not even know we are here. Though my voice screams at me to help Shahram it is better for all of us if we do not cause more fuss.

Because of all the noise, the entire community gathers in the house. They do not come in through the same entrance as we did. They must be rushing in through the garden or the rooftop, entrances that only locals are aware of. This brings back memories of Shiraz. When there was a dispute or argument, everyone would show up to watch and take sides. To me these men look strange, and they take the smugglers' side in the argument. Interesting: only men are coming by. Not one woman shows up. The men are confused; they do not know whether to turn to Shahram, trapped in the garden, or stare at our dirty, exhausted, angry, and uncovered faces, visible in the door to the garden.

Squashed Nose whispers to the blob. She disappears through the front door as he stands guard at the garden door. She runs back in, holding a rope. It does not take a genius to figure out what the rope is to be used for: they want to secure Shahram until he pays what he owes Squashed Nose.

Squashed Nose barks before leaving the room, "Give us the note!"

His voice is so loud that Shahram hears him from the other end of the "house."

Shahram yells, "Don't give them the note! They're going to hurt me and send me back!"

"Give us the note or we won't tell Keyvan you are here!"

Shahram shouts again, this time a different message, "They are going to hold me here. They are going to kill me! Please! Give them the note. Get Keyvan. Go, Go!"

Farah and I yell, "Are you sure this is the right thing to do? They will hold you hostage! Are you sure?"

"Yes, yes, just write it!"

We have no idea why Shahram changed his mind. We can't talk to him. Farah writes the note and signs it. She passes it to me to sign. Squashed Nose grabs the note. Looks at it. Can't read it. "Are you sure this is the right note?" he says, pointing to the note.

"Yes. What are you going to do to Shahram?"

In sign language, he rubs his fingers together for the sign of money, then rubs it against his throat and slides his hand in front of his throat. These symbols are international. Though we do not speak the same language, it is clear. Shahram's life is indeed in danger.

"Kill him? He is not an animal! What is wrong with you?" screams Farah. I squeal. There is no price for human life. Shahram will be dead if the money is not here within twenty-four hours. Oh, my God. How are we going to save his life?

The woman sends one of the men to look for Keyvan. We are officially free. The sun is setting, its gold and amber hues mocking us as it sinks below the roof level of the house. The house is quiet. All the men have left with the exception of two: one man who stays in the room with Shahram, and a second man who stands guard behind the door.

We sit in front of the door in the house facing the alley. No children play here, in contrast to the alleys in Shiraz, which are always alive with the sounds of children's shouting and laughter.

Farah and I hold hands, squeezing them from time to time. Farah exclaims, "We did it. Good job, sister!"

I reply, "You were my strength in all this. We are still not free. Keyvan will be here soon."

Keyvan emerges from the shadows as we are looking down the alley.

He is with another man. He is bearded and grey, like the man he is with, and like all the Pakistani men we have seen so far.

Farah and Keyvan run toward each other. They embrace, holding tightly to each other. Hearing Farah shout Keyvan's name, the woman of the house and Squashed Nose come to the door and stare at this public display of affection, Squashed Nose looking as though a pornographic scene were being played out in front of his eyes. When Squashed Nose arrived with us, he did not acknowledge his wife at all. There is a world of contrasts in the different cultures our little group represents. How differently the two couples interact with each other.

Farah and Keyvan are ecstatic. Their faces are glowing; their smiles are wide. Their skin is flushed. Their transformation is instantaneous. Farah and Keyvan are thrilled to be together again.

Keyvan introduces his friend, Akbar.

Farah says, "Keyvan, it has been so rough without you. We have so much to tell you."

Keyvan looks worried seeing just the two of us and, turning to Squashed Nose, demands, "Where is Shahram?"

Squashed Nose yells in Urdu. Akbar translates, "You find the money to pay what he owes, and bring it here within twenty-four hours or we will kill him." I swallow hard. It would be a nightmare forever if they kill Shahram. I will not be able to live with myself. But unless Shahram allows us, we are not to mention that we are holding all his money.

All this is being translated by Akbar, who speaks perfect Urdu.

Keyvan yells, "I have to see Shahram before I leave. Where is he?" Squashed Nose is reluctant to let Keyvan into the house. Maybe he does not want to let Keyvan see Shahram because he is injured. But Squashed Nose soon realizes there is no way we will leave unless the two of them talk.

Keyvan, alone, is taken out to the garden. One minute passes; two minutes . . . fifteen minutes later, Keyvan comes out. "You won't believe this. Shahram is bleeding. But he still does not want to let the smugglers know he has money. He will try to escape. We need to stall the smugglers. Let's go!" We dash out the smugglers' door, while they yell, "Come back with the money soon!"

We walk down the alley. Keyvan's eyes are fixed on the ground. Then he notices my feet and gasps with disbelief, "Sima, what on earth is wrong with your shoes?"

"My toes were killing me, so I had to cut the stupid tops off so that my toes are free and I can still walk. These were soccer shoes. Now they are open-toed sandals."

~~~~~~

Exhausted, frustrated, and angry, we walk on. The street is dark. There are no trees in the streets. Something is odd about this place. Its streets are narrow and dirty. Our first impression is that everything is grey: the clothing, the buildings, the mood. The buildings are unimaginative and unadorned. Maybe it is the uneasy feeling of dislocation that makes us see the scene only in shades of grey. But I am convinced Quetta really is a grey city. There are not many cars on the road; actually there are more animals on the road than cars. Animals—goats, sheep, chickens, and roosters—roaming on the main roads with the cars. Why? It's not as if they are grazing.

Keyvan flags down a taxi. It is black, the colour of death. In Shiraz, our taxis are bright orange. These taxis drive on the wrong side of the road. I am scared to get into this taxi.

Keyvan, a twenty-four-year-old, overnight becomes a husband to Farah and a father figure to me. He wants to make light of the situation and cracks a joke.

"Farah comes with a dowry. You're her dowry!"

I do not like the joke, but now is not the time to complain.

I insist, "We have to call Mamán."

Keyvan smiles, "Excuse me, do you think you've come to a palace? You want a telephone booth? You can't call yet."

"We still need to call Mamán. This is urgent."

The black taxi takes us to the university. Keyvan's friend, Akbar, who is a medical student, has a phone in his room. We call Mamán. She just wants to hear our voices. "How are you, Mamán?" We need not talk much. It is understood. We are safe. How we arrived here is of no importance. We assume when she returned to Shiraz without us, Baba figured out what happened immediately and was worried for our safety as well.

Mamán sighs, "I've been glued to the phone since I came back. Don't talk too much. It will be expensive. Be in touch. Go. Go. Go. Don't worry for your plants, Soraya is watering them."

"How is Baba?"

"Don't worry, he is okay. Be safe. I will invite all the family for dinner on Thursday."

We understand. This is what she usually does. This is the Shirazi Jewish custom once a person has overcome adversity. A feast is prepared for the entire family and a donation—a *Nazr*, a wish—is given to the needy. When Mamán is under stress, when she dreads the outcome of an event, she makes a *Nazr*. *I am making a wish for my daughters' safe journey. If that wish comes true, I'm going to invite the entire family for dinner.*

Seeing my toes is a daily reminder of that painful exodus. I am told by Akbar that the foot is symbolic of the direction we take in our lives. The grey toenails are turning darker; they represent the darkness I am leaving behind. The future regrowth represents the new direction my life is taking. It will be a slow healing process.

Life in Pakistan

We take a black taxi again, to the hotel where Keyvan has rented a room for us. As the taxi drives through the city, I decide that Pakistanis had no imagination when they built these buildings. There is no outstanding architecture, nor are there any rich colours. The stores' signs are in Urdu. I can read Urdu—the alphabet is similar to Persian—but I do not know what I am reading. Some of the stores are closed with the metal pullover security door, and they are covered with graffiti. Quetta is a very small city; it is more like a small village in Iran: Old and decrepit street signs point to old and decrepit buildings. In my city, we preserved the old and were proud of it. This is the kind of age that needs to be cleaned up and renovated. It is repulsive.

The putrid smell of cigarettes hits me like a thick, black fog. Every man I see is smoking.

Keyvan has rented a hotel room for the three of us on the only street that is the downtown area. As we walk into the hotel, Keyvan informs us that this is all there is to downtown Quetta.

The owner of the hotel, a man in his thirties, is dressed in a long tunic with matching pants, with a head scarf wrapped around his head. He stands behind the wooden counter in the lobby. He has the same round face and the same fat nose as the men in Zahedan. As he approaches the front desk, he does not take his eyes off of Farah and me. He must be curious as to why Keyvan has the privilege of escorting two young girls. He looks at Keyvan and then at us. His thoughts are crystal clear: he wishes he were our escort instead of Keyvan.

Keyvan tells him in English: "My wife and my sister-in-law," pointing to Farah and me. He glares ferociously at the owner and says very clearly, "Stop staring and do your job. Just give me the key."

We walk up two flights of dark, winding stone stairs to our room. I've already had the frightening experience in Shiraz of falling and cutting my lips on the edge of stone stairs. I have no intention of repeating that experience. With my eyes wide open, I carefully watch every step of this dim staircase. A narrow outdoor balcony stretches from the staircase door along the front of the building, giving access to four rooms. From this second-floor balcony, we look down on the main road. The street is silent. There are no people. Few cars are on the road. A downtown street as quiet as this is strange. Keyvan struggles as he opens the metal door of our room with the big key.

The walls, whitewashed many, many years ago, are now dull, dark grey, and brown, as much from cigarette smoke as from filth. As in the lobby, a strong stench pollutes the air in our room. To make matters worse, opening a window is not an option, as there are no windows to open, only the door. The room is furnished with two single beds, covered by unwashed grey blankets. The rusty, bent metal legs of the bed are the tell-tale signs of plenty of use. It looks as if it is infested with lice. What am I going to do if I am infected? There is no way to change a pillowcase or pull out a blanket from our luggage. We have no luggage. The sight of this repulsive room with these filthy beds makes me sick to my stomach. But however uncomfortable this bed will be to sleep in, it will be better than where I have been sleeping this past week. I should be thankful; after all, I am the one imposing on Farah and Keyvan's honeymoon. It would not be wise to start complaining right from the start.

Once in the room, I realize that I have not showered for more than seven days. My undershirt sticks to me like a second skin. A shower becomes an urgent necessity. Looking around the small room, I realize there is no bathroom.

"Keyvan, where is the bathroom?"

"There is no shower in the room. Let's heat up the water on the heater, to warm the room. Then you both can take a shower with it."

The room doesn't have a bathroom!

Keyvan fills a kettle of water in the bathroom in the hallway and then places it gingerly on the heater in the cramped room.

Farah and I still have our gold coins and the American paper money taped to our bodies. We remove the tape very carefully to make sure the American currency is not shredded to pieces. It is a relief to see that the coins, although hot from our bodies, have not rusted. The American money, wet from our sweat, is still in one piece. This money will be used only to leave Pakistan, which we hope to do tomorrow. There is nothing to like about this city so far.

Farah and I venture out to see the shower. A common bathroom for the four rooms sits off the outdoor balcony adjacent to the staircase. The tile floor is ancient. There is no way to guess its original colour. There is a round metal tub with a rusty dripping faucet, each drop plinking on the rusted metal below.

It takes a team of three people to have a so-called shower. Keyvan stands outside the door to make sure nobody walks in. Farah trickles warmish water from the kettle over me as I rub myself free of the week's sweat and dirt. I don't have soap or shampoo. Only one kettle of water . . . another will take half an hour to heat. I am just appreciative of the water. This is our first experience of luxury in Quetta. I wash off the sand, dust, cigarette smoke, and sweat, hoping I won't carry the scars of the desert crossing for too long. The only towel is small, thin, and grey. There is no way it will dry both of us.

I have no clothes to change into after the shower. Keyvan lends me one of his shirts and a pair of pants. Farah stands behind the hotel's shower door to stop anyone from opening the door.

I hand-wash my pants and my shirt in the same tub in which I showered. Don't waste the water. It's a great commodity here. In a short time, we've devised several plans: the shower operation, the washing and the drying of clothes. The heater will be strategically placed at the edge of my bed and I will hang our clothes close to it to dry them. They will be dry by morning. Life in Tehran comes to mind. The difference is that now I am in a foreign country with even more primitive bathroom facilities. It is impossible to think that it could ever get worse than this.

After another half hour, there is enough warm water to trickle over Farah's soap-less body. Farah is now clean and wears a fresh outfit, courtesy of Keyvan. All three of us are in the room. Water is dripping from Farah's long, tangled black hair. It usually takes a blow-dryer and a sturdy brush to comb and dry her thick hair. Asking for that is like asking to go to the moon. She is shivering and clutching her sheet; I am shivering.

We look like chickens with their feathers stuck to them, just rescued from drowning.

The first priority was to take a shower. This is now accomplished.

The growling noise in my stomach speaks to the second priority: it grows louder every second, so loud that it is embarrassing. Now my stomach screams of hunger. It can't be ignored. An entire band is playing its repertoire in my belly, and the sound escalates minute by minute.

Not only are Farah and I improperly dressed, but it is late at night, it is cold, our hair is wet, and everything is closed. Our only option is to eat in our room.

Keyvan is busying himself with some cans and a can opener, on top of the bed, which serves as our table. He spreads newspaper on the bed as our tablecloth. He shares with Farah and me the best food he could serve us under these circumstances. Farah and Keyvan sit cross-legged on one bed, while I sit on the other bed watching and salivating over the new dining discovery.

"I know you will like it," he says. "This is condensed sweet milk out of a can, and this—" pointing at a pile of something dry and brown, "—is Melba toast." The best supper we've had since we left Shiraz. Mamán would be fuming to see us eat this for supper: the opposite of her instructions. I love it. The sweet milk is silky smooth as it rolls down my throat. At least this resembles food. It is certainly better than rice with roaches. Baba always says, "To a hungry man a stone will be delicious," and it is definitely true today.

Like a balloon emptied of air, there is no energy left in my body. I tumble into bed, exhausted.

〜〜〜〜〜

Baba has decorated our garden with lights, and there are many tables to seat the guests. Our garden looks just like it did the day Ammeh Nilofar was married years ago. Keyvan is walking with Farah. Farah is a beautiful bride dressed in her white gown with a tiara on her head. The white mesh covers her face. Many happy faces surround them, singing and dancing. The palm of her hand is dyed with henna from the party two days ago. I can have as many chips as I want because it is my sister's wedding, and the mean old cook, Bashi, can't say anything. Aria and Cyrus are running around as always. Soraya and I are dressed in matching flowery dresses sewn by Mamán. The garden and our clothes do not look as good as they did for Ammeh Nilofar's wedding, but that does not matter. Farah is the star tonight and she is gorgeous. It is her dream come true. She had many obstacles to overcome to see this night.

The surprise is that Keyvan's parents and siblings are happy to be here, too. His mother and sisters are distinguishable in the crowd because they are dressed in their colourful pink, red, and orange costumes with layered skirts and matching bandanas. Everyone is cheerful.

The food is served on tables in the garden by male waiters. Farah dances with Keyvan's mother. How come we never met his entire family before? There is no exchange of gold; nor is there a big dowry for Farah and Keyvan. Their strong love is all they count on. Farah wants a hundred red roses.

A hundred plump red roses are placed in a magnificent crystal vase. The sweet smell of the roses, the vividness of the red colour, the sound of the laughter, the sky full of stars make this evening unlike any other evening I have seen. It is breathtaking. Usually the roses bloom on the bushes, but tonight is a special night, and the hundred roses are in a vase at the head table where Farah is sitting with Keyvan, his parents, and Maman and Baba.

Farah moves to place the filthy blanket over me. I wake up, startled. I must have fallen asleep as I was eating. I wish I could see the rest of the dream.

Keyvan, wide awake, is sitting up in bed. Farah is telling him the story of our desert trek.

"Farah, you won't believe it. I just had the most beautiful dream."

My dream was prettier than the grey bed, in the grey room, with the grey bed covering. In my world, the two of them had the most beautiful wedding.

Tonight is Farah and Keyvan's "wedding night."

Traditionally, if this were in Iran under normal circumstances, lingerie would be laid out on the bed of the bride by the groom as a gift. It was believed that figs, dates, and nuts are aphrodisiacs, so these would be laid out in the room in which the bride and groom were supposed to consummate their marriage. The newlyweds would be followed into the room by relatives, singing and dancing their joy. The bride would remove all the gold jewellery she had received that evening from her groom and the guests. The mother of the groom would stand behind the door, to assure the consummation of the marriage.

Here, in a faraway land, there is no lingerie, no jewellery except what we brought from Shiraz, no dates, no figs, no nuts, and no mother-in-law.

There is no singing and no dancing. It is quiet and bare. But Farah and Keyvan are both blissfully happy.

There is a big problem: me. Keyvan could not trust the men here to have a separate room for me. Though there is no mother-in-law standing behind the door, there is a sister-in-law in the room, sleeping in a bed two feet away!

Sadly, I am their chaperone. How awkward for all of us.

Here is the joke: They both know that when Sima sleeps, nothing can wake her up. Two years ago in Shiraz, a building was bombed. The whole city was shaken by the explosion. I was asleep on my cot under the stars at night in the garden. Once my head hit the pillow, I was fast asleep. I didn't hear a thing then and neither did I on the first night of my sister's honeymoon.

Still, it must feel bizarre to them to have me in the same room in such circumstances. I can't thank them enough for tolerating this and making no fuss.

In my dream that night, Shahram follows me: "Help me. I do not want to die."

"What help can I offer you? I can't speak Urdu; there is nowhere to go for help."

I wake up with heaviness in my heart. I should be happy, I am free. But I am not happy. Shahram's life is in danger. Although I did not know him for long, I shared one of the scariest five days of my life with him. Aren't the people who share our toughest times supposed to be our most cherished friends?

Shahram has not come by yet. This means he hasn't been successful in escaping.

December 12, in the morning

We are frightened for Shahram's life. Are they going to kill him? How terrible to survive the hazardous escape across the inhospitable desert, only to be killed when he reaches his destination. He helped us to escape; now he is a hostage.

Shahram believed it was only fair to have a free ride because of his translation skill. But nothing was discussed in advance. I imagine Shahram under torture, busy reciting his poems to lessen the pain. Although Shahram always asked the host in the tent to give him a pack of cigarettes, he smokes so fast that surely he has none left. Cigarettes are his oxygen, his food, and his love. He is a chain-smoker. The twenty hours that he did not smoke during the escape were excruciating for him. As soon as we were safe in Pakistan, the first thing he pulled out of his pants pocket was his cigarettes. He never stopped smoking during the entire car ride. The inside of the car was thick with the smoke, so thick that had someone looked inside the car they could not have seen us. I can't imagine how he will survive without them, especially now, with the threat of being murdered hanging over his head. Not having any cigarettes left will drive him crazy. There is no way Squashed Nose would offer him a cigarette, unlike when we were in the car. They were too friendly about sharing their rolled-up smelly tobacco then but things are different now. There is a war between them. Squashed Nose will not be kind to the enemy, Shahram.

We confess to Keyvan that we have Shahram's money. Wouldn't it be a good idea to ask Shahram to hand in the money and move on?

"Has anything like this ever happened here?"

"Not that I know of, but it may have."

Keyvan leaves us in the room, ordering us, "Don't go out of the room. Something has to be done before they kill Shahram."

Farah is worried. What if they not only hurt Shahram but in the process they harm Keyvan, too? What are we going to do in this city? We don't know the language, don't know our way around in this strange city, and have no family or relatives. We are doomed, crying hysterically and aching all over. We cry for our situation, for Shahram's life, and for our unknown future.

In this part of the world, human life has no value. The smugglers are willing to kill Shahram over money. What are they going to gain by doing that? It will be a lose-lose situation.

Keyvan returns in the late afternoon. He looks like he has been terribly traumatized. "There was a lot of shouting going on between Shahram and the smugglers. Shahram looked terrible. The smugglers are adamant that unless they are paid in full they will kill Shahram. Shahram looks like he lost a lot of weight overnight. He looks awful and is incoherent. Akbar was the smugglers' mediator on behalf of Shahram."

The smugglers did not want to negotiate at all. Finally, Keyvan says, "I asked Shahram to consider using the money you are holding for him to pay the smugglers to buy his freedom. He agreed reluctantly."

Shahram asked for an extension of three days, supposedly so we can collect the money for him from his family in Iran. He is planning to escape again; if he fails, then he will use his money to pay them as a last resort.

I am too confused. Both sides are right. How would Shahram feel if he was in the smugglers' shoes? Fair is fair. I do not like to be taken advantage of but I also do not like to take advantage of others. He should have discussed the details before he embarked on this journey. But then he also has a point: because of his translation the smugglers made an easy two thousand dollars.

The smugglers agree on a two-day extension. Shahram will be freed once they are paid.

～～～～

We haven't been here two days and every little step is a big ordeal: the shower manoeuvres, the canned food, the Shahram hostage crisis, the cold weather, the lack of shoes and coats. Will this ever get better? I had no idea what would happen when I arrived in Pakistan. There are too many things that no one can prepare for in advance when one is a refugee.

Keyvan takes us to meet his friends at the university dormitory. Quetta's damp December weather gives everyone the chills. Hoshmand, one of the dorm students, offers Farah and me each a coat.

No shops sell women's clothing. Do women make their own robes? Wearing a man's wool coat, which is too big for me, is not going to bother me. Warmth is what I care about now. The last thing we want is to get sick in a foreign land.

All the students we meet are men—not one female among them. This is not surprising. Women can only survive in Quetta if they are hidden away and invisible.

"I have had enough of visiting students and seeing the dorms, let's visit the city," I announce.

Keyvan is not so enthusiastic about taking us sightseeing. He keeps stalling. Why?

～～～～

The faces in the street are sad, scowling. The men's eyes jump nervously from place to place. No one smiles. There something very wrong with this place. It is bizarre; half of the population is missing. There are no women on the streets!

Only mean, angry looking men are around. How is this possible? There must be women somewhere. Where are they hiding? Why are they hiding?

Even the streets are steeped in mourning. No colourful carpets. No bazaars. No life.

The damp grips us with its chilly fingers. The cold rain adds to our misery. It is bad enough to have no warm clothes; but lack of closed shoes makes the cold temperature more difficult to endure. I am not going to borrow shoes. That is where I draw the line. Mud covers my feet and blackened toes. My toes make me look like a creature from another planet. I hate to look at them and feel terribly responsible for the insult I bestowed upon them on that unforgettable night. I wear the open-toed soccer shoes that I traversed the desert with. It's not as if I can go buy a pair of shoes. There is no women's clothing in this part of the world. Women don't exist!

I point out a black thing to Keyvan. "What is that?"

He looks at me strangely. "It is a woman. She's wearing a burka."

She looks like a moving black telephone booth without windows. Black mesh covers her face. Is it for this sort of existence I struggled across the desert? Is this the life of every woman in this city? It is shockingly dreadful. My reality is put into new perspective. In comparison, Iran is a paradise. Here the women have no shape, no expression, and no colour. I can't even see their eyes. It is a living death to be a woman in this city.

Ten ramshackle shops make up the main street. A dead cow hangs on a hook in a butcher shop. There are no flies buzzing around. It is even too cold for the hungry flies. The customers, all men, stab at the still-dripping cow to pick the section of meat they want. The butcher trims their selections on his small, blood-stained wooden block next to the dead cow.

The carrots, potatoes, and beets have seen better days. What is available is unappetizing and not fresh. The small apples at the fruit stand look rotten.

Farah suggests, "Keyvan, buy some oranges. That is the only fruit that looks edible." Pastry shops like we had back home in Shiraz are non-existent.

The sidewalk is cracked, broken asphalt, narrow and plagued with potholes full of water. It is a difficult task to simply walk. Old, broken-down navy Hondas and Toyotas roam the streets. Keyvan mutters under his breath, "Those who have a car are considered the wealthiest of the wealthy."

As Keyvan, Farah, and I stroll along the main street, Farah whispers, "Sima, don't look back. We're being followed." We are still paranoid that someone may have followed us from Iran.

"What do you mean?"

"Don't look, but there's a line of men behind us. Let's go into a shop and you'll see what I mean."

We stop. As we enter the fruit store, a line of men that stretches about half a block also stops. We buy some more oranges. Leave the store. The men start to follow us again.

"Keyvan, what's going on?"

"Do you see any women walking around here?"

I look around, and at last spot a black telephone booth masquerading as a woman on the street. "Oh . . . there's one."

"Tell me how she's dressed?"

She has on full black body covering; her face is masked by a black mesh net.

"Now do you understand why they are following you? They've probably never seen a woman's face before. To them, you look like you're walking around naked. Maybe they even think you are prostitutes. Who knows?"

Me?

Naked?

Prostitute?

His voice echoes in my head.

It is incomprehensible. I wish the earth would open up and swallow me. These stares are too hard to take. It is like they are ripping my clothes off with those beady, lustful eyes. If I were in Shiraz I would first curse these men, then I would zigzag though the alleys to safety. Here I can't speak and don't know my way around. The buildings are closing in on me. The men's burning eyes follow me no matter where I go. There is no way to ignore them. Slouching make me smaller. Sima, disappear. Where can I disappear to? There is nowhere to go. I am trapped.

Covering my hair is not enough. Despite our *hijab*, long pants and long-sleeved loose shirts, men follow us like cats behind a fish wagon. I am not used to the blatant stares or the belligerent behaviour.

Don't they work? They sit along the street or lean on lampposts smoking their reeking, rolled-up tobacco. How do they feed their families? Their faces are wrinkly, like ancient crocodiles. Men in Iran do not behave this way. I could not have imagined such a different culture. Pakistan was once part of the Persian Empire. We all come from the same culture. What has gone wrong with them? A major genetic mutation happened here. We usually evolve for the better. We progress, but these people have regressed drastically.

I want to hide, similar to the rest of the women in this city. The men are a nightmare. They are so obvious in their stalking that it is impossible not to pay attention to them or to pretend they do not exist. Facing their stares and smelling their foul cigarettes is suffocating.

But I don't have this luxury.

⟩⟩⟩⟩⟩

"When are we going to leave Quetta? Why are we still here?"

Keyvan's answer is not promising. "Farah and you are not safe here. You have no identification. Tomorrow morning I will take both of you to the United Nations office to apply for political refugee status."

Not . . . safe? What do you mean?

It never occurred to me that I don't have a passport and that the Pakistani police can arrest me.

Everything is new to me: the stares, the smells, the condensed milk, and now my stay in this hotel and my safety in Pakistan.

The metal springs in the bed poke me all night. But I cannot bother moving; the part I lie on is the softest part of the bed. I can't sleep. What if the police break in as I am sleeping? Will they deport me back to Iran? What if the police stop us when we are on our way to the United Nations?

Am I becoming a drama queen? Is it really this bad? I don't want to try to find out what happens if I am stopped by the police.

December 13, morning

Keyvan flags another black taxi. I do not like these black cabs; I feel like I am going to a funeral. The steering wheel is on the wrong side. Keyvan tells the taxi driver to take us to the UN office. The part of the city we are now passing is a different shade of grey. I am depressed just looking around me.

The driver's eyes are locked on us from his front mirror the entire ride. His behaviour is no different than that of the other men in this city. He stops in front of a one-storey building. This is the famous United Nations? I had pictured a beautiful, sophisticated office building with a fancy gate. But what is in front of us is small and plain. We open the door, and right across from us is a man sitting at a wooden desk, typing. The walls are painted cream, and they are clean. I can actually see the colour of the walls. There is no sound other than the occasional clacking of the typewriter. No one listens to music. No music, no life.

The United Nations employee is a native Pakistani man in his thirties. "What can I do for you?" This is a good start. He wants to help us.

"I refuuugggeeeee, p . . . ol . . . it . . . ic . . . al." It is what I say—or think I say—with my broken English. Keyvan comes to the rescue. "They are here to apply for United Nations political refugee status."

The UN employee nods his head, puzzled. "There have been many Iranians these days, but I have not yet seen Iranian women here." He hands each of us a registration form printed in English and asks us to fill it out, pointing out a table with chairs, near the wall behind his desk, with a couple of pens on it. Farah and I march over and sit down.

I have never seen such a detailed form with so many questions. Even if the questions were in Persian, I am not sure I could answer all of them. But the form is in a foreign language, English. It is impossible. I have some knowledge of English because of the English classes in elementary school, but all that I can remember is the response to "What is your name?" and "Where do you live?" Well, I have to try.

The questions are as simple as my name, my parents' and grandparents' names and their country of birth, their addresses and their professions. I try many times, rewrite the answers many times, tear up the form many times, until I finally manage to answer most of the questions. Every two seconds, we prod Keyvan with a question. His English is as poor as ours, but he has filled out the form before. We count on his help.

One question in particular is none of their business. What is my religion? Jewish? Muslim? Christian? None of the above? I have to check one of the four choices. This is the United Nations office. They do not have to know. They will probably guess. But I will not tell them. I do not like the idea that my gender, and now possibly my religion, will create prejudice against me. This is the United Nations. Why does our religion make a difference to the UN? I leave it blank.

The forms are completed. Farah and I hand them to the man. He tells us to come back in two days for an interview.

"Why in twoooo days? Why no now? No one else waaaaittt here."

"The person in charge is out of the office. He will be back in two days. Meanwhile, make sure you do not leave your hotel room for too long because you do not have proper documentation. If the police stop you, you do not have protection."

I want to shout at him, "This is the United Nations! My life is in danger! How come there is no one to replace this important man? What if I am stopped by the police?" There is no choice. We have to accept this.

But I can't put two sentences together. I force myself to say, "Ttttank you," and leave with Farah and Keyvan.

Would Mamán and Baba be angry at me for not telling the truth about my religion? I am devastated about my current situation. I can't go back. I can't go forward. I have to wait. And wait. And wait. That is all I do. I am an expert at waiting. I have to wait two long, dreadful days to have an interview to *maybe* be eligible for the protection of the UN. What if I am *not* eligible? What do I do then? I do not want to go outside of this room. I can't cook. I can't crochet. I can't read books. All I can do is to sleep. My back is sore from all the springs poking into me from the bed.

Farah and Keyvan are newlyweds, and I have nowhere to go to give them privacy. Keyvan is kind. He brings us food. Melba toast and condensed milk have lost their novelty. That is all I eat for breakfast, lunch, and dinner. Thank God for the occasional orange. I've never been a fussy eater, but condensed milk is spouting out of me. It is monotonous.

This room is unappealing. There is nothing to look at. It is enough to make anyone go mad. But I will not allow this wait to drive me crazy.

I dream.

I dream of a day I do not have to be sleeping in the same room with Farah and Keyvan.

I dream of a day I will be accepted as a citizen of a free country.

I dream of a day I will be able to go to university.

I dream of a day I can see Mamán and Baba and they will be proud of me.

My brain is racing around the world and I am chasing it. It is a great distraction from reality. I love dreaming. When I dream, this room comes alive with my hopes.

December 15, morning

Two days in the small room is suffocating. We walk out of the "hotel." Fresh air feels good to my nostrils. I am alive. Black Taxi is our best friend, now. At the UN, the same man greets us happily. He is expecting us. "I remember you." He motions us into a private room off to the side. Another UN official sits at the desk, perusing our completed forms. He is a white man, blond, heavy-set, who speaks perfect English. He must be either European or American; he looks like the backpacker tourists in Iran before the Revolution. The ones I always practised my "perfect" English on.

We trust Keyvan to be our translator. Maybe because he had already filled out the same forms before, he is confident. The UN official asks the same questions as on the form, our dates of birth, address, father's name, mother's name . . . Does he think we lied? Why does he have to check the information again? I am getting nervous.

We sit quietly. Keyvan translates for us as we answer the official's questions for an hour. He does not ask anything about our religion. This is a good sign.

"Why did you leave your country?" to determine under which category we would be protected. There are many categories. "We were not able to go to school. Our aunt and a friend were executed."

He pulls open a drawer and withdraws a file. Opening it, he picks up two papers, and hands them to us. Written in both English and Urdu are the words "Protected under the United Nations."

We look up, puzzled. The UN official explains that this is the documentation that protects us under the United Nations international ruling. "You are now officially a refugee. In all countries where the UN has an office, asylum is guaranteed to any political refugee. You fall under political refugee status." As excited as I am by having this piece of paper in my hand, I am overwhelmed by a million more obstacles to overcome; but every step conquered is a step closer to freedom.

Again he rummages in his drawer, and pulls out an envelope. "Here are 300 rupees, your monthly UN allowance, for all your expenses." How generous of the UN.

I ask Keyvan, "Why is he keeping cash in the drawer? Isn't he afraid of thieves?"

He responds, "Do you have a bank account here?"

"No," I reply, regretting the question.

"That is why he gave you cash."

Keyvan informs the official, "We will move to Lahore in two days. Please forward their files to the Islamabad UN office." Keyvan's file has already been sent to Islamabad.

We are back at our hotel. Shahram is sitting at the entrance waiting for us. The smile on my face is as big as it can ever get. I scream, "How did you manage to get out?" A miracle happened today. This is the best day since my departure from Shiraz. I have the full protection of the United Nations. It is also the day Shahram is liberated from the smugglers.

The city is so small that it is easy to figure out where we are staying, in the only local hotel in town. "I came by to thank all of you for the relentless support and the help you offered me. It was smart of you not to mention that you were hiding my money."

"Our pleasure. You also helped us."

It is easier to leave Quetta knowing that Shahram is a free man at last.

December 17, 1982

It is Friday, but how are we to mark our Shabbat? Are there Jews living in Pakistan? We aren't even sure we want to look for them. It makes me very sad. We don't tell anyone we are Jewish. Keyvan keeps it quiet, too. It is easier that way. We don't want to complicate matters. I keep my secret close to my heart, reminiscing about the smell of fried fish, the glow of the flickering Shabbat candles, and the entire family gathered together to recite the blessing over the wine. I keep the ritual alive in my heart. It is not as colourful as it was in Shiraz, but for now this is my best option.

If I had wings, I could fly to Shiraz and sit on top of the pomegranate tree and watch Mamán as she prepares for Shabbat, as Naneh Jaan-Jaan brings lunch, as Baba returns from the farm. I choke up, but I can't cry anymore. Reality crashes into my consciousness. There is no way to have wings, and I have paid a huge price for this so-called freedom, which I am now beginning to question. Maybe it was all a mistake!

I have not been at all impressed with Pakistan so far. Quetta is backward. The men seem to have nothing to do other than stand around in the street and stare at passing flapping black telephone booths or ogle and undress any woman who walks by. I will be happy to leave this place. It has served its purpose: it had the closest UN office to Zahedan. I will never come back. A few days here is enough not just for this lifetime but for the next ten lifetimes.

I am dressed in the same clothes I crossed the desert with, with a head covering and my open-toed soccer shoes. My black toenail is staring at me. *Look, look, I am the evidence of your desert trek.*

We leave Quetta at noon by train for Lahore.

This is the first time I will be travelling by train. There are no trains in Shiraz.

The train is massive, all metal and black. It is humongous. Frightening. It approaches the station and shrieks to a stop. The image of the train in my mind clashes with the reality that is in front of me. I had seen pictures of trains in magazines when I lived in Shiraz, but what is in front of me does not look like what appeared in the magazines.

We climb the dirty steps into the car. The pictures I had seen always showed bright red plush seats with plenty of leg room. These seats are brown and black and are so dirty that it is hard to guess what the original colour was. I'm sure they have never been cleaned. And there is no leg room. In the pictures, there was a colourful tray of food in front of the passenger. Here, there is no attendant, no sign of food.

People travel with their children and their chickens. Here, between the caged chickens and the little girls and boys scampering about, I curl into a fetal position. The women wear the cumbersome black sheets that cover them from head to toe, including their faces. The men stand out as individuals. The women are anonymous. It must be hard to travel when you are encumbered with all this cloth. It is not easy for them to keep their restless little boys from disappearing down the aisle. They must feel suffocated. I had that feeling when I wore the *chador*. Relating to their predicaments and frustrations is easy for me.

It is a good day's train ride to Lahore. As we move northwest, the dramatic mountain terrain we saw around Quetta grows flatter, and a greener, gentler landscape emerges. Thank God, there is still colour left in the universe! Keyvan has packed his backpack with Melba toast, condensed milk, and oranges. We dine on this elegant meal.

We enter Lahore's train station. Walking out of the train station, I am left speechless. This scene feels familiar, as though I have been here before. The downtown square is similar to Shiraz's main square, with its dancing water fountain of coloured lights. The ornate buildings, intricate architecture, the cleanliness, the streets lined with green trees, and the freedom of men and women to walk on the street without being stalked is a sight for sore eyes. This is a testament that the city was once a cultural capital. There is no way anyone could compare Quetta to Lahore, and if one would even attempt to do so, it would be like comparing day to night. This is the way Iran looked before the Revolution.

Keyvan tells us, "I lived here for two weeks before I came to meet you in Quetta. We will go to an affordable hotel until we figure out what to do next." I can't forget that this is Farah and Keyvan's honeymoon.

Apparently, there is no plan. We will devise one as we go along.

Here we meet again with students. Keyvan keeps nagging me, "Don't be too friendly with the students. Don't talk too much." I understand his reasoning. But I do not like it when he orders me and corrects me so many times in one day.

We are walking down the street when Keyvan suddenly stops to converse with a stranger. He had done this many times. "Do you know a man by the name of Mohammed? He is from Shiraz."

"Yes, there is a man by that name and he is from Shiraz. He lives in Rawalpindi."

Keyvan tells us later, "Mohammed knows many people here. He's lived in Rawalpindi since the Revolution. We have to move to Rawalpindi to find him. We will go there until we figure out how to leave this country."

Our stay in Lahore lasts a day. Though I love this city, we need to go chasing Mohammed in the hope that he will help us find a way to leave Pakistan.

December 18, 1982

In less than three weeks, we have seen so many cities in Pakistan. We most likely have seen more of Pakistan than some natives in this country. We travel by bus from Lahore to Rawalpindi, the fourth-largest city in Pakistan. At noon on a warm, sunny Saturday afternoon, the bus station is so crowded with people that it brings back memories of Tehran. Is there enough air here for these hordes to breathe?

Hundreds of merchants have dragged their donkeys, laden with goods, to prime sites in the middle of this busy thoroughfare, intent on selling their wares. People push through the crowds in all directions. We are jostled, elbowed, bumped, as if we are invisible.

This is already a million times better than Quetta, a good start. I may actually like it here. There is action in the street.

No more walking telephone booths!

I can get lost in this crowd and not worry about the staring eyes that rip my clothes off me. Women are not hidden. They are dressed in saris, their faces showing. Their long, straight, black braided hair falls freely down their backs or frames their faces. Colour is everywhere. Men don't notice us. We are freaks no longer.

It is dirty and noisy. Garbage, newspapers, and food wrappings cover the ground. Mysterious red patches litter the pavement everywhere we walk. "What are all these red spots?" I ask Keyvan.

"The locals, at the end of their meal, chew a digestive called paan.[7] It is red and it stains their mouths and lips. When they are finished, they spit it out, mostly into the street, on the pavements. What you see is spit spots of red dye. See the man there? He is chewing some." Disgusting!

He continues his explanations, "Welcome to Pakistan. They had paan spots all over Quetta, too. You were too busy thinking about the stalkers to notice."

This random red tapestry is topped by different-sized lumps of animal feces, smelly and awful. I have to look not only right and left as I cross the street; I have to look down, too. I don't want to step into this muck.

Crossing the street in Rawalpindi is a life-threatening experience. Every time I cross, I am grateful that I have not been flattened by a car. A short stroll along the sidewalk challenges every sense. Cars weave their way around and through crowds of people and animals. When not weaving, they drive on the left side of the road, which is the opposite of how they drive in Iran—one more thing to look out for besides donkeys, chickens, people, and paan. The air is intensely hot and thick with the smells of animals and sweating humans. Drivers curse pedestrians and animals; pedestrians hurl insults back at them; and animals complain and birds squawk indignantly. Dust gets in the mouth and eyes. Colours assault the eyes.

---

7   A betel nut concoction.

Keyvan has done his homework. He has asked the students in Lahore advice on renting a hotel room. We walk for fifteen minutes; he motions us to follow him quickly, which is impossible. Walking has never been so torturous. The location tells me we are overpaying a lot for the convenient location of this hotel. Keyvan must think this is what we need. We follow him like sheep. Whether he knows what he is doing or not will become apparent as we go. Is this the blind leading the blind?

He enters a foul, gloomy, local hotel. We follow. The owner slithers toward us from the direction of a room behind the counter. This is creepy. Does he sleep here? This three-storey attached building must cost a fortune in the centre of town. Every square inch is used for rental.

Strangely, the owner does not want to see our documents. Not that we have any documents, but usually in any hotel they ask to see some form of documentation. He must think we are Pakistanis visiting Rawalpindi. Keyvan rents a room with two single beds for two weeks. The owner hands us the key.

Our room is on the second floor. As we walk up the stairs, the low-voltage light bulb flickers, announcing its last breath. We open the door to a dark room with a high ceiling and walls painted dark brown. Keyvan flicks on the light. It barely illuminates the room. The one small window is high up and faces a brick wall. The brown and red-striped blinds are pulled halfway down, further robbing the room of light. This room is unhealthily dark. At least there is a private bathroom here, with a proper shower and sink. Luxury at last! Farah and Keyvan will sleep together in one of the single beds. I will settle far away, five feet away, in the other corner of the room. I am embarrassed for both Farah and Keyvan.

December 19, 1982

I am tired all the time. Even after twelve hours of sleep, I wake up exhausted. This is not normal for me. We spend most of the time in our hotel room sleeping. Farah and I have no desire to leave the room.

Keyvan buys a single-burner stove, a pot, a knife, three spoons, and three metal plates. Metal plates! That is disgusting. Prisoners are fed with metal plates. It will have to do. I am a fugitive. I can't expect any better.

We are now equipped to cook for ourselves. It is easy to shop here. Keyvan buys the essentials from the shops in the street downstairs. The grocery store provides us with tomatoes, rice, onions, and we make our first hot meal since we left Zahedan.

We prepare vegetarian food, rice with tomatoes. To boil water takes forever, and the element is slower than a turtle. In the future, we will have to start cooking early in the morning, and then we might have something ready by suppertime. This stove is intended for keeping food warm, not cooking. Too much time is wasted cooking this way. It is not as if we have anything else to do or someplace else to go, but it still bothers me.

While waiting for the meal to cook, we distract ourselves by sleeping, to recoup the energy lost to the physical and emotional stress of the journey. This is demanded by our bodies, and we are too worn out to disobey or to argue. Walking over one hundred kilometres through the desert that first night alone was both physically and emotionally taxing. Sleep is wonderful; endless hours of it are recharging us like a battery plugged into a power outlet.

December 21, 1982

The room is unusually quiet for mid-morning. Keyvan tiptoes out of bed. I whisper, "Why is Farah not up yet?"

"She is sick. High fever. She needs a doctor."

Keyvan leaves. I am alone with Farah, whose skin is boiling hot. I put cold compresses on Farah's forehead. This is all we need now. Little things that I took for granted have new meaning now. If we were in Shiraz, I would have made her orange juice or chicken soup or asked Naneh Jaan-Jaan for help; she would have had some concoction to bring down the fever. I have nothing to offer her.

She wakes up in the late afternoon. She is hot, red like a watermelon, and lethargic.

"Where is Keyvan?"

"He went to look for a doctor. He will be back soon."

She wobbles as she goes to the bathroom, screaming with pain. I am deeply alarmed. Fear has been revealing to me its monstrous face with the many different masks it wears. Today's version wears the fever mask. I pray for Farah—the prayer I always say when I have no other resources at my disposal.

Keyvan returns. We leave for the hospital by taxi. It is our first experience with taxis in Rawalpindi. The poor driver has a difficult task manoeuvring around. There is no distinction between the roads and the sidewalks. Looking out from the taxi, I note that the signs on the shops are all in the Persian alphabet; I can read them but cannot understand them. There is no order to the shops, many of which are filled with fabrics; colourful saris float on the hangers in shop entranceways. The fruit stand is next to the clothing shop, which is next to the butcher shop. This is chaotic. I am accustomed to a proper ordering of shops, as in Iran. The shops that sell fabrics are next to each other; the rug shops are next to each other. But here, simply looking at the variety from a taxi makes me dizzy.

The men wear shirts unbuttoned almost to their navels. Why bother putting on the shirt?

Finally, we reach the hospital. The patients are howling, screaming, rolling on the ground. Is the world coming to an end? This looks like an early 1900s hospital with no renovation since its construction. The walls are dirty. The chairs are broken. The staff is too busy.

With this many people here before us, will Farah be seen before she passes out? Finally, it is her turn.

A blood test is ordered. We are told it takes two weeks for the results to come. Two weeks! Farah could die in that time! The doctor prescribes antibiotics.

Keyvan takes the prescription to the pharmacy near the hotel. Within a couple of hours, he comes back with the medications. Nothing is done quickly here. Our patience is tested every minute of every day.

Farah starts taking the antibiotics and slowly begins to feel better. She must have picked up something along our journey. She is never sick. But the escape must have been too hard on her in addition to the extra responsibility for my welfare. She has never complained, not then and not now.

I write to Mamán: Please send me a new pair of shoes and some clothes. Mail it to Mohammed's address. He has a permanent address.

I would like to meet him. Why is he not coming to visit?

❧❧❧❧❧

Keyvan announces, "My friend Mohammed is coming to meet you this afternoon."

Mohammed arrives in mid-afternoon in a great rush, as if the house were on fire and he is the fireman sent to put out the flames. He is

Shirazi, dark-skinned, short-haired, with a heavy Shirazi accent that can't be missed from a kilometre away. In the Shirazi accent every word is dragged out. It is not that we stutter; it is for poetic effect that we drag out every word. We have done it for so long that we do not realize we do it.

Is this payback time? Because in the past, everyone had to wait a long time to hear a sentence from us; that is why our patience is being tested so much. We are getting a taste of our own medicine.

"Hi, how are you?" He looks down at the ground as he talks to us. Why so shy?

He is impressed by the courage and the quick thinking we showed when we encountered the Pakistani police.

He hands us a bag. "I know you will like this book; an elementary English grammar text with Persian instructions. Start learning English. It will come in handy."

"*Mamnoon*, it is kind of you to help us."

Farah asks for directions to the United Nations.

"The United Nations headquarters is in Islamabad. It is a fifteen-minute walk to the public bus stop from here. A half-hour bus ride and a half-hour walk to the UN office. Present yourselves to the UN as soon as possible." He gives directions in his slow Shirazi drawl but at an accelerated rate, as if he is being chased by a lion and is running for his life. But as generous as he is with all the goodies he brought us, he is that thrifty with his words.

Why is he speaking so fast? He is too rushed. Is it because he visits all newcomers to this part of Pakistan? I dare not ask all the questions that pop into my head. He dashes out of the room as fast as he walked in.

~~~~~

As I venture onto the streets of Rawalpindi, I cannot stop thinking about how much I miss my family, my beautiful garden, the familiar faces, and my neighbourhood. I am lost here. Today I venture out to buy body soap and when I return to the hotel I see that it is laundry soap. Never would this happen to me in Shiraz.

In Shiraz I knew every twist and turn of the streets, but here in Rawalpindi I have no idea how to get from one place to another, to read the signs or bargain with the shop owners. Half the time, I am not sure what I am buying. To buy shampoo, there are too many choices, and all the labels are in Urdu and English. Both languages are foreign to me. The street vendors speak only Urdu, and I don't speak any.

In addition to physical fatigue and the culture shock of Pakistan, I am troubled as to how to continue my studies or how to get to a country where I can do so. The future is blurry and has been so for too long. Insecurity is my worst enemy. It carves a crooked path in my psyche and gnaws relentlessly at me. It is my constant companion. The only secure thing in my life now is this small burner that can cook the food ever so slowly. That is why, every third day when it is my turn to cook, I get up early and start working the snail-paced stove to have supper ready by evening. There is no routine or structure. It is a terrible feeling when every day starts and ends like this.

To live with newlyweds is awkward. In Shiraz, when we did not want to be in the company of someone, we would refer to them as a "donkey's head": their presence was as useless as a donkey's head. This is how I feel living with my newlywed sister. I am too scared and too tired to leave to give them their privacy. I have nowhere to go.

I am a helpless foreigner here. The locals must regard me the way I looked at the Afghanis in Shiraz. Displaced. Not belonging. A burden to society? I hope not. Keyvan leads the battle to get us out of this situation.

Wearing the same clothing day in and day out is tiring. For many weeks, I have been wearing the same clothes that I left Iran with; the shirt will soon have holes in it. Its colour has mutated from navy to grey, and the seams are beginning to unravel. I begged Mamán both by phone and by letter to send me clothes. They will arrive, but not soon enough for me.

Farah is slowly regaining her strength. Today we will venture out, following Mohammed's directions, to the UN.

December 22, 1982

The UN office is a fifty-kilometre bus ride from Rawalpindi. Buses are cheap and frequent; every ten minutes another bus loads up. As we enter the bus, the driver shouts, "Men to the rear, ladies in the front." We could have been back in Iran. Though there are no walking black telephone booths in Rawalpindi, there are still definite gender restrictions. Men and women can't mix here, either. How will we know when to get off the bus? We will have to keep turning around to make sure we and

Keyvan leave the bus at the same time.

Islamabad looks like yet another country. From the bus window, the roads are cleaner, and there are no masses of people milling around the squares as in Rawalpindi. There are no animals on the streets, and little traffic. Wizened, bent old trees line the boulevard. It is December, but the leaves are lush. I haven't seen such greenery and cleanliness in Shiraz since long before the Revolution. The women in the street are dressed in gorgeous saris, or in what I assume are the latest European styles of jeans and dresses. It is a sight for sore eyes. The freedom of dress, the beautiful pinks, oranges, and yellows of the saris, the cleanliness, and the orderly street, bursting with vibrant trees and flowers, is a 180-degree turn from my experience in Quetta. Trees! I missed them so much, for so long. The weather reminds me of northern Iran and the Caspian Sea. This is what European cities must look like. It is a lovely sight from the bus.

There are still red spots on the pavement, but not as many. I would much prefer to be living here than in Rawalpindi, which is so different from what I am accustomed to.

We walk briskly toward the UN office, following the instructions that Mohammed gave us. The UN supported us in Quetta, and we expect the same here.

We pass stately homes with marble columns, locked behind steel gates; winding stone paths lead up to the house. The cars are much newer here, and we recognize many prestigious makes: Mercedes, Toyota, Jeep. This is the capital of Pakistan, and it is obvious by the amount of money riding the roads.

After a thirty-minute walk, we arrive at the UN office, a white building with majestic columns on either side of the entrance. Keyvan, Farah, and I enter through the garden to the front door. From the lobby, we see many doors. People passing through are dressed in suits.

None of them wear head coverings.

UN officials? Dignitaries?

"We are here to update our status." The receptionist picks up a phone and calls someone. We wait at the side of the desk. About ten minutes later, we are ushered into a waiting room where our social worker will come to get us.

Social worker? Mamán used to be a social worker as well as a nurse. She would drop in unexpectedly on her assigned clients, always women, to make sure they were running their home properly and taking good care of their children. Is this social worker going to come for surprise visits and find out how we live? It would be mortifying if she sees how we cook in our hotel room and wash the dishes in the shower.

The social worker informs us that there are many Iranian refugees here. We follow her silently across the lobby to her office. There is another waiting room outside the office with many people milling about. Take a number and sit down; dozens of people are ahead of us.

We listen to the chatter around us: Persian! Now Farah and I are smiling. We are among our own. I ask a man sitting next to me, "Where are you from?"

He answers, "Isfahan."

A woman inquires, "Where are you from?"

"Shiraz." Now we are included in the conversation.

People are eager to talk, about their experiences, about their families, about their lives. We pass the time Shirazi style, peppering one another with questions. How wonderful to speak in my mother tongue! We blend in. No one asks about our religion. We do not mention it.

We meet many people from Iran who are applying for political refugee status. They are full of horrific stories about friends and family members who were arrested and executed back home.

Keyvan recalls, "Yes, my brother was brilliant, but he was shot for no reason. The Hezbollah goons didn't even question him first. You're guilty if they just think you are guilty. It is madness."

A gentle-looking woman with long, silky, black hair and no *hijab* introduces herself as Sakineh Khanoom. "They killed my brother the same way," she says. "They gave no reason. They accused him of being a counter-revolutionary. We all fought for freedom. Once they took the power, they took the freedom to serve themselves. They are free to commit brutalities, murders, rapes. It is crazy. No one other than themselves, whatever his politics, is safe."

An older man in his fifties cries bitter tears as he recounts his story. "I am an engineer. I worked many years during the Shah's reign. I built a good fortune. All my assets were confiscated and I lost my job, just because I am Baha'i. My bank account was frozen. I've worked all my life and I am left with nothing. I am lucky to be alive." He must be suffering a lot. An Iranian man never cries in public, especially not in front of women. He looks ninety years old. He has so many wrinkles. The last three years have not been kind to him.

"Our aunt was picked up at midday from work one day. She didn't come home . . . nobody knew where she was, but her name was announced on the radio the next day among the executed," Farah recounts.

A slim woman in her late twenties, with short, cropped hair, speaks accent-less Persian; she must be from Tehran. But why is she here? Why didn't she escape through Turkey? "They came to my house while I was hiding to arrest my brother. They took him. We never saw him again and there was no record of where they took him. I still don't know if my brother is dead or alive."

Sheyla's story flashes before my eyes. "They picked up my friend's two sisters one night. A few weeks later, it was announced over the radio that her family had to come pick up their dead bodies. The voice on the radio sounded so jubilant. A few days later they came back for my friend, and I never saw her again. That's when I stopped going to school."

Farah asks Afsaneh Khanoom, "We are now staying in a hotel in Rawalpindi. Do you know anyone we can rent a room from?"

"How many of you are there?"

"Me, my sister and my husband."

"I have a two-bedroom apartment with my husband. I will rent you one of the bedrooms as of January. I have sleeping bags. You can share my pots and pans, too."

Today I am a lucky person to have met Afsaneh.

We thank Afsaneh. "We will not be able to move until the end of the month anyway, because Keyvan rented the room in the hotel for two weeks. We didn't think we would be so lucky to find a place so quickly. We will meet you here next week."

Farah and I are stunned at Afsaneh's kindness. How could she trust us to share her apartment with us? She did not even ask us our last name. We tell Keyvan about our discussion with her. Although he does not usually like it when we are too friendly with strangers, he is proud that we have found a place so fast. "Well done. I am happy to move out of that stinking hotel room."

There is something special about Afsaneh, and both Farah and I trust her completely. It is in her eyes, in her voice. "When you look at the eyes, they tell the truth." Maybe there is truth to this. We will soon find out.

"Farah and Sima!" At three o'clock, our social worker summons us into her office. She greets us in Pakistani-accented Persian. "I will be your social worker. Call me Mrs. Maria." She is old, dressed in a skirt suit, her long, black hair in a ponytail. She updates our documents. We are to meet her if there are any changes in our address. She informs us that our monthly UN allowance will be available at the end of every month. "Make sure you are here early in the morning because there will be a long lineup."

We are moving to Islamabad! At last—a light at the end of the tunnel. I can't imagine Afsaneh's apartment being as dark as the room we have in Rawalpindi.

Anticipating that we will be moving at the end of the month, we can tolerate the inconvenience of our room in Rawalpindi more easily. I begin to appreciate little things: reading any books I want, the little burner, cooking our own meals no matter how painfully slow-paced. Hope gives us comfort and keeps us going.

We travel to Islamabad to go to the UN office again on Monday. As planned, Afsaneh is waiting for us, excited. We visit her second-floor apartment, consisting of two rooms connected to each other by a door. Thankfully, each room has its own exit to the outside corridor. Four bare walls and an off-white tile floor stare at us. No window again. It looks like a prison cell.

In this room, we will not know if it is day or night. We are not lucky enough to have windows. I love to see sunshine spilling into a room. There is no fragrant flower-filled garden to look into. A window is a luxury we can't afford now. The kitchen is only slightly better equipped than our present facility. There is a two-burner stove next to a sink. If a space was too tight to move in, Mamán would say: "It is like a casket." The bathroom is so small that it feels like a casket with a sink and a shower.

"Don't take a daily shower. This apartment is rented out to two people, not five. If the owner finds out we are five living here, he will kick us out."

At least she is honest in disclosing the rules before we move in. A Persian expression comes to mind: "It is better to fight at the beginning about the details and be at peace later." She could have easily omitted this detail and left it to when we moved in.

The deal is done: 300 rupees per month for the rent. We move on January 1. Even though this room is by no means deluxe, it is much better than the hotel room in Rawalpindi. For one thing, there is no odour of rotten rat associated with it.

We return to our Rawalpindi room. We meet Afsaneh a couple more times at the UN office, our social network, the only place we meet other Persian speakers.

January 1, 1983

Today is packing day. In less than two weeks, we have accumulated cooking gear, two big shopping bags' worth of shampoo, soaps, bottles of oil, salt, spices, metal plates, and our fancy burner. We are packed like mules. The bags are heavy, and we balance them happily, overjoyed to move out of the dark, noisy, featureless room in Rawalpindi and travel to Islamabad to live with Afsaneh.

A wave of homesickness engulfs me as I move, again, from one city to another, from one dark room to another. I am homeless. I have nobody to go to other than Farah and Keyvan. No way out. Will I rot in this country? We are all in the same boat, living subhuman lives. Darkness wraps itself around me like a thick black cloud. I do not like when I feel this dark. I want to run away from myself. But there is nowhere to run to.

The bus stops. Farah pokes me. "We are here. Wake up!"

I wish I could tell her that I was not sleeping. I have nightmares even when I am awake.

Afsaneh greets us. "These are the sleeping bags. You need to buy towels and bedsheets."

Our room is adjacent to Afsaneh's on the second floor. It is too close; we might as well all be living in one room. We hear every move she makes. She must also hear every move we make. When we lay out the sleeping bags Afsaneh gave us, we barely have any room in which to move. The room is ten feet by ten feet square. Farah and Keyvan still have no privacy. I take a corner of the room as my spot. They settle in the corner diagonally opposite to me. If I could disappear every night and come back every morning, I would do it. Though neither Farah nor Keyvan say anything, I am not comfortable to be this close to them at night.

Afsaneh comments on our one-burner stove. "It is smart to have the extra burner." She is relieved that we won't be using her stove too much. Her cooking is the only outlet she has to calm her nervous energy. She loves to cook and is always in the kitchen. She jumps at every bit of noise. Neurotically cooks and cleans. Generously offers us a plate of cooked food. We are allowed to use the kitchen only after she is done cooking. She eagerly shares recipes with us. Farah is becoming a great cook under Afsaneh Khanoom's supervision.

"Come, I will show you where you can go grocery shopping. There is a local fruit market a short way from here. Buy your vegetables only there; he has the freshest produce and the best prices in the neighbourhood."

Afsaneh's refrigerator is in her bedroom and is too small to share. We have to buy fresh groceries to cook every day.

We experiment with some of the native produce and spices and gradually come to like the main spices in Pakistani cuisine — curry, cardamom, and cinnamon, particularly in rice dishes. Cinnamon is hardly ever used in Iranian cooking. When it is mixed with cardamom, it makes a great combination for rice. We try different variations of the new-found spices in our various rice dishes with lentils, raisins, and shredded carrots. The spices make the old, familiar dishes taste so different. When Mamán used to make lentils with rice, she never added cinnamon to it, but Afsaneh Khanoom's recipe requires it, and that makes the dish more sophisticated.

Though there is no window in our room, we are blessed with a balcony right outside the room. From our balcony I can see a schoolyard. One of the few legacies the British left in Islamabad is the school system. The children enter the schoolyard between seven-thirty and eight a.m., walking with the pride of getting an education. They line up to enter the school in the morning, looking neat and well-dressed. Their uniforms always look clean and pressed; the girls' hair is always neatly combed, and even the boys look tidy. The ease and confidence of the schoolchildren impress us, especially in light of what we have just gone through ourselves in Iranian schools.

～～～～～

Keyvan comes home carrying a box in his hand. He visited Mohammed and this parcel had arrived at his house a few days ago. Mamán sends love packages to us through Mohammed. I jump up and down with joy. We carefully open the box, which is taped so heavily that it could have been mailed to Mars.

In it are clothes for Farah and me. Black pants; two long-sleeved shirts; a beautiful brown purse with a delicate flower embroidered on the flap, with a matching wallet; white sneakers. I no longer have to wear the same shirt day after day. Now I have two shirts. She includes a bag of pistachios in the parcel. The scent of Shiraz is packed into the parcel. Mamán packed as much love as she could into this box.

Mamán packs in the parcel things I know she will deny herself. She never fails to demonstrate her love for us.

We have to call Mamán to let her know the parcel arrived. I dress up in my new clothes, feeling like a princess. My purse looks wonderful on my shoulder. No one will ever guess that I am a destitute refugee. If only Mamán could see how happy I am wearing the clothes she has sent me.

It has become our ritual to call Mamán from the telegraph office in Rawalpindi at least every two weeks each Wednesday. The bus ride is long. Considering my new pants, I do not want to sit on these dirty black seats that will stain my clothes. I do not want to walk in the muck of Rawalpindi, either, but there is no choice. We still have to return to this city despite the disgust we feel for it. There is no telegraph office in Islamabad that we know of. On the bright side, there are public buses running every few minutes to Islamabad. The fare is a few rupees. Reasonable.

It is extremely dark. Why is it so dark inside every building we enter? Is it because electricity is too expensive? The office is also much more crowded than the one in Shiraz. I don't know if people come here because it is a place to hang around and meet friends, or whether everyone is here to make phone calls. We have to push our way through and try to find the phone lineup. We don't move. In fact, the line in front of us stays the same length. We see people make their calls and leave. The locals must be butting into the line. How do they cut into the line? We wait for hours, tired, hot, bored, and thirsty. We have to stay here to make the call or come back and wait again.

We have been lined up for at least three hours. Finally it is my turn; I have to pay in advance for the estimated minutes I will be talking on the phone. In English, I ask the teller, the only man working in the telegraph office, "How much will it cost for a five-minute call?"

"Ten rupees." I reach into my purse to pay him.

There . . . is . . . no . . . wallet . . . in . . . my purse . . . No, no, no! My wallet has been stolen!

The purse is a tote bag of thick brown material with a handle that goes over my shoulder. Nobody I know has a purse like mine. I felt so lucky and fashionable when I carried this purse on my shoulder with the wallet inside; I felt Mamán was with me.

I am in tears. Sobbing, sobbing, sobbing.

My wallet has been stolen!

There is no way the person who stole it is more impoverished than I am. But whoever it was thought I was rich because the purse is so beautiful. They anticipated a wallet full of money. Thank heaven I did not keep my UN paper in there.

Farah says, "It is only your wallet. You still have the purse. We've lost more than this."

No amount of consoling calms me. It sounds ridiculous to grieve so much for the loss of a wallet. But it is not just the wallet. This is the last straw. I am sad about all the losses in my life: missing Mamán and my whole family. Not having privacy. Not going to school. I miss Soraya. I miss my flowers. I miss the scent of Shiraz. I feel like a ticking bomb, ready to explode from the accumulation of these losses.

I blame myself for not being careful. I do not deserve fine things anymore. It is my own fault that God does not like me. I am devastated, not over the wallet but over its sentimental value. I can't hold myself up anymore. I want to sit down, hide my head between my knees, and cry until I fall to sleep. But I can't do that. There isn't an inch of clean space around me, from chewed-up paan, to sheets of newspaper, to cigarette butts, gum, and spit. It is a revolting sight.

How can these Pakistanis outsmart me? Nobody stole anything from me all the way across the desert from Iran; but a simple walk into the telegraph office, and someone manages to snatch my wallet from under my nose. I have let my guard down. I have lost so many things in my life that the loss of this little thing seems intolerable.

Keyvan comes to the rescue; he gives me money to call home.

Mamán asks, "Have you received the two parcels?"

"Yes, I received the shoes, bags and wallet. Have you sent another parcel?"

"Yes."

"What was in the parcel?"

"Some nuts and the navy blue coat you made in Tehran in the dress factory with Shah Gholam. I sent the two parcels at the same time weeks ago."

Something is wrong. Usually it takes two weeks to receive the parcels. My heart sinks. I love this coat. I am so proud of it and now someone else is enjoying it. It has most likely found itself a new owner. I hope for a miracle that it will show up somehow. I do not want to accuse Mohammed of stealing the coat and maybe selling it. But Keyvan tells me we can't trust anyone. Since we are all in such bad circumstances it is easy to give in to temptation. I dare not bring it up with Mohammed. A double whammy of a day.

Two losses in one day. This is too much to digest.

We never discover the whereabouts of that parcel. Somewhere along its route someone is wearing my lovely coat.

Mamán tells me, "Soraya wants to visit Keyvan."

We understand what she is trying to tell us. Be ready, Soraya is joining you. Soraya writes us in her letters that she is unhappy. She's not going to school. She is envious and longing for us. We are so lucky to have left. Mamán asks, "Do you not think she is too young to go alone to visit Keyvan?"

"Mamán, you know there are mice everywhere. [This is our code for "the walls have ears."] Write me a letter."

Now it all makes sense. Soraya writes us, "I stay in bed until noon. I am not interested in cleaning or crocheting anymore. It was fun when you were here and we had competitions. I miss you both."

Soraya is miserable. There is no solution to her misery except for her to join us here. We recognize this through the letters and broken telephone conversations.

We, as well, feel incomplete without her. The three musketeers can't stand being separated. I am missing a limb. It will be more difficult for Farah and Keyvan to have Soraya around, but I will have someone to keep me company. I also miss our little competitions. When Soraya comes, we will have a competition to learn more English words every day. We always did that; we always pushed each other.

Will this be a good move? I hope. Only time will tell.

She is too young and has no idea how bad our living conditions are. It will be a challenge for all of us, particularly for Keyvan. He is not only a husband to Farah; he has become a father/older brother to me.

He corrects me all the time, from my accent in English, to the way I laugh and the way I speak to others, especially men. Mamán used to say the same thing. I like to talk to everyone; this is my way of coping. I need to be more reserved. Seeing me in a strait-jacket would make Keyvan happy.

~~~~~

Mamán knows her youngest and last remaining daughter will inevitably have to leave. Afraid to go to school, her life is just as limited and frustrating as ours had been. At one point, Mamán writes in a letter, "Soraya will leave sooner rather than later. There is really no other choice."

With the next phone call, Mamán, concerned about a tap on the phone line, tells us, "Soraya will be seeing Keyvan soon. She will travel the same way. Remember Amir and Khatereh. She will go with both of them to visit Keyvan."

We are ecstatic. Soraya will use the same escape network we did. She will be travelling with Amir, a man whom my family has known for a long time and our hiking friend. I stayed with his aunt Zari when I was on the run in Shiraz.

Baba is definitely not going to be let in on this escape, either. He answers the phone when we call, he says hello, and he hands the phone to Mamán. We don't have a chance to tell him we are free and looking forward to the future, a real future, since he refuses to talk to us. Being so far away, we would love to hear words of love and encouragement from him. It won't happen. We are sad about this rift with Baba. I am thick-skinned, but I am homesick and yearn for his love.

I pray that God will grant Mamán enough courage and strength to be able to accompany Soraya out of the house without Baba stopping them. She will have to escort another beloved daughter to Zahedan, a trip she undeniably dreads. It may bring Baba's wrath down on her head. Again. If their relationship was difficult before, it must be impossible now. She could have done nothing. But she opted for freedom for her children. My admiration for her willpower increases daily. I am profoundly indebted to her for the audacity and self-sacrifice she displayed in helping us escape then and Soraya now. Words are too weak to describe her devotion.

Freedom . . .

What would have been my fate, if she had not helped? I do not want to imagine.

The days drag on as we wait. Trying to learn English at this time is frustrating and unsuccessful. Our minds are not on the task. Thoughts of what could go wrong during the escape haunt me day and night. Is Soraya really with Amir and Khatereh? Can they protect her from the smugglers if they want more than promised? I relive the horrible nightmares of our escape. Soraya is young but she is resilient. She was right with us during the revolution. She also knows what her chances are of any kind of normal life in Iran. This will give her the strength and determination to deal with any setbacks. I wish I could be with her, help her survive, support her, cheer her with thoughts of a bright future. I wish I could lighten her burden but I can't.

No one can.

At least I can take comfort in the fact that Soraya's toenails won't turn black because Mamán now knows that cleats are not the best foot-wear for the desert.

Our only connection to smugglers is through Akbar in Quetta. He calls Mohammed, who tells Keyvan, who passes the updates on to us. Life should only be so simple that one could just make a phone call from home directly to us.

It isn't. It is painfully long, waiting. And waiting. And waiting.

~~~~~

I call Shiraz. Cyrus answers the phone. He says, "Mamán and Soraya have gone to Tehran to visit Khaleh."

Farah and I calculate the length of the journey based on our expe-rience. Each escape cannot follow a rigid schedule. We were delayed because the driver was arrested. We have no way of knowing. But Soraya should arrive in Quetta in less than three days.

She does not. No news. No way of getting in touch with the smug-glers to find out what is causing the delay.

Bad news travels fast and no news is good news. But I can't help it, I can't be at peace until I hear from Soraya; as a result, we are in a state of terror for several days. Once again, our patience is tested. But we have no more patience left. We have reached rock bottom.

Keyvan is not at home. Farah and I are going crazy. Mohammed comes to our room in the late afternoon. At the sight of him, we both shout, "Is she safe?"

"Yes," he replies, smiling hugely. "They have arrived in Quetta. She will stay there for two days to complete the UN documentation. Soraya, Amir and Khatereh will take a train for Rawalpindi on Thursday after-noon. If all goes according to the plan, she will be here on Friday, late afternoon, at the train station."

Farah and I jump up and down, hugging each other. Sounds of our laughter and crying fill our room. The people living on the first floor must hear the two hysterical girls screaming and wonder why.

It is over. Soraya is coming. Farah and Keyvan, Soraya and I, all living in a ten-foot by ten-foot room . . . in this room, we will be packed worse than sardines in a tin can. Sleeping at night in this small room will be a challenge. It is too crowded to sleep on our backs. We will have to take turns even in our sleeping positions.

If only Soraya could come to Islamabad directly. It is a beautiful city but there is no train station. Soraya will be as appalled with the scene at the train station as we were.

I long to see Soraya, to talk to her, to hug her. To tell her how proud I am of her for having the courage to take a chance on her future. Reality hits again. There is no way I can see her until she arrives on the train. The restrictions in my life are stifling. I am frustrated and discouraged.

Another long, torturous week is ahead of us. The best way to pass the time is to keep busy. We return to our English books. Now we are more successful. "Afsaneh, our sister is joining us on Friday!" She has no more sleeping bags. The sleeping bags are spread out, for covers, to be used as a cover, and our mattress is the blanket on the floor. There is no other way.

To devise a better sleeping arrangement takes a lot of imagination.

We have lots of imagination, but this room cannot stretch to accommodate us and we are constantly adding more people.

On Friday morning, Farah and I go grocery shopping in the shop near our apartment, to celebrate Soraya's arrival in Islamabad. No fancy tablecloth, no porcelain china dishes and not even more than one dish will be offered to Soraya. What to make for a welcome dinner? "The meek one gives you a green leaf as a gift, not because he is cheap; it is because that is all he has." This is our truth. The best of what we have is offered to Soraya.

Keyvan's invention of the perfected rice dish with tomato is the dinner. This is what we eat all the time. He has supervised us so many times that now no one can tell who the cook is. It is brilliantly red and delicious. Soraya will like it.

Soraya will be stunned when she sees the size of the room and all of us manoeuvring to sleep without hitting one other. She has no idea what to expect. We have not disclosed our living accommodations to her. All four of us will be living in this small room.

If Keyvan and Farah did not have privacy before, it will be worse now.

February 11, 1983

In the afternoon, Keyvan, Farah, and I wait anxiously for Soraya at the train station in Rawalpindi. I miss her so much; it feels like I have not seen her in years. Every faint face in the distance promises Soraya's arrival.

I see the shape and figure, the head with uncovered hair, the so-familiar way of moving, the way she glances around the station as if looking for someone.

"There she is!" I shout. I point her out to Farah, and the two of us push our way through the crowd to her, calling out her name.

She hears and turns toward us. Farah and I fall on her, wrapping our arms around her and kissing her. She starts to laugh, and then we all laugh. Tears are brimming in our eyes, threatening to slide down our faces. Keyvan rushes up and hugs her. She is thinner than she was when we last saw her. Her eyes are red-rimmed. She is brimming with excitement. She is also totally exhausted. I hold her face in my hands. "You're okay? We were worried sick about you. I'm so glad you're here."

The three musketeers are reunited. Soraya's arrival starts a new chapter in our lives. We are uncertain where it will lead us but we are stronger for her being with us.

The thick crowd is difficult to push through as we exit the train station, and it is too noisy for talking. As soon as we are outside on the street, Soraya commences to tell her escape story.

She is still wearing the same clothes in which she left Zahedan. Her long-sleeved brown shirt has a thick layer of dust on it. "Mamán stayed with me in Zahedan for seven days before we were able to set out on the walk. The smugglers moved our group from one safe house to another three times. The final time, they said we had to rush, that there were Hezbollah on the way to find us. They ordered us to leave our bags and come instantly. They promised someone would come later and collect the bags and get them to us in Quetta. I had so many gifts for you. But we had to leave them behind. The bags never arrived in Quetta. I don't think we'll ever see those bags again. They just took advantage of us, because they could. There's nothing we can do."

We've learned from others that this is a common phenomenon on the escape routes, the smugglers scamming the fugitives.

"But poor Amir—remember him, Sima? You stayed at his aunt's house in Shiraz."

"What happened to him?" I asked.

"He sold everything he had. I mean everything—furniture, his land, his shop. He turned everything into cash so he could start a new business when he finally settles somewhere. He hid all the money in his briefcase. When the smugglers rushed us from one house to the other, he grabbed the briefcase. He had been sitting on it almost the whole time we were in the safe houses. He was really paranoid about it. But they said, "No, there's no room in this car for this bag. It will come with the next car." He tried to argue, but they wouldn't let him get in the car with it."

"They did it on purpose!"

"Of course they did. It wasn't hard to see that he never let go of that case. They knew something valuable was in there."

The smugglers know what to look for. They have seen enough fugitives to recognize people's attachment to certain objects.

"I tried to console him, to make him feel better. His problem was way worse than mine. I have blisters all over my body from the money I was hiding, but he has no money left to him at all. That briefcase was his future. He is completely devastated. He looks like a haggard old man now. He's decided to wait in Quetta a few more days in the hope of getting back his bag. He's not being very realistic. Even I know he's never going to get that money back. I'm really upset about what happened to him."

We walk in the direction of the bus station to catch the city bus to Islamabad. Soraya is so busy talking that she is totally unaware of the movement around us: the cars, the donkeys, the ugly red spots on the ground. When we arrived, we found this scene very exciting. Soraya is still too absorbed in her recent experiences. She can't stop talking.

The telegraph office is the first stop. To call Mamán is top priority, though there will be a long wait. It is better to call now than to come back later. Mamán is worried sick.

No need to say much. Once Mamán hears Soraya's voice, she knows Soraya is safe.

"How did Baba react to our disappearance?" I ask Soraya.

"He is still sad, in his silent way."

Mamán is happy for us. She has sacrificed so much. Baba does not like change. He is like a bear that hides his head under the snow hoping there will be no snow left when he raises his head. This hell is not going to disappear that fast.

At the bus terminal, we have to wait for our bus. When it arrives, Soraya wants to sit in between Farah and me to go to Islamabad, but the bus driver insists that Soraya should go to the end of the bus. Because Soraya is petite, dressed in jeans and long-sleeved shirt, and has very short, cropped hair, the driver assumes she is a boy. Men and women do not mix on the bus. Soraya is devastated. What a welcome!

We sit at the back of the women's section, and Soraya sits in the first row of the men's section. She hasn't stopped talking. I manage to squeeze in a word. "How are my plants doing?"

"Your poor plants," she responds. "Mamán came back from Zahedan to celebrate your escape. Your plants were blooming until the day all the guests came for the party. Everyone was stunned when they saw the plants. The family realized what a terrible life you had been living. They saw the plants as a testimonial to the hope you had been carrying for months. The plants started dying soon after. Their purpose in life had been achieved. I felt awful, because I knew how much you loved them. They just gave up on living."

Soraya glances around her. "Do you live on another planet?" she asks.

"Wait and see."

We are almost there.

Soraya's jaw drops when she sees our room. She looks around to see where the rest of the house is. There is nothing for her to see. "This is where we live, sleep, and eat."

"How can we all fit in here?"

"No worries, Soraya. At night we use this blanket as a cushion under our sleeping bag. In the daytime, it works as a carpet. We're not on vacation, sister. We are refugees!"

Soraya is not enthusiastic about our prize tomato and rice dish. She is quick to figure out the one-burner stove on the corner of the room. We don't need to explain anything else.

"I want to take a shower and go to sleep. It has been a long trip. Can you come with me to the bathroom with scissors?"

Soraya takes off her clothes, and we cut away the tape where the money is taped to her waist. The skin under the tape is raw and red. It never ceases to amaze me how, when one is faced with a life or death situation, pain and irritation become irrelevant until the threat is long gone. Soraya is surprised to see how irritated her skin is.

Exhausted, she lies on the hard floor. It is not at all what she expected. But the details of our living situation are not something we are proud of, nothing to brag about in our letters. If Mamán knew where we lived and how we live, she would have never agreed to send Soraya to Pakistan. This is short-term pain for long-term gain. At this moment, with Soraya's innocent face deep in sleep, I honestly can't see the light at the end of the tunnel.

~~~~~~

Soraya demands an explanation, "What have you been doing in the past few months?" She already plans to leave Pakistan. There is no response. She thinks we are holding things back from her.

"Soraya, you think we haven't asked ourselves and everybody we meet what we should do and where we should go and how we should leave here at least a thousand times? We're four people among hundreds, maybe thousands, of refugees, all in the same boat. There are no answers right now. When we figure out what to do, you'll be the first one to know."

"Then for now, we have to have a goal. Let's learn some English."

Mamán sent us English books and Persian-to-English dictionaries. We study English on our own. Learning at least twenty new words by the end of each day is the goal we are committed to until such time as we leave Pakistan. It is not that easy to read the dictionary. But the simple phrases we learn help us ask for our needs. We are all familiar with the English alphabet because we had an hour of English every week during the Shah's reign. No matter where we end up, we are certain that knowledge of English will be to our advantage. I still can't pronounce "th" and "s." When I say the words "stop sign," Farah and Soraya laugh. It comes out "eestop sighn." I can't make my tongue pronounce the "th" sound to say "Mother," "Father," or simply "the." "Mother" comes out as "Modder"; "Father" comes out as "Fadder"; and forget about how to pronounce "the"! It is funny. I've never been able to say it right. My pronunciation drove my English teacher crazy and now it is driving me crazy. I must be missing a muscle in my tongue.

February 28, 1983

Farah and Keyvan, the newlyweds, now have two chaperones at all times. They sleep in the same room with us. Everywhere they go, we go with them. They are never alone. They have no time for themselves.

Although we are under UN protection, we do not dare stray out alone too far from the house. We are in a country whose culture is different from ours. We don't know whom to trust, whom to be wary of, what type of behaviour might arouse anger, what districts are unsafe to walk in, what to do if we are in danger. We worry about being mugged, beaten, or kidnapped. We have no family to back us up, to worry if we are late or don't turn up. The paranoia is shared. We feel safer when we are all together.

Though we can't follow the street signs properly, since the desert crossing we seem to have GPS installed in our heads. We can find our way anywhere, in any foreign city, with any foreign language.

Each day crawls by as slowly as the previous one. We develop a routine. We take turns shopping, cooking, cleaning, and then practising our English.

Our one break is the biweekly visit to the UN office. These are our only social outings. We are no closer toward our goal of leaving Pakistan today than the day we first arrived; we still do not know how to improve our situation. Every time any one of us meets someone new, we ask if they know of a way we can enroll in some school, or of any country that accepts political refugees.

In Islamabad there are many tea houses. Kebabs are cooked over charcoal on every corner. Mohammed tells us the food here is too spicy. The Pakistanis use many spices and also hot chili, which is rare in Persian cooking.

The restaurants are packed with men. An old, dark-skinned man stands behind a charcoal grill just where the sidewalk meets the opening of the restaurant and grills lamb on a skewer. Its aroma fills the entire street. The same restaurant also serves tea all day. It has metal roll-over doors that the owner uses to close the restaurant at night, but during the day there is no visible door. One particular restaurant downtown is especially busy. That is where the beggars congregate.

They look very old, small, wrinkly, and crippled. How are these old men with no legs or arms able to get here every day? Someone must bring them. Or do they sleep on the ground? What do they eat? It's a mystery to us. The police make sure that none of them come near the government offices and the embassies. The government does not want foreigners to associate Pakistan with poverty.

Pakistan is a country of extremes. On one side, there are the beggars. They are so poor that even I, who have nothing, feel compassion toward them. Then a few blocks away are the magnificent hotels that look like palaces, with an armed guard always on duty. As much as we would love to explore these enticing hotels, we are not permitted, as we are not guests. When foreign dignitaries come to Pakistan, they inevitably come to Islamabad and stay in these glamorous hotels. I did not see such grandiose hotels in Shiraz.

From our balcony, we see the school buses coming, and they are always on time. How lucky these children are to be able to go to school. Do they know it? Does it ever occur to them that there are children the same age elsewhere who are unable attend school? I watch them arrive and enter the school and am envious that they have such a privilege.

I stand under the overhang on the balcony. It is winter. It rains often. The dampness reminds me of northern Iran, where it is misty all the time. The fog and the mist are inexplicable, just like our future. The rain takes different forms. Sometimes it drizzles, and sometimes there are big drops that plop down on the balcony floor. On rainy days, we are stuck in our room. There is not much to do. There is no TV, no radio, no music. Watching the rain fall is a form of entertainment. We don't know if the rain is going to stay light or if a heavy storm is coming or if we will see the sun later on. Will there be strong winds? It is best not to venture out into the streets or walk to the bus. There are puddles everywhere. I do not want to get splashed with mud by buses going at high speed. On such days, we are more agitated and more aware of our pitiful life. There is no one to talk to. How many times can we retell our stories to each other?

〜〜〜〜〜

Hijabs are rarely seen; most women wear vibrant red, pink, and orange saris and they look breathtakingly magnificent. Occasionally I see a woman in jeans or a skirt, but for the most part, traditional, modest, but colourful, clothing is the norm.

We like the saris. There is a flow to them. The women who wear them display their femininity. We are tempted to buy our own. This is a little extravagance we allow ourselves from the monthly UN allowance. The three of us go on a sari expedition. The shop owner is a man who speaks perfect English. Since almost everyone here speaks English, we don't have to learn Urdu. This language is useless for us since we are not planning to stay here for long. He estimates our sizes and pulls out a few styles for us. The soft, flowery sari fabric feels lightweight and care-free. The thick, embroidered band at the bottom of the *chalwar khameez* reveals my slim ankles. The band is supposed to be tight-fitting but it isn't, in my case.

We bargain, since we are buying three. We each buy a sari. Mine is baby blue, Farah has a pink one, and Soraya's is orange. They are stun-ning. We enjoy blending into the environment for the first time since our arrival.

We visit the UN office more often than we are supposed to. Life is extremely uneasy. The UN made it clear that we cannot go to school in Pakistan. We can't work. We have no rights. Every time we are in the UN office we encounter other refugees, mostly Iranians. We pepper them with questions. "Do you know anybody who left Pakistan? Who are they, where do they go, how do they leave?" We arrive before the office opens and stay there until we are hungry, our stomachs rumbling like ferocious lions.

Persian is the only language in which we can express ourselves fully. "Why do you think the UN is giving us a monthly allowance? But they don't want us to go to school or find a job. Why don't they make some effort to teach us English? They are not helping us to change our status. We can't live the rest of our lives taking handouts from the UN!" The paper the United Nations has given us is now useless. They want to keep us as refugees. They want to make us parasites of society. They don't show us any way out of our situation.

We aren't there to mooch off some foreign government. This is not the way I see myself. Nor do my sisters want to live that way. We will find a way out or die trying.

We are deeply disturbed by our situation. Although I am learning twenty new English words a day, I still can't hold a conversation with anyone or even make myself understood. Our frustration is voiced to our social worker. She responds, "That's how it is. There is nothing more we can offer."

They are professional bureaucrats doing their jobs. We can't count on the UN to improve our circumstances. It is up to us to come up with a new plan. I have no regrets about visiting and seeing all the cities in Pakistan so far, but enough is enough. My patience is running out, and I am becoming increasingly anxious.

Soraya is restless. "You brought me here so all four of us can live in one room? So what if we're free? We're as tied up here as we were in Iran." The words she utters are exactly what I am thinking. At least back in Iran we had our own rooms and a refrigerator, which would be a luxury at this point. We had a family, and we had a telephone. It has been months we've been living like this in one room with no plan. We don't know where we are going. We only know we can't go back to where we came from.

"Soraya, I've heard of many people who've left Pakistan. We just have to find a way. Have you forgotten how bad it was at home? If we forget what brought us here, we'll be in real trouble. Now we have to stick together and not lose hope."

Living in such close quarters puts a strain on our relationships. Farah and Keyvan have the worst part of it. Keyvan is doing everything he can. He's making all sorts of inquiries and trying to reach all kinds of people who might be able to help us.

One evening when Keyvan comes home, I am excited to share with him all the new words I learned during the day. He is not at all enthusiastic. "Of course, while I am running around to get all of us out of here, you are improving your English."

He is resentful about my learning English. If I don't study, he thinks I am wasting my time and if I study, he is resentful. It is too confusing. We are too close, invading each other's personal space.

Days turn into nights and nights into days, and the cycle repeats itself endlessly. There is no structure in our lives. There is nothing to look forward to. There is no hope.

~~~~~

Keyvan often meets Pakistani university students when he drops by the university to speak with Iranian student friends. Rachid's curiosity is immensely piqued by three Jewish girls in Islamabad. He does not know any Jews who live in Pakistan. Rachid's family wants to know what we are like. We have our first invitation for a dinner at the home of a Pakistani.

Rachid introduces us to his parents and siblings. The mother is dressed in a sari; the younger sister is wearing pants and a shirt. The parents are in their fifties, Christian. They, too, are a minority in Pakistan. Both Rachid's older brother and his sister are university students.

We walk through the house to enter the garden that is at the back. There are no carpets in the rooms we pass through. The floors are white tile. There is no decoration on the walls except for a wooden-framed family photograph. It is poorly furnished.

A few orange trees are in the garden, and the scent of orange blossom surrounds us. It is as if I am back in Shiraz. The air is fresh, and spring is almost here. Dinner is served on a big wooden table in the centre of the garden. Rachid's mother, a short, skinny lady with big eyes and dark skin, is a great cook. She serves us chicken and a rice dish. The rice is aromatic. The combination of cinnamon, cardamom, and cloves is so pleasing to me. There is fruit for dessert. They serve us more food than we can ever imagine eating.

The entire family is interested in hearing our story. It is unfathomable to them that young girls are forced to escape from their home and country, and that a mother has encouraged it. With my broken English, I string together a few words: freedom, democracy, execution, revolution, and maybe I make enough sense to be understood. They are kind, patient, and sympathetic with us. They are fluent in English.

We ask, "Is there any way we can continue our studies?" We receive the standard answer that we have to have a student visa or be a permanent resident.

Total strangers have opened their home to us graciously. We are grateful for their generosity. In a different country, far away from home, kindness reaches out to us, and we find links that bind us together.

"Is there a Jewish community in Islamabad?"

"Not here; there may be a small community in Karachi."

Rachid urges us, "Leave Pakistan. There is no future for foreigners here. Don't stay long. Don't depend on the UN, either. You would be better off going to Karachi. There you will have a greater chance to find a way to leave." It is past midnight, and we are deeply immersed in the conversations. Rachid's mother offers us tea. I love Pakistani chai, black tea simmering with condensed milk and cardamom; I never get enough of this tea. We have tried to make this tea ourselves, but it never comes out quite like this.

We leave their house late at night and catch the last bus to our small, depressing, crowded room.

This encounter has given us a new direction to follow. We realize we are not making progress here, and maybe we are in the wrong city. We have to move to Karachi. We don't have any idea what life is like there, where we might find a place to stay, how much it might cost. Maybe Keyvan should go ahead and find out what we need to know. Is it selfish of us to send him off? It certainly will be hard on Farah.

~~~~~~

Keyvan has, in some mysterious way, made friends with a key figure of the Afghani consulate in Islamabad, who is posted here with his wife. They are kind people and invite us over for dinner. Unlike the Pakistani houses we have been to, there are sofas, a table for dining, and gorgeous Iranian wall-to-wall carpets. Afghanis have always looked up to Iranian culture, since their culture derives from the same origins. We are able to speak Persian with them.

We are served a vegetarian rice dish with cauliflower. I ask our hostess how she made this recipe. She is not willing to share. "It takes too long to make. The secret is in the spice." Apart from that, their hospitality is beautiful. Dessert is a fruit bowl with oranges, apples, and grapes. Grapes! Where do they find grapes? I am embarrassed to ask. It will remain a mystery. They are very expensive and way beyond our budget.

A lively discussion on education springs up. So many brilliant, educated people are being imprisoned in Iran. We were unable to continue our education. What does this attack on education and the educated mean for the future of the country?

Pakistan is only a bridge to somewhere better, somewhere we can't really name at the moment. The consul and his wife pity us because they keep asking us how old we are. But when Soraya tells them she is only fifteen, they nearly fall off their chairs. She looks much younger than her fifteen years. In fact, she really is too young to be going through all this. A fifteen-year-old's place is at home with her family and a life of security—not in the land of far-far-away, not knowing what tomorrow brings. The uncertainty is hard and draining. It is likely written all over our faces.

The husband expresses his concern about the state of affairs in Afghanistan. "Muslim extremists are on the rise in our country, too, and it is frightening for us. I hope Afghanistan does not follow the same path in its politics as Iran. We despise this group."

We commiserate with them and the changes that are happening in their country.

"Islamabad is not the right location for you to find your way to another country. You don't have diplomatic connections here, do you? This is a capital city but not a real international city like Karachi. You will be better off making inquiries there."

It seems to be widely known among Pakistani citizens and foreign officials that Karachi is the only place from which one can leave Pakistan. We take our leave of our generous host and hostess and make our way home.

On the bus ride back to our room, I can't stop thinking about their advice for leaving Islamabad. We contemplate the idea of going to Karachi. How are we to manage it? We are familiar with Islamabad. We've lived here for three months. We argue over the advantages/disadvantages of a move to Karachi. This is not home, but we've been here longer than anywhere else . . . Another move, another city, another dislocation, and another "opportunity" to start from zero.

We are comfortable here, in that we have some knowledge of where to go for our daily essentials. We decide that the three musketeers will stay in our semi-secure place in Islamabad while Keyvan checks out the situation in Karachi.

~~~~~

Iranian New Year is approaching. It is the first time in all my life that I have lived in another country. In Iran, this time was the time of much food preparation, decorations on the table, ancient symbolic customs to fulfill, all sorts of family and community events. Here, we are helpless to even consider a celebration. In our room there is no table, no chair, nothing to decorate, no family. Every corner is piled with stuff, from clothing to books to a slow, one-burner stove.

Afsaneh has tears in her eyes and can't talk. She is as miserable as we are. Her husband had gone to Karachi weeks ago and is still not back. The separation is hard on her. It is bad enough to be in a totally different country during the New Year, but worse to have to celebrate it without her husband. She understands the logic, but her heart is heavy.

"Please join me for the New Year. It is too lonely for me."

The traditional fried fish and herb rice dish is a standard New Year's meal. Remembering the past, all of us are nostalgic about missing our families. Lives have been turned upside-down. This ending is not what any of us ever expected in our wildest dreams.

Though our backgrounds are different, loving the spring and the New Year is the common thread between us. Talking about it brings back warm memories of the past we do not want to let go of. It sustains us. We had a family of our own, with whom we celebrated all the holidays. Here, our family does not extend beyond four and that is lucky in comparison to other refugees who have no one. Poor Afsaneh does not even have one family member now.

The Iranian refugees who come to the UN are organizing an outing to celebrate the New Year. Keyvan plans to travel to Karachi to collect more information but he wants to stay for the picnic in two days' time. We will all be safe with Afsaneh. A change in scenery will be good for us, too, before he leaves.

On a foggy, misty Friday morning, laden with bags of food—egg sandwiches and fruit— Keyvan, Farah, Soraya, Afsaneh, and I take a bus to go to Mari, a national park in the mountains close to Islamabad. Shahram, Amir, and maybe a dozen or so other Iranians are also there to celebrate. Soraya is the youngest one. Most refugees are in their twenties.

Mari Park is a tranquil oasis on a mountainside, far away from city noises and traffic. Green trees are everywhere, but they are evergreens, not fruit trees, as I was accustomed to see on our outings from Shiraz. The sky is covered by a thin layer of cloud. The sun fights to come out, peeking at us flirtatiously. This type of weather is foreign to me. Farah and Keyvan take advantage of this moment to take an unaccompanied walk. They must be happy to be alone, without their chaperones.

We greet each other with laughter. The men gather branches to make a fire, just as we did years ago during our hiking trips. How I miss those days! No matter how hard I try to avoid thinking about my family, I am not successful. I miss them. They follow me everywhere I go.

Unlike our outings in Shiraz, there is no grill, no feta cheese with halva, and no nuts at this picnic. Everyone has brought sandwiches, and we eat them together.

Underneath our brave chatter, we feel anxious and uncertain about our future. Gradually, the glittery veil drops, and we start to talk in earnest. Despite differences in age, sex, and religion, we have much in common. All of us have left Iran because of the brutality of the Islamic government. Every one of us has lost friends or family members, a familiar lifestyle, a home. Every one of us is scared and scarred. Misery loves company, and unfortunately, this celebration has become an occasion for airing our misery and despair, our dreams and aspirations. We want to change from this parasitic dependency on the UN and become members of a society where we can contribute in some way to this world.

"I want to go to America."

"Wishful thinking! There is no way for any of us to get there."

"Spain is open to Iranians."

"Maybe I can go to France."

"No way, France's border is very restricted."

My only wish is to be out of Pakistan by this time next year. That is my greatest desire, my only desire! But I am resigned to waiting. I know by now that nothing happens quickly. Where I will end up, I have no idea, as long as it is not Pakistan.

Interesting — of the twenty refugees present, not even one claims to be happy living in Pakistan. That alone speaks to how terrible our lives are in this corner of the world.

As refugees, none of us can make a life for ourselves in Pakistan.

March 24, 1983

Keyvan leaves by train for Karachi from Rawalpindi, where the train station is located. He trusts Afsaneh and asks her to keep an eye on us. He is supposed to return no later than seven days from today. There is no way to keep in touch. There is no phone number that we can call, no person to ask, no way to communicate with each other.

The days go by. Farah is sad, nervous, and sick with worry. "What if he is hurt? What are we going to do? I am a newlywed and look at me: I am stuck alone babysitting my two little sisters. This is just too much! If it weren't for you, I would have gone with Keyvan to Karachi. It's so unfair! I am too young for this."

She is right. We are dragging her down. We don't want to be a burden to her but we are. She feels responsible for us. If anything goes wrong with us, she's the one who has to answer to Mamán.

It is not as if Keyvan left us here to go partying in Karachi. We are barely surviving, financially, emotionally, psychologically.

If Farah had some way to be in touch with Keyvan, it would not be so difficult for her. But there is no communication at all between them. This is what makes it so difficult to cope. We have to wait and hope he will return with some good news.

I can't concentrate on learning my twenty English words anymore.

We are too depressed over our future and Keyvan's safety. All we do is sleep. This is our therapy and refuge. If only we had a radio, we could listen to music. We don't even feel like going to the UN anymore. The novelty is gone. When people see us there, they will ask where Keyvan is. We don't feel like answering questions.

Being in limbo is our state of life, our state of mind. No family to visit, no school to attend. Only waiting. Staring at each other. Pitying ourselves. Time and routine lose their meaning. I used to love being the first one up in the morning. Now I dread the morning. I dread the nights. When is the time for breakfast when you sleep on and off all day and night? When is lunch? We need to have at least one meal a day.

The day is long.

Yesterday was long.

Tomorrow will be long, too.

Seven interminable days have passed, and we have had no news from Keyvan.

Pray again. It is time, a voice says. It has worked in the past. Listen to the voice. I've been so caught up in the drama of my life that I have ignored the most powerful weapon I have at my disposal. Now is not the time to lose hope.

April 9, 1983

Keyvan finally returns. We have spent two and a half weeks in hell. Farah is beside herself with joy! It seems that there is sunlight outside for the first time since he left.

He has good news, he says. He tells us he has met with countless Iranians in Karachi. His new friend, Piroz, an Iranian, is renting an apartment for us. The plan is for us to move in two days to Karachi. Piroz is a student who has taken it upon himself to help Iranian political refugees. He disapproves of the Islamic government. He moved to Karachi in 1978 to continue his studies just before the universities were closed. He is fluent in both English and Urdu.

Saying our goodbyes to Afsaneh is not easy. She has become as close as a family member could become in a distant land. Holding back the tears is impossible. Goodbyes are dreadful. This is yet another ending. It is painful. Every time I say goodbye, our last moments with Mamán in Zahedan haunt me.

Tears roll down our cheeks. We sob hysterically as we embrace each other. Afsaneh, too, has had more than her share of goodbyes. We tease her, "You will have all this room to yourself and the kitchen, too." She is inconsolable. Maybe she will find another tenant at the UN, she says, but no one can take our place.

Amir and Shahram accompany us to the train station and we say goodbye to them. Train stations, bus stops, deserts. We have been moving for so many months. We are no further ahead today than five months ago when we arrived in this country; and now, yet another long train ride in the hope of finding my New Home.

On the train to Karachi, the flashbacks begin. I can't stop these flashbacks, which are so intense that they seem real . . . as if I could really converse with the people in my head. It is strange to see Soraya, sitting across me enthusiastically anticipating what is awaiting us in Karachi, when she has just appeared in my mind in a totally different context. I am living in a time warp.

It is April. This time of year used to be my favourite time in Shiraz. I always looked forward to Passover . . . the white orange blossoms, the pink apple blossoms, shopping for nuts and roasting them, grinding the turmeric and black pepper with a mortar and pestle. The Passover preparations were endless. The actual morning before Passover, Baba Esghel would come to our house, flashlight in hand, searching for *chometz*. Not even a crumb of *chometz* could hide from his scrutiny. My favourite part of the holiday was when thirty or more of the aunts, uncles, and all the cousins gathered for the first night; and when the time came to say *Dayenu*, we would hit each other with green shallots. The long, green shallots would be broken into tiny, crooked pieces by the end of the night. Laughter erupted again and again. I relive those days in my mind; that is the closest I can come to the holiday. There is no way to have the Passover celebration here. When is Passover? We don't even know that!

But I fear it no longer exists as I used to know it, because I am so far away from my home. I cannot imagine that the celebrations could continue without my being there. As for me, I move in a bubble in the present tense, disconnected from the past or from what is happening beyond the walls of my bubble, something I never could have dreamt of in my worst nightmares.

I am only seventeen. Why am I talking to myself as if I am a ninety-year-old? The events of the past three years could have been spread over a lifetime. Even for ninety years, it is too much. Too many losses. Too many goodbyes. Too many horrible scenes in the last three short years.

We have not lit Shabbat candles in months. I anticipate the day that I can celebrate the holidays. It is not so much for religious reasons, but I love to do it anyway because it connects me to my roots.

It has been hours we are sitting in this train. I am on another planet. The landscape changes from hilly to flat. Occasionally, animals cross a country road.

After yet another train ride, we arrive in Karachi and meet with Piroz, who, as he promised, has rented a two-bedroom apartment for us.

April 13, 1983

Piroz, who is dressed Pakistani style, is in his thirties and has hazel eyes and thin, light brown hair; he looks like a lighter-skinned version of the locals. Had he not spoken Persian to welcome us here, there is no way I could have guessed he is Iranian. Keyvan introduces us to Piroz, but we are dripping with sweat, distracted by the heat, and can't concentrate on proper formalities.

It is humid and muggy. Fire is coming out of the sky. An egg will fry on the sidewalk within a minute in this boiling heat. With humidity from the coastal waters, the temperature must be at least 50°C. Sweat is dripping from all parts of my body. I am drenched, soaking wet within minutes of arriving in Karachi.

Piroz, whom we had never met, is the breed of Iranian to whom I had been accustomed. He is the person who travels an extra mile just for the sake of helping. The bond between us is the betrayal by our government and native land. I am pleasantly surprised by his warmth and concern; it is impressive.

Soraya gives voice to what we are all thinking: "How can we live in this heat? We will die. It is too hot." Living in desert heat is easy compared to this. The humidity makes breathing difficult. Before we can say anything to Piroz, he flags a taxi for us.

Unlike Islamabad, Karachi is crowded, dirty, and noisy. "Why are the drivers honking their horn all the time? Aren't you deafened by all the noise?" I ask Piroz.

"You will get used to it. Don't worry."

We are delighted with the small two-bedroom apartment on the ground floor of a three-storey building. Soraya and I are happy to have our own room, with a window that opens onto an artificial pond in a park. The extra room finally affords Farah and Keyvan some privacy. They must be ecstatic to have some privacy!

Piroz is smart. He knows how dirty this place is but also sees the potential it has. He provides us with cleaning gear. Soraya and I offer to clean it thoroughly. Farah and Keyvan spend the rest of the day at Piroz's apartment and sleep there. This is the least Soraya and I can do to thank Farah and Keyvan for all their sacrifices.

~~~~~

Thick layers of filth covering the walls and floors are the only furnishings. The colour of the tiled floor is impossible to figure out . . . it looks dark brown from the dirt stuck to it. The walls are supposed to be white, but the colour is nearer to dark grey than white. The stove is invisible because it is caked with leftover food.

Soraya and I pull up our sleeves and get to the task. We sweep, clean, polish, and wash every corner of this apartment. The water pressure is too low. The water is dripping drop by drop from the faucet in the small bathroom. It takes forever to fill the pail. I can only imagine how long it will take to wash my thick hair with this kind of water pressure. This city is near water; how can there be a shortage of water?

Now we can at least see the rooms: a bathroom and a kitchen, which contains a stovetop and a small sink. Both rooms face the pond. The apartment is very compact. No extra room such as a dining room. There is no garden. Exhausted, we fall asleep in the middle of the night on the floor. We are used to this by now. It is hot. There is no air conditioner or fan. Soraya and I leave the windows open, hoping to catch a breeze, just as we had in Shiraz.

The next morning, the doorbell startles us awake. It is Piroz. "What on earth happened to your faces?"

As far as we know, nothing has happened to our faces.

"What? What's wrong?"

"Look at your faces!"

Soraya's face looks horrible, like a cut-up, ripe watermelon. Thousands of tiny bumpy red spots cover her face. Apparently, vicious, hungry mosquitoes spent the night feasting on our fresh, clean blood, determined to leave no part of our faces unkissed. Soraya's reaction to my face is as horrifying as my reaction is to her face. We don't need a mirror; a glance at Soraya's face is proof enough of how hideous my face must look. Sleeping on the floor wasn't bad enough; now we can't even go out, looking like this. My inner voice cuts in: *Poor girl, you have not yet recovered from the black toenail and now you look revolting with all the red spots on your face.* Though this is true, I do not like it when my voice is so honest and has no compassion for me.

This is awful! People will be scared to look at us. Will this lead to some rare disease? Beauty is not a concern, but I am terrified of the consequences of these bites.

I am too devastated to console Soraya . . . Soraya, my little sister, her beautiful face now red and swollen. Piroz warns us, "It is itchy and you will want to scratch yourself. Don't, because if you get an infection, it will not heal for a long, long time. The pollution is very bad here. To heal an infection takes forever." Soraya and I wash our faces with the rationed water frequently and hope for the best.

Luckily, Farah and Keyvan are spared because they stayed with Piroz. This is an instant and bitter lesson about Karachi. Never leave the windows open at night, no matter how hot the weather.

Taking a shower in the morning one would think is a normal thing to do, but not here. There is no water pressure at all during the day; it is only available for two hours, from four a.m. to six a.m. This is inconvenient. Welcome to Karachi.

No matter how much we want to avoid being seen outside this apartment, there is too much to be done, and we must venture outdoors. Our bodies rebel against the heat and humidity of Karachi. The jarring noise hits us like a thunderstorm. Having lived in Tehran, I thought I had seen the ultimate in crowded streets, where I had to push though walls of people block after block to get from one end of the street to the next. Here, it isn't just the crowds—people jump in and out of cars, buses, and trucks while the vehicles are in motion. Any minute now, I expect a passenger to jump off a bus and knock me over, or a car to run over a pedestrian and squash him flat. The constant honking shrieks in my stomach . . . it is poisonous both to my body and to my soul.

This is hell in every aspect. The heat, the dirt, the racket: These conditions would drive anyone crazy. Patience is not simply a virtue, here; it is essential for survival. The only way one is able to live in this city without going crazy is to step back from the chaos and breathe. That is what we are going to have to do.

Nobody has noticed our blotchy faces. They are too busy surviving on the street.

The majority of the women are dressed in saris. Some who dress in skirts and blouses cover their faces with white powder. They walk around with umbrellas. It is not raining. Umbrellas for the sun? How peculiar. Never have I seen anything like this. But umbrellas offer protection from the sun. Most men are dressed in tunics with pants, though some men are dressed in suits. These men are the ones working in foreigners' offices or in banks. Those suits must be incredibly hot!

Karachi is full of rickshaws. Two big, black, wooden wheels in the back with seats for passengers and a metal oval harness that is pulled down across the stomachs of men and boys who are often painfully thin and frail-looking. These men weigh far less than the load they are pulling. Many locals use these rickshaws instead of taxis; it must be cheaper. Tourists also use them, but I find it demeaning and physically devastating for the rickshaw drivers, given the extreme heat and the terrible noise. It isn't a very moral choice. Piroz comments that a rickshaw driver makes good money for an unskilled labourer.

〰〰〰

Soraya wakes up in the morning looking extremely pale.

"What's wrong?"

"I didn't sleep all night because of a stomach ache." To watch her writhing in pain on the floor is excruciating. Dysentery is a dreadful condition. Since we do not eat any food from the street vendors, we thought we were safe. Soraya's pain confirms we have not been vigilant enough. Hospital bills are costly.

Keyvan asks Piroz. His advice: "Make sure to give her liquids. This is usually the case for newcomers to Karachi. I will bring her a painkiller later on today."

Karachi's water is impossible to drink without first boiling. We boil the water for a minimum of twenty minutes; by then, the full pot of water is reduced to half. There is already a shortage of water, but we have no choice. Farah and I stay at home with Soraya for three days to keep her company.

Since there is no water during the day, we can't cool off by taking a shower. The humidity is impossible to bear, intensified by the thick smog covering the city. Breathing the noxious air is a constant struggle. Give me dry heat, I adore that. Being from Shiraz, dry heat is what my body can thrive on. It is never too hot if it is dry. But this humidity suffocates me.

The biggest grocery shopping of the week takes place on Wednesday at the Sadar open-air market. Farmers from the surrounding areas bring their goods for sale to the market: chickens, goats, sheep, nuts, vegetables, fruit, clothes . . . it is a loud, brilliantly coloured Asian fair. Whatever anyone can carry to sell is here. The vendors wear moist, white, cotton head coverings to keep cool. They dry so fast that you can see steam rising out of them. A bucket of water stands next to each vendor; they splash the water on their faces often and wet their head coverings. I do not want that water to get near me. If by any chance it gets close to my lips, dysentery will be my unwanted guest. I will be as sick as Soraya.

From the corner of my eye, I see mangos. I love mangos and had been on a mission many times in Shiraz to find them in the market. I was never successful. Here in the Sadar market, heaping piles of succulent, perfumed mangos bring me to heaven: sweet, juicy, mouthwatering.

I take one and hold it in my hand to smell it. In that moment, I am blessed by the love of Mother Earth, so graciously feeding me this mango. I thank her for this wonderful, unexpected treat. I have not tasted mangos for years. Mangos do not grow in Iran. When Arab tourists from the Persian Gulf visited Shiraz, they would bring them for us as gifts. The old male vendor tells us they are locally grown; bananas also are in season. They are the best we have ever tasted. This is one of the two good things about Karachi. Their mangos are absolutely the best. Mangos and bananas!

Karachi is a city of extremes. The rich are exceedingly rich, and the poor are totally destitute, with both classes living next to one another. Expensive shops, restaurants, hotels, brand-name cars—Mercedes, Land Rovers, and Peugeots—crowd the more upscale part of the city where the consulates and the UN are located. The Hilton and the Ritz–Carlton hotels look like palaces: grand, ornate, with stone carvings on the walls. Policemen with guns guard these hotels, in addition to the usual doormen. The government wants to be sure that tourists are not approached by beggars or thieves.

Young children run around shoeless on the boiling hot pavement. A woman sits on the sidewalk under the blazing sun, breastfeeding her newborn. Mosquitoes cover both the mother and the baby. The beggars are as young as three or four years old, or very old, crippled, disfigured men and women. One beggar hangs onto my legs for money. Piroz warned me not to give money to them because if I give to one there will be a dozen others descending on me within seconds.

There are armed police in plain view to discourage crime. Armed marshals control the city. No one is allowed to be out on the streets at night. Karachi is not a safe city. That is why we always travel in groups. Going out of the house in the evening is out of the question. It is just as bad as Iran. The noise, the dirt, the undrinkable water, the humidity, and the fact that the passengers jump out of moving buses make the city just too dangerous.

Mamán and Baba send us money from time to time through the network of students. We are in contact with home, mostly by letters. Mamán sends letters to us via Piroz. Many Iranian students in Pakistan had left Iran when the schools closed prior to the Revolution. At that time, each student could be sent one thousand American dollars per month for living expenses by their families no matter which country in the world they studied in. If the students left Iran prior to 1979, the Islamic government still honoured the exchange rate of seven *tooman* to the dollar. The foreign student exchange rate under the Shah is still respected by the Islamic government.

Iranian currency has depreciated a lot. The American dollar is now sold for forty *tooman* per dollar—more than a fivefold increase since 1979. The students living abroad are still able to purchase American currency at seven *tooman* to the dollar. The thousand dollars are more than enough for three months' expenses. Their surpluses come in handy for us. That is the only way Mamán can send us money.

The money Mamán sends us is to be used only to leave Pakistan. Day-to-day expenses are paid from the allowance given to us by the UN, which is 300 rupees per month per person. Our rent is 1,000 rupees per month. There is not a lot much left over for food. We are indeed on a tight budget.

Rent is much higher here compared to Islamabad, yet the monthly allowance from the UN is the same as in any other part of Pakistan. At the UN, we have discussions with other refugees about the money we receive. This is not enough; we can't pay our rent with just this. We can't work, either. We are stuck between a rock and a hard place, our hands tied behind our backs.

The UN frustrates us. They want us to be parasites. If I could work, I would not need their handouts. Don't give me a fish — teach me how to fish. This will free us both. But something is seriously wrong with the UN.

The UN office in Karachi is much bigger than the one in Islamabad. A huge garden surrounds the complex. The old, curvy trees, green grass, and wilting white flowers welcome us as we enter the UN compound. Just like in Islamabad there are white columns on either side of the entranceway. We walk up a step onto the white tiled floor before we reach the actual office.

There must be at least a couple dozen employees working here. Our social worker, a man in his forties, a native of Karachi, is unsympathetic to our issues. As far as he is concerned, the UN has fulfilled its duty. "You are too demanding and ungrateful," he scolds, wagging his finger at us.

"How are we to live with such privations?"

No, our social worker does not want to hear our ideas. We talk among ourselves, write down our ideas in Persian and hand out copies as refugees mill about the office. "If you are interested to hear more, please join us tomorrow to discuss it further. Let your friends know and join us."

The next day, fifty frustrated refugees join us for the complaint session. Keyvan, Piroz, and a few other refugees lead discussions in the United Nations' garden. A short, husky man shouts, "We have to organize a hunger strike!"

A scrawny man screams, "You are crazy! We will lose our protection from the UN. Don't bite the hand that feeds you!"

Piroz's voice fights to be heard. "The UN Refugee Commission is supposed to recognize our needs. If we don't collectively voice our demands, how will they know what we need?"

Soraya, the youngest one in the audience, yells, "This is not life. The UN has to at least listen to us. Unless we scare them with a hunger strike, we will not be heard."

Soraya has stood for justice since the day she could talk. All eyes are fixated on her. The men are shocked at the courage of a fifteen-year-old who would suggest a hunger strike. She looks much younger than her years.

We angry refugees talk furiously among ourselves. Hassan, one of the many frustrated men in the crowd, shouts, "I would like to see UN workers live on the amount of money they hand us every month and taste the troubles we are having!"

Hunger strike at the UN? This is the last place anyone would think refugees are mistreated.

"Do you think we can get more people to join us?"

"Will the strike get through to these bureaucrats?"

"We're not being ungrateful. Give us the right to work, so we can make our own money."

"Some people around here speak good English, so why don't they allow us to organize an English course? Let them give us a room so we can improve our skills and give ourselves more options for the future."

A few refugees warn us, "Do not waste your breath. It has always been this way and it isn't going to change. How long are you planning to continue a hunger strike? You are not going to live here long enough to create any change."

"This is true. We are not going to be here for too long, but, the UN's existence is based on supporting refugees. Let them actually do what they stand for, not just for us but for future refugees."

"It is not about us. It is about really helping those who need help. It does not even cost the UN anything. They can certainly give us a room for classes: there are so many empty rooms in this building. The office people here are rich." One refugee points to the fancy cars at the side of the garden. "They can't be poor and driving the Peugeot, Benz, and Toyotas."

"We don't even want a room. Let them just announce an English course on Monday in the garden. At least we would be able to use each other's talents to improve our situation."

Excitement and enthusiasm fills the air.

An additional terror hangs over the Iranian refugees. A new face shouts, "Have you heard of the new agreement that has been signed between Pakistan and Iran to deport all political refugees back to Iran? The protection of the UN is not an exception to this agreement."

As soon as he utters those words, it is as if a bomb has fallen in our midst. The fear becomes palpable. We are not safe here, either.

This alone would be a reason for a hunger strike. Now is a good time to ask for everything we know will benefit us refugees.

The furious debates, in the dusty heat of Karachi, remind us of the early days of the Revolution. Something good is at work, here, regardless of the outcome. Electric, vibrant energy pulsates through the air. Fifty refugees are gathered on the grounds of the UN at eight o'clock on Monday morning. Two other Iranian women and the three musketeers are the exception to the male majority.

A bond quickly develops between us. The other two women, single, and much older than us, both feel responsible for our well-being. Though this crowd is mostly men, it feels good to have the five of us representing the women.

We are as frustrated as before, but now we feel empowered to voice our demands. The pros and cons, the fervent argument rolls on. The husky man shouts, "Let's take a vote. That is the only way to solve this dilemma. Those in favour of a strike, raise your hand."

Forty hands are raised in favour of the strike.

Piroz announces the result of the voting. "We should not burn our bridges behind us yet; the UN is not the enemy. I will write our demands. If they do not respond within two days, then we will go on a hunger strike."

1.   No refugee should be deported back to Iran.
2.   Give us a room to have the refugees teach other refugees English.
3.   Either help us leave Pakistan or help us go to school or work here.
4.   Increase our monthly allowance by fifty rupees per month.

I am thrilled to be part of this group, excited that we are able to voice our dissatisfaction. Considering that we are in the UN building, I hope they respond quickly to our request. Memories of student council and my elementary school principal float back to me.

No one in the UN is interested in hearing our requests, let alone responding to them. They laugh at us. They do not think we will carry it further. Our pleas fall on deaf ears.

The raw anger is evident in each face.

"No one came out of their office to talk to us. Their job is to take care of the refugees. But they are not interested in speaking with us. They follow the rules set down by well-fed men in a big building in Geneva! They have no idea how those rules constrict our lives and make a future impossible. And they don't care! Hypocritical bureaucrats."

As the rage is displayed by the refugees, the atmosphere becomes ugly.

"Is anybody interested in going on a hunger strike?" Hassan asks.

A loud roar of "Yes, yes, yes" fills the air.

The unanimous decision is made: "Wednesday morning at 8:30 we're going on a hunger strike."

May 4, 1983

Wednesday morning arrives swiftly. Fifty Iranian refugees from far-flung corners of Iran have common demands. We sit under the overhang in front of the entrance to the office, blocking the employees from entering. The UN officials are taken aback to see us there. No one has ever done such a thing here. Our representative, Kiomarse, a man from Tehran, speaks perfect English. He hands in the paper with our demands and asks to speak to the UN chief.

"I hope it will not be as disastrous as the Iranian Revolution."

"Do you think they will kill us here, too?"

The UN chief comes out of hiding and addresses us all. A husky white American man in his forties, he scolds us in an authoritative voice booming with confidence and privilege.

"The United Nations helps as much as possible. Our hands are tied. No more help can be offered. To change policies takes a long time. You're wasting your time and our time. Please leave." He races back and forth to his office and to the garden where all the refugees sit many times during the day. He takes note that it is long past lunchtime and no one has eaten. Soraya is the youngest in the crowd. He is concerned for Soraya more than anyone else.

"You should eat," he pleads with Soraya.

She shakes her head. "Until everyone eats I will not."

Toward the end of the day, he starts to be uncomfortable. Our social worker looks at the crowd, in disbelief that we are participating in the hunger strike.

The UN employees roll their eyes; their heads shake in disapproval. If the roles were reversed, I wonder if they would have done anything differently than what we are doing.

Though we are far away from the real enemy, the Islamic government of Iran, nothing has changed. We feel like parasites in this society. We are handed a meagre monthly allowance, but there is no way to crawl out of the hole we have been dropped in. We can't work and we can't study. Life is not supposed to be lived this way.

The UN employees look surprised. Didn't they hear when every single one of us voiced our discontent with the way we have been treated here?

No!

They are concerned for their international image. Not about us.

Starving refugees at the United Nations! Makes for an international public relations nightmare.

The men can go without food, but the girls, these little kids, especially Soraya, cannot be seen going hungry at the UN.

Local reporters and a video camera arrive to film us, and our spokesman Kiomarse reads our manifesto with its demands. The news team confirms, "Those aren't many demands. Why couldn't you organize something yourselves?"

"We need permission to use the UN grounds. There is nowhere else we can meet."

Group morale is strong.

We have been betrayed by the UN. We are concerned for the safety of other refugees. If it were not this hot, it would be easier. Soraya brings water to splash on our faces.

The UN official orders Indian food. Fifty metal domes cover the hot dishes stacked up one atop the other, leaning against the wall close to where we sit. All fifty hungry refugees smell the mixture of cinnamon, cardamom, and curry. It is torture. It's not bad enough that we are all hungry, but now temptation wafts a few feet away from us.

They have money to order us fancy food from a restaurant but they can't put more money toward our monthly allowance.

No one touches the food. It will rot. It is much too much waste in a city where so many are hungry for a decent meal. My stomach growls, and my heart aches to witness this much waste.

I am outraged by the UN's insult. Not only do they ignore us and dismiss our demands, they are adding an emotional stress of temptation to the physical stress we are already suffering.

How dare they insult all of us in this way?

At night, we sleep on the tile floor in the UN.

Members of the group start cursing the UN officials and their inhumanity.

If the UN is on a tight budget, how could they order so much food for all the refugees sitting on strike? Prepared food must cost a fortune.

The second day is harder. Everyone looks pale and messy. Their breath stinks. My breath must also stink but I am unaware of how bad it is.

We are holding our ground.

Soraya becomes ill.

Keyvan suggests, "Soraya, you are too young for this. The group appreciates your support but break your strike. It is okay."

"I will not break my hunger strike like a coward."

Today, the food smells even better than yesterday. The expression, "To the hungry man everything is delicious" is certainly true in this context. The next day, they order pizza for us, for lunch and dinner.

The mixture of rotten food and the fresh, hot meal is a real torment for our group. The UN officials know exactly what they are doing. They are hoping there will be a crack in the group that will end the strike. When the group loses its unity, that is when we lose and the UN wins.

"Do you think they will change their minds?"

"They have to! This is the UN."

"Do you know how bad it will look when this strike is shown on TV around the world?"

I am fainting from hunger. Keyvan insists that all three of us eat.

"What about you?" I ask him. "You have a stomach ulcer. Do you have any idea what this will do to you?"

Keyvan snaps at me, "Now is not the time to argue with me. Just eat the food that is here. I am speaking for the whole group. Farah, Soraya, and you will still be here but you are all too young for this."

Farah repeats what Keyvan said: "Soraya and you should eat." To be honest, I am happy to have permission to eat, but it is awkward to eat in front of all these hungry, sick-looking men.

Soraya states we will eat only one meal a day to respect the other members of the group.

The UN's chief officer smiles happily at us. He is proud there is a crack in the group.

As the days go by, the men become hungrier, sicker and paler. The crowd's energy diminishes.

An atrocious odour of empty stomachs pervades the garden. The combination of the stench and the humidity make it almost impossible to breathe.

One of the men says, "Ironic, isn't it? I survived the Islamic government only to die on the UN grounds!"

It is not so much the hunger that bothers the refugees but the food that they order every day to weaken the spirit.

The men drink only water.

As the days pass, one by one, our members get sick. The UN calls the ambulance to take them to the hospital.

The guard stands by the front door and does not let any Iranian refugees return once they leave.

I can't help but think that the only place in the world that could offer us help is unwilling to do so. They would rather we get sick and take us out by ambulance one by one than offer any help to actually improve our living conditions.

Would people who help the UN financially know what this organization really stands for?

What is offered to us is not the real help we need to empower us refugees to change our lives. It is about holding us hostage at the bottom of society. The monthly allowance is a sad substitute for what we really need. Even that is not enough for us, who are sharing an apartment and expenses for four. How could it be enough for someone with no ties to anyone else? It does not make sense.

There is anger from both the UN employees and the refugees in the UN garden. Both sides are convinced that they are right and have not been treated justly.

But it is the UN officials who have the power, not us.

Many refugees have been taken to the hospital. Many are lying prone on the ground, without enough energy to stand up. They are prepared to martyr themselves here to make their point, so that maybe future refugees will find it easier. The mood is grim. Our hope that the world's peace organization would stand by us has been dashed to bits.

At the end of the week, the chief officer marches into the garden, and looks about in disgust at the human wreckage scattered around the building. We stare up at him, hope and hatred flickering across our faces. He opens a folder in his hands, and waits until everyone's attention is on him. He has an ultimatum and a final offer from the organization.

No political refugees will be deported to Iran and there will be an increase of fifty rupees per month for the refugees residing in Karachi. There were weak shouts. What about the other requests? What about English classes, about work permits, about helping us emigrate?

He answers that he'd spoken to the main office somewhere in Europe, and they really couldn't do anything about it. Now, he commands, if we don't disperse quickly, he will call the police, and we will lose our refugee protection from the United Nations. He has lost his patience, and he means business now.

He has tried to reason with us, he has tried to bribe us with food, but he is at the end of his rope. He gives us two hours to decide, and the group comes to a unanimous decision to give up and leave.

>>>>>>

Harsh reality hits us. The United Nations will not do anything else for us. The only way out of Pakistan is through our own ingenuity. Our time is now spent trying to find out how we can leave Pakistan without papers. Which country will accept us as refugees?

During the hunger strike, Ali confides in us, "My friends went to Spain a few weeks ago."

How did they go to Spain if they were refugees? We are excited about this possibility. It would be trouble free to go to Spain. One could easily settle and stay there. None of these people had passports. They must have had some kind of forged documents.

For a moment we daydream.

"Spain . . . I could take Spain."

"We'll speak Spanish, learn to dance flamenco, and watch bullfights."

Flamenco dancing is one thing I know about Spain. When I was under house arrest I made needlepoints of many flamenco dancers. I can't wait to actually see them dancing. They must be fascinating people, full of spirit and excitement.

A glimmer of hope comes to us. Soraya and I discuss this latest possibility.

"Would you like to go to Spain?"

"It is a fabulous idea. How soon do you think we'll be there?"

"Do you think maybe next week at this time?"

"That would be fun; how can we prepare all the documents in time?"

"We don't have passports; there is no way we can leave here."

Keyvan announces, "We can live together for a little while in the new country. Then you and Soraya will have to find your own place. I need some privacy with my wife. After all, I'm only twenty-five and I feel like your father."

Soraya and I are happy because Keyvan has faith in us that we are responsible enough to take care of ourselves. Does he think we are a burden? Most likely, but it is hard for us to accept. No one wants to be a burden.

As we are busy counting our chickens before they hatch, Hassan shouts, "Didn't you hear? Last week Spain deported the refugees back to Iran."

The blood runs cold in my body. Spain isn't accepting any more Iranians. The Spanish government is keeping a very close eye on the airlines now and deports anyone they suspect of trying to find refuge.

To obtain passports and possibly visas is a huge undertaking—the one task we have not yet succeeded in accomplishing.

We are not fussy. Any Western country that will have us, we'll gladly head for. A country where we can become citizens with some rights to study and work is all we long for. It is not too much to ask, but without passports or visas in hand, it becomes an impossible dream.

There must be a way to buy documents on the black market. Of course, Iranian refugees carrying forged passports run a big risk. We have heard that if one is caught with a fake passport, there are severe punishments, even possibly deportation. It would be a serious decision that we would have to make, if we had the chance to get a false passport.

With great dismay, I realize there is no country in the world I can call my own. Farah tries to cheer me up. "Sima, please keep in mind the end of a long, dreadful dark night is the sunrise at dawn. Don't lose hope. We've just won a small victory. There may be others coming. We have come too far to be depressed now."

Although we try to stay optimistic, there is no way out of here.

Is Pakistan our stepping-stone or our final destination?

The freedom to read about other lifestyles and schools of thought amazes me, and I appreciate it with a new-found gratitude. This is exactly what the religious fundamentalists in Iran will not allow us to do. Dictators all around the world prefer to keep citizens uneducated, uninformed, and under restrictive laws. They fear the knowledge of the general public; they know that readers will learn that other points of view exist. To the people who want to control the minds of others, ignorance is a blessing. The more they keep people uninformed and ignorant, the more control they have over them.

Ever since I started reading *The Little Black Fish*, I have been devouring books. I would read voraciously, partly because of the times I was forbidden to read. Freedom of the mind is among the greatest freedoms imaginable.

But now I can't even enjoy reading a book. That has been my way to keep my hopes up; now I have such terror about our future that I can't calm down enough to read. Will I die here of old age as a refugee? Will all my dreams of going to school, of making a contribution to mankind remain only wishful thinking? Will I be filled with despair at the end of my life that I did not do anything worthwhile with it? I can't get rid of these questions that fill my head; and even more, the emotions they arouse in me. I am filled with dread.

‑‑‑‑‑‑‑

Keyvan leaves the house early every morning and comes home in the evening expecting us to serve him. He arrives exhausted and hungry. We are frustrated and angry by his lack of concrete results. By now, I have read and reread the book I love the most, *The Little Black Fish*, and memorized it, word for word. Since there is nothing else to do, I stare at the walls and study every crack for hours. I can describe every crack and crevice in the four walls of this room in my dreams. This can't go on much longer.

Cooking and cleaning, which I did not mind doing, and actually liked, are now chores I loathe. Why did I have to leave my country if all I do here is less than what I could do there? At least in Shiraz, I could stroll through the garden and enjoy the smell of the orange blossoms, or keep my plants company, watering them and encouraging their growth. Here, going out alone is out of the question. The humidity is driving me crazy. My clothes stick to me like a tight corset, and all my curves are accentuated. The apartment is too small. Are Farah and Soraya having as difficult a time of it as I am? I dare not ask because that would be opening a can of worms. I am going mental. In this mood, I avoid talking to the others.

In addition to my unvoiced frustrations, Farah, Soraya, and I take turns doing Keyvan's household chores. I resent it.

I do not care anymore and can't keep all these thoughts inside or I will explode.

The best way to demonstrate my discontent is to not do his chores. Soraya and I stay in our room the entire day. No more cooking, no more cleaning. There is no cooked food for him to eat. We are on strike. Since we had agreed on the division of household responsibilities, we are sure he will understand our point of view.

Keyvan returns home, glances around the apartment, stares at us. "Why is this place so messy? Where is dinner?"

"It is your turn to cook and clean this week. We have done more than our share for many weeks now. We are not your slaves in the kitchen while you are out all day."

Keyvan listens carefully at first, staring, eyebrows shooting up. His neck veins start to throb. He erupts. "I am out all day, putting my life in danger, trying to find a way out of this hellhole for you! I've had it! I can't deal with this anymore! You are on your own!" pointing at Soraya and me.

"Do you think my husband is your butler?" Farah yells.

Farah and Keyvan are furious at us. They leave our room and slam the door shut behind them.

Soraya and I exchange nervous glances. We are frozen with shock. There is nowhere to go. No one will deal with girls. How are we to leave this country? We will rot in Pakistan.

Soraya huddles in one corner and cries herself to sleep. There is nothing to talk about. A thick, black *hijab* of fear hangs over our room and spreads throughout the cramped apartment. There is nothing in the room to distract us. Two sleeping bags, an English–Persian dictionary, and *The Little Black Fish* are the only objects in the room. Otherwise it is bare. I am so lonely. So vulnerable. So sad. Never in my life have I felt so crushed.

Going back is not an option. If our future is to live here, I'd rather die than remain here, a useless appendage for the rest of my life.

Complete silence hangs over the apartment. Farah does not speak to Soraya or me. I am sick to my stomach. I can't sleep, although I stay in bed the entire day. I have not eaten since this argument started. I want to die. It is a slow, painful death. Soraya and I are in the room, trying to make ourselves invisible to Keyvan and Farah.

The worst thing that could have happened to us has now happened. Together we would have had more power and may have had a chance to leave; but now, divided, there is no way to get out of Pakistan. Mamán used to say, "No matter how hard you try, you can't clap with one hand. United you are powerful, alone you are not." Why is Keyvan so angry at us? Why is he overreacting? There must be other reasons. I need to find out.

After two long days of being completely ignored, both Farah and Keyvan knock at our door. Keyvan stares at the ground, avoiding eye contact. "I spoke to Mamán." Why would he call Mamán without telling us? Surely he told Mamán only his side of the story and Mamán is mad at us.

He pauses for a few long breaths. "She wants to talk to you!"

All four of us walk over to the telegraph office. Keyvan is annoyed and avoids any conversation. Mamán screams at me over the telephone. "Keyvan is totally in charge of you and Soraya. Period. You have to listen to everything he says and follow his orders; otherwise, he told me, he will leave you behind. I begged him to reconsider because your future is at risk. Work it out and call me back!"

Keyvan is happy now. He has set many new rules, AND he wants a written, signed promise from Soraya and me. We are to obey the rules without question:

We are to listen to him at all times.
We are not to speak until we are spoken to.
We are to do the housework when he is out.
We are not to ask any questions.

Keyvan complains, "It is too hard to be only twenty-five years old and a father to two teenagers. You are naive. You start talking to men and they think you are interested in them. You can't trust any men. I know what they are like. They are wolves looking to pluck you little lambs and eat you alive. I have to make sure you are safe."

Talking to any men in the UN is off-limits. We are to do Keyvan's household chores with pleasure. There is no fun. No music. No family. Days drag into nights and the nights drag on and on.

We have a new level of respect for Keyvan now. He has won. We have been led to believe that our future lies solely in his hands. He is well aware of it and rubs it in our faces.

Mamán's words, "You are so bitter that even a gallon of honey will not make you sweet," apply to my situation now. But I do not want to feel this bitter. I look to see what is good around me.

Karachi has a magnificent waterfront. I wish we could visit it. We are too demoralized to even attempt it. I used to love to be in nature, to meet people, to read. Now I do not care about any of this. The sum of my life in Karachi is breathing and existing.

With glimmers of hope around us, we are excited, but once we weigh our options and realize the impossibility of leaving Pakistan, we sink back down into the dumps. One thing is certain: going to the United States is completely out of the question. Since the hostage crisis in 1979, the American border is much more tightly controlled for anyone of Iranian origin. An Iranian without papers would not stand a chance. Iranians who oppose the Islamic government are also in trouble. All Iranians without papers—Jews, Muslims, Baha'i—are painted with the same brush. The expression that the enemy of my enemy is my friend does not apply here. I would have loved to have the option of going to America. There, opportunities exist for both women and Jews. But it is out of the question.

Our only option seems to be Canada. We do some research and find out that Canada is so cold that one can freeze there. Our Iranian refugee friends at the UN joke with us.

"You're going to go there for real? You'll freeze to death just walking across the street. It's like Siberia, it's so cold."

Jamshid, a recent refugee, pipes up, "Their dollar is stronger than the American dollar. Their economy is soaring. My uncle lives there. It is cold, but they have a great system to fight the cold. I am going to Canada."

"My uncle went to university there. They have the top university in the world. They will let you go to school. They will even pay you to go to school. They give loans and bursaries to the best students!"

You mean they pay us to go to school? This Canada must be

paradise. I've never heard of such a thing. In Iran even if I wanted to pay they would not let me go to school. In Canada, they pay the tuition and living expenses for the best students to attend school.

I love Canada already.

Jamshid is an Iranian movie star in his early forties. He is well built, with thick, long black hair: strikingly handsome. His command of English is surprisingly good. Canada appeals to him as a place to pursue his dream. He is the best thing that came out of our hunger strike.

"Maybe this is not such a bad idea. We don't care about the cold. We can dress warmly."

"What's the catch?"

"If it is really such a great country, why do they still look for newcomers?"

"You don't understand. It is so cold no one wants to live there."

"They are looking for new people to work and pay taxes."

"I'd love to go there. If they help us I'd love to pay taxes."

"Maybe our whole family will be able to come."

The smile is back on my face.

To live in a land where we will be accepted in spite of being foreigners and Jews is a miracle. I think I sense a rainbow through the thick clouds of our many months of darkness.

Keyvan finds out from his well-informed sources that Turkey and Canada have a reciprocal agreement. Both countries welcome visitors from the other, as long as the tourists have return tickets to the city of their departure. This agreement allows visitors to land in Canada without visas. This is the best news ever. Luck is on our side.

We have no passports and no visas. All we have at our disposal is a burning desire to go to school and to work. To maybe one day call our new place "home." To go to a country that welcomes us. To go to a country that permits us to grow and allows us to be contributing members of society. The thick cloud has thinned a little, and a bit of the rainbow shows through.

But Keyvan is still frustrated. Every time he comes home, we jump all over him to find out any bit of news.

"There is no news, as usual. Do not to ask me questions anymore. I will let you know when I have news. You have no idea how many brick walls I encounter every day. Just when I am certain that I am about to meet the right contact, the deal falls through. It is a living hell every time

I step out of this apartment."

Keyvan explains that as kind as everyone seems to us, we are all in the same boat. People will share their information only after they succeed. No one will give away a secret for fear it will jeopardize their own escape. Makes sense.

Piroz is in a one-of-a-kind situation, since he is not planning to leave yet. He is a student, and that is the reason he is so well-connected. He gives Keyvan guidance on where we might be able to purchase Turkish passports on the black market. Piroz strongly warns Keyvan to keep quiet about his contact if he is successful in obtaining passports. "Do not disclose this information to anyone until you leave."

We are becoming just like everyone else. Selfish. Or is it self-preservation?

We have to protect ourselves. The kind, outgoing, friendly three sisters are becoming cynical. Charity begins at home. We will help other refugees as soon as we get out.

Keyvan announces, "Dress up. We need to take pictures for the passports."

"What? We are going to have passports? Why do you keep such important information from us?"

"I've been working on this lead for a couple of weeks. I wanted to be sure before I shared it with you."

We do not have fancy clothes; it doesn't matter since the photograph is only a head shot. Smiles are back on our faces. We may have taken one tiny step, but there are still many obstacles facing us. "Patience. Rome was not built in a day. This is the first step."

The Pakistani photographer is old. The last time I went to a photographer's studio was shortly after the Revolution. The photographer was a Christian who was the father of my classmate. I wore my best shirt and my headscarf. Mamán stood in the room to make sure I posed to her liking. It is so different now.

Keyvan watches us carefully to make sure the photographs turn out well. My hair is uncovered, and I am wearing the beautiful red polyester long-sleeved shirt that Mamán sewed.

Mamán is not here, but I sense her presence. We each take turns having our pictures taken for Turkish passports. I am sad that I have no Iranian passport. Even if I had one, the current Iranian government is detested around the world, so it would be useless. I am thrilled at the possibility that our Turkish passport opens doors for Keyvan, Farah, Soraya and me. Though this calls for celebration, we dare not celebrate. We do not want to invite bad luck. Until we are in the new land, we will not celebrate or tell anyone of our plans.

Next morning, Keyvan puts all the photos in his pants pocket. What if they become sweaty and turn into garbage?

By now, I have studied Keyvan's behaviour so much I can tell when he is nervous. He paces back and forth with his hands intertwined behind his back, staring at the floor. He is as filled with fear and excitement as we are.

"Keyvan, we have a better idea. Let's wrap the photographs in plastic in case you have to wait a long time; we do not want them to get ruined."

He responds, "Wish me luck." Today is the day he has to buy the passports. He puts many one hundred American dollar bills into his front pants pockets. We are not allowed to go with him or ask him where he is meeting the dealer. It is top secret, and he acts like a top-secret agent. "I will be back as soon as I can. I hope the man who sells the passports shows up. I have to meet him at noon."

Farah pleads, "Please come back as soon as you have them. Don't wander around with those things on you."

Farah is a wreck, terrified for Keyvan. Worst-case scenarios pop into my head, unasked-for and unwanted. We can't do anything. Pretending to sleep does not work anymore.

Today we may have the passports and if that happens then we may be able to leave this dreadful place.

The next steps depend on this.

There is no way to buy airplane tickets unless we have passports.

Canada is our only option.

Please, God, help Keyvan stay safe.

Considering how things could go wrong, I pray that God will protect him.

Late in the afternoon, Keyvan comes home beaming with excitement. He is our prince in shining armour. He flashes the four Turkish passports he pulls from his pants pockets. At the sight of the passports, we start screaming, sobbing uncontrollably, embracing each other.

I never imagined a passport could change the course of my life.

It just did.

We will be able to leave Pakistan after all!

Each passport cost US $250. The young Turkish man who sold the passports does not want to deal with women. We are not going to argue. The fact is now we have passports, four dreamt-of miracles.

Keyvan hands me my passport. I am happy to hold my passport to freedom and to life. It has another name on it. I am able to read it, but I do not understand what I am reading.

Our next challenge is to find a way to buy tickets and pay off the gate agents at the airport.

~~~~~

The person who sold the passports to Keyvan insisted that they are authentic Turkish passports. Our new passports have common Turkish names. We memorize our names and our "parents'" names. The ages marked on the passports are close enough to our actual ages. No eyebrows will be raised.

One part of the puzzle is solved, but our photos are not yet in the passports, and to change the photos is an intricate job; it takes the right person to do it. How Keyvan finds these people is never discussed with us. We only know that a lot of money is exchanged in the process. Thank God for the money Mamán and Baba sent. They must be in the poorhouse because of our flight for freedom. I never take advantage of Mamán and Baba's money, knowing how hard they work for every *tooman*. I count every dollar I spend; I haven't bought any new clothing other than the saris since leaving Shiraz. The food is the same boring rice with tomato or another vegetable, day after monotonous day. I rarely go out to eat; I've never seen a movie in Pakistan. There is no way to squeeze more money to save. All the money that Mamán and Baba send has been saved to help us leave Pakistan.

Once I arrive in our new country and am able to work, I will no longer ask Mamán and Baba to send me money. I will do whatever it takes. I will clean houses to support myself and to pay for my studies, the one thing that matters the most to me.

Farah's and Keyvan's birthdays have passed unacknowledged, as has my eighteenth birthday. When I was a child, I always imagined what my life would be like on my eighteenth birthday. I would certainly be in medical school studying to be a neurosurgeon on my way to becoming a cardiologist before I became a school principal. At this moment, simply attending any university would be a big achievement.

I miss Mamán, who always made my birthday so special with her educational gifts. She bought me a set of Canon cameras before the Revolution. Now, in this part of the world, everything is meaningless, even birthdays.

Soraya will soon be sixteen years old. She has seen enough drama for her age. What am I to do for her birthday?

"Soraya, you will be sixteen, soon. What are your dreams?"

"The best gift is to have the opportunity to leave this country, to study and work. That is all I want."

"What do you want to study?"

"First let me finish high school; then I will decide."

"It is great to hold onto dreams, Soraya. That day is not far off. It will become reality."

The best birthday gift for all of us will be that of having real opportunities in life.

That day has arrived.

Each passport has our photo in it. Keyvan shows us the passports. "It took a very long time for the Pakistani man to glue your pictures on. No one can tell the difference. He did a great job." This is a dream come true. How could a small booklet, this passport, change the destiny of one's life? Tears of happiness roll down my cheeks. I thank Keyvan.

"Not yet . . . we are not done yet. There are more obstacles to overcome."

He is right.

But we are inching closer to leaving. The proverb "Be careful what you wish for because you might get it," reverberates in my mind. Yes, it does take perseverance, hard work, and much luck. Dreams come true for those who do not give up, no matter how bleak the circumstances.

If it is a Turkish passport taking us close to our dream, let it be. If holding this piece of paper will bring me to my goals, I will hold it. I am no less Iranian by holding this document. I still know where I came from. I still know my heritage. I still know who I am.

We pepper Keyvan with questions. "What are we to do with this passport?" "Where are we to buy the tickets?" "When are we leaving?"

"Hold on. Were you born at four months? I will let you know when I have more news."

I am so eager to hear the details of our next step. But like so many times in the past year, we have to keep our million questions to ourselves. The future will unfold at its own pace. Until then our only option is to wait.

~~~~~~~

We find out that getting refugee status in most of Canada's provinces is difficult. The province of Quebec is less stringent in applying the law because it needs immigrants.

Keyvan waits until we stop talking. Then he responds slowly and patiently, "The same person who sold me the passports told me to go to a specific travel agency to purchase return tickets to Montreal, Canada. They work in collusion with airline employees. They have to be paid to look the other way when we show up with our passports before boarding the plane."

Bribery!

We will pay whomever we have to pay to buy our future. There is no price too high for a person who wants to follow her dream.

It is time to call Mamán and Baba.

The telegraph office here in Karachi is quieter than usual. What a surprise. As soon as we arrive we are able call Shiraz.

Cyrus picks up the phone. He calls out, "Mamán, it is Sima."

"Mamán, we are going to Canada!"

"You will freeze there. Can't you go anywhere better?"

"That is the only place we can go. We will let you know when we get there. Please pray for us."

Passports are all in order. Airplane tickets are bought. Arrangements have been made to leave at the right time, with the right guard on duty at the airport. Whatever we could do in advance is done, but the uncertainty hangs over our heads.

How am I to sleep with so much anticipated danger that lies ahead? A monumental achievement if all goes well; if not, the consequences could be devastating. My imagination for the worst-case scenario becomes excessively vivid. Where will I be sent if I am caught at the airport? The UN will not be able to do anything. Will I be sent to Turkey? The prisons in Turkey are as bad as the prisons in Iran. When I think of all that could go wrong, my body freezes with fear. Will I ever see Mamán and Baba again? While these thoughts hang over my head, time slows down even more. Tonight is even more torturous than the night of the desert crossing. Then I had to keep moving, and that distracted me, but here in this hot and humid room, there is no distraction.

I look the fear right in the eye and command her to shut up. Whatever happens, I have no choice. I will accept the consequences of my actions graciously. At least I am with my sisters and Keyvan. There is power in our group, and that makes the terrible circumstances more bearable.

Flight to Freedom

As you start to walk out on the way, the way appears.

Rumi

June 4, 1983

Goodbye time. Again. I dread saying goodbye, leaving people I know behind, leaving bits of my heart behind. Saturday was also the day I left Shiraz . . . our lucky day, with one big difference: this time, I am leaving Pakistan, I am leaving Asia; I am leaving the Middle East—and the past—behind me.

Piroz, our guardian angel. How am I to thank him for his unwavering help? Words fail to describe his loyalty not only to me but to my entire family in Karachi.

Piroz looks straight into my eyes. "Leave. Follow your dreams and never forget the hell you lived in. This will help you overcome all obstacles."

Keyvan, Farah, and Soraya thank him for his kindness at the door. Tears, laughter, and joy fill the room . . . but the scent of fear, fear of the unknown, is pervasive. The finale is so close I can almost touch it. An emotional roller coaster is now my normal state of being.

What if we are unable to leave? We have one last favour to ask Piroz. Keyvan hands Piroz the key to the apartment and tells him to hold onto it until we have left the country. And another proviso: Feel free to give whatever is left in the apartment to the next group of refugees.

We have nothing to take with us. There is nothing of value here. I left Shiraz with nothing and I will do the same here. No need for luggage. Travelling light is what I do.

For the flight out of Pakistan, I wear the jeans and T-shirt that Mamán sent from Shiraz and the brand-new, dark red sandals that I bought for this special occasion. Unlike when I left Shiraz, Zahedan, and Quetta, there is no need for the *hijab*. I discard it with pleasure. I should never have been forced to wear it. The only meaning this piece of material has to me is one of oppression and regression. I respect those who are wearing it based on their free will and beliefs but I never chose it. It stifled me from the first day I wore it.

The jeans, T-shirt, and sandals are the best clothes I own and have saved to wear for the day I leave Pakistan. And that day is today! In my mind, I picture the best-dressed tourists, elegant and confident, when they fly to Western countries. With these clothes, we can blend in at the airport like regular passengers.

No problem squeezing the four of us into the taxi; we have only the one suitcase. As the taxi driver manoeuvres crazily between pedestrians and donkeys scurrying across the road, I am consumed with the memories of the seven months of my youth left behind in Pakistan, and the steps it took to bring me to this farewell to Asia.

Keyvan informs us we are to meet John, who will help us clear immigration. Who is John? How powerful is he to be able to help us leave? I can't wait to meet him. If we are able to clear all the obstacles, we will have a chance to arrive in Montreal . . . eventually. But we have some scary stops on the way. I do not even want to think about the stops because if I do, I will not be able to go to the airport. How on earth will we pull this off? Farah, Keyvan, Soraya, and I are carrying Turkish passports, yet between the four of us, none of us knows one word of Turkish. We need John to make this deception work.

The taxi stops in front of the airport. Pakistani men in traditional native costume run to the taxi to empty the luggage out of the trunk of the car, expecting to be tipped. *No, we only have one piece of luggage. We don't need any help.* It is impossible to get rid of the men. Dozens of beggars stick to us like flies trapped in honey.

No family member escorted us to the airport and no one is here to wish us safe travel; but John is waiting, rigid as a stone statue, by the entrance. He holds a sign in his hand announcing his name.

He is Pakistani, so why is he called John? I ask myself . . . then remember: for foreigners, all Pakistanis are named "John." He is a muscular man in his mid-twenties. We spot each other right away, three girls and a man coming out of a taxi. What are the chances of a mistake? He works in conjunction with our travel agent. His job is to accompany us through the various stages of departure in the airport. To make sure we board the plane. He speaks perfect English. He orders us: "Sit down on this bench. Do not move until I arrange all your documents."

By now, we have learned to follow instructions. All four of us sit as one on a cold metal bench. Waiting, waiting . . . praying and waiting. The airport is filled with travellers: Pakistanis dressed in local costumes, foreign backpackers, men in three-piece suits, and women in elegant dresses with matching hats. Stewardesses pass us wearing uniforms of orange, red, and blue. I've never seen stewardesses before. I stare at them: glamorous, exciting, and adventurous women, flying all around the world.

The airport is much cleaner than the streets in Karachi; there is rancid, overflowing garbage lying around, but the white tiles are visible. There are not as many signs of chewed-up red paan on the ground. These tourists are too elegant and sophisticated to be chewing paan.

Soraya whispers in my ear, "We have been waiting here so long! What if they do not let us get to the gate? What if we leave Karachi but are deported to Turkey?"

I have no answer for her.

I am also terrified.

Soraya remembers what Mamán would do when she was nervous: pray.

I am choking with fear; my throat is bone dry, I can't swallow, and can barely talk. However, prayer will not require talking. It is silent and powerful. Let's pray and ask for help.

I can't look at the other visitors anymore. Planes take off one after another. The Pakistani baggage handlers carry the luggage for the travellers. There are many crying children. So many people pass in front of us, and no one seems to encounter any problems. How can they be so fortunate as to pass security while I am glued to this cold metal bench for hours? My body is frozen with fear. Has John been arrested in the process of helping us? Something has gone seriously wrong. I ask a woman, "What time is it?"

"Four o'clock."

I start to shiver. It is past our departure time. A cold sweat breaks out and rapidly covers my body.

John reappears a few minutes later. I thought he had forgotten about us. "I tried my best to put you on that plane and I couldn't. The gate agent who was supposed to help us through his barrier called in sick today."

No! Please, no! We are *not* going back to live in Karachi. We *can't*.

My feet turn to lead, unable to move, unable to leave the airport, unable to leave the possibilities that await us. Disappointment shadows Keyvan's, Farah's, and Soraya's faces.

John insists we leave the airport. Is he telling the truth? Or does he want more money? With smugglers, one never knows. It is all about money. Money solves everything. The more you want something, the more you have to pay. This is not the first time we are dealing with smugglers.

John promises us, "You will be able to leave soon. Your travel agent will arrange it for you."

Keyvan calls a taxi. None of us says a word in the taxi. The only sound is the quiet sobbing, sobbing, sobbing, until we cannot cry anymore.

We have to stop at Piroz's apartment to retrieve our key. He is in disbelief, staring at the ground, to avoid our eyes and his sadness. No amount of consolation will remedy our newest wound. But he tries hard. "It is not unusual to fail on the first try."

I do not care what happened to other people in the past.

We have failed.

There is no hope.

I want to hide. The thick, black layers of darkness drop over me again. I was so close to leaving this hell — so close — and it was snatched right out of my hands.

I dash to my room and spend the entire evening pretending to be asleep but unable to close my eyes, caught between the possibility of living my dreams and the actual reality of this hot room that looks and feels like a prison cell. I ponder our entire previous attempt for freedom: from Shiraz, to Zahedan, to Quetta, to Islamabad, and all the way to here. The one thing that I want is to be able to make my own choices.

❯❯❯❯❯

The next day, Keyvan returns to the travel agency to exchange the tickets. Fortunately, even though we paid many times the price of the airfare for these tickets, they were open tickets. This means that if we can't leave, we don't have to purchase new tickets. Or pay a penalty. The travel agent charged us two thousand dollars of Mamán's and Baba's hard-earned money for each ticket. This was the cost of our yet-to-be successful departure from Karachi. From Pakistan. From this oppressive part of the world. From the country that is standing between us and our future.

The days leading to the departure are painfully long. The humidity is at its maximum. I had vowed to myself never to come back to Karachi; but as it happened, I haven't even left, and now I am back in this hell. Is there something I am missing or not paying attention to? Or am I being unappreciative, and that is why I am stuck here? No matter how bad Pakistan was and is, it is still a bridge to connect me to a better world, and for that I have to be grateful.

I start counting the positives of living in Pakistan. The negatives I have evaluated many times. I was forced to be independent in Pakistan, to trust my gut feeling. The only way to transcend a position is to pass through it. I am thankful to have hit rock bottom and to spring back when the opportunity arose. The words that helped me cross the desert revisit me: "At the end of a long, dreadful night is a bright, sunny day. Keep your hopes up."

Since our first attempt to leave, I have developed a serious infection in my toes. What is it about me and my shoes whenever I leave a country? The new red sandals that I bought for this trip rub and blister my toes. I have no other shoes to wear. My feet throb and yellow pus oozes out. I am reminded again that the path to freedom is an agonizing one.

Piroz brings me antibacterial cream. "Be careful. Because of the heat and humidity, infections take forever to heal." I apply the cream daily and keep off my feet as much as possible. The damn infection does not heal. Are the bacteria using the ointment as food? How am I to walk to the airport without limping?

An agonizing week has gone by, and at last . . . tomorrow will be departure.

June 11, 1983

The four of us are back in a taxi, on the road to the airport. The voice in my head reminds me not to say that I will never be back in Karachi because I may still return. The goodbye to Piroz is not as elaborate as the first time. Few airplanes are up in the sky today, but I want to be in one of those sleek, silver birds looking down on the city.

The taxi driver zigzags through the traffic toward the airport. The blare of a police siren directly behind us cuts through the noise of the human, animal, and mechanical traffic. It forces the driver to slow down. My heart races, and my legs tremble like chickens about to be slaughtered. Is the police car following us?

Keyvan whispers to us, "Do not act nervous. Try to appear as calm as possible." Mamán's voice reverberates in my head, "To a cat who is watching to steal your meat, any sound scares her." If the police stop the taxi and ask us for our identification, we are doomed. Keyvan asked us to leave the UN papers in the apartment. We have no identification other than our forged Turkish passports. The police car's siren grows louder and louder every millisecond. I try to devise a story that will be close to the truth, because I can't lie; but my brain is paralyzed with fear. There is no way to cover this one. Turkish passport, on the way to the airport with the tickets and of Iranian origin—it will not take a genius to work out that we are escaping.

Farah is pale, and Soraya is freaked out, her eyes bulging out of her face. The silence in the car is electric. No normal traveller would be filled with anxiety if a police car came up behind them. Will the taxi driver be alarmed and co-operate with the police, handing us over like hot diamonds? Or is he unaware of our internal turmoil, doing his best to tackle the traffic and the police car that is right behind us? Every move he makes, I jump. He can't drive faster, but if he drives at this crawl we will never make it on time to the airport to meet John. This airport ride has already taken twice as long as the last time we drove there. Are the police going to arrest us?

Finally, at the exact intersection for the airport, the police car turns right as our taxi driver continues to International Departures. What a relief! We lean back exhausted against the seats as the stress subsides. Keyvan gives the driver an extra tip because he is thrilled that we all made it to the airport. The driver looks puzzled.

John is waiting at the front door—the same spot as last time, but he isn't holding the sign. He instructs Soraya and me to sit down. Seeing John perturbs me. For some unknown reason, every time I see him, my body tenses. I develop goosebumps and start to perspire profusely, as though I am deep in the *hammam*.[8] My clothes stick to me like a glove from all the perspiration. Then the voice in my head says, "You are getting yourself in trouble; no normal tourist is so nervous." I quickly wipe away the beads of sweat and proceed as if nothing were happening. We should look as happy as all the other travellers.

Farah and Keyvan will accompany John to process our departure. I want to ask him why we have to wait but I hold back; I can't afford to upset him, since he is our only hope now. Soraya and I sit on the cold metal bench again. A minute goes by, another minute, ten minutes, an hour; I am going crazy. Soraya squeezes my hand so hard that I jump up from my seat; she is also apprehensive. Time plays its ugly game with us again.

Dozens of intercom announcements call out exotic destinations for departing flights, Flight 688 to Paris at Gate 21, Flight 724 to London at Gate 34, Flight 555 to Qatar at Gate 15. Men and women rush in front of us, singly, in couples, in groups. Clusters of women wearing different, colourful uniforms with matching blazers and hats, stride by purposefully. Mamán believed that in order to be a stewardess, one had to be strikingly beautiful with a perfect figure. She is right; these women are slim and move confidently. "Look at me, aren't I gorgeous?" In contrast to these stunning women in Western dress are Pakistani women wrapped in their saris, trailing behind their husbands. Interestingly, not even one Pakistani woman is walking side by side with her husband; they are all following, and the distance of two feet apart is always observed. It baffles me that I noticed this phenomenon only today, after seven months of living in Pakistan, and the only reason is because I am stuck to this cold metal bench under strict orders not to move.

I can't look at the passengers any longer. I have been patiently waiting here for three long hours and Farah and Keyvan are not in sight. I am ready to scream from frustration.

Tension and anxiety build up inside of me; I am about to explode. Resorting to my prayer is the only option. "Soraya, let's pray." A feeling of jealousy, foreign to me, grips me as I witness other travellers passing ahead of us. I can't look at them anymore. It is too agonizing. I close my eyes and in my head I repeat my prayer endlessly. These are the longest three hours I have ever waited. For anything. For anyone.

---

8   Steam bath.

Keyvan shakes me, forcing my eyes open, frustration written all over his body. Farah's eyes well up. It is four o'clock, past our intended flight time. We have failed again. Our flight took off while we were still waiting. We were so close, but again flight is snatched out of our hands. This inevitability is just one more disappointment we have to deal with.

⌇⌇⌇⌇⌇

This new wound is too raw. Keyvan mutters under his breath, "I will go to the travel agent on Monday to plead with him."

Farah, Soraya, and I come up with a better idea. "We will come with you this time. If the travel agent meets us, he might have more sympathy for us. He will try harder to make our departure happen." Reluctantly, Keyvan agrees.

The travel agent's office is situated in an affluent part of Karachi, lined with embassies, and unlike the rest of the city, it is quiet and clean. In this modern building, we enter the elevator. The elevator alone distinguishes this building from the rest of the Karachi we know. This is the first time I have been in an elevator in my life. Keyvan pushes the button to the third floor. *I am claustrophobic in this metal box; what if it stops in mid-air? How do I get out?* My voice needles me. But the ride is so fast; the chatter in my head doesn't have much time to torture me. As we leave the elevator, I make sure not to walk on the crack between the elevator and the ground. Keyvan warns us, "Do not speak too much, but do whatever you think has to be done."

The travel agency is right in front of the elevator. No receptionist greets us. This is a one-man operation. The agent, a heavy, dark-skinned, bold-looking Pakistani man in his fifties, sits behind a huge mahogany desk. He does not get up from his throne to welcome us. He claims to be a well-travelled man, but when he speaks with us it is in broken Persian and he brags that he also knows Italian, French, and German. He looks at Keyvan and then at each of us, wondering, "Why are you all here?"

We speak to him in our broken English.

"Help, vvvv . . . eeee leevvveee. Pleeease."

On his desk sits an ashtray full of cigarette butts. He continues to smoke as we discuss how we can ensure that our next attempt to leave will be successful. He asks, "Where are you from?"

"Shiraz."

"I visited Iran in 1976. I enjoyed my visit to Shiraz."

Farah asks, "You have child?"

She knows when to ask the right question. I understand where she is going with this.

"Yes."

"Is how old?"

"I have three girls your age and an older son. They all live here in Karachi with my wife and me."

"T'ink wee like your child. Help leave Karachi. No like Karachi. Pleease. We ccrazzy now."

He puffs violently at his cigarette. We choke with the smoke wreathing the room in noxious grey clouds. Now is not the time to make a fuss over the smoke. He sits deep in thought.

Silence hangs mournfully in the room.

Farah starts to cry. Soraya and I follow. It is not a quiet cry. Hhhh, hhhhh, hhhhhhhhhh, we weep desperately.

"Enough! Stop it! I promise this will be the last time you have to go to Karachi airport." His tone conveys his sincerity; he means it this time. Maybe it is the tears, maybe he sees how young and innocent Soraya is, maybe it is the extra cash Keyvan hands him. We'll never know but we believe that our insistence to meet him pushed him to make a more serious effort to help us.

June 18, 1983

Third time's the charm . . . we hope. We again say our last goodbyes to Piroz in the apartment we have lived in since April.

There is no reason to repeat the previous instructions. "Piroz, you will know we are gone if you do not hear from us by the end of the day."

On a very sunny, hot day dripping with humidity, we leave our apartment for the airport. Again. I look at the city with more intensity, hoping it is for the last time. I will be out of this country and off this continent, leaving behind my childhood and adolescence to embrace the unknown . . . willingly. I arrived here as a seventeen-year-old, a teenager, never dreaming that I would end up bearing such responsibilities at my age, and I am leaving here, having taken on more than my share of the challenges of adulthood.

Farah and I arrived here on our own and now all four of us are leaving together. The size of my family has shrunk from hundreds to just four. This is the most precious family that I have now. I am leaving everything behind, yet I'm happy to face what is awaiting me. If someone had to learn to be patient, Mamán would say, "It takes the patience of Job." If she wanted to teach us to be patient she would say, "If you are patient, you can make halvah out of sour grapes." Both these adages apply to our situation now.

John is waiting for us at the airport. Once more. The airport is crowded with people going to destinations around the world, as well as people arriving from foreign countries. And then there is us: Farah, Keyvan, Soraya, and me. To everyone else, this day might be typical; to us, this day could be the turning point in our lives. Today is a day of hope and despair. A simple plane ride will make all the difference between living in freedom and living in persecution. John signals to us to follow him as quickly as possible. We head toward the direction he is pointing, making sure not to walk too fast, yet maintain a steady pace. This simple walk lasts a few minutes, but it seems as though a lifetime has passed.

I try to blend in with the other travellers as much as possible, to mirror what everyone else is doing, but I can't. My toes are infected, and as a result, I am limping. I aim to remain under the radar, to be visible to Farah, Keyvan, and Soraya but invisible to everyone else. Easier said than done.

With John leading the way, we are instructed to pass many people who are waiting in line. We are reluctant, but John insists that we hurry, and make it through the security check before the officer's shift is over. We make it to the front of the line for ticket validation. All of the other passengers stare angrily. Guilt overcomes me. Who am I to cut in front of all these people, who have been patiently waiting their turn? But I have to cut in if I want to make the flight and escape.

Within minutes, we are following John, passing the security gate. I am perspiring from head to toe, avoiding eye contact, keeping my gaze glued to the ground. I avoid looking at Farah and Soraya; they must be tormented, too. A Pakistani guard with an incredibly large belly, wrapped around tightly with a belt, sits on a stool. He glances at our passports, and quickly grabs the one hundred dollars tucked away in each. He motions with his hand to move along swiftly. One by one, we pass in front of him as rapidly as possible. I let out a sigh of relief, moving away from him. Thank God he is on duty today. This is the man who prolonged our tortured existence in Karachi for two excruciating weeks.

John accompanies us to the gate. We can't thank John since we do not want to attract attention to ourselves. We wink at him as he melts into the crowd.

A miracle, indeed.

Our travel agent has kept his promise.

Silently, Farah winks at me, smiling imperceptibly.

I nod quietly. This time we are sitting at the actual gate where we are supposed to board the plane. A huge, impersonal plane waits outside on the tarmac, but to us this plane represents freedom. It emanates warmth and safety. The name Alitalia, written in red letters, assures me that we are in the right place. I have never been this close to an airplane in my life, and now I am within walking distance of one. The planes circling in the sky look so minuscule compared to this monstrosity.

Soraya and I sit in one row, Farah and Keyvan in another. I try to avoid eye contact with the other passengers and the possibility of conversation. As I look around unobtrusively I do not see any other "suspicious" people. Most other travellers seem calm and relaxed. Or are they putting on a facade just as we are? A woman plops herself next to me. Is she suspicious of us? I dare not take a chance.

Farah waves, smiling at me. *Come sit closer to us.* I shake my head. I don't want to take any extra chances at this point.

I feel frustrated and helpless, with no control over my destiny. On one hand, I am ecstatic, practically jumping out of my own skin, because freedom seems to be just hours away. On the other hand, I am scared that at any second an officer will come to recheck my passport.

I whisper in Soraya's ear, "Let's pray quietly." The same prayer that I uttered on the night of the desert crossing, the same prayer Mamán used to say when she could not do anything else.

An announcement floats over the terminal: "All the passengers for Alitalia board the plane."

A Persian proverb comes to mind: "I hobbled all the way to India on foot." I hobble on one foot and run enthusiastically on the other one. Farah and Keyvan lead the way, while Soraya carefully watches every step I take and makes sure I do not fall. The other passengers have carry-on luggage and many other bags with them. We have no bags and no carry-on. Will this blow our cover? We walk outside to board the plane and for the last time, I breathe the hot, humid air of Karachi.

A short climb up the metal stairs, and I am greeted by stewardesses, smiles plastered on their faces. One of them checks our tickets. "Go right and follow the numbers." Where are the numbers? Keyvan and Farah are just as clueless as I am.

A cool mist blows down from the vents above the seats and over my sweaty body as I stagger down the aisle, looking for the number. The monstrosity I witnessed while looking from behind the window does not match the tight aisle inside. Every centimetre of space is carefully planned. To experience this moment has taken many months of perseverance and determination coupled with patience and much luck. It took the patience of Job. I thank heaven for being able to finally board the plane.

I am terrified beyond imagination because we are stopping in Riyadh, the capital of Saudi Arabia, one of the most backward countries in the Middle East. We will have a brief transit before changing planes. If caught here, we will be handed over to the Iranian government, and I do not want to think about what would happen next.

Our seats are toward the back of the plane. A blanket and a pillow await us on each seat. How considerate, what great service. Such luxury is beyond me. I settle next to Soraya, cramped in my small seat and still hyperventilating from the most recent encounter with my internal voice that can't shut up. Farah and Keyvan remain in front of us.

Horrific images have never been completely vanquished during the months in Pakistan. We are travelling on Alitalia, we are carrying Turkish passports, and yet between the four of us, we speak not one word of Turkish. What if a Turkish-speaking flight attendant is on board? It seems very likely on a Pakistan-to-Saudi Arabia-to-Italy flight. What if one of the flight attendants addresses us in "our" native tongue? To avoid possible detection, we don't talk to each other at all, covering our faces fully with the blankets. We plan to pretend to sleep during the entire flight.

The plane is full. After agonizing minutes, the door is shut, and we are safe for now; no one came to recheck our passports. The stewardess demonstrates the emergency procedures, and though she speaks in both Urdu and English, it sounds like gibberish to me, and I have no idea what she is talking about. The buckle in her hand is similar to the buckle in my seat; this must be a security precaution. I am too excited to be able to concentrate on her demonstration. Though the plane is still on the ground, in my head I am already flying to a faraway land of freedom and hope where the possibilities are endless.

As this huge metal monstrosity taxies smoothly down the runway, I am humbled by its size, by this complex technological creature. This is my first experience of flying.

The plane takes off. The higher the plane flies, the smaller the city looks. It is like an aerial map in a textbook. The clouds surround us, balls of ephemeral fluff. No sign of earth. I am floating up in the sky among the white clouds . . . feathery, giant cotton balls. It is liberating, this sensation of being up in the air, speeding silently away from the shackles of Asia. My voice reminds me to be thankful for all the people who participated in helping me arrive at this moment: Mamán, Baba, Naneh Jaan-Jaan, Zari, Farhad, Khatereh, Ammeh Nilofar, and all the people in Pakistan. This flight will be etched into my psyche for the rest of my life. This is the flight of freedom and hope. This is the turning point in my life and, just like the plane battling to keep steady in the air, I have been battling for a freedom that has almost materialized. From now on, whatever happens is all up to me; no one will decide for me what to wear, what to do, what music to listen to. I will live as a free woman and use my freedom to the best of my ability, constructively and with appreciation. I will face my challenges just like this plane; I will follow through with persistence and determination.

From the corner of my eye, I notice the stewardess pushing the meal wagon down the aisle. The smell of hot food is impossible to ignore, and I begin to salivate. But I do not want to look at the stewardess or speak to her in case she is of Turkish origin. As she passes the aisle, my stomach growls at me for not feeding it. Hunger pangs gnaw at me.

Outside my blanket hiding place, someone is smoking a cigar. I choke from the thick layer of dark smoke enveloping me. What is wrong with people? Don't they realize that the smoke cannot escape the plane and we are all trapped here with the noxious odour making breathing impossible?

The silence makes the noise in my head louder and louder. The fear revisits me on a minute-to-minute basis: How stupid could I be to believe that I can fly safely to Canada with a Turkish passport? I do not like this voice; it is negative and unreasonable. It has nothing good to offer. When it grips me, I feel debilitated. Keyvan must have been crazy to think we can pull this off. If anything goes wrong, he will never forgive himself, and Mamán will neither forgive nor forget him.

I might have dozed off, because an announcement on the intercom wakes me. The stewardess moves along the aisle, efficiently picking up the passengers' trash. The captain announces that we will be landing shortly in Riyadh.

As we are about to disembark in Riyadh, a flight attendant asks Keyvan in English, "Where are you from?"

"We are from Turkey."

She starts to address Keyvan—in Turkish! We are stunned, rooted to the ground by fear. Our worst nightmare has come to life. Keyvan doesn't answer. He can't. She looks at all of us, puzzled, eyes narrowing, but she can't make out what is wrong with us. I am trembling, praying that she will leave us alone and walk away. A colleague calls her to help a sick wheelchair-bound passenger. She walks away. There are miracles when one prays.

The women here look as badly off as the women in Quetta; they are of the black walking-telephone-booth variety. The head, the face, the eyes are all covered. The telephone booths walk a few feet behind their husbands. We wait in the airport. I am suffocating with the heat and fear. I have never felt such heat! The two-hour stop feels like an eternity.

Keyvan is too pale and nervous; I hope his ulcer does not act up now because it will be a disaster for all of us. Ever since the Revolution, he has had bouts of bleeding ulcer, usually aggravated by stress. We all live with stress differently. Under this amount of stress, my arm is numb, and I am afraid it will fall off and out of the shoulder socket. Farah and Soraya are as white as ghosts. We do not want to be seen here. We are in the worst country to be given any consideration if we are caught. Three of us are women. Jews. Illegal refugees. False documents. *Please, God, help us get through this!*

This time, only our tickets are verified as we enter the plane. As the plane takes off, we are leaving the Middle East behind us . . . at last! We are to fly overnight, and if all goes according to schedule, we will arrive in Rome in the early morning. There will be an eight-hour stopover until we leave for Canada.

We disembark in Rome. We are free to walk around the sparkling, absolutely spotless airport. The floor is so clean one can eat off of it. Whenever I turn a corner, I see yet another round, silver, metal can. It is clean and sprinkled with sand. What could this be? There are so many of these things around the airport. A man rubs his cigarette in it. It must be a garbage can and an ashtray. It looks like a piece of art compared to the rancid overflowing bins in the Karachi airport.

In this airport, there is no smell of sweat; instead, we are surrounded by different perfumes, floral, sensuous, fruity, as women and men stride by. I am in heaven already. If the airport is so mesmerizing I can just imagine what the modern city of Rome looks like. I am tempted to take off and explore the city. But circumstances and limitations warn me against the temptation. I promise myself to return one day under better conditions and tour the city, see the luxurious hotels, and window-shop the exquisite clothing boutiques that I am sure exist here.

The sight of wonderful, well-dressed, well-groomed passengers is bewildering. No head scarves, no saris, no red paan on the ground. The boutique sells Italian brands of clothing and purses—a sight for fashion-starved eyes. The men are clean, handsome, well built, and fashionably clothed. It has been too long since I have seen anything like these men.

The women are tall, slender, and fully made up from head to toe. And the skirts are so tight! I wonder how they can walk on those high heels with such tight skirts. There is no way I can do that; I would be falling on my face with my first step. My head spins around in all directions, taking in all the sights. Seriously, why are their skirts so short? Are these ladies just typical Italian women or they are prostitutes decked out in their professional wear? In the airport? How bizarre.

Keyvan whispers in Farah's ear, "We should mail our return tickets to Pakistan; maybe another refugee can use them."

Farah is baffled by the idea. "Where are we to find an envelope, a stamp, and a mailbox in the airport? Even if we do find everything, what will happen if we need the return tickets to board the plane?"

"There is no way I will hand my return ticket to Keyvan now," I whisper to Soraya. Soraya shakes her head, too. Keyvan changes his mind; it would not be a smart idea to mail the tickets now. We will wait and find a way to do so on the way to Canada. We have to get rid of them somehow before landing there.

The last and final part of the flight to Montreal is approaching. Already I have missed two meals and have no idea when I will be eating again. My stomach groans with every step I take. I feel an agonizing pain in my midsection. I am running on pure nerves. Keyvan, Farah, and

Soraya are in the same state. We will eat once we are in Montreal. No one will die from not eating for a day. The voice in my head returns for a visit. *How are you going to find anything to eat? Do not be so sure you will be eating so soon. You'll be lucky if they do not send you back.* I scream back silently, *Just shut up, I do* not *want to hear your words of caution anymore.*

As we enter the plane for the third time in the past twelve hours, the same disaster-prone scenarios begin to pop up in my head again. It will be another seven hours of agony before landing. Again, I will have to pretend to be asleep; this is becoming more and more difficult to do. I wish sleep would overcome me, but my body is wide awake with electric energy pulsing through it. Fear keeps me alert all the time; the possibility of danger is real. Subjecting my body to such abuse will end as soon as the plane lands. Although this airplane ride is going to be nerve-racking, it will be very quick, and I should consider myself lucky that I did not have to cross the world on horses or camels or, even worse, on foot.

The question of the return tickets hangs over my head. How are we to salvage the return tickets? Unless we speak to a stranger and ask her to mail them to Pakistan for us, we will have to tear them into pieces. That is like tearing money. I can't do it; neither can my sisters and Keyvan. Keyvan tries to speak with the woman who is sitting next to him. She is Canadian and asks him, "What brings you to Montreal?"

Is it intuition, or just stupidity on his part? He trusts this lady and tells her our story in his fractured English. I have no idea how much of our story was understood by this stranger. I am convinced that she understood the gist of our story. He requests, "Please to mail envelope," pointing to the tickets. She agrees. An angel has appeared from nowhere. Thank God.

I sit on the side with Soraya and Farah, watching as Keyvan discusses our lives with a total foreigner, who agrees to help us. But the voice in my head goes crazy and starts shouting uncontrollably, saying, *You have all come so far to take a chance; why are you letting Keyvan do this? You are insane!* But I can't listen to this voice anymore; there are more important things to attend to.

As the plane makes its way across the Atlantic, the most crucial part of our journey is yet to occur. Before the plane lands, we will all have to tear up our passports. If we land without papers or identification, we can claim refugee status. Canadian Immigration cannot deport us. There will be no evidence of where we came from, and therefore no country to which we can be deported. This is the hardest part of our plan, because this passport, though it can now cause major problems for me, was my salvation to freedom. Now it is time to flush it down the toilet and brace for the unknown.

As soon as it is announced that the plane is approaching Montreal, we take turns visiting the bathroom to tear up and flush away our passports. Keyvan goes first, then Farah, and now it is my turn. My body is as heavy as Mount Everest. I can hardly take a single step forward, let alone make it to the bathroom. I only have to walk ten steps, but it feels as if I have to walk to the moon. Finally I am in the lavatory. I feel as though the walls of this tiny box are closing in on me and I can hardly breathe. My heart pounds erratically. Is it my imagination, or am I about to die? I take the passport out of my jeans pocket. I stare at my photo and stop. Close my eyes. Rip each page to small pieces. Flush it away fast. The pieces of paper swirl down with the water, taking my Turkish identity with it. Whoosh!

Soraya's turn is next, and I do not want her to miss her chance.

There is no turning back.

I have no paper trace to my past.

There is nothing to prove where I come from other than the memories that I hold close to my heart.

It is late; Soraya sits beside me squeezing my hand. She looks so innocent. Her eyes are tearing up, and so are mine. But we can't cry. We don't want anyone to be suspicious. Why would anyone cry as they land? If they are visiting Montreal, there is no need for tears. If they are coming home, there is no need for tears, either. I push the tears down my throat. I will have plenty of time to cry later. But I hope they will be tears of gratitude, tears of happiness, and hopeful tears of seeing Mamán and Baba one day soon.

The stewards are running back and forth to prepare for landing. The descending plane hits the runway with a bump. A scream of ecstasy rises in my throat, but I swallow it.

So many months of sacrifice, planning, perseverance, and prayer to realize this dream! And now I am finally here.

People are preparing to disembark. They line up in the aisle. I have nothing to pick up, no purse, no suitcase, no gifts. I sit. In contrast to the excitement of the other passengers, my legs are pillars of solid, unbendable steel over which I have no control. They are the symptom of my fearful anticipation of facing the Canadian authorities.

Will I ever be able to prove to Canadian immigration that I am an innocent teenager who had to escape to be able to continue my studies?

Issues that I have been struggling with since I left home come flooding back. What's going to happen if they let us stay? Will I be worthy to be granted the freedom to study and work?

Will Mamán and Baba be able to visit me in my new country one day?

How is Sheyla? Is she still alive?

My brain is now running a marathon with my heart. I have no idea which one will win but for now I know one thing: unless I stop and pray I will go crazy.

I swear to do everything I can, to be good to this country, and make all the people who know me proud. I will do whatever it takes on my part to pay my debts, both to my parents and to all those who helped me along the way.

Please, God, help me fulfill my dreams.

PART THREE

Homecoming

Dance, when you're broken open.
Dance, if you've torn the bandage off.
Dance in the middle of the fighting.
Dance in your blood.
Dance, when you're perfectly free.

Rumi

Montreal

June 19, 2003

Baba is coming to visit us in Montreal! He vowed to be present to dance at Cyrus's wedding and this time he was true to his word. Over the past twenty years, he had promised us many times that he would come to visit but now he is really flying over the oceans for us. One of Baba's favourite expressions is, "When someone truly loves you, he will do anything to see you; he will climb the mountains and cross the oceans," and he is doing just that. This is a double celebration: Aria's engagement as well as Cyrus's wedding. He will dance at two *simchas* in less than three weeks. One trip, two celebrations.

How am I to greet Baba, against whom I hold such deep resentment for not being part of my life for so long? How I am going to recount to him what it took to arrive here? Where are the family members he knew? Who are these new ones?

My voice warns me, *Contain yourself; get ready for a bumpy ride ahead.* Baba was never one to admit that he needed a vacation; that is not the reason for his visit. I am convinced the trip is a quest for forgiveness and reconciliation; it is now or never. It will be the most significant meeting to mend our relationship with each other; unless we play our parts whole-heartedly, it won't heal our deep wounds from decades of separation. Baba must also have mixed feelings toward us. I anticipate many explanations and apologies. I pray not to be filled with too many regrets, too much guilt. These two sentiments I despise: they make me weak and helpless. A waste of energy. My voice convinces me: *All this has been arranged by God; just be patient and watch the events as they unfold before you.*

Cyrus drives Farah, Leah, and me to the airport in the early evening to greet Baba. Silence envelops us, but the background of Persian singing on the car radio breaks the stillness. Each of us has struggled with our individual turmoil, and over the years we've fought our private battles without Baba's presence. The last time I saw Baba I was seventeen. Today I am thirty-eight years old. He has not been part of the fabric of my life for my entire adulthood.

~~~~~~

Scenes of my life replay in my mind as though I am watching a bitter-sweet movie. I am gripped by the memories of the past twenty years . . . the happy memories, the painful ones, the exquisite joys, the deep sorrows.

If someone survived many perils, Baba would recite the Persian expression, "They are like cats and have hundreds of lives." Since I have so far survived so many, I feel as though I am a cat.

. . . I almost died one night. That particular night, in the winter of 1986, I had to wake up early for a physics exam. While sleeping, hallucinations about fire roared through my head. The angry, red-hot flames trapped me, and I could not escape. What struck me the most was the awful smell of the fire; it was hard to breathe, and I was choking.

I had not yet adjusted to the cold, bitter, Montreal winter. The depression that had dominated my life during my last years in Iran and during the escape, and the challenge of making a new life for myself in Montreal while suffering from culture shock, were expressed during the night, when my mind was free to roam unfettered. A nightmare about fire fit in.

The brnnnggggg brrrrrnnnnggggg brrrrrnnnnnggggg of the alarm clock startled me out of a fiery nightmare, out of bed, and sniffing the air. Smoke! I opened the door of the apartment to spot deadly, black fumes escaping under the door of my neighbour's apartment and heard her cat scratching frantically behind the door. Terrified, shaking, I rushed back into my room and dialed 9-1-1, then ran down the hall and pulled the alarm. Tenants stormed out of the building, a stampede of frightened, screaming humanity—all except for my neighbour, who had lit a cigarette in bed and fallen asleep, her mattress slowly catching on fire, wrapping her in smoke, choking off the air, ending in a slow, painful death. Her cat survived the fire.

... I think back to our own arrival in Montreal. When Baba arrives, he will find us waiting for him. It was very different for us when we arrived in Canada. There was no one to greet us at the airport. It took twelve hours after landing in Montreal to locate a Persian translator so that we could claim political refugee status. We were detained for two weeks at a Hilton Hotel in Laval that Immigration Canada was using at the time for political refugees. The rooms had thick, red, shag carpets, clean bedspreads, and huge glass windows facing the green landscape, exactly as I had seen in the movies.

Farah and Keyvan were separated from Soraya and me, and we were placed in a separate room. We were not allowed to see each other or talk to each other.

We had to stay in our rooms and were not allowed to leave unless we were escorted. Guards paced back and forth down the hall to ensure that we did not escape. We had no privacy. Our doors had to remain open at all times, and we were constantly under surveillance. We left our room only when we were transported to the immigration office near Mirabel Airport. There, we were asked the same questions over and over. "Where are you from?" "What are your parents' names? "Where were you born?" "What is your date of birth?"

The only other time I was able to free myself from detention was when I had to be taken to the hospital over the growing infection on my foot, which was becoming critically discoloured. An armed man kept me company. I was more scared of him than worried about my infection; the presence of any policeman brought back dreadful memories of the Hezbollah.

Though both Farah and Soraya insisted that they wanted to come along, they were not permitted. I hated being by myself with no one but the security guard. I tried to ignore him and stared out the car window. What struck me the most was the greenery in Montreal; it felt as though we were travelling along a country road. The armed man drove the car for some time and finally stopped. Maybe it was the guard, maybe it was my luck; we did not wait more than an hour to see a man in a white lab coat.

The guard spoke a few words to the doctor, who did not ask me anything about my problem. Due to my extreme fear of the guard standing beside me, I could not have explained myself anyway. I had forgotten the little English that I knew to begin with and had turned into a mute. All I could do was point to my feet. In addition, I was secretly terrified about the hospital bills, as the total of our worldly wealth was sixty dollars, and Keyvan (who was not with me) was the one who actually had it in his hands. I feared the repercussions of my not being able to pay the hospital bills. I worried that I would be forced to start washing hospital bedsheets; that I would be thrown in jail; that I would never see my family again, would never know the freedom that was so close I could taste it. The doctor was sympathetic; he reminded me of the doctor who had treated me in Shiraz. He checked my leg thoroughly, reassuring me that my infection would heal quickly; there would be no permanent damage. The guard took care of the bill and brought the prescription to my room a few hours later.

The two weeks spent in detention seemed endless. Every day was more tedious than the last, with no activities and no one to keep us company. But worst of all was the food. We were fed three times a day, within eight hours. The food looked like plastic and tasted like it, too. It had no flavour and no spices. I could not eat the food. As a result, my stomach grumbled the entire two weeks.

We were finally in the land of liberty but we were trapped in a cage, unable to taste the sweetness of freedom.

The first night after we were released, we spent the sixty dollars to stay at a youth hostel. The struggle to survive and make ends meet started the next day. An Iranian couple representing Iranian refugees, with whom we had become acquainted during our two weeks under investigation, invited us to their home and told us about an organization, SAVI, which was dedicated to helping refugees.

The SAVI social worker asked us our religion. We had not mentioned our religion since we left Iran and did not know if we were safe to reveal the truth. But the three musketeers took a chance and decided to declare ourselves honestly. With shaking voices, we replied, "We are Jewish." She then strongly suggested that we go to JIAS—Jewish Immigrant Aid Services.

JIAS became our family in Montreal and helped us settle in. We were assigned an Iranian translator, Mitchell, who took care of us as though we were his sisters. Quebec government policy stated that new arrivals had to learn French. During the day, I attended French school and in the evenings went to McGill University to learn English on my own. But it was painfully long and slow. I needed a new plan.

JIAS helped me find jobs.

My first job was as a nine-to-five live-out nanny. I looked after three Jewish children aged three, five, and eight. Before Chanukah, they wanted to buy gifts for their parents and needed my help for the purchases. Gifts for adults for holidays! Unbelievable! I suggested that it would be better if they wrote a poem or made a drawing to thank their parents. What — no gifts for parents? A proper nanny knows better than that! That advice landed me in trouble because shortly afterwards I lost my job.

Then I was a cleaning lady in a house that had seemingly not been cleaned for months. The dirty dishes were piled up in the sink, the clothes hamper was full to bursting, and the lady of the house expected me to clean everything in less than four hours. Even a professional cleaning lady would have taken a week to clean up that mess. I lasted one day in that job.

My most exciting job was in a French grocery store as a clerk behind the cheese, cold cuts, and baked goods counter. My English was not good enough and my understanding of French was even worse. To me a pie was a pie! There was no difference between strawberry, blueberry, or raspberry pie. The poor customers went home many times with the wrong orders. Worse yet were the blue cheeses, which were smelly and mouldy. I never dared to taste them and could never understand the fuss customers made when I gave them the wrong blue cheese.

But the most terrifying part of my job was the slicing of cold cuts. The electric slicer's round metal cutter whirred angrily when it was turned on. Every time I used it, I was petrified that I would chop off my fingers along with the meat. As a result, I made sure to use the machine as little as possible. If the customers wanted half a pound of meat, they got a thick slice of it. Anything to avoid using the machine too long.

These first jobs enabled me to save enough money to take intensive English courses, which cost one thousand dollars. Sounded like a million dollars to me at the time because I was earning only four dollars an hour. Finally, I had saved enough money to attend the intensive courses, which enabled me to pursue my full-time studies.

〜〜〜〜〜

I loathe going to airports because they make me restless. Still tormented over the devastating return trips to Karachi's airport, I did not return to an airport until the day Mamán arrived in Canada with Cyrus and Aria in April 1988. Mamán had the stark choice of staying in Shiraz and facing the fact that Cyrus and Aria would be sent to fight in the Iran–Iraq War and possibly be wounded or die, or escaping without Baba's approval or knowledge.

We contacted our friends in Pakistan, who helped us to make the arrangements. Would Baba ever forgive Farah, Soraya, and me for arranging the escape of our mother and brothers from Iran in the summer of 1987? How abandoned Baba must have felt when he came back to the house that day! The furniture, dishes, and Persian carpets were intact. But the house was empty; the only living creatures were the cats and his chickens. Mamán was too afraid of the consequences to even leave him a note. It would have been too risky.

Mamán, Cyrus, and Aria were also told by the smugglers, as they had lied to us, that they would have to walk for only a short distance. Little did they know that they would have to traverse an entire desert on foot. They were not prepared for the painful, long journey. Mamán had never exercised in her life, and with every step she took, her legs screamed, making each step more difficult than the last. Mamán realized what dangers she would have to endure if she were caught. Not only was she fleeing the country illegally, but she was taking along Aria and Cyrus, who were supposed to enlist in the army shortly. If she was apprehended, she would be tortured and killed.

When the pickup truck finally arrived, Mamán was ordered to sit in the front. My brothers were commanded to lie face down on the open back of the truck, under a tarp. It was a warm July night in the desert, and the road surface was rough and uneven. Every time the truck drove over bumps in the road, their faces, arms, and legs would smack against the rough, cold metal floor. As time passed, the bruises became bloody wounds. Underneath that airless covering, the heat, sweat, and taste of blood on their faces became unbearable.

Suddenly, they heard a gunshot. The driver sped up, zigzagging back and forth across the road. One of the men in front screamed back at them that they were being followed by several Hezbollah police cars.

In a panic, they drove off the road, switched off the headlights, and continued to drive. Half an hour later, the truck slowed, and Mamán and my brothers were told to jump off and to lie quietly, face down in the sand. One of the smugglers stayed with them as the truck drove off into the darkness. For an hour, they lay flat, their bodies and faces pressed into the sand.

After the desert crossing, Mamán and my two brothers, disguised as girls with full head coverings, drove in a rickety truck for four days to Quetta.

They organized their United Nations permits to stay in Pakistan.

Ten days after they left Shiraz, they arrived in Karachi.

Living in Karachi also held its dangers. Iranian refugees were often blamed for bomb explosions in Karachi, which caused a lot of suspicion to fall on any Iranian refugee living in the city. The Pakistani police raided Mamán and my brothers' hotel a few times, where the rooms were searched for guns and jewellery.

"Why jewellery?" I asked Mamán.

"Because jewellery is given as a donation to anti-Islamic groups to be sold, and the money used to buy guns. That happened to a few refugees. They were arrested because they had jewellery on them." Mamán's voice shook in recollection.

Mamán cooked every meal in the hotel room, as we had, on a one-burner heater. She felt obligated to feed the other single Jewish boys in the hotel, who were also refugees. My family's departure was delayed many times because of the restrictions on Iranian refugees at the time. Mamán lost hope. She felt she would never be able to leave Pakistan, that Pakistan was her final destination.

Inexplicably, 108 Iranian Jewish refugees, including Mamán, Cyrus, and Aria, were escorted by Pakistani police to the Karachi airport and airlifted out of Karachi to Amsterdam by plane at the end of October 1987. They had to wait an anxious twenty-four hours for proper paper-work to arrive legally in Austria.

Mamán, Cyrus, and Aria finally reached Montreal ten months to the day after they left Shiraz.

My family was the one thing that I missed the most. I had been longing for them all these years, but homesickness would shortly be a thing of the past. My family would soon be here, next to me. I would no longer be alone on holidays. The excitement of having a family again kept me up many nights prior to Mamán's arrival.

We kept in contact with Baba by letters and minimal phone calls. Baba was relieved once he found out that the boys and Mamán were safe. He had no choice but to accept the fact that his family had chosen to leave the hell Iran had turned into under the Hezbollah.

᷿᷿᷿᷿᷿

It was one of the happiest days of my life when I spotted Mamán in the crowd at Mirabel Airport. But I almost missed Cyrus and Aria. When I left Shiraz, Cyrus was only twelve years old; now he was six feet tall, a broad-chested man with mustache and beard. Aria had been only ten years old and four feet tall; now he was over six feet tall, and movie-star handsome. Though Mamán was young by Canadian standards, only forty-four years old, she looked old, with too many wrinkles. True to Naneh Jaan-Jaan's favourite expression, each of these wrinkles told a story.

At the baggage claim, we were stunned to face four six-foot-high boxes that Mamán had lugged along with her. They had left Iran without anything; however, Mamán was determined to buy us as many gifts as possible in Pakistan and Austria. They managed to accumulate heaping piles of stockings, skirts, and shirts in different sizes and colours. Our social worker at JIAS, Rivka, was astonished at the enormous boxes that were stacked up in front of us. Clearly, she had never seen an Iranian mother bearing gifts. Manoeuvring the boxes to my apartment was a tougher job than I had imagined. We had to rent a special truck to deliver the boxes, and a delivery man was needed to drag them up the narrow staircase and into my apartment on the third floor.

Laid out on the floor on top of a tablecloth were heaping platefuls of rice, stew, and chicken that the three musketeers had prepared for our family. We purposely prepared the kinds of food with which they were familiar. A feast to welcome them to Canada, not realizing that our cooking on an electric versus gas stove, and the spices we used, were not exactly as Mamán had shown us six years before. Our taste buds had evolved. Mamán, Cyrus and Aria stared at what we had prepared, and then stared at us. The food that we had cooked was too Canadian for their liking. They preferred Mamán's traditional Shirazi cuisine.

Mamán happily took over the kitchen and the one-bedroom apartment the next day. We stayed together in my tiny apartment. It was an often humorous struggle to coordinate bathroom and shower schedules between the five of us. We took turns sleeping on the one bed; every four nights it was my turn to sleep in it. The irony was, none of us complained. We were well aware that it would be short-term pain for long-term gain.

All three of them started working immediately. Cyrus was working during the day and going to university in the evening. Aria was going to school during the day and was working on the weekends.

〜〜〜〜〜

My niece, Leah, had been born in December 1984. Mamán was always present when her sisters gave birth, but in Canada, poor Farah gave birth to Leah without Mamán's support. Soraya and I were there but we were useless to Farah. When Mamán arrived in Montreal, Leah was four years old. They developed a strong bond. Mamán was determined to make up for lost time with her. Leah enjoyed being the apple of Mamán's eye, the first, and the only, grandchild for a long time.

Mamán once again chose the welfare of her children over her own comfort and social status. From the day of Mamán's arrival in Montreal, she recreated Shabbat for us. There was no reason good enough not to attend her Shabbat dinners. She worked tirelessly as a companion for a ninety-five-year-old Canadian woman on weeknights and looked forward to our Friday night dinner and day of rest on Saturday. Though it was years later, she continued the Shabbat tradition, carried with her all the way from Shiraz. The spicy smell of fried fish and stew filled the apartment every Friday.

Mamán was unhappy for many reasons. She felt emotionally alone in supporting her five children. She thought being a companion was not a good use of her credentials as a nurse and her hard-won skills. Though she had our total support and love, she was too angry at Baba for his lack of support, of which she repeatedly reminded us, day in and day out. Mamán never forgot and neither took responsibility for her role nor forgave Baba. In her eyes, Baba had done wrong, and nothing could make it right. She insisted on constantly rubbing it in our faces that she had sacrificed her life for us.

Mamán wrote to Baba infrequently. She made sure to tell him how difficult her life was in Canada. But she consistently forgot to mention how much she was loved by all five of us. To Mamán, the glass was always half empty.

〜〜〜〜〜

I moved out of town in September 1988 to pursue my lifelong dream of studies in health care. Baba's suffering had made a strong impression on me. I wanted to find the underlying cause of the pain and I believed this was the answer to my prayers; to continue my studies, to be able to serve and make a difference in the lives of others. I rented a room in a house owned by a middle-aged single Englishwoman, Julie.

Studying was very demanding on all the students, but I had an additional handicap, my English, which was still not on a par with the others. I had to work much harder than the other students to understand and learn the material. It was the most exciting time in my life because finally I was studying in the field I loved, and that alone gave me tremendous energy and drive to do whatever it took to succeed. Julie would say, "I leave the house in the morning and you are studying and when I come back late at night you are still studying. Don't you get sore from sitting so long?"

Though I was eligible for both loans and bursaries, I also had to work to support myself adequately. I survived on a very tight budget of four hundred dollars per month, of which three hundred went for the rent. The remaining one hundred dollars was spent frugally; every cent counted. I was lucky at times to have a few dollars left at the end of the month so I could go to cheap Tuesday night movies with Soraya, who had joined me to pursue her studies a year after me, and to splurge on a coffee-and-muffin treat for a dollar.

My excitement of the week was when Julie, my landlady, took me grocery shopping with her very early on Saturday mornings before it was too crowded. I had no car and the grocery store was a long distance away. (Not quite the distance of the Iranian desert, but far by North American standards.) This grocery store was known for better quality grade B fruits and vegetables. While she was shopping at the regular shelves, I was glued to the door where the lower-quality fruits and vegetables were sold for one dollar per package. I stayed by the door so I would have the first choice to pick the best of these goods. Julie was the richest person I knew. Her grocery bill was fifty dollars; mine was under ten. I dreamed that one day I would be able to shop for regular goods and spend fifty dollars on groceries. That was a dream that seemed far from my grasp at the time.

Julie was raised in a refined, disciplined British household, and consequently had definite rules of conduct. No talking on the telephone after nine o'clock; no guests staying over; and, more important, no cooking with spices, because that would smell up the house. Her family were cultured people who loved going to concerts on a regular basis; for my birthday, they invited me to a performance of the symphony orchestra. She was kind to include me and Soraya when she invited her family to Sunday dinner at her house.

The years flew by, and my family, minus Baba, was present at my graduation ceremony. That day I felt as if I had wings, that I could fly up into the air, singing with ecstasy that hard work, perseverance, and keeping my eyes on the goal had paid off.

All along I had dreamed of coming back to Montreal to be with my family. Montreal had embraced me when no other city in the world accepted me; and I had to pay back my debts. This city allowed me to follow my dreams and it was time to be of service to the community. Nineteen-ninety-four was a new beginning in my career, the opening of my own clinic.

Simultaneously, Mamán developed a strange burning sensation in her stomach, the kind of pain that did not subside and progressively worsened. My whole world was shaken when she was diagnosed with the terrible "C" word. Cancer. Cancer of the stomach. She underwent an operation to remove the tumour. I was devastated over Mamán's illness and petrified by the possibility of the cancer's return. I went on a mission to find out why she had developed cancer and how to ensure her health. The more doors I knocked on, the more people I asked, the more I realized that there were no answers to my questions. I faced a brick wall. I was told repeatedly by both medical professionals and alternative therapists that her cancer was a matter of bad luck.

She was strong and determined to live, though she never fully regained the same zest for life she had prior to the illness. It was as if she was on borrowed time and the hourglass had been turned over.

⌐⌐⌐⌐⌐

On Father's Day 1995, I met Eugene on a blind date arranged by a friend who thought we would be perfect for each other. I had been on blind dates before and did not anticipate this one being any different from my past experiences. Boring. However, I did have my rules about blind dates. A date had to take place in the daytime, and I did not want to be picked up at my house, in case he was a weirdo. The date and the time were set: Sunday morning at eleven o'clock.

I was as hungry as a starving wolf. We went to a French restaurant on Laurier Street, and sat outside under the shade of a tabletop umbrella, where I ordered an appetizer, a main course, dessert, and a large café latte. Eugene ordered only a main course and watched me eat as if I had just been released from a starvation camp. He remarked that ladies do not eat much in public, but I dismissed his comment. After brunch, we went shopping, as he wanted to buy a gift for his sister, Gloria, who lived in Ottawa. I found this interesting, because he cared to buy a beautifully wrapped gift that pleased his sister. From the beginning, presentation and finesse were two characteristics that stood out in my relations with him.

Eugene was a handsome, fit, and kind Canadian with tremendous joie-de-vivre and an excellent sense of humour. The son of a Holocaust survivor, he had learned to take nothing for granted and enjoyed life with its many small blessings. Unfortunately, I never met his mother, since she had passed away a year before we met; but the serene nature themes and soft colours of her paintings are a testament to her gentle spirit.

During our second date, I was more apprehensive. I was strongly attracted to him; I cared and wanted to make a good impression on him but feared I might have blown my first chance two days before. Was it too late to remedy how I had behaved? I had gorged like a pig the first time we were together. But our second date went smoothly, and since this time I was not so hungry, I could ask more important questions. I explained to Eugene I was not interested in having a casual relationship forever. As I did not play games with people and wanted to be treated the same way, I suggested setting ourselves a time limit of three months. After that period of time, we would know if we were compatible and deeply attracted to each other, or if we weren't, we would know that as well. Either way, no hard feelings if it did not work out.

During dinner, he told me how he had found out about me. A friend of mine, Franceen, gave him my phone number. He couldn't make out from my name where I had come from, so he called another friend, Rosy, whom I knew casually, and asked her: "Do you know anyone by the name of Sima? Is that an Indian name? Is she Jewish? Is she thin?"

Rosy answered most of the questions correctly but added, "She is not thin and she has an afro."

Learning this from Rosy, I had worn a loose dress on our first date so Eugene could not make out if I was fat or thin. Being fat is not a label that ever fit me. It was Rosy who said I was fat, but it was also Rosy who insisted he call me immediately after our first date to ask me out again.

On our third date, we went for dinner and a walk. He wanted to know about me, about my background. And he showed a great deal of concern as I manoeuvred through the narrow, cobblestone streets of Old Montreal. Every few seconds, I would hear, "Sima! Be careful! Watch out for the cobblestones!"

I appreciated his concern but eventually became annoyed and reminded him rather vehemently that I had managed to escape from Iran without his assistance and felt more than capable of handling the streets of Old Montreal on my own. He never forgot that response and reminds me of it often. He is the love of my life.

Between Eugene's Jewish Canadian background and my Jewish Iranian background it felt as if we were from two worlds that when mixed together would produce an exquisite blend. We were engaged in August and married on January 20, 1996, with Mamán and all my siblings present. Baba was invited and supposed to attend because it had become easier to travel abroad from Iran. But he never made it to my wedding. A major disappointment and yet another open, raw wound from Baba that I had to shore up in my heart. My sister-in-law, Gloria, tried to comfort me as I was crying under the *chuppah* (the marriage canopy). "You will meet your father again one day; do not give up hope." But I never believed that day would materialize.

My niece, Leah, celebrated her bat mitzvah in the spring of 1996. In Iran, there was no such thing as a bat mitzvah. Even the boys' bar mitzvahs, celebrated only by a Kiddush in synagogue, were modest affairs. In Canada, however, any occasion to celebrate was reason enough to do so. We danced all afternoon. Farah was beaming with pride and excitement, and Mamán, who was very close to Leah, could not have been happier. Keyvan and Farah had lived separate lives for many years by the time the bat mitzvah rolled around. Farah worked during the day and continued her studies at night and raised Leah.

My first son, Eric, gave me the crown of motherhood in February 1997. This was a blessing that taught me patience and gave me sleepless nights for a long time. Surprisingly, I would wake up from the slightest noise Eric made. Farah teased me: the Sima who could sleep through anything, including her sister's honeymoon, had changed. Eric became Mamán's obsession; every move he made, Mamán recorded.

Daniel was born in June 1998, and Eric displayed his love passionately from day one. Soon after Daniel's birth, Soraya, who was working with me, went on a vacation, where she met her future husband, Kiomarse, also of Iranian Jewish descent, and decided to move out of town permanently. On February 27, 1999, Soraya and Kiomarse were married.

>>>>>

The oncologist pronounced perfect health for Mamán at her five-year checkup in December 1999: a promise of a long life. We no longer had reason to be concerned about her well-being.

Unfortunately, our optimism was short lived. Mamán went to help Soraya during her first pregnancy. She developed mysterious rashes all over her body in February 2000. She shortened her visit and returned to Montreal to further investigate the reason behind her constant rashes.

It took a few long weeks before she was diagnosed with liver cancer. My whole world came crashing down on me. Though I am not one to cry easily, crying was all I did. I was devastated. We were informed Mamán's days were numbered. Never had I imagined having to deal with losing her at the young age of fifty-six.

Those were excruciating days when nothing could lighten my burden. There was no light at the end of this tunnel. Darkness and gloom had found its way into our family. Eugene was in the habit of filling our home weekly with flowers; these would usually make me happy, but now the fragrant blooms offered no joy. He was also reliving his mother's loss through my loss. I was defeated and had it not been for Eric and Daniel I do not know if I could have gotten out of bed or stopped crying.

On the last day of Passover, the phone kept on ringing. Family members and friends from around the world called to speak to Mamán. She took her time and spoke softly to everyone who phoned. Baba also called, and Mamán spoke to him as well. He wanted to have her forgiveness. I do not think Mamán granted him his heartfelt desire. Mamán phoned Aria, who lived out of town, and asked him to come to Montreal on Thursday night, a day earlier than planned. It was as if Mamán was planning to go away on a long trip and was taking care of all the details. She waited to celebrate the last day of Passover with us. Three days after Passover, she died at her home on May 1, 2000, six days short of my thirty-fifth birthday. I was sitting shiva on my birthday. I did not just lose Mamán. I lost my best friend and my confidante.

Poor Soraya had to deal with this tremendous loss without her siblings. She was nine months pregnant at the time and was not allowed to attend the funeral in Montreal. She gave birth to her daughter, Lily, on May 22.

After Mamán's passing, Baba became very worried about my brothers' welfare. Both by phone and by letter, he let us know that we should find a bride for Cyrus, who had been living with Mamán; her death was a tremendous loss for him. Aria was alone in another city pursuing his career. Baba, who had lived alone for a long time, could relate to the boys' predicament.

When he heard that Cyrus was engaged to Rivka, an Iranian-American Jewish girl from New York, Baba promised he would attend the wedding, no matter what obstacles might arise. Baba had to present Cyrus's wedding invitation to a special office to get permission to leave Iran. Since he was already seventy years old, had all his assets in Iran, and was leaving with very little money, he was granted the exit visa.

The first of his two top wishes was to dance at his son's wedding. But considering that he had just turned seventy years old, had never left Iran, and did not speak a word of English, we didn't believe it was possible. This time, we were proven wrong.

Baba finally realized that he had some unfinished business with his family. He had not made it in time to see Mamán and resolve the conflicts in their relationship and maybe he was alerted by that missed opportunity. There was no way for us to meet him in Iran. Time was getting short. To miss this happy occasion would have been foolish. He could not live with himself and the consequences unless he walked Cyrus down the aisle. Cyrus and all of us needed to reunite with him.

It was now or never.

It is past eight o'clock in the evening. The arrival screen indicates that Baba's plane landed more than an hour ago. Standing here, waiting for Baba, I see reunited families embracing, hugging each other, families in every direction. A man holds a big bouquet of red roses in anticipation of his loved one's arrival. Another family holds a decorated bristol board to welcome their visitor, and the dozens of balloons obstruct my anxious view. Although I do not know these people, it is blissful to witness these expressions of love and happiness. With every passing second, I grow more and more impatient. Every time the door opens, I hope to see Baba's face.

Will Baba recognize me in the crowd? Will he be shocked to see how beautiful and grown-up Farah's daughter, Leah, is? Farah, Cyrus, Leah, and I have been standing in the same spot for the past two hours.

There is no sign of Baba.

I worry for Baba; he can't speak a word of English, and he left Tehran more than twenty hours ago for Austria. He had had a ten-hour stopover. How did he manage? This is the first time he has left Iran and the first time he has travelled by plane. Even if he has made it on the plane to Montreal, how is he going to fill out the declaration form to pass immigration? I could not do it when I arrived here and I'd had some knowledge of English. Poor Baba!

Ironically, we can now fully understand the French and English announcements on the intercom. The day we arrived here, we had no idea what was being spoken over the intercom, nor in what language. Today is not just a celebration for Baba's arrival; it is also a celebration of our twenty years in Canada.

My heart pounds fiercely as if it wants to fly out of my chest; I can't do anything so I do what I always do at times like this. I resort to my secret weapon, my prayer.

Finally, I see a familiar face shuffle slowly out of the terminal, dressed in his white, long-sleeved polo shirt. "Daddy, Daddy," I shriek. My voice echoes in the airport and all eyes are focused on me, implying with their stares, "Why did they let the crazy one out of the mental hospital?"

My mind's image of Baba, of the strong, muscular man I had last seen in Shiraz, is a far cry from the man who is now approaching us. Baba has aged considerably; he has a big, overhanging belly, and limps as he walks. His hair is completely white and his thick, black moustache has also gone completely white.

What happened to my handsome, fit Baba?

How cruel time has been to him. I start to weep. Love and forgiveness flood my entire being.

The tears cleanse me internally, a cascade of emotions that releases past resentments and allows me to embrace Baba completely. In retrospect, this was one of my best gifts from him, one of my best gifts to myself, to open my heart to Baba unconditionally.

We are reunited . . . thank you, thank you, thank you, God!

As we arrange the rope-wrapped luggage to wheel out to our car, we need a knife. Baba reaches into his pocket and pulls out a Swiss army knife. We are astonished and amused at airport security in Iran and Austria. He hadn't been checked at security leaving either Iran or in Austria, where he had a stopover—or maybe leaving Iran and Austria with a weapon in hand is normal?

We thought the two huge pieces of luggage that Baba brought with him were packed with clothing and personal items. But those bags are crammed with gifts for us: carpets, blankets, nuts, Iranian silver crafts, and some miniature scissors for my sons. He has also brought Persian children's books and many sheets of Persian poetry and expressions. Baba, who could never part with even a piece of paper or an old shoe, has brought nothing for himself but a few days' worth of new clothing: suit, pants, shirts, and silk socks.

June 20, 2003

We spend our first Shabbat dinner together after more than twenty years. While preparing supper, memories of my last Friday night dinner in Shiraz float unbidden over me. Baba follows me around all day as if tied to my apron strings. He loves the food I serve him, can't get enough of it, and thanks me frequently. This evening, he is also reunited with Aria, who has driven up from out of town with his future wife, Hanah, a Canadian Jewish girl.

Baba has had so much bad luck lately. He had lost his land through trickery and by fighting for his rights in a country where rules and regulations are enforced only for ordinary citizens, where government officials are exempt from these same regulations.

He had lost time, precious time, with his family. Maybe he is the one to be consoled; maybe I am the one to ask for forgiveness for not being there for him during his many years of solitude. Baba is the one who missed out the most. It is written all over his body. What is important is that we are together at last and we will celebrate Cyrus's and Aria's happy occasions as a united family.

Farah is on a high; she is tireless and gladly takes on tour guide duties for Baba. Baba and Farah forgive each other and express their love for each other openly.

Soraya flies in from out of town to visit at the end of June, to be joined later by her husband. Baba is ecstatic to see Soraya, his princess, and meet her family for the first time. She has two children: a daughter, Lily, and a son, Mathew.

July 1, 2003

The whole family drives to Ottawa for Aria's engagement party because his bride, Hanah, was born and raised there. Baba is the life of the party. He dances like there is no tomorrow. I've never seen my Baba dance before. The angry, reserved man I had known has been transformed into a jolly, fun human being.

Baba shares with me his basic philosophy of life. Quoting verses and sayings from our ancient Persian poets, Sa'adi and Hafez, he stresses the importance of taking care of one's family, of oneself, and of appreciating the important things in life: loved ones. He also urges me to strive to live life fully, to prioritize my life accordingly, and to hold no grudges or nurse any resentment. He warns me against gambling, alcohol, and other habits that would ultimately cause grief.

In a dispute, there are at least three versions, one on either side and the third one, which is the truth. Your job is to hear the entire story, make up your mind, and be as honest and as truthful as possible. These are the priceless gems shared from a long, painful life. I love Baba.

After so many years of being distanced from Baba both physically and emotionally, a new and deeper love for him is blossoming. I admire his determination and courage to take the monumental step in coming to visit us. He confesses that he did not know if we would be there at the airport to greet him or what our feelings toward him would be. But he took the chance. This proved, as well, to be the most important experience to heal our deep, raw wounds, not just for him, but for us, his children. I no longer hold onto the bitter, deadly poison of resentment that would have eventually killed me like an acid that dissolves anything it touches. Forgiveness sets me free.

It is another turning point in my life. I forgive and forget every bad feeling I have harboured against Baba for so many years. A heavy burden is lifted off my shoulders. His actions are also proof that he forgives us for having abandoned him. He, too, had wounds to heal.

He insists on visiting Mamán's grave often. The ambiance and tranquility of the cemetery make an impression on him that borders on obsession. Are the frequent visits to ask for forgiveness for his shortcomings with Mamán? Is it to have a clean slate with her? I will never know, because Baba is not one to demonstrate his feelings.

~~~~~

July 4, 2003

As is customary, before the wedding I hold the Shabbat dinner at my house. Farah and Soraya help me with the cooking of traditional Iranian dishes; Soraya is the expert chef of Iranian cuisine, unlike me. I relish every second of this day; it is as if a guardian angel is watching over me to make sure everything moves along seamlessly.

Having fifty people for dinner is not an easy task under any circumstances, but to cook from scratch makes it even more challenging. I received the miraculous gift of Baba's presence and am elated and given unlimited energy to do whatever it takes to have a meaningful time with him and my family.

As I light the Shabbat candles freely, of my own choice, I have an epiphany: how blessed I am to be a Jew. I have healed the wounds of many years of considering myself a second-class citizen because I am a Jew, because I am a woman, because my family name is Goel. All those handicaps and burdens propelled me to flee the prison of Iran and to come to terms with my true shining essence, a proud Jew at last. I accept my birthright with joy.

This is the happiest time I've had with Baba since Ammeh Nilofar's wedding in our garden in Shiraz more than thirty years ago. Baba shimmies with the dazzling belly-dancer in my living room, the surprise gift to the bride and the groom from the three musketeers.

July 5, 2003

The next morning, Saturday, Baba accompanies Cyrus to synagogue, where he is given the special honour, as father of the groom, to read from the Torah in front of the entire congregation. He is especially thrilled to have been awarded this privilege when attending his son's wedding—one of his two greatest wishes. None of us thought we would ever live to experience this day.

The wedding day is quickly approaching, and Baba will be returning to Iran in less than three days. He reveals to me, "I wish I could stay longer, but I have to attend an appeal court hearing in Tehran over the loss of my land. I will be back. I promise."

July 6, 2003, 6:00 a.m.

I accompany Baba to the Baron de Hirsch Cemetery to visit Mamán's grave early in the morning. There is a lot to be done today, and no minute can be wasted. The cemetery is tranquil and misty. No one else is here. The tall poplar trees stand in a row, welcoming Baba like a familiar friend. His love for nature is as strong as ever.

Mamán's black granite tombstone reads, "Your devotion, strength, and love are ever-lasting." Baba points to it and I translate it for him. Again.

"The Jewish cemetery in Shiraz is nothing like this; and there are no tombstones, either." He sighs deeply. Then he continues, "I love this place. Look at these beautiful trees; we don't have any trees like this in Shiraz's Jewish cemetery." He looks into my eyes and out of nowhere he proclaims, "I am proud of all of you." Tears roll down Baba's cheeks.

The words I have longed to hear for so many years are uttered from Baba's lips, here in the middle of a cemetery in Montreal, as he leans on an old poplar tree. Tears roll down my cheeks, too. I can no longer hold them back. They are the tears of joy, the tears of reconciliation with Baba, and the tears of genuine love from me to Baba, from Baba to me.

Baba had never praised us, fearing we might become arrogant and boastful. From early childhood, I yearned to hear him acknowledge me, to know that he is proud of me. Baba's few words reassure me of his deep love toward me. Baba must be tormented to be crying in front of me. Is he crying because he is returning to Iran in two days? Is he crying because of all the years of suffering apart from us? I will never know, no matter how many times I ask the questions.

Baba accompanies me to a kosher bakery. "Look at him, a shop owner wearing a *kippah* and actually advertising his Jewish faith. No one can ever do that in Iran. Can I hug him?" Before I have a chance to answer, he is in the personal space of the shop owner and about to hug him. The shop owner is somewhat taken aback by Baba's exuberance, but I hastily explain that Baba is from Iran, where such freedom does not exist.

July 6, 2003, noon

Mamán's grave in the cemetery exerts a magnetic attraction for Baba today. He returns to the site twice more, once with my brothers Cyrus and Aria and for the third time with his own brother, "the Doctor."

Over the past sixteen days, Baba has hardly slept. He rarely talks about the past, content to live in the present and enjoy every moment he spends with us. When there is a strained relationship between a parent and a child, the child will always wonder if somehow the fault is his or hers and that the estrangement is a just punishment. So it is with me. Baba arrived here with no expectations, with nothing but an open heart. I have never seen a seventy-year-old with so much vigour. He was always energetic but at his age I would think he needed more sleep or rest; instead, he is the last one to bed at night and the first one up every morning.

July 6, 2003, 3:30 p.m.

We meet at the synagogue for photographs. Baba is wearing a suit with a bowtie. He had never worn ties, even to synagogue, complaining, "I am choking." But Cyrus has convinced him to wear a black bowtie for his wedding. Baba is especially happy to wear the white boutonnière as a member of the bridal party. He poses elegantly with his five children and his five grandchildren. He has never beamed with such happiness. Never has he been so proud. For the first time in his life, he glows with ecstasy. He is no longer "Dr. Goel's brother, Bijan," under the shadow of his accomplished older brother. He is Bijan Goel who has five wonderful, healthy, and successful children. He is a person in his own right and his own achievement, surrounded by his family. Baba is blissfully joyous. It is written all over his body.

July 6, 2003, 5:30 p.m.

Baba participates with effervescent delight during cocktails. He thinks the hors d'oeuvres are the dinner, and is puzzled why dinner is served so early. He is astounded by the opulence of the entire affair. The quality and quantity of food, the sushi station, the smoked meat station, the Chinese station, the rotating hot hors d'oeuvres and the open bar are beyond his wildest imagination. Not even at the wedding of royalty in Iran would there be such a feast.

Cyrus gives Baba the responsibility of holding the gift envelopes. He does not fully understand why people are giving envelopes, because in Iran, gifts for the newlyweds are household items, but he walks around proudly with the brown cotton bag full of envelopes. For him, it is an honour to have been asked to carry out this duty and he feels that he is being helpful.

July 6, 2003, 6:30 p.m.

Seated before the wedding canopy are relatives and friends who have travelled across the globe. There are many friends from Montreal with whom Cyrus wants to share his joyous day. This is a very important event for him, and he spent the entire year preparing for it, meticulously planning every detail. Thirty family members walk down the aisle. Cyrus is accompanied by Baba alone. There is not a dry eye among the relatives, as everyone is sadly aware of Mamán's absence.

July 6, 2003, 8:00 p.m.

Baba has never seen so many young and old men and women dance so enthusiastically. Dancing in Iran was for young girls looking for a husband, but here it is for everyone. He joins in the party wholeheartedly.

In life, there are times when a split second in our existence becomes so vivid and so heightened that everything makes perfect sense. You want to cherish the moment and accept the gift of the present with utmost gratitude. This is exactly how I feel at this moment. All my life, my entire journey, with all its peaks and valleys, has led me to this split second. I pinch myself hard to make sure I am not dreaming, that this joy is really happening all around me and that I am part of it.

I glance around to find Baba at the other end of the room, asking for a drink. Do I have any reason to be worried? No, not at all; this night is a fairytale wedding that is coming to a happy ending. What could go wrong now? *Stop it, Sima, you ruin all the fun.* I pinch myself again and start dancing with Baba.

July 6, 2003, 8:30 p.m.

Baba honours us by reciting the blessing for the bread. At Cyrus's request Baba recites the Twenty-third Psalm: *The Lord is my Shepherd . . .*

I have never heard Baba sing so magnificently, his voice ringing out loud and clear.

Dinner is being served, and it is time for toasts and speeches. My husband, Eugene, addresses the newlyweds and the guests. In his poem, he writes about Baba. Since Baba can't understand English, I translate for him. He looks at me and demands, "Walk with me to the front where your husband is, so everyone will know who I am." Next to the bride and the groom, he is the shining star tonight.

Baba has been acknowledged as the most important guest, something that is entirely foreign to him. He has never been acknowledged in his life. Tonight, he is the luckiest man alive. He holds his head high and stands as a blessed man. Nothing else matters. What is important is that we are celebrating together, and I am the happiest person to be dancing with Baba to the strains of Persian music at Cyrus's wedding. Baba is elated.

July 6, 2003, 9:15 p.m.

A few minutes later, Baba lifts Mathew, his youngest grandson, onto his shoulders and dances lightheartedly around the floor. Concerned that Baba might be feeling tired, Farah takes Mathew down from his high perch and tells Baba, "I want to dance with you as soon as I give Mathew to Soraya."

As Eugene and I are dancing, shortly after sundown, THUMP! something heavy falls. My heart drops like a boulder.

The music stops, and all the guests on the dance floor gather in a ragged circle around someone on the floor. My eyes fly around the room searching for Baba. I can't find him!

Darkness engulfs me. Instinctively, I know that the heavy thud involves Baba. I sit down quickly on a chair to avoid falling myself. Things start to move in slow motion. I rise and push my way through the ring of guests gathered around that spot on the floor. It *is* Baba, lying flat on his back on the floor. I can't bear to look; I close my eyes and start to pray, shaking uncontrollably, hoping this is just a bad nightmare that will dissipate into thin air.

Among the guests are doctors and nurses who do what they can. They administer CPR, mouth-to-mouth resuscitation. Guests call 9-1-1 and Hatzoloh, the Jewish ambulance service. Within minutes, Hatzoloh screeches up to the synagogue, long before the municipal paramedics. They quickly roll Baba onto a stretcher and drive him to the Jewish General Hospital. I drive my car to the hospital, frantically following the ambulance, with Farah keeping me company.

The bride and groom return to the sanctuary, open the Ark, and begin to pray. Cyrus has planned everything, but this is not part of his plan.

Within minutes of reaching the hospital, a number of guests arrive to advise us as to the proper religious protocols should Baba not survive. The Hatzoloh ambulance paramedic comes to ask for Baba's Hebrew name. This religious Jew wants to pray for Baba's soul.

We know we are in trouble and I start praying, "May God's will be done." Shortly afterwards, we are officially informed by a doctor that Baba has passed away. He had passed away in the synagogue. The doctor does not know Baba; he does not know that what he has told us has changed our lives forever.

A major twist of fate! My whole world crumbles to pieces. I grieve for the loss of Baba but respect his choice of not wanting to return to the hell that was awaiting him in Iran. It was Baba's choice. He fulfilled his most important desires, and his mission was accomplished.

As angry as I am at his death—and as unfair the timing of it—he left us as a happy, blissful man. Not many people have the chance to dance their way to heaven. Only a *tzaddik*, a holy one, is granted this privilege.

Farah and I consult our rabbi, who had followed us to the hospital, and decide that as difficult as it is, we must continue with the wedding; Cyrus and Rivka have only one night to be the bride and groom. Under no circumstances will we spoil their special night any further.

Farah and I make the funeral arrangements by phone while we are still at the hospital. We return to the wedding and announce to the entire gathering that Baba is fine and resting comfortably. This is indeed the truth!

We do not break the news to the bride and the groom. There is no way I can give the speech I had prepared; I don't have the strength. My tears hang on the edge of my eyelids, threatening to spill over.

I am convinced that God uses me and delivers the speech to the newlyweds through me. Unquestionably, this time Divine Grace carries me.

As the guests leave late in the evening, we tactfully let them know of Baba's death and the time of the funeral. Only at the end of the evening do we have a chance to confront our loss, and at that, we do not tell Cyrus and Rivka of Baba's death. Farah, Soraya, Aria, and I are able to cry freely when Cyrus asks one of his many Persian friends to sing Mamán's favourite song. A love song that translates as: *I am coming to see you, my beloved, with many bunches of flowers. Meeting you is as important as air is to my lungs and food is to my flesh . . .*

All four of us insist to Cyrus, "Unplug your phone. Do not to answer any calls. The wedding was so successful that people are going to call to congratulate you for it."

These orders are to spare him the sorrow of this night. In the morning, we will let him know the catastrophic news.

But modern technology beats us to it. Cellphones and e-mails ping to Iran, Israel, and the United States at the speed of light. At five o'clock in the morning, Cyrus storms into my house because of the phone calls he has received.

"When did Baba pass away? Have you buried him yet? When should we sit *shiva*?"

He is incredulous that we did not reveal the news to him and Rivka and organized the funeral on our own. Despite his grief, Cyrus thanks us profusely for not ruining his wedding.

᠈᠈᠈᠈᠈

Baba sang and danced his way into heaven and left us with the memory of a blissfully contented man. We made up for twenty years lost in sixteen days. What lives on in eternity is the legacy we leave behind. Baba left me the legacy of seeing him as a happy man at last.

July 7, 2003, 11:00 a.m.

The Persian poet and mystic Jalaladdin Rumi wrote these words of grace and wisdom: "Don't grieve. Anything you lose comes around in another form."

As we bury Baba, each of my siblings and I take turns throwing earth on Baba's coffin, as is the Jewish custom. In doing so, Baba's second wish, to be buried by his children, is fulfilled. Despite the fact that we lived oceans apart, Baba's top two yearnings were granted against all odds.

Three white butterflies danced gracefully around us. The butterfly is a symbol of freedom. These butterflies signified Baba's freedom and this is the form in which it manifested itself.

Freedom . . . freedom at last, for all of us.

To this day, whenever I see a white butterfly, I know Baba is somewhere near me, saying hello.

Conclusion

I am convinced that Iran, bordering the Caspian Sea and the Persian Gulf, is a jewel of the Middle East. Its rich soil, its oil, its ancient civilization, its world-renowned poetry, and its wonderful variety of climates make Iran worthy of being an incredibly prosperous country, not only for a few privileged members in government but for the entire Iranian population. I wish Iran would take a stand as a peacemaker in the world, especially in the Middle East, and refrain from threatening the world with nuclear annihilation.

There is no easy road to freedom anywhere, as I learned in Pakistan. Freedom is won not just by removing one's own shackles, but by living in a way that complements, enhances, and transforms the freedom of others.

What I wish for Iranians is a country that allows its citizens to be free and to contribute to the improvement of mankind. If there are dreams about a magnificent Iran, there are also paths that lead to that dream. In the late Nelson Mandela's words, "Let freedom reign. The sun never sets on so glorious a human achievement." A government that supports the merit of a man is based on its benevolence, hard work, and contribution to a higher cause. A government that empowers its citizens is based on the beliefs of love, peace, and acceptance. I dream of an Iran that is at peace with itself and the world.

While writing this book, I went back to dark places that I have tried not to visit for decades, since they caused me so much pain and anguish. I am eternally grateful for the freedom of expression we have here in the West. While in the East some people may look at Westerners with envy, wishing they could be living here, I wonder if we really know how blessed we are to be living in this beautiful country. We can be who we are at any given time.

If I had to live my life over again, I would not change anything. All that has happened in my life helped me to become who I am today. I am grateful to all the people whose paths crossed mine, for a season, for a reason, or for a lifetime. You have made my life meaningful.

I believe that in each of us there is a seed of greatness that, once it is tapped into, can blossom to express our unlimited potential.

I wish to thank each and every one of you, my committed readers, who have travelled alongside me throughout my journey. I hope you feel as enriched as I did in opening my heart and soul to you, making my life into an open book.

In Thomas Paine's wise words, "That which we obtain too easily we esteem too lightly; it is dearness only which gives each thing its value."

I cherish my freedom.

Sima Goel
Montreal

Acknowledgements

To my four siblings, Farah, Soraya, Cyrus, and Aria, who have been my best friends in good times and bad; my deepest appreciation and love. I am proud of all of you. We have come a long way.

Special thanks to my eldest sister, Farah. We trekked across the desert together; you have been by my side in the best and the worst times of my life. I am grateful for the details that you shared with me of our life in Shiraz.

To my wonderful sons, Eric and Daniel, who insisted that I write the story of my family and my journey, for them and for future generations. They encouraged me on the days that I wanted to give up on writing this book.

To Rivka Augenfeld, our social worker at JIAS, whose commitment, devotion, and humanity was not bound by her office hours. We were blessed to have you in our lives.

To Joyce Yedid, our lawyer, our heartfelt appreciation.

To Mr. Abe Abraham, the head of JIAS when we came to Canada, your vision to unite our family is greatly cherished.

To Howard Reitman, thank you for believing in me and my story and for being the catalyst for the birth of this book.

To the board of Combined Jewish Appeal Women's Campaign 2008–09, thank you for giving me a chance and a forum to share my story with a great audience. I will forever be grateful for that opportunity.

To Sandy Cytrynbaum, my thanks for your tireless support from the conception of the idea until the very end. Your bountiful energy and zest for life inspires me.

To Lesley MacLeod, thank you for insisting that I pursue this project.

To Rachel Alkallay, who undertook the difficult task of editing the first version of the book, I offer my thanks. Her keen questions and interest in my story helped me get in touch with many long-buried, often painful memories, which became some of the most frightening, as well as deeply sentimental, threads in this memoir.

My grateful appreciation to General Store Publishing House team: Tim Gordon, publisher, who took on this project and believed in its potential; Jane Karchmar, my editor, for her keen editorial skills, kindness, and being always available when I needed her; Magdalene Carson, the art director, whose great talent and sensitivity captured the essence of the book; Andrea McCormick, publicist, for her enthusiasm and willingness to offer guidance to this novice author who is embarking on an unknown path.

To my extended family and friends, thank you for being there for me.

To all those people who illuminated my path in the days when I didn't know if I could continue further, my heartfelt appreciation.

To the reader, I hope that the obstacles I encountered and my persistence in overcoming them will serve as inspiration in your own life. It is my belief that within each of us lies the ability to reach a greater potential than we are aware of, and with perseverance, we can achieve our dreams.

And last but not least, to my beloved husband, Eugene, who patiently watched me give birth to this book. He has shown me it is possible to love a man without losing one's own identity. He is happy to have his wife back after five years. He has my eternal love and gratitude.

About the Author

CLAUDE CHARLEBOIS

*D*r. Sima Goel has been practicing chiropractic since 1994. She obtained her wellness certification in 2006 and is currently working toward a post-doctorate degree in functional neurology. Dr. Goel gives workshops on optimum health and well being and writes a weekly column on health and wellness for a local newspaper. Dr. Goel lives in Montreal, Canada, with her husband, two energetic teenage sons, and a sweet Boston terrier.

TO ORDER MORE COPIES:

GENERAL STORE PUBLISHING HOUSE INC.
499 O'Brien Road, Renfrew, Ontario, Canada K7V 3Z3
Tel 1.800.465-6072 • Fax 1.613.432.3634
www.gsph.com